Forensic Science Advances and Their Application in the Judiciary System

Forensic Science Advances and Their Application in the Judiciary System

Edited by

Danielle Sapse and Lawrence Kobilinsky

CRC Press
Taylor & Francis Group
Boca Raton London New York

CRC Press is an imprint of the
Taylor & Francis Group, an **informa** business

CRC Press
Taylor & Francis Group
6000 Broken Sound Parkway NW, Suite 300
Boca Raton, FL 33487-2742

First issued in paperback 2020

ISBN-13: 978-1-4398-2959-2 (hbk)
ISBN-13: 978-0-367-77857-6 (pbk)

Visit the Taylor & Francis Web site at
http://www.taylorandfrancis.com

and the CRC Press Web site at
http://www.crcpress.com

I would like to thank my family, Estelle, Hayley, and Ben, for allowing me to pursue this book and to especially thank Danielle Sapse, who worked diligently to make this significant project a success. It has been a great pleasure for me to work with her.

Lawrence Kobilinsky, PhD

I dedicate this book to my beloved father, Marcel Sapse, who passed away in 2004.

Danielle Sapse, JD

Table of Contents

Foreword

Forensic science is an umbrella discipline incorporating many fields such as document examination, toxicology, pharmacology, serology, ballistics and explosives analysis, arson investigation, trace evidence (e.g., hair/fibers, glass, soil, paint), pathology, anthropology, and odontology. Chemistry is a component of each of these disciplines. The tools of the practitioner range from the common light microscope to the most sophisticated analytical instruments. Regardless of the specific instruments that criminalists use to solve crimes, the one clear need is that the scientific method be used to try to exclude or associate a suspect with a crime scene or victim. This will insure the reliability and admissibility of scientific evidence in the courtroom. The analysis of physical evidence identified at a crime scene can be critical to solving any crime. Observation of items of importance and their documentation, collection, and packaging, followed by experimental analysis in the laboratory, can often either prove or disprove a hypothesis. Test results can contribute to an understanding of what occurred at the crime scene, prior to and during the commission of the incident. Crime scene investigation must be done properly and thoroughly for laboratory personnel to acquire the most accurate information about the evidence and crime scene.

Over the past decade many achievements have been made in forensic science and there have been exciting advancements in the technology available to crime scene personnel and laboratory analysts. Many of the newer methods employed by criminalists are based on sound scientific research and have extraordinary sensitivity and specificity. Wherever possible, analysis of evidence should provide quantitative data, which can subsequently be analyzed statistically. The analysts' unbiased conclusions are then made based on sound scientific principles utilizing the scientific method.

This book describes such methods and provides insight into their impact on forensic science and criminal justice. For example, nuclear magnetic resonance (NMR) and quantum chemistry are now applied to certain problems related to forensic science such as the analysis of licit and illicit drugs. For the results of analyses to be useful to jurors in criminal cases, this scientific evidence must be deemed reliable and admissible by judges who serve as gatekeepers of novel scientific evidence. The results must add to the understanding of the jurors and assist them in finding a defendant guilty or not guilty. To explore in depth the role of forensic science in the judiciary process, the first chapter of the book discusses scientific evidence, describing several criminal cases whose outcome has been largely decided based on forensic evidence analysis.

Forensic science has played a very important role in the litigation of cases involving illicit drugs. Chapters 2 and 4 present the legal and chemical aspects in the detection and analysis of a major class of abused drugs, the methamphetamines. Some of the methods used to clarify the circumstances in which a crime has been committed are related to DNA. Chapter 3 describes new methods used for the analysis of DNA obtained from botanical evidence as well as from insects. Such evidence can sometimes be used to determine the identity of the victim or suspect after a crime has been committed.

The next few chapters discuss new applications of chemical methods to forensic science. Among those, quantum chemistry calculations as applied to systems of forensic interest, such as toxins, fingerprinting agents, and the synthesis of methamphetamines, are comprehensively discussed in Chapter 4.

Chapter 5 describes various legal aspects of the utilization of DNA in the analysis of biological evidence. Different cases are presented in which DNA analysis is used either for convicting a criminal or for exonerating an innocent person who has been wrongly accused. This chapter also contains quantum chemistry calculations on the complexes formed by DNA fragments and methyllithium and their potential future use in forensic investigations.

A description of NMR methods and their application to physical evidence analysis in forensic science is contained in Chapter 6.

Some of the most useful procedures for solving homicide cases are the postmortem investigations. Chapters 7, 8, 9, and 10 address this issue, from different points of view. Chapter 7 discusses pharmacogenetics and its role in forensic science. Chapter 8 describes "virtual autopsy" methods, consisting of scientific noninvasive research applied to the bodies of murder victims, with special emphasis on cross-sectional imaging. Another look at the studies of human remains is provided in Chapter 9, which includes DNA studies of ancient remains such as Egyptian mummies.

Chapter 10 discusses postmortem chemical changes that take place upon death of an individual. Forensic and legal issues related to animal cruelty are presented in Chapter 11. Indeed, abuse of animals appears to be strongly correlated with the abuse of women and children. Some of these issues are addressed in this chapter.

One of the purposes of this book is to help solve some of the problems related to forensic investigations. It is hoped that the issues raised and the methods described will contribute to strengthening forensic science in several of these areas.

Contributor List

Delphine Allorge, PD, PhD
Service de Toxicologie-Génopathies du Centre de Biologie-Pathologie du CHRU de Lille
Université de Lille
Lille, France

Elise Champeil, PhD
Department of Sciences
John Jay College of Criminal Justice
New York, New York

Angelique Corthals, PhD
Department of Sciences
John Jay College of Criminal Justice
New York, New York

Fabrice Dedouit, MD, PhD
Service de Médecine Légale

and

Laboratoire d'Anthropobiologie
Toulouse Cedex, France
Service de Radiologie
CHU Toulouse-Rangueil
Toulouse, France

Marie Faruch, MSc
Laboratoire d'Anthropobiologie
Service de Radiologie
CHU Toulouse-Rangueil
Toulouse, France

Catherine Fressigné, PhD
IRCOF
Université de Rouen
Mont St. Aignan, France

Francis Joffre, MD, PhD
Service de Radiologie
CHU Toulouse-Rangueil
Toulouse, France

Kimora, PhD
Law and Police Science Department
John Jay College of Criminal Justice
New York, New York

Jacques Maddaluno, PhD
IRCOF
Université de Rouen
Mont St. Aignan, France

Philippe Otal, MD, PhD
Service de Radiologie
CHU Toulouse-Rangueil
Toulouse, France

Joseph A. Prahlow, MD
South Bend Medical Foundation
Indiana University School of Medicine–South Bend
South Bend, Indiana

Robert W. Reisman, DVM
Bergh Memorial Animal Hospital
ASPCA
New York, New York

Daniel Rougé, MD, PhD
Service de Médecine Légale
CHU Toulouse-Rangueil
Toulouse, France

Hervé Rousseau, MD, PhD
Service de Radiologie
CHU Toulouse-Rangueil
Toulouse, France

Anne-Marie Sapse, PhD
Department of Sciences
John Jay College of Criminal Justice
New York, New York

Danielle Sapse, JD
Law and Police Science Department
John Jay College of Criminal Justice
New York, New York

Charles F. Siebert, Jr., MD
New Jersey Office of the State Medical Examiner
Woodbine, New Jersey

Norbert Telmon, MD, PhD
Service de Médecine Légale
CHU Toulouse-Rangueil
Toulouse, France

Gilles Tournel, MD, PhD
Institut de Médecine Légale
Faculté de Médecine de Lille
Lille, France

Margaret Wallace, PhD
Department of Sciences
John Jay College of Criminal Justice
New York, New York

Victor W. Weedn, MD, JD
Assistant Medical Examiner
Maryland State Office of Chief Medical Examiner
Baltimore, Maryland

Scientific Evidence

1

DANIELLE SAPSE

Contents

Introduction

At a trial, the culpability or innocence of the defendant is established in different ways. Some of these ways involve the use of forensic science.

Forensic science, the science in the service of the law, comprises many different specialty areas. The area that comprises all the aspects having to do with full-service forensic science laboratories is called criminalistics. Criminalistics involves the identification and interpretation of physical evidence found at the scene of a crime. This evidence can be separated into biological evidence analysis, material evidence analysis, fire debris and substance identification, and pattern evidence such as fingerprints, footwear, and others, and presented to the court during the trial.

Evidence is studied through recognition, identification, individualization, and reconstruction. Recognition takes place at the start of an investigation, and then the physical evidence has to be identified and classified. Chemical evidence is classified in the forensic laboratory by the use of chemical or instrumental techniques. To be of use to the prosecution, and to be accepted by the court, these classifications have to be performed.

Experiments are particularly important when they result in exclusion or disassociation. Indeed, a negative result can be an absolute, while a positive result has to be viewed in terms of probability. For instance, if a fragment of glass is found at the scene of the crime, it may be suspected of belonging to a certain car's headlights. When tests show it to be different, it is clear that it does not belong to the car. If it is similar to the car's headlights, there is always the probability that another car features the same headlights.

Individualization can be the recognition of an object as unique among a certain class, or an unknown item can be identified as having a common origin with a known object. Reconstruction uses the analysis of physical evidence to shed light on the events that took place. Reconstruction might have a speculative aspect, which can lead to an incorrect interpretation. As such, it is used cautiously.

All the relevant findings at a crime scene can be introduced at trials either by the prosecution or the defense and constitute evidence. The use of scientific evidence in court is subject to certain laws.

Evidence law is based on principles and regulations for admitting proof in court. These laws can vary depending on the state. In federal court, rules of evidence are found in a code called the Federal Rules of Evidence, which was developed in 1975 and is used for both criminal and civil cases. There are also individual state codes, which apply to state court cases. This includes both testimony and physical evidence. In criminal cases, the state has the burden of proof to assert that a defendant committed a crime. There must be proof beyond a reasonable doubt that the crime was committed and that the defendant committed it, and this information can be proven by using evidence.

Evidence can be categorized in several different ways. Testimony is spoken evidence, given by witnesses under oath in court. Real evidence is "evidence furnished by things themselves, on view or inspection, as distinguished from a description of them by the mouth of a witness" (Black's Law Dictionary 1990). Some examples are the physical appearance of a person or place, inanimate objects, weapons, and tools. A subcategory of real evidence is scientific evidence, as used in forensic investigations, which will be discussed later.

Another way to classify evidence is whether it is direct or circumstantial. Direct evidence is evidence that proves a fact directly, without having to make any assumptions. For example, if a witness actually saw a crime happen, rather than if he heard about it from another person, that would be direct evidence. Circumstantial evidence is evidence that is not based on personal firsthand knowledge, but rather on other collateral facts. Circumstantial evidence can be admissible, especially when it is combined into a collection of different types of evidence.

One type of evidence that is not usually admissible is hearsay, which is secondhand testimony. That is, the witness does not have personal knowledge of a crime, but he or she heard about it from another person. The reason why hearsay evidence is not usually admitted into court is because the opposing party cannot cross-examine the person who first made the statement. Without cross-examining a witness, it can be difficult to find out if he or she is telling the truth and is accurate. There are, however, certain exceptions as will be shown later.

For evidence to be admissible in court, it must be relevant and trustworthy. Relevant evidence is evidence that can prove, for instance in a criminal case, whether the defendant committed a crime. For example, in many situations, prior convictions might not be relevant, because they would not prove whether the defendant committed the crime for which he is on trial. Information such as this may also wrongfully influence the jury.

Evidence also has to be trustworthy, that is, competent. It cannot violate the exclusionary rule. The exclusionary rule is the rule that states that if evidence is wrongfully obtained, if it is obtained in a way that violates the rights given in the U.S. Constitution, it cannot be admissible and must be excluded from the trial. For example, the Fourth Amendment prohibits illegal searches and seizures. If a police officer conducts an illegal search, such as one that is performed without a warrant or consent, when necessary, the items found cannot be admissible as evidence. A landmark case on this subject is *Mapp v. Ohio* (1961). In that case, police officers conducted an illegal, warrantless search of Ms. Dollree Mapp's house, while searching for a person suspected of a crime. While searching, they did not find the suspect they were looking for, but they did find some obscene drawings, and Ms. Mapp was charged and convicted for their possession. On appeal, the U.S. Supreme Court overturned the conviction, because of the illegal search.

Evidence, as mentioned before, can be physical evidence or testimony. Testimony, evidence spoken by witnesses, can be of different kinds. There is testimony any time a witness saw a crime happen. In some cases, there are also expert witnesses.

An expert witness is a witness in court who knows more about a certain subject than other people would. An expert witness can talk about both the facts and his or her own opinion, and also help the jury understand technical evidence. There are several rules about the use of expert witnesses in court.

According to the Federal Rules of Evidence, Rule 702, "If scientific, technical, or other specialized knowledge will assist the trier of fact to understand the evidence or to determine a fact in issue, a witness qualified as an expert...may testify thereto in the form of an opinion or otherwise."

The judge has to decide if it is appropriate for someone to be an expert witness. First, if the evidence is something easy to understand, an expert is not necessary, such as in a case in which an expert had to say that the reason no fingerprints were found on a car was because the person used gloves or wiped away the prints. Expert witnesses are used for information related to science and medicine, but also for any issue where people cannot be expected to understand everything, such as mechanics and vehicles.

There are several ways in which the expert witness might know about the facts of a situation. For example, if the expert is a doctor, he might know the patient's condition because he examined him, because he got his files from another doctor, or by what he hears in court. Sometimes the lawyers will explain a situation to an expert and ask him to give his opinion about it in court. The expert might be questioned in a hypothetical way. For example, a doctor could be asked, "What if someone worked with benzene, and then they get a high fever?" "What is your opinion?"

There is one situation in which an expert is not allowed to give an opinion: "Whether or not the defendant had or did not have the mental state or condition constituting an element of the crime charged or the defense thereto." This is from Federal Rules of Evidence 704(b), and it usually applies to psychiatrists. The reasoning is that the expert can talk about any mental disease that the defendant might have, but only the judge or jury can decide if the mental disease can be a defense to the crime committed.

There is a process that takes place in the court when an expert witness participates in the trial. First, the expert is asked questions by the party who called him or her to court. After the direct examination, the expert goes through a cross-examination, which is conducted by the other side. During the cross-examination, the expert's memory, knowledge, and opinion might be challenged. If the witness makes any statements that are not consistent, it is harmful to his credibility. Also, the examiner might try to find information that would contradict what the expert says (for example, if the expert is a doctor, and the examiner finds contradictory information from a medical book).

As previously stated, *hearsay* is a legal term referring to the use of out-of-court statements as evidence. It is evidence that is not based on the witness's own personal experiences, but on matters that he was told by another person. Normally, hearsay evidence is inadmissible in court, but there are several exceptions.

Some exceptions are when the declarant gives a statement of his state of mind at the time he gave the declaration, or an "excited utterance," which is a statement made under stress during or immediately after an unexpected event. Also, business records and public records can serve as evidence that an event occurred, since these records are usually kept carefully and accurately, in a routine way.

Another exception, in homicide cases, is the "dying declaration." If the declarant gives a statement while believing that he is about to die, about the reason for why he would die, the statement may be admissible.

A hearsay exception important for scientific evidence is that for "learned treatises." This exception is for written material like textbooks, journals, and periodicals. These can be on a number of different subjects, such as science, history, medicine, and engineering. This type of material can be discussed as part of the questioning of the expert witness, since even though they were written "out of court" they can be assumed to be reliable since they were written by professionals and also evaluated and used by other professionals. For this kind of evidence to work well, the court has to know that the writing is reliable (usually by using an expert) and it must be brought up and discussed during the trial.

Another type of hearsay evidence that is admissible is a declaration of one's physical condition. These are statements that are made to anyone, not just a doctor, that relate to symptoms that the person is feeling at that moment. Statements about past symptoms, the reason for the symptoms, and medical history, are only admissible if they were made to a doctor or other medical professional while in the process of diagnosing and treating the condition.

Description of Scientific Evidence

Physical scientific evidence involves such procedures as fingerprint identification, DNA typing, glass fragment identification through refractive index measurements, and others. Fingerprint analysis and DNA typing are discussed in greater detail in separate chapters.

When scientific evidence is presented at a trial, jurors have to be told about information pertaining to testing errors and also information about the error rate of the laboratory where the tests were done. This is especially important for DNA evidence, which may identify a person. For example, a DNA test might show that the probability of two people's DNA matching is one in a million. However, the probability that the laboratory made a mistake in the testing is one in 500. The jury should be informed of this possibility of error. Most of the time, courts will accept testimony about the statistics of a DNA match.

Most courts allow testimony regarding the statistical possibility of a coincidental match and leave the question of accuracy of the figure to cross-examination. There are controversies related to the fact that population databases are too broad. For instance, if a defendant is part of a specific group featuring a certain genetic pattern in one in 10,000 people, but he is also part of a smaller group which features the pattern in one in 1,000 people, considering the probability as 1 in 10,000 is unfair to the defendant.

Indeed, if a defendant is a member of an insular group, the probability might work in his favor. However, if that group is not the suspect population, the statistical testimony has to be accepted.

For instance, in the case *People v. Mohit*, Dr. Morteza Mohit, a physician in Westchester County in New York State, was accused of raping one of his patients. The defendant was from a town in Iran, Shushtar, where there were people of Persian descent and there was much inbreeding. Being Shiite Muslim, Dr. Mohit claimed that for religious and traditional reasons, inbreeding is very common. However, this is not relevant in a crime committed in New York State. If the crime would have been committed in a region inhabited by Shushtar Shiite Muslims, the probability that the semen belonged to Dr. Mohit would have been much smaller.

Another type of evidence that can be used for identification is voiceprints. Courts do not all agree on whether voiceprints should be admissible. Courts are more likely to accept voiceprints as evidence if the proper methods were used and if the expert is certified by the organization of voice examiners. The cross-examiners can try to show a problem with the evidence. In one case, for example, the government wanted to use voiceprint evidence against a defendant. The defense tried to prove that the background voices in the sample could have caused a mistake.

Expert witnesses can be psychologists and sociologists. They are sometimes called on to testify as experts to explain a person's behavior. For example, some people involved in criminal activity may have Battered Woman's Syndrome or Child Abuse Syndrome, which can show a pattern of typical behavior by abused women or children. This type of evidence is not always admitted.

Another technique used in forensic research is neutron activation analysis (NAA). Neutron activation analysis is a technique for the analysis, identification, and comparison of physical evidence. This elaborate process can isolate and measure very small traces of all kinds of materials such as gunpowder, narcotics, hair, alcohol, and other substances.

The identification and quantitative analysis of the material are accomplished by measuring the gamma rays emitted after the sample has been irradiated by bombardment with neutrons in a nuclear reactor. This method is expensive and requires complicated nuclear equipment, but it is exceedingly accurate in identifying substances and has the advantage that the material analyzed is not damaged and can be preserved for courtroom exhibition.

A party intending to use NAA results as evidence has to offer one or more experts who will testify as to the validity of the process. It is advisable and mandatory even, in a criminal case, to give the other party pretrial notice of the intended use of NAA test results.

In some trials, the degree of intoxication of the suspect plays an important role. Chemical means are used to determine the subject's level of intoxication, for such crimes as drunk driving or crimes supposedly committed under the influence of alcohol. Measurements of the breath, blood, or urine can be used to indicate the approximate amount of alcohol that has reached the brain.

For example, a level of 0.05% or less of blood alcohol means that the subject was probably not under the influence of alcohol. A finding of 0.1% or more shows that the accused is probably intoxicated.

In addition, detection of narcotics use may also be necessary. The drug Nalline can be used to detect the recent use of narcotics (see Figure 1.1). When the drug is injected in a subject, the eye pupils of a recent user dilate.

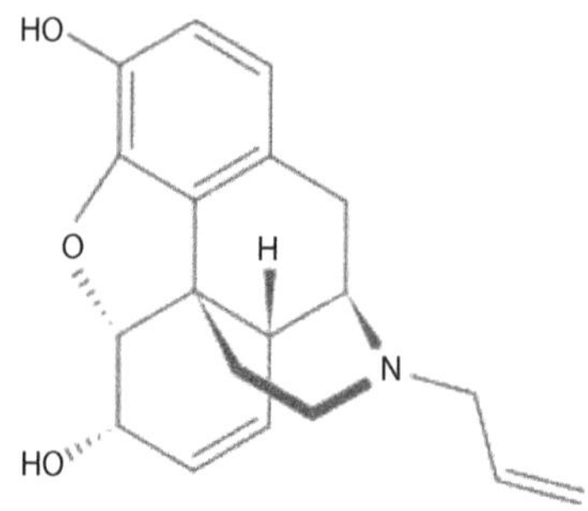

Figure 1.1 Nalline.

The courts have been receptive to Nalline tests. Another test is enzyme multiple immune assay testing of the subject's urine.

Two Landmark Cases: *Frye* and *Daubert*

One of the first major cases that dealt with the issue of the admissibility of scientific evidence was *Frye v. United States*, 293 F. 1013 (D.C. Cir. 1923). This was an appeal of a second-degree murder case, in which the defendant was convicted. At the trial, one piece of evidence was testimony, by an expert witness, about the use of a polygraph test.

A polygraph test, which is also known as a lie detector test, is meant to discover if a suspect is lying or telling the truth. The test works by measuring the suspect's blood pressure along with his respiratory rate and perspiration, while he answers questions. Experts believe that blood pressure depends on the change in the person's emotions. When they show emotions such as fear or anger, their blood pressure will increase. If they are purposefully lying, or if they feel guilty, they will fear being discovered, and their blood pressure will increase. Sometimes, the test might seem to indicate a lie, but in fact, the suspect's blood pressure went up because he is nervous. However, in that case, the blood pressure will eventually return to normal, while if the person is actually lying, the blood pressure will continue to increase.

The *Frye* case attempted to decide if polygraph tests could be admitted as evidence in court. Expert opinions are admissible in court whenever there is an issue that is too intricate for most people to understand and form an opinion about.

This case set an admissibility standard for scientific evidence. The standard states that "a scientific theory or piece of evidence that was accepted by only a minority of specialists would not be admissible at all." The only scientific theories that are admissible and can be presented to the jury are those that were generally accepted by the suitable scientific community. To decide if a procedure is "generally accepted" as necessary, the courts look at previous judicial decisions, as well as books and articles on the subject.

The *Frye* test states that it is important to locate the stage development of the given technique. There are several possibilities. When a technique is first discovered, the scientific community has to examine it. Then, if they agree that it is well founded, it is considered to have been accepted by the scientific community and, therefore, can be admitted into court. Some of the techniques that were evaluated under *Frye*, besides polygraphs, were voiceprints and neutron activation. Neutron activation is the technique of bombarding specimens with neutrons (a particle found in the nucleus of atoms) and measuring a ray of energy emitted by the nucleus called a gamma ray.

The reasoning for the *Frye* test is that it is necessary to make sure that qualified people will decide if the conclusions of a method are reliable and should be used in court. Sometimes, it can be hard to conclude when a discovery has been accepted and is no longer in the experimental stage. The *Frye* case decided that the blood pressure test was not adequately accepted and recognized. Consequently, the court could not admit the results as scientific evidence.

Since the *Frye* case, in 1923, courts decided to change the test due to the many new advances that the scientific community might not have completely accepted. If scientific, technical, or other specialized knowledge will assist the trier of fact to understand the evidence or to determine a fact in issue, a witness qualified as an expert by knowledge, skill, experience, training, or education may testify thereto in the form of an opinion or otherwise, if (1) the testimony is based on sufficient facts or data, (2) the testimony is the product of reliable principles and methods, and (3) the witness has applied the principles and methods reliably to the facts of the case.

Some of these changes occurred with the case *Daubert v. Merrell Dow Pharmaceuticals, Inc.*, 509 U.S. 579 (1993). In this case, the families of two children born with birth defects sued the company, Merrell Dow Pharmaceuticals, Inc., which made Bendectin, a medication that the mothers took while pregnant. The evidence included testimony from several expert witnesses. One doctor testified, stating that no other birth defects related to Bendectin were seen in studies of over 130,000 patients. On the other hand, some of the plaintiff's witnesses testified that they believed Bendectin could cause birth defects, based on experiments done with animals. The district court ruled in favor of the defendant, stating that scientific evidence is admissible only if the principle on which it is based is "sufficiently established to have general acceptance in the field to which it belongs." This was the standard used in *Frye v. United States*. The Court of Appeals affirmed.

The case went to the U.S. Supreme Court, which disagreed and reversed the lower courts' decisions. It set forth a new standard, which said that the test of admissibility should be whether the testimony includes "scientific knowledge" that was tested, and not only evidence of generally accepted principles.

The Supreme Court's opinion was that since Rule 702 was written after *Frye*, it could overrule the *Frye* standard. It does not require a standard as high as "general acceptance." Therefore, the trial court judge can decide whether the evidence is reliable and should be admitted.

Some of the factors that *Daubert* examined to decide if testimony should be admitted were how well the theory was tested and how reliable it is, whether it was published, whether the expert has a respected position in the scientific community, and whether another expert could use the technique to get the same result.

At this time, the *Daubert* decision is only binding on federal courts. However, many states use it as well. Other states use the *Frye* standard or another standard altogether.

Several years later, *Kumho Tire v. Carmichael*, 526 U.S. 137 (1999), used the *Daubert* standard and extended it to technical evidence, rather than just scientific evidence. That case applied the ruling in *Daubert* to a situation where the testimony was of nonscientist experts, specifically a tire failure expert. This case started when there was a car accident in which the tire of a minivan blew out. The accident led to one death and several injuries. The plaintiff, who was the driver of the car, sued the tire's maker and distributor (Kumho Tire). Part of the plaintiff's case included testimony by an expert in tire failure analysis, as previously mentioned.

Class Action Lawsuits

One of the examples of weighing expert testimony takes place at the class certification stage in a class action lawsuit. A class action lawsuit is a lawsuit in which the plaintiffs have a common legal position against the opposing party. Instead of each plaintiff bringing a separate action, they are combined into one, which leads to a much more efficient result. If it is relevant to the case, an expert witness may be called by each side.

As shown by H.P. Scribner, to become certified as a class action, the plaintiffs have to prove that they have common issues to resolve. The class certification stage is a separate stage from the trial. The merits of the case itself are not relevant at this point and cannot be taken into account, according to the U.S. Supreme Court.

The problem is how to decide if the expert witness's testimony should be admitted. Some courts are concerned that evaluating the expert witness at this point would lead to a speculation of the case's merits, which is not allowed at that time. For this reason, some courts do not evaluate the experts at this point. Other courts look at how material and reliable the testimony would be, but not how persuasive it would be. Still other courts look at the materiality and reliability of the testimony to decide if it should be admitted and then decide if the expert witness testimony makes class certification suitable.

Medical Device Cases

In the case *Fuesting v. Zimmer, Inc.*, 2009 WL 174163 (C.D. III., 1/26/09), the plaintiff had a knee implant made by the defendant. Seven years later, he started to have pain in the knee, and the prosthesis had to be removed. The plaintiff sued, arguing that his knee implant failed because of an error made in the sterilization process. The prosthesis was sterilized by gamma irradiation in air. The plaintiff used an expert witness who testified in court. The expert witness, a doctor (Dr. James Pugh), stated that this process caused the prosthesis to oxidize and delaminate and that this led to its failure. The jury ruled for the plaintiff, but the judgment was vacated on appeal, because the court believed that the expert's testimony did not meet the standards of admissibility from *Daubert* and Fed. R. Evid. 702, which is that expert testimony has to be reliable and relevant.

As shown in *Daubert*, the following factors must be examined:

- Whether the scientific theory was tested
- Whether the theory was published and peer-reviewed
- The theory's rate of error
- Whether the theory was "generally accepted" by the scientific community

At the remanded trial, the plaintiff brought another expert witness, Dr. Robert M. Rose, to testify. However, the court found that Dr. Rose's conclusions did not clearly follow from the accepted principles. He did not actually show that the sterilization process resulted in the failure of the prosthesis. To accomplish this, he would have had to show that the causal chain must be characteristic of the plaintiff and each step in it should be supported by scientific arguments.

For example,

- the amount of radiation that causes oxidation
- the amount of oxidation that causes delamination
- whether the polyethylene used in this case, which the defendant claimed to be oxidation-resistant, can be subject to delamination
- whether the placing of the prosthesis in the body can affect the rate of oxidation

The plaintiff's expert witness did not know of any relevant scientific articles that show if there is a difference between oxidation rates for implants sterilized by GIA as opposed to other procedures. Also, it was unclear if additional oxidation may have taken place after the implant was removed. Since the court decided to exclude the expert's testimony, the defendant was granted summary judgment.

A similar situation, with the same defendant, occurred in *Jaske v. Zimmer Inc.*, 2009 WL 150946 (N.D. Ill., 1/20/09). The plaintiff also had a knee prosthesis that failed, and he sued the manufacturer, Zimmer. The plaintiff brought in experts in polymer science as witnesses. However, although they were qualified, they depended on a test that was not reliable in this case, a Fourier transform infrared (FTIR) spectroscopy.

The court decided that the testimony was not reliable for two reasons. First of all, proteins and lipids from the plaintiff's body may have permeated the product. Also, the test results did not establish when the oxidation took place. The plaintiff moved for reconsideration.

At the new trial, the plaintiff supplied additional evidence, showing that the oxidized polyethylene and any biological material found would absorb the infrared radiation used in the FTIR at different frequencies. He also presented the fact that the FTIR is an accepted standard of the American Society of Testing and Manufacturing. Originally, the court objected that the FTIR spectrum gave information about the amount of oxidation only at the time the test was done. However, the plaintiff showed that his expert witnesses used the FTIR results only to support their theory, since it is a recognized fact that gamma irradiation sterilization in air causes oxidation.

This case shows the eventual dangers of the *Daubert* challenge. If the *Daubert* motion caused the plaintiff to lose his case, and he is given a second chance, he would know what problems to address.

Daubert Hearing Cases

A number of recent cases, such as *United States v. Lopez-Martinez*, 543 F.3d 509 (9th Cir. Sept. 10, 2008) (No. 07-10174) and *In re Scrap Metal Antitrust Litigation*, 527 F.3d 517 (6th Cir. May 15, 2008) (No. 06-4511), show the discretion a trial court has in deciding to have a *Daubert* hearing. As seen before, the case *Kumho Tire Co.* stated that the trial court judge's "gatekeeping" obligation applies to testimony based on types of knowledge that are technical, even if not scientific.

United States v. Lopez-Martinez was a case in which the defendant was charged with the crime of smuggling illegal immigrants into the United States. This occurred after a member of his party was left behind in the desert and died. At the trial, the government used an expert witness, a border patrol agent, to testify as to "patterns and methods common among smugglers in the Yuma area."

The defendant appealed, claiming that the court should not have admitted the expert testimony without first determining if it is reliable by holding a *Daubert* hearing.

The court, relying on the decision taken in *Kumho Tire*, stated that under FDRE 702, the trial court has wide discretion to decide reliability. The court decided that since the testimony did not refer to very complicated science or technology, a formal *Daubert* hearing was not necessary, and also it was not necessary for the agent to describe each step in the process. The expert was considered to have been experienced and could be a reliable witness.

The other case was *In re Scrap Metal Antitrust Litigation*. This was a civil case about antitrust conspiracy related to scrap metal. The expert witness was an economist who testified about harm due to the fact that competition was restrained during eight years. The admissibility of the expert testimony was questioned. However, no formal *Daubert* hearing was held.

The jury entered a judgment of more than $20 million against the defendant. The defendant appealed, claiming that the court should have held a *Daubert* hearing. The Sixth Circuit disagreed, believing that the court was correct in admitting the evidence. The expert presented valid arguments and explanations, and so it was appropriate that the testimony was admitted. Again, it is seen that the trial courts have wide discretion in deciding when to admit expert testimony, even without holding a *Daubert* hearing.

Other cases that involved this issue include *United States v. Kenyon*, 481 F.3d 1054 (8th Cir. 2007), a child abuse case where the expert was a professor of pediatrics. He testified as to the characteristics of children who were victims of abuse, based on experience with about 5,000 victims. He explained in court that victims might not always show signs of physical harm, that they may hide the abuse and have problems describing it. Also, the abuse may worsen over time. The court decided that the fact that there was no *Daubert* hearing would not be an issue. The appellate court held that if a district court finds that an expert has the right amount of training, education, and experience, it could admit the testimony without a preliminary hearing.

Another case that dealt with this problem was *United States v. Spotted Elk*, 548 F.3d 641 (8th Cir. 2008), which was a drug conspiracy case. In that case, the defendants ran a drug trafficking business on a Sioux reservation. The crimes they were charged with were drug conspiracy, drug distribution, and firearm crimes. One of the forms of evidence against them was fingerprints found at the defendant's premises. The trial court allowed a fingerprint expert to testify about the prints. Since the expert had thorough training in fingerprinting and the methods he used were accepted in the scientific and legal community, the testimony was admitted.

As with the other cases, the defendant believed that the evidence was wrongfully admitted since there was no *Daubert* hearing.

United States v. Pena, 586 F.3d 105 (1st Cir. Nov. 17, 2009) (No. 08-1407), was another case that involved fingerprints as evidence. There, the crime was illegal weapons possession and possession of cocaine base with intent to distribute. The defendant ran away after he was approached by officers. The officers then apprehended him and found bags of cocaine base, $2,800 in cash, and a loaded .357 Magnum revolver. The fingerprint expert had evidence that showed a match from the defendant's fingerprint to a partial latent print on the weapon. The defendant objected, but the court said that he would have to have data and experts to show why the evidence should not be admitted. This type of evidence has usually been admitted, and there were no precedent cases to show that it should not be.

The court allowed three troopers from the state police who were trained in fingerprint analysis to testify that a print on the weapon matched the defendant. They used the ACE-V methods (analysis, comparison, evaluation, and verification).

The jury convicted him, and he was sentenced to 120 months in prison. The defendant appealed, stating that the ACE-V method is not reliable and is not a valid scientific method.

As shown mainly in the chapter about DNA, DNA typing has become a major tool for proving the guilt or innocence of a suspect. DNA fragments found at a crime scene in tissues such as blood, semen, saliva, and others can be compared to the DNA database to identify a specific person. The value of this powerful method is now decreased because of some recent discoveries.

Fabrication of DNA

Scientists in Israel, at a company called Nucleix, found out that it is possible to fabricate DNA evidence. They showed that if they have a DNA profile, they can use it to create a sample of DNA that matches that profile, without actually obtaining tissue from the person.

There are several ways in which fabricated DNA can have serious consequences. First of all, it can be used to wrongly implicate a person for committing a crime. Also, it can lead to an invasion of privacy, especially for celebrities. Scientists such as Dr. Dan Frumkin, from Nucleix, believe that soon criminals will start producing fake DNA, and that it may have already happened. According to Dr. Frumkin, the equipment needed is not expensive, and an undergraduate biology major is qualified to use that equipment.

There are two ways in which DNA samples can be made. One way requires, to start, a small amount of real DNA, which can be taken from any easily obtained source such as hair or a cup the person drank from. Then, genome amplification is used to increase the amount.

In one example, blood was taken from one person and centrifuged so that only the red cells (which do not contain DNA) remained. Then, DNA was taken from another person's hair and added to the red cells. This way, all the genetic material was from the second person. Finally, the researchers sent the sample to a reputable laboratory, which found a profile of the faked DNA.

The American Civil Liberties Union and other groups found these facts disconcerting. They deplore the facility with which DNA can be planted at a crime scene. This is in contrast with, for instance, fingerprints, which are much more difficult to plant.

The other way DNA samples can be made is by using known DNA profiles, which are kept by the police. Scientists can take many samples of DNA, clone small snippets representing common variants, and mix them together to create a sample that would match any profile. Four hundred twenty-five different DNA snippets would be a sufficient amount to fabricate any profile.

Nucleix developed a test that can differentiate real and fake DNA samples. Amplified DNA, which is used in either of the two methods, is not methylated—it does not have certain molecules that are usually attached to the DNA to inactivate genes.

To counteract this problem, the police ensure that DNA is not the only evidence used. If someone's DNA is found at a crime scene, but that suspect has an alibi and no criminal record, he may not be indicted.

Chimera DNA

Another problem arising using DNA typing for forensic purposes occasionally occurs. Indeed there are a few individuals whose DNA possesses a special property. Most people have cells that all have the same DNA. However, some people are made up of cells that are different from each other. Such people are called chimeras, named after the mythological creature Chimera, which had body parts from different animals. Most human embryos develop from one egg. However, sometimes, there are two eggs. If they become fertilized by two sperm cells, they will usually develop into fraternal (nonidentical) twins. If, however, the two cells fuse together, only one baby develops, but he or she would have cells of two different types, and would be a chimera. Usually, chimeras do not look different from the general population, except that each of their eyes might be a different color.

Another category of such people includes mosaics. Mosaics are different from chimeras in that they start by having the same set of DNA in each cell. However, at some point in life, some of their DNA changes and becomes different. This happens to some degree in many people, because of the sun, chemicals, and possibly illness. However, these are minor changes.

For a more serious difference, the change in the DNA would have to occur early in development, for example, when the first cell divided into two, and one of them has a change in the DNA. Then, with further development, half the person's cells will be different than that first cell.

However, with mosaics, the difference in the cells is not usually that significant. (It is less of a difference than for chimeras.)

These conditions can have an impact on DNA that is used to identify a criminal. One example would occur if a suspect is accused of a homicide, and blood is found at the scene of the crime and checked against the suspect's cells. If the suspect is a mosaic, the cells will probably be similar enough to believe that they came from the same person. If he is a chimera, the cells could be different enough that no proof is possible.

Two Criminal Cases Involving Scientific Evidence

Michael Peterson was a writer and journalist who was accused of murdering his wife in 2001, after she was found dead at the foot of the stairs in their house. He claimed that she fell and hit her head, and he found her unconscious. At first, the medical examiner thought this might be true. However, investigators believed that, judging by the evidence, she had been killed by beating, especially after an autopsy was performed. It was thought that the number and type of injuries were not in agreement with falling down the stairs, but rather with being severely beaten.

Soon after, Mr. Peterson was charged with murder. He and his attorney claimed that even if his wife was murdered, he did not commit the act; an intruder could have come in (which had happened several times previously) and committed the murder.

While Mr. Peterson was waiting for his trial, two issues came up. First, it was found out that a woman who was his neighbor and friend when he lived in Germany had also died by falling down stairs. (The Petersons had taken custody of her daughters afterward.) Also, evidence was found that Mr. Peterson was exchanging e-mails with a male prostitute.

A few months later, a scientific investigation was done in Peterson's house. Luminol was found to have been sprayed on the walls. Luminol is a chemical that is used to detect blood. When it is sprayed on a surface, light is produced, and blood patterns can be seen even in a dark room. Also, hair and tissue-like material was found on some of the furniture.

According to the prosecution, the patterns of stains on the wall indicated that there was an attempt to clean off the blood. However, the defense stated that the patterns were caused by luminol spraying.

Some of the evidence on the victim's person included lacerations, brain hemorrhage and other brain damage, and contusions on the head, back, arms, wrists, hands, and face. These findings were inconsistent with a fall but indicated a possible lethal beating.

At the trial, the judge, Judge Orlando Hudson Jr., allowed the prosecution to use almost every piece of evidence that the attorneys for the state wanted. It was also decided to exhume the body of the woman in Germany, Elizabeth Ratliff, which led to a finding that she also was murdered. Some of the evidence that would help the prosecution was the similarity in the deaths of Mrs. Ratliff and Mrs. Peterson. This is a type of evidence that sometimes might not be admissible in court to prove guilt. (Usually events from the defendant's past are not admissible.) However, in this case, the judge allowed it, because of the similarities between that situation and the present case. On the other hand, some evidence for the defendant is the fact that there were no witnesses, weapons, or motive in either case.

The forensic expert Dr. Henry Lee was called by the defense. His findings seemed to be more indicative of one or two falls than of a beating. These findings included bloodstain patterns and the fact that the crime scene might have been contaminated by the police.

The defendant used several arguments to help his case. First of all, he argued that the police used fake affidavits to acquire the search warrant. They may have done this because Mr. Peterson criticized them in the columns that he wrote. Other arguments were that there was no probable cause to search his car, and that the grand jury should not have convened until the autopsy report was done.

Some of the people who testified at the trial for either side were financial experts, firefighters, police officers, medical examiners, DNA specialists, and many others. The motive for the crime was unclear, but it could have been related to money or the fact that Mrs. Peterson found out about the e-mails with the male prostitute.

The prosecution's case was stronger than the defense's case, and the jury found Michael Peterson guilty of first-degree murder. He was sentenced to life in prison without parole.

Another famous case concerned a crime committed by a man called Scott Peterson, who was convicted of killing his pregnant wife. When Mrs. Laci Peterson went missing, Mr. Peterson called his mother-in-law. The police arrived and searched the neighborhood.

The police were suspicious of Mr. Peterson, because he was away on the day of the disappearance (Christmas Eve) on a fishing trip. Mr. Peterson allowed for a search of their cars, their house, and his workplace and boat. These searches were legal under the Fourth Amendment, because he gave his consent. Also, interviews of family members were conducted. It was found out later on that the house itself had not been dusted for fingerprints.

About four months later, the bodies of a woman and a baby were found near the water, not far from where Peterson was fishing. DNA testing identified them as Mrs. Peterson and her baby. Scott Peterson was arrested, even before the final test results, because the police were afraid he would try to flee.

There was a certain amount of evidence for both the prosecution and the defense. One important piece of evidence for the prosecution consisted in a number of phone calls from Peterson to Amber Frey, with whom he had been having an affair. Ms. Frye testified that Peterson told her, a few weeks before the disappearance, the same day that he bought the boat, that he had "lost his wife" and that this would be his first holiday without her.

Amber Frye testified in court about her conversations with Peterson, regarding the fact that he said he was not married and lied about taking business trips. When Ms. Frye realized that he had been lying and had a wife who was missing, she decided to help the police by taping her phone conversations with him.

Evidence that was found in Peterson's shed included a tarp he used while fishing that was soaked in gasoline and another that was covered by fertilizer. According to the district attorney, both gasoline and fertilizer destroy DNA and make it difficult for dogs to pick up a scent.

Another piece of evidence for the prosecution was the fact that there were inconsistencies in Mr. Peterson's statements and actions. Among those was the fact that Mr. Peterson claimed that he and his wife were watching the Martha Stewart show on the day that his wife disappeared. However, there seemed to be an inconsistency about the episode shown that day.

Several witnesses testified for the prosecution. Mrs. Peterson's sister testified that Mr. Peterson had planned to play golf on the day that he went fishing. A detective testified that Mr. Peterson denied having an affair and also that police officers found a gun in Peterson's truck.

Some of the testimony brought by the prosecution was that the two bodies were found near where Peterson said he had fished, that Peterson visited the area several times afterward, and that he could not have caught sturgeon (as he had claimed) because of the type of equipment and boat he had with him. In addition, he could have chosen a fishing spot much closer to his home. Another contradictory piece of evidence was that Peterson said it rained the day he went fishing, but the marina harbormaster said it had not.

Evidence at the preliminary hearing included a strand of hair on pliers found in Peterson's boat. Only mitochondrial DNA molecules can be taken from one strand of hair. This is a type of evidence that is not usually used in California because, while it can show a likelihood of identification or rule a suspect out, it cannot specifically identify someone. For that, nuclear DNA is needed.

Therefore, Peterson's lawyer tried to get that piece of evidence excluded because it could be unreliable. However, the mitochondrial DNA found could only be found in one out of 112 white people.

On the other hand, there was another reason to suppress the evidence. A hair could have gotten onto the pliers when Peterson brought them into the house, or if Mrs. Peterson handled them.

The defense presented a number of arguments. Some of these arguments were based on testimony by witnesses whose statements seemed to indicate that another person committed the crime.

- Two men and a woman saw a woman who looked like Mrs. Peterson walking a dog while Mr. Peterson was fishing.
- A former police officer saw some "scruffy"-looking men putting a woman who looked like Mrs. Peterson into a van.
- One of the Peterson's neighbors saw a "suspicious" van in the neighborhood shortly before Mrs. Peterson disappeared.

There were also other pieces of evidence that could be used for the defense. For example, the print markings on the boat matched those on buoys in the marina, which indicates that he was indeed fishing at that time and place.

A hypothesis that would have supported the defense was that members of a satanic cult committed the crime. However, a forensic pathologist testified that Mrs. Peterson's body was in the water for several months, and that the baby was probably separated from her for a few days only. This information contradicted the idea of a satanic cult having committed the crime, since they would have cut the baby away from her body.

A difficulty in this case was that there was no direct forensic evidence to prove that Peterson committed the crime. The most important pieces of evidence were the age of the fetus, and whether the rope around his neck was purposely applied. The other evidence, such as the wiretaps, mitochondrial DNA, and other pieces of evidence, could also be used in court against the defendant, with the participation of expert witnesses, such as the medical examiner.

At the trial, Scott Peterson was found guilty and sentenced to the death penalty.

Conclusion

From the cases described above, it can be concluded that scientific evidence plays a crucial role in the determination of the guilt or innocence of a defendant. However, in certain cases, the conclusions derived from the examination of the scientific evidence can be subject to argumentation. All in all, eventually justice is imparted largely due to forensic discoveries.

Bibliography

Books

Black's Law Dictionary. 1990. St. Paul. West Publishing Co.

Calvi, J.V., and S. Coleman. 2004. *American Law and Legal Systems*, New Jersey. Pearson Prentice Hall.

Champion, D.J., R.D. Hartley, and G.A. Rabe, 2008. *Criminal Courts*. New Jersey Pearson Education, Inc.

Gaensslen, R.E., H.A. Harris, and H. Lee. 2008. *Introduction to Forensic Science and Criminalistics*. New York: McGraw-Hill Companies, Inc.

Lee, H.C., and J. Labriola. 2006. *Dr. Henry Lee's Forensic Files*. Amherst: Prometheus Books.
Sapse, D. 2007. *Legal Aspects of Forensics*. New York. Chelsea House.
Waltz, J.R., and R.C. Parks. 1999. *Evidence Cases and Materials*. New York: Foundation Press.

Articles

Federal Evidence Review. 2010. Full Daubert Hearing Is Not Always Required to Admit Expert Testimony. http://federalevidence.com/blog/2010/february/full-daubert-hearing-not-always-required-admit-expert-testimony-part-vi.
Dye, N. 2006. Understanding Genetics, The Tech Museum, Stanford University. http://www.thetech.org/genetics/ask.php?id=172.
Ilani, O. 2009. Israeli Scientist Says DNA Samples Can Easily Be Forged. Haaretz.com, http://www.haaretz.com/print-edition/news/israeli-scientist-says-dna-samples-can-easily-be-forged-1.282271.
Kaye, D.H. 1993. DNA Evidence: Probability, Population, and Genetics in the Courts. *Harvard Law Journal* Vol. 7.
Pearson, H. 2002. Human Genetics: Dual Identities. *Nature* 417, 10–11.
Pollack, A. 2009. DNA Evidence Can Be Fabricated, Scientists Show. *New York Times*. http://www.nytimes.com/2009/08/18/science/18dna.html?_r=1.
Scribner, H.P. 2008. Rigorous Analysis of the Class Certification Expert: The Roles of Daubert and the Defendant's Proof. 28 Rev. Litig. 71.
Springer, J., 2003. Did Prosecution Meet Its Burden? http://news.findlaw.com/court_tv/s/20030908/08sep2003123255.html.
Wajert, S. 2009. Daubert Lessons from Two Medical Device Cases. Mass Tort Defense. http://www.masstortdefense.com/2009/02/articles/daubert-lessons-from-two-medical-device-cases/.

Legal Cases

Daubert v. Merrell Dow Pharmaceuticals, 509 U.S. 579 (1993).
Frye v. United States, 54 App. D. C. 46, 293 F. 1013.
People v. Mohit, 153 Misc. 2d 22 (1992).
Kumho Tire Co. Ltd. v. Carmichael, 526 U.S. 137 (1999).
Fuesting v. Zimmer Inc., 2009 WL 174163 (C.D. III., 1/26/09).
Jaske v. Zimmer Inc., 2009 WL 150946 (N.D. III., 1/20/09).

Trends in Legal Aspects of Methamphetamine

2

KIMORA

Contents

Introduction

Chapter 4 discusses the application of quantum chemical calculations to the study of methamphetamines. Indeed, methamphetamine (meth) use is a serious concern in the judiciary system. Many states and the federal government have begun to enact legislation to combat the use and production of methamphetamine in the United States. Many states have instituted programs to reduce the rural methamphetamine problem. Harm reduction as a public health alternative to the criminal model of drug use, reliance, and habit is viewed as a viable advance in forensic science in 2011. The Addiction Institute of New York and

Reality House, Inc., of New York are two agencies who are implementing forms of harm reduction as a public health alternative to aid methamphetamine clients.

Methamphetamine Abuse and Treatment in Rural America

Methamphetamine is a highly addictive stimulant that can have serious effects on a user's physical, mental, and social health. The National Survey on Drug Use and Health (NSDUH) reports that nearly 12 million Americans have tried methamphetamine. Methamphetamine uses as recorded by the Substance Abuse and Mental Health Services Administration's (SAMHSA) National Survey on Drug Use and Health includes prescription preparations and nonprescription illicit methamphetamine. For the purposes of this chapter, the author will concentrate on the implications of illicit rural usage of methamphetamine. The National Institute on Drug Abuse (NIDA) reports that increased methamphetamine availability and production is being found in rural areas of the United States.

The following avenues to reduce methamphetamine use in rural areas will be explored: cognitive behavioral interventions; as well as child and teen programs, such as high-quality pre-kindergarten, in-home-parent coaching, and after-school activities.

What Is Methamphetamine?

Methamphetamine belongs in the stimulant family of drugs of abuse. It is a sympathomimetic drug, a phenylethylamine, and its chemical structure closely resembles epinephrine and pseudoephedrine (Levounis & Ruggiero, 2006). Methamphetamine is easily manufactured from pseudoephedrine-containing over-the-counter medications and household solvents. Crystal methamphetamine, also called "crystal meth," "ice," or "glass" on the street, is produced by recrystallizing powder methamphetamine and is then smoked like crack cocaine.

Ice is a colorless, odorless form of concentrated crystal methamphetamine that resembles a chip of ice or clear rock candy. Some samples of ice sold on the street have been up to 98 to 100% pure amphetamine (Kaminski, 1992). It is sold as a "safe" alternative to crack cocaine (Mayo Clinic Health Letter, 1989). Pharmacologically, methamphetamine inhibits the reuptake of synaptic dopamine, which is similar to the effect of cocaine on the dopamine system. However, methamphetamine also directly promotes dopamine release, which may be implicated in the unique neurotoxic effects of the amphetamines on dopamine and serotonin neurons (Levounis & Ruggiero, 2006, p. 76).

How Is Methamphetamine Related to Amphetamine?

Methamphetamine is amphetamine with a CH3 molecule attached. Drug users prefer it to amphetamine because the methyl group apparently allows more of the drug to cross the blood-brain barrier. Methamphetamine, like amphetamine, exists in two forms, d- and l-. The molecular structure of the two forms is identical, but they are mirror images (Avis, 1999, pp. 87–88).

What Is Amphetamine?

The amphetamine family of drugs is one of the more powerful groups of central nervous system (CNS) stimulants (Jaffe, 1990). In addition to acting on the brain, the CNS stimulants affect a number of other body systems. The amphetamines and similar drugs (Ritalin, for example) improve the action of the smooth muscles of the body (Weiner, 1985). Because these drugs thus have some potential for improving athletic performance, at least to some degree, they are often abused for this purpose. However, these effects are not uniform, and overuse of the CNS stimulants can actually bring about a decrease in athletic abilities (Weiner, 1985). The amphetamines are thought to be able to achieve a calming effect by enhancing the function of the reticular activating system (RAS) of the brain, the portion of the brain thought to be involved in focusing attention (Gold & Verebey, 1984). The RAS is believed to "screen out" extraneous stimuli to allow concentration on one specific task. Children who suffer from hyperactivity are believed to have an underactive RAS and so are easily distracted. The amphetamines are thought to stimulate the RAS to the point where the child is able to function more effectively (Doweiko, 1996).

The amphetamines have also been found to be the treatment choice for a rare condition known as narcolepsy. Narcolepsy is a lifelong neurological condition in which the person is subject to sudden spells of falling asleep during waking hours (Harvard Medical School Mental Health Letter, 1990; Mirin, Weiss, & Greenfield, 1991).

The class of drugs that derive from amphetamine has been used medically (and recreationally) since the beginning of this century. Amphetamine was provided to both sides during World War II, resulting in epidemics of amphetamine use in Japan and Scandinavia when huge quantities of the drug were dumped on the open market. In the United States, amphetamine was used by truck drivers, housewives, students, and anyone else who wanted to stay awake or lose weight. Realization of the dangers of amphetamine was not long in coming, and by the 1970s its medical use had been restricted to treatment of narcolepsy and attention deficit disorder (Avis, 1999, p. 86). Doghramji (1989) describes narcolepsy as an incurable disorder thought to reflect a chemical imbalance within the brain. One of the chemicals involved, dopamine, is the neurotransmitter that the amphetamines cause to be released from neurons in the brain. It is possible that amphetamines can partially correct the dopamine imbalance that causes narcolepsy.

How Widespread Is Methamphetamine Abuse?

According to the 2007 Monitoring the Future Survey—a national survey of 8th, 10th, and 12th graders—methamphetamine abuse among students has been declining in recent years. However, it remains a concern. Survey results show that 1.8% of 8th graders, 2.9% of 10th graders, and 3.0% of 12th graders have tried methamphetamine.

In addition 0.6% of 12th graders were current (past-month) methamphetamine abusers in 2007. Decreases in past-year abuse of methamphetamine were seen for 8th (from 1.8% to 1.1%) and 12th graders (from 2.5% to 1.7%) from 2006 to 2007 (NIDA, 2008).

In 2006, there were an estimated 731,000 current users of methamphetamine aged 12 or older (0.3% of the population). Of the 259,000 people who used methamphetamine for the first time in 2006, the mean age at first use was 22.2 years, which is up considerably from the mean age of 18.6 in 2005. From 2005 to 2006, lifetime methamphetamine abuse increased among those 26 and older, particularly among those 26–34 years of age. Rates of past-year methamphetamine use among persons aged 12 years or older were the highest in the Western United States (1.6%), followed by the South (0.7%), Midwest (0.5%), and Northeast (0.3%) regions of the country (NIDA, 2008).

Increased methamphetamine availability and production are being reported in diverse areas of the country, particularly in rural areas, prompting concern about widespread use (California Attorney General's Crime and Violence Prevention Center, 2008).

Until recently, methamphetamine was not a significant medical problem on the East Coast. Now methamphetamine use is becoming a prevalent problem within the New York City gay and bisexual community, thus allowing it to be defined as a countrywide epidemic (Rawson, Simon, & Ling, 2002). In 1998, a telephone survey conducted by Stall and colleagues found that 7.4% of men who had sex with men in New York City used methamphetamine (Stall, Paul, & Greenwood, 2001). In 1999, Halkitis and colleagues found that 10.4% of gay men with human immunodeficiency virus (HIV) and gay/bisexual HIV-negative men, who had been recruited from gay mainstream venues, had used methamphetamine (Halkitis, Parsons, & Sturratt, 2001).

Why Is Methamphetamine Such a Problem in Rural Areas?

Seventy-one percent of the methamphetamine offenders, according to the Minnesota Department of Corrections, are from rural areas.

According to Aubrey Madler, Roxanne Vaughan from the Department of Biochemistry and Molecular Biology at the University of North Dakota School of Medicine and Health Sciences, and Michel Knopp, project coordinator of Rural Methamphetamine Education Project, there are a number of reasons that methamphetamine is such a problem in rural areas:

1. There are many abandoned buildings in rural areas. Some of these buildings house meth labs.
2. Anhydrous ammonia is one of the key ingredients in producing methamphetamine. It is easily available in rural areas because farmers use this chemical as fertilizer.
3. Children in rural areas who are around the methamphetamine labs get exposed to toxic chemicals that present health and environmental issues. The Partnership for a Drug-Free America reports that children who are removed from such areas have methamphetamine in their bodies.
4. EMS personnel can get injured when they arrive on the meth site by the hazardous substances as well as the people who are under the influence of methamphetamine. Meth users can be highly volatile people to deal with in this situation.
5. Law enforcement personnel are overworked. Meth lab manufacturers avoid police because labs can be portable and so are easily dismantled, stored, or moved. Those people who are arrested fill up crowded jails and strain the police resources.
6. Meth orphans can result when one or more of the parents die or are in jail due to methamphetamine abuse. Many grandparents raise their grandchildren due to problems that methamphetamine can cause with one or both of the parents.
7. The ingredients to make meth are cheap and can be purchased in local stores. Meth can also be cooked at home in kitchens and garages.

8. Methamphetamine abuse during pregnancy can cause prenatal complications such as increased rates of premature delivery, abnormal reflexes, and extreme irritability and may be linked to congenital deformities. Methamphetamine abuse by those who inject the drug and share needles can increase the user's risks of contracting HIV/AIDS and hepatitis B and C.
9. Treatment for meth use may be hard to find in rural areas. It is very common for rural areas to have fewer health facilities and treatment options.

What Are States Doing to Help Combat the Rural Methamphetamine Problem?

Communities are attempting to stop the spread of methamphetamine use through education programs, increased law enforcement efforts, and addiction treatment programs. Forming partnerships with local and state agencies to help combat methamphetamine use is beneficial (Madler, 2009).

The Meth Watch Program is designed to help stop the theft and suspicious sales of pseudoephedrine products, as well as other common household products used in the illicit manufacturing of methamphetamine in small, toxic labs. Meth Watch is a program sponsored by the Consumer Healthcare Products Association (CHPA). A key goal of this program is to promote cooperation between retailers and law enforcement to prevent the diversion of legitimate products for illegal use. Several states have started their own Meth Watch programs, including Iowa, Kansas, Georgia, Michigan, Minnesota, Mississippi, Oregon, South Carolina, Tennessee, and Washington.

Meth Watch

Meth Watch was started in Kansas as a public-private partnership between the Kansas Department of Health and Environment, the Kansas Bureau of Investigation, the Kansas Methamphetamine Prevention Project (part of the nonprofit statewide drug prevention system), and Kansas retailers. As news spread of its success, other states wanted to create a similar model to combat the methamphetamine problem.

The Kansas Methamphetamine Prevention Project (KMPP) was implemented in October 2002 in response to the devastating consequence Kansas communities were experiencing as a result of methamphetamine production and usage. KMPP provides training, technical assistance, strategies, and resources for addressing the methamphetamine problem at the local and state levels. They provide effective, efficient approaches for reducing the supply of, and demand for, meth in communities throughout the nation. Prevention strategies target groups such as retailers, rural populations, home visitors, youth, parents, and children affected by their parents' meth use and manufacture. The Kansas Project has become a national model. Fundamental to the success of KMPP are partnerships and collaborations developed with local and state agencies in Kansas. KMPP partners with agencies from numerous fields of expertise, including prevention, law enforcement, district attorney's offices, government, and rural agencies. The Kansas Methamphetamine Prevention Project is a project of Shawnee Regional Prevention and Recovery Services, Inc., and is a not-for-profit agency. It is partially funded by the Federal Edward Byrne Memorial Justice Assistance Grant Program, awarded by the Federal Bureau of Justice Assistance, as administered by the Kansas Criminal Justice Coordinating Council.

A statewide network of agencies partnered to make the Kansas Methamphetamine Prevention Project successful. The agencies are Kansas Department of Health and Environment (KDHE), Kansas Bureau of Investigation, Prevention and Recovery Services in Topeka, Kansas Social and Rehabilitation Services, Kansas Regional Prevention Centers, Kansas State University Research and Extension, and the Kansas National Guard, to name a few.

The KMPP conducts "train the trainer" sessions throughout the state to increase awareness of Meth Watch and other prevention strategies. The people involved in the KMPP learned early on that local participation is the key to successful implementation of the Meth Watch. They achieved widespread community involvement through an ongoing mini-grant process. The Kansas Department of Health and Environment (KDHE) distributes Meth Watch materials to retailers and other interested parties statewide on a regular basis and nationwide as requested (T. J. Ciaffone, Kansas Department of Health and Environmental Bureau of Environmental Remediation Response Unit, and C. Cain, KMPP project coordinator).

Meth Watch outside Kansas

The CHPA has made funds available to help support state and local Meth Watch programs. In addition to the Kansas program, a number of additional states have taken the Kansas model and implemented their own Meth Watch programs, including the following:

Georgia
Indiana
Iowa
Kentucky
Maine
Michigan
Minnesota
Mississippi
Montana
New Mexico
North Carolina
Oregon
Pennsylvania
South Carolina
Tennessee
Texas
Virginia
Washington
Wyoming

In this chapter, the author will comment on the Meth Watch programs and/or similar methamphetamine prevention and treatment programs in the following states, due to the proliferation of information about the various programs:

California
Iowa
Kentucky
Maine

Michigan
Minnesota
Mississippi
Montana
Nebraska
North Dakota
South Carolina
Tennessee
Oregon
Washington

California–Butte County Meth Treatment The Butte County Meth Strike Force, located in Oroville, California, reports in 2009 that Butte County estimates that 80% of crime is related to methamphetamine use. They also point out that 40%–50% of the children in the foster care system are there due to methamphetamine abuse. Therefore, various outpatient and inpatient programs are located inside and outside the Butte area to combat the methamphetamine problem in Butte County, California. Drug counseling, basic awareness, initial recovery, and relapse prevention are covered in the treatment facilities.

Iowa Meth Watch Program Jerry Fleagle, president of the Iowa Grocery Industry Association, indicates that Iowa Meth Watch provides training and preventive tools to any retail establishment that sells products that later can be used to manufacture methamphetamines. The Center for Substance Abuse Prevention (CSAP) gives retailers a kit that includes a training video, shelf display markers, and other educational tools, as well as report materials to provide information to local law enforcement officials. The goal is to have the community working with law enforcement to slow the production and distribution of methamphetamine in Iowa. The program began in 2007.

Kentucky's "Walk Your Land" Program Since the illegal production and use of methamphetamine is reaching epidemic proportions in Kentucky, the University of Kentucky Cooperative Extension Service, Pennyrile Narcotics Task Force, and East Kentucky's Operation UNITE are collaborating in an effort called "Walk Your Land" to educate all property owners about methamphetamine production and then get them to monitor their own properties. People are encouraged to look through their trash for fruit jars, glassware, plastic spoons, and other items that are used to produce methamphetamine. Citizens are encouraged to call law enforcement officials and their county extension office and not tamper with the items themselves. Operation Safe Land provides removal of methamphetamine related waste from rural properties.

Maine Methamphetamine Prevention Project This is an educational program designed to increase awareness about the harm associated with methamphetamine production and use, and to increase capacity of key institutions and community members to prevent the production and use of methamphetamine in Maine. With Maine's vast rural landscape, it is important, they state, to look for meth labs that may be going undetected. As of November 1, 2005, Maine law restricts the sale of pseudoephedrine, which is a precursor ingredient to pharmacies only. The Federal Combat Meth Act also restricts products containing pseudoephedrine. Citizens are encouraged to contact local police or sheriff for help if they encounter a meth lab.

The Michigan Meth Watch Program The Michigan Meth Watch Program has events all over the state of Michigan to inform the public about the dangers of methamphetamine. It is a collaborative initiative begun in 1997 to reduce meth lab activity in the state. It is illegal to steal or purchase precursor products (meth products) in the state. Many businesses cooperate to prevent the theft, fraud, and abuse of legal products to make methamphetamine. Michigan claims in their "Michigan Meth Watch" website that the prevention program is a success in the state because businesses collaborate.

Minnesota Meth Watch The Minnesota Department of Corrections is working to reduce meth-related recidivism through (1) Challenge Incarceration Program; (2) Thistledew Camp; (3) partnerships; and (4) treatment.

The Challenge Incarceration Program (CIP) is an innovative boot camp that uses cognitive skills, physical labor, and military drills to prepare drug offenders for reentry. The reconviction rate for CIP graduates is 2%.

Thistledew Camp hosts a pioneering juvenile methamphetamine and chemical dependency program that started in 2005. According to the Minnesota Department of Corrections, this "unique treatment program is cognitive behavioral skills-focused and addresses a wide range of risk factors including psychological needs and criminal thinking" (Minnesota Department of Corrections, 2005).

The Minnesota Department of Corrections has *partnered* with (1) the state Human Services and Public Safety Departments to develop treatment programs; (2) Hazeldon Publishing on a chemically dependent treatment journal; and (3) the Minnesota Department of Corrections facility at Shakopee for female offenders to receive treatment.

The Minnesota Department of Corrections offers methamphetamine treatment to those who suffer from addiction to the drug. The department reports that "research indicates that meth users need about a year to start to recover from the cognitive damage to their brain. For that reason, much more time-intensive treatment is needed than a traditional 30-day program" (Minnesota Department of Corrections, 2005).

Mississippi Meth Watch Program Mississippi utilizes the Meth Watch Program to curb the spread of methamphetamines in that state. As in other states that have adopted Meth Watch, the Mississippi Meth Watch Program helps to stop the sale and theft of household products used in the illicit manufacturing of methamphetamine. Retailers form the cornerstone of the program in Mississippi too.

Montana Meth Project

> The Meth Project is very simply changing the nature of crime control in Montana. As of 2005, the Montana criminal justice system was overwhelmed by the consequences of meth. If we are able to continue to make the kind of progress we have seen in the past two years, methamphetamine will have changed from a crisis to a manageable problem. (Montana State Attorney General Mike McGrath, 2009)*

By using consumer marketing and advertising strategies as the basis for its outreach, the Montana Meth Project has been repeatedly cited as a powerful private sector response to a devastating social problem. It was recently recognized by the White House as one of

* www.methproject.org/About_Us/results.php

the nation's most powerful and creative antidrug efforts. Recent statewide survey data, including data from the Centers for Disease Control and Prevention and the Montana Department of Public Instruction, as well as national survey data demonstrate that attitudes and behaviors toward meth have changed substantially since 2005, before the Meth Project initiated its preventive campaign. The Montana attorney general has also issued data showing that meth use and related crime has been on the decline in this same time frame (Montana Meth Project, 2009).

Teen methamphetamine use is decreasing in Montana. The 2009 *Montana Youth Risk Behavior Survey* reports that lifetime meth use by teens in Montana has dropped 44.6% since 2005. This decline is greater than any other observed across all risk categories measured by the survey (Montana Department of Justice, 2008).

The Montana Meth Project's theoretical framework is based on the prevention principles that individuals who believe that the use of a particular drug involves risk or harm and/or who disapprove of its use are less likely to use that drug. Combined with other enforcement, treatment, and prevention efforts, the Montana Meth Project's education campaign has had dramatic prevention effects. Virtually all Montana citizens are aware of the dangers posed by meth. Early results show that drug use behavior has been altered in the short term. For example, during the period of 2006 and 2007, for patients 20 years of age and younger, admission for those citing meth as their drug choice dropped by 42% (Montana Department of Justice, 2008).

University of Nebraska-Lincoln The University of Nebraska-Lincoln publishes "NebFact," a document that outlines how citizens of Nebraska can fight meth in Nebraska. The fact sheet contains strategies for individuals and communities to deal with the meth epidemic. The goal, according to Marilyn Fox and Sue Brown, University of Nebraska Extension educators, is not just to educate the family on the hazards of meth, but "also to protect them from the many other hazards posed by meth use and production" (Cooperative Extension, Institute of Agriculture and Natural Resources, University of Nebraska-Lincoln, 2004). The program emphasizes the following points: (1) assess the situation; (2) identify the priorities; (3) develop a work/action plan; and (4) implement the plans.

North Dakota (Rural Methamphetamine Education Project) The main goal of the project is to develop and deliver a public awareness and education campaign to children, schools, teachers, parents, and communities. The public awareness campaign is a multifaceted approach involving the printing and dissemination of materials regarding methamphetamine to the direct delivery of schools, victims, former users, and treatment counselors. Presentations are also available for community stakeholders (i.e., public officials, teachers, business leaders, and parents) and the general public to learn about how methamphetamine is affecting the state and their community and how they can respond to it (Minot State University, Rural Crime and Justice Center, 2009).

South Carolina Meth Watch Program Sponsored by the CHPA, the Meth Watch Program has been formed to respond to the recent incidents involving methamphetamine labs in the city of North Augusta in South Carolina. The business community is very involved in curbing the methamphetamine use through monitoring and purchase limits on products that can be used to create meth in labs. Citizens are urged to contact law enforcement officials if they see suspicious customers (North Augusta, Department of Public Service, 2009).

Tennessee Meth Watch Program Methamphetamine is destroying Tennessee communities at an alarming rate. In 2000, the Federal Drug Enforcement Agency reported 239 clandestine lab seizures in the state. For the first six months of 2004, that number had skyrocketed to more than 1,000, not including those labs seized during the latter part of the year. At least 700 children were removed from their homes in 2005 due to their parents' meth use. The Tennessee Bureau of Investigation's (TBI) Drug Investigation Division is responsible for investigating all drug offenses within Tennessee, including violations related to meth. As a result, the Division is spearheading the TBI's response to this scourge. There is a commitment of highly trained agents and other investigative resources to the identification, dismantling, and prosecution of meth distributors and organizations. The TBI has also developed four highly specialized meth response trucks that are dispatched to meth labs across Tennessee. The Drug Investigation Division also recognizes that children are often the innocent victims of meth. As a result, the Drug Division is complementing its enforcement efforts by partnering with other agencies and the National Alliance for Drug-Endangered Children (Tennessee Bureau of Investigation, 2009).

Oregon's YouthLink—Methamphetamine Awareness Project In 2002, YouthLink piloted the Methamphetamine Awareness Project (MAP), an innovative drug prevention project funded by the Center for Substance Abuse Prevention (CSAP) to reduce, delay, and prevent teen methamphetamine use in targeted communities in Yamhill County, Oregon. MAP provides after-school programming that combines drug-prevention education, team-building skills, and community service with the art of filmmaking. They show the film titled *Meth: Don't Go There*, a 16-minute documentary about the devastating community impact of meth abuse. In 2004, Newberg, Oregon, students produced two broadcast-quality service announcements targeting methamphetamine. In 2003, YouthLink began the Community Drug Awareness Project (CDAP) to reduce, delay, and prevent teen club drug use in Jefferson High School. The Oregon Meth Watch website is dedicated to providing Oregonians with up-to-date information on how methamphetamine is affecting that state (Oregon Meth Watch Program, Oregon Partnership, 2009).

Washington Meth Watch Program The Washington Meth Watch Program is a collaborative initiative, which began in Spokane County by the Greater Spokane Substance Abuse Council (GSSAC) and the Spokane County Meth Action Team to curtail drug lab activity by making the theft or purchase of precursor products more difficult. Since inception, it has grown from a core of retailers using signage, educating employees, and reporting suspicious activity to a broad membership of businesses linked together to prevent theft, fraud, and abuse in the community. The group consists of grocery markets, drug stores, convenience stores, auto parts stores, pet/farming supply stores, banks, credit unions, security firms, property managers, and storage facilities. The strong community partnerships and proactive involvement of business owners and citizens alike has made this prevention program a success throughout the state of Washington (Washington Meth Watch Program, 2009).

Short-Term and Long-Term Effects of Methamphetamine Abuse

The National Institute on Drug Abuse (NIDA) reports that methamphetamine "increases the release of very high levels of the brain chemical dopamine, which is involved in motivation, the experience of pleasure, and motor function, and is a common mechanism of action for most drugs of abuse" (NIDA, 2008). Chronic methamphetamine abuse significantly changes how the brain functions. Noninvasive human brain imaging studies have shown alterations in the activity of the dopamine system that are associated with reduced motor performance and impaired verbal learning (Volkow et. al., 2001).

Methamphetamine is a Schedule II stimulant, which means it has a high potential for abuse and is available only through a prescription. It is indicated for the treatment of narcolepsy, which is a sleep disorder. Methamphetamine is prescribed by some physicians to treat attention deficit hyperactivity disorder as well. We need to understand that the medical uses of methamphetamine are limited. In addition, the doses prescribed to treat narcolepsy and attention deficit hyperactivity disorder are usually much lower than the amount typically abused.

What Are the Short-Term Effects of Methamphetamine Abuse?

The short-term effects of methamphetamine abuse may include the following, according to the National Institute on Drug Abuse:

- Increased attention and decreased fatigue
- Increased activity and wakefulness
- Decreased appetite
- Euphoria and rush
- Increased respiration
- Rapid/irregular heartbeat
- Hyperthermia

The elevated release of dopamine produced by methamphetamine is also thought to contribute to the drug's deleterious effects on nerve terminals in the brain (NIDA Research Report Series, 2006).

What Are the Long-Term Effects of Methamphetamine Abuse?

The National Institute on Drug Abuse reports that the long-term effects of methamphetamine abuse may include the following:

- Addiction
- Psychosis, including paranoia, hallucinations, and repetitive motor activity
- Changes in brain structure and function
- Memory loss
- Aggressive or violent behavior
- Mood disturbances
- Severe dental problems
- Weight loss

With chronic abuse, tolerance to methamphetamine's pleasurable effects can develop. In an effort to intensify the desired effects, abusers may take higher doses of the drug, take it more frequently, or change their method of drug intake. Withdrawal from methamphetamine occurs when a chronic abuser stops taking the drug. Symptoms of withdrawal include depression, anxiety, fatigue, and intense craving for the drug. As mentioned earlier, chronic methamphetamine abuse also significantly changes the brain. Recent studies in chronic methamphetamine abusers have also revealed severe structural and functional changes in areas of the brain associated with emotion and memory, which, according to the NIDA, may account for many of the emotional and cognitive problems observed in chronic methamphetamine abusers (NIDA, 2009).

The Methamphetamine Production Prevention Act of 2008

The Methamphetamine Production Prevention Act of 2008 became law on October 16, 2008. This act replaces the Combat Meth Act by requiring electronic logbooks to be kept rather than written logbooks. These logbooks contain information related to the sale of drugs commonly found as meth ingredients, such as pseudoephedrine. According to the Rural Assistance Center, individuals can purchase limited amounts of this drug, and they must present a government-issued photo identification card and sign the seller's logbook after they have reviewed it to verify its accuracy.

Combat Methamphetamine Epidemic Act of 2005

The Combat Methamphetamine Epidemic Act of 2005 (CMEA), according to the U.S. government's website on methamphetamine information, was signed into law on March 9, 2006, with the implication that the law would regulate retail-over-the-counter sales of ephedrine, pseudoephedrine, and phenylpropanolamine products. This includes daily sales limits and 30-day purchase limits, placement of product out of direct customer access, sales logbooks, customer ID verification, employee training, and self-certification of regulated sellers. The CMEA is found as Title VII of the USA Patriot Improvement and Reauthorization Act of 2005 (Public Law 109-177). The CMEA was passed to curtail the illicit production of methamphetamine.

Assessment of Impact of Drug Courts in Methamphetamine Cases

Although drug courts have enjoyed considerable empirical, anecdotal, and political support, there is a growing call to assess whether drug courts impact different types of offenders equally (Goldkamp, 1999; Longshore et al., 2001). This is particularly important in light of research that has found there is no difference in outcomes among drug court participants and nonparticipants (Deschenes & Greenwood, 1994; Granfield, Eby, & Brewster, 1998, Listwan et al., 2003; Wolfe, Guydish, & Termondt, 2002) or that drug court participants have higher recidivism rates in contrast to nonparticipants (Miethe, Lu, & Reese, 2000). Findings suggest that drug court participants who had any history of using meth may have more serious substance use histories but less serious criminal records. Stoops, Tindall, Mateyoke-Scrivner, and Leukefeld (2005) examined differences between drug court participants who had ever used meth and participants that never used meth. They discovered that meth users were more likely to have tried multiple illicit substances and to use multiple substances in a single day. In terms of criminal behavior, participants who had ever used meth were more likely to self-report theft, selling drugs other than marijuana, and breaking and entering into someone's home or vehicle. However, those who had never used meth had significantly fewer "weapons charges, probation violations, nonsupport, and other charges on their criminal records" (p. 267).

Huddleston (2005) has proposed that drug courts can be an effective strategy for communities experiencing problems with meth. In his review, he references three drug courts that primarily serve meth users. The Butte County (CA) Drug Court identified 87% of their participants as meth users, with 15% reconvicted during the follow-up period. Similarly, 60% of the Orange County (CA) Superior Drug Court participants test positive for meth use and 26% of its graduates recidivated. Finally, an evaluation of the Salt Lake County (UT) Felony Drug Court, which primarily serves meth users, found that drug court participation significantly reduced drug arrests. It is worth noting that none of the studies reviewed explicitly compared outcomes of meth users with those of non–meth users, nor did they distinguish regular meth users from experimental or sporadic meth users.

Harm Reduction Is a Public Health Alternative to the Criminal Model of Meth Drug Use, Reliance, and Habit: The Addiction Institute of New York

It is time that we stop penalizing meth users, sellers, and abusers by incarcerating them. Prison is not a viable option since the abuse of any drug needs to be viewed as a public health issue.

During an interview with John Bellamy Taylor, director of the AINY Evaluation Clinic of the Addiction Institute at Roosevelt Hospital in New York City, it was clear that the Addiction Institute is committed to viewing harm reduction as an alternative to the criminal model of meth drug use, reliance, and habit. There are six precepts of Harm Reduction (HR): (1) Harm reduction is a public health alternative to the moral/criminal and medical/pathological models of drug use, reliance, and habit; (2) harm reduction endorses and embraces both abstinent and nonabstinent strategies and treatments in pursuit of positive change; (3) harm reduction has arisen primarily as a "bottom-up" approach, driven by consumer advocacy and authorship, rather than a "top-down" policy driven by politicians and pundits; (4) harm reduction promotes and provides low-threshold access to supportive services as an alternative to traditional high-threshold criteria; (5) harm reduction is based on the tenets of compassionate pragmatism as opposed to those of moralistic idealism; and (6) harm reduction is a process, not an outcome, and therefore recognizes positive change, however gradual or incremental, from a client-centered point of view (Taylor, 2010).

How Does the Evaluation Service of the Addiction Institute of New York Aid Clients?

At the Addiction Institute of New York, state-of-the-art treatment begins with both sensitive consultation and comprehensive evaluation. Their focus is on personal motivation and collaborative engagement in a process of cognitive-behavioral change. Clinical assessments are provided by a team of experienced and expert medical and mental health care professionals within a framework of research-supported placement criteria and evidenced-based practice guidelines. They share a commitment to (1) developing a panoramic picture of a client's psychotropic substance use pattern, its emotional and psychological context, other strengths and liabilities, level of functioning, and quality of life; (2) identifying a most commensurate but least restrictive level-of-care for initiation of an effective treatment; and (3) communicating and coordinating with referring and otherwise involved professional providers, as well as concerned family members, with regard to optimal treatment planning (Addiction Institute of New York, 2010).

Resiliency, Hope, and Integrity (RHI) Philosophy and Reality House Philosophy Aid Methamphetamine Clients

Harm reduction as a public health alternative to the criminal model of drug use, reliance, and habit is viewed as a viable advance in forensic science in 2010 at Reality House. I interviewed Onaje Mu'id, clinical director of Realty House, in April 2010. The mission statement of Reality House is as follows: (1) Provide chemical dependency treatment services through traditional and social justice models; (2) endeavor to achieve cultural competency throughout the agency to respect each client and treat them in a dignified manner; and (3) engage stakeholders in a collaborative process to ensure feedback and continuous growth and excellence.

Mu'id also outlined the Resiliency, Hope, and Integrity (RHI) Philosophy at Reality House that is integral to application of the harm reduction model outlined by John Bellamy Taylor of the Addiction Institute of New York. The RHI Philosophy and Reality House Orientation encompass a human-centric strength-based leadership approach in recovery-oriented systems of care (ROSC). As Lenard Hebert, director of Reality House, puts it, "We are a community, not just a clinic ... let the healing begin."

The RHI organizational goal involves the following points: Develop cutting-edge leadership in the areas of (1) organization cultural wellness, (2) cultural competency, (3) social justice, (4) clinical excellence, (5) progressive supervision, (6) trauma-informed, (7) strength-based family services for an evolving recovery-oriented behavior health care system.

Onaje Mu'id summarized the importance of adopting harm reduction as a public health alternative to the criminal model of drug use, reliance, and habit in the following statement: "Authentic leadership is the ability to translate the ideal about oneness of humanity into tangible actions for its realization."

Conclusions

Methamphetamine is a highly addictive stimulant that can have serious effects on a user's physical, mental, and social health. Approximately 10 million people have tried methamphetamine at least once. This is an astounding number of people who are using a drug that can infuse whole communities with social ills, crime, child neglect, and domestic abuse. Short-term and long-term effects of meth use are discussed. Many states and the federal government have begun to enact legislation to combat the use and production of methamphetamine in the United States.

Many states have instituted programs to reduce the rural meth problem. Methamphetamine abuse can be prevented through aggressive education programs like the Meth Watch Program, which is sponsored by the Consumer Healthcare Products Association (CHPA) and is designed to help curtail the theft and suspicious sales of pseudoephedrine products, as well as other common household products used in the illicit manufacturing of methamphetamine in small, toxic labs. A key goal of this program is to promote cooperation between retailers and law enforcement to prevent the diversion of legitimate products for illegal use.

The Kansas Meth Prevention Program (KMPP) began as a public-private partnership formed in October 2001 to develop a statewide infrastructure to fight the methamphetamine problem in Kansas communities. The program received funding through the Substance Abuse and Mental Health Services Administration (SAMHSA) in 2002.

A statewide network of agencies partnered to make the KMPP successful. The CHPA has made funds available to help support state and local Meth Watch programs. In addition to the Kansas Meth Program, a number of additional states have taken the Kansas model and implemented their own Meth Watch programs.

The Combat Methamphetamine Epidemic Act of 2005 (CMEA) was passed to curtail the production of methamphetamine.

Harm reduction as a public health alternative to the criminal model of drug use, reliance, and habit is viewed as a viable advance in forensic science in 2011. The Addiction Institute of New York and Reality House, Inc., of New York are two agencies that are implementing forms of the harm reduction model as they work with clients who have suffered from methamphetamine use and abuse. More research needs to be directed in the area of harm reduction.

References

Addiction Institute of New York, 2010.

Avis, H. *Drugs and Life*. Boston: McGraw Hill, 1999.

California Attorney General's Crime and Prevention Center report on Stopdrugs.org, 2008.

Ciaffone, T. J., and Cristi Cain. Kansas Department of Health and Environment, 2009.

Cooperative Extension, Institute of Agriculture and Natural Resources, University of Nebraska, Lincoln, NF04-608, October 2004.

Deschenes, E. P., and P. W. Greenwood. 1994. Maricopa County's drug court: An innovative program for first-time offenders on probation. *The Justice System Journal* 17: 99–115.

Doghramji, K. 1989. Sleep disorders: A selective update. *Hospital and Community Psychiatry* 40: 29–40.

Doweiko, H. E. *Concepts of chemical dependency*. New York: Brooks/Cole, 1996.

Gold, M. S. & Verebey, K. 1984. The psychopharmacology of cocaine. *Psychiatric Annuals* 14:714–723.

Goldkamp, J. S. 1999. Challenges for research and innovation: When is a drug court not a drug court? In W. C. Terry (Ed.), *The early drug courts: Case studies in judicial innovation* (pp. 166–177). Thousand Oaks, CA: Sage.

Granfield, R., Eby, C., & Brewster, T. 1998. An examination of the Denver drug court: The impact of treatment-oriented drug offender system. *Law & Policy* 20: 183–202.

Halkitis, P. N., Parsons, J. T., & Sturratt, M. J. 2001. A double epidemic: crystal methamphetamine drug use in relation to HIV transmission among gay men. *Journal of Homosexuality* 41(2): 17–35.

Harvard Medical School Mental Health Letter. 1990. *Amphetamines* 6(10): 1–4.

Hebert, L. 2010. Interview with Lenard Hebert on April 5, 2010, at Reality House, Inc.

Huddleston, C. W. 2005. Drug courts: an effective strategy for communities facing methamphetamine. Alexandria, VA: National Drug Court Institute.

Jaffe, J. H. 1990. Drug addiction and drug abuse. In A.G. Gilman, T. W. Rall, A. S. Nies, & P. Taylor (Eds.), *The pharmacological basis of therapeutics* (8th edition). New York: Macmillan.
Kaminski, A. 1992. *Mind-altering drugs.* Madison, WI: Wisconsin Clearinghouse, Board of Regents, University of Wisconsin System.
Levounis, P. and Ruggiero, J. S. 2006. *Primary Psychiatry,* 13(2): 76.
Listwan, S. J., Sundt, J., Holsinger, A. M., and Latessa, E. J. 2003. The effect of drug court programming on recidivism: The Cincinnati experience. *Crime and Delinquency* 49: 389–411.
Longshore, D., Turner, S., Wenzel, S., Morral, A., Harrell, A., McBride, D., et al. 2001. Drug courts: A conceptual framework. *Journal of Drug Issues 31*: 7–26.
McGrath, Mike, Montana State Attorney, speech. 2009. Location unknown.
Madler, A. Rural Assistance Center, 2009.
Mayo Clinic Health Letter. 1989. America's drug crisis. Rochester, MN: Mayo Foundation for Medical Education and Research.
Miethe, T., Lu, H., and Reese, E. 2000. Reintegrative shaming and recidivism risks in drug court: Explanations for some unexpected findings. *Crime and Delinquency* 46: 522–541.
Minnesota Department of Corrections. 2005, December. *How is the Minnesota Department of Corrections working to reduce meth-related recidivism?* http://www.doc.state.mn.us.
Minot State University, Rural Crime and Justice Center, Rural Methamphetamine Education Project, 2009.
Mirin, S. M., Weiss, R. D., and Greenfield, S. F. 1991. Psychoactive substance use disorders. A. J. Galenberg, E. L. Bassuk, & S. C. Schoonover (Eds.), In *The practitioner's guide to psychoactive drugs* (3rd ed.). New York: Plenum.
Montana Department of Justice April, 2008. *Methamphetamine in Montana: A follow-up report on trends and progress.*
Montana Meth Project, 2009.
Mu'id, O. 2010. Interview on April 19, 2010, at John Jay College of Criminal Justice.
National Institute on Drug Abuse (NIDA), September 2006. Research Report Series.
National Institute on Drug Abuse (NIDA), June 19, 2008. *InfoFacts-Methamphetamine.*
North Augusta, Department of Public Service, South Carolina, 2009.
Oregon Partnership, Oregon YouthLink, 2009.
Rawson, R. A., Simon, S. L., and Ling, W. 2002. If a US drug abuse epidemic fails to include a major East Coast city, can it be called an epidemic? *Journal of Addiction Dis.* 21(1): 1–4.
Stall, R. Paul, J. P., Greenwood, G., et al. 2001. Alcohol use, drug use, and alcohol-related problems among men who have sex with men. The Urban Men's Health Study. *Addiction* 96(11): 1589–1601.
Stoops, W. W., Tindall, M. S., Mateyoke-Scrivner, A., and Leukefeld, C. 2005. Methamphetamine use in non-urban and urban drug court clients. *International Journal of Offender Therapy and Comparative Criminology* 49: 260–276.
Street drugs: A drug identification guide. Plymouth, MN: Publishers Group, LLC: 2005.
Taylor, J. B. 2010. Interview on April 5, 2010.
Tennessee Bureau of Investigation, Nashville, Tennessee, 2009.
Volkow, N. D., Chang, L., Wang, G. J., et al. 2001. Association of dopamine transporter reduction with psychomotor impairment in methamphetamine abusers. *American Journal Psychiatry* 158: 377–382.
Washington Meth Watch Program, 2009.
Weiner, N. 1985. Norepinephrine, epinephrine, and the sympathomimetic amines. In A. G. Gilman, L. S. Goodman, T. W. Rall, & F. Murad (Eds.), *The pharmacological basis of therapeutics* (7th ed.). New York: Houghton-Mifflin.
Wolfe, E., Guydish, J., and Termondt, J. 2002. A drug court outcome evaluation comparing arrests in a two-year follow-up period. *Journal of Drug Issue* 32: 1155–1172.

New Frontiers in Molecular Forensics

Identification of Botanical, Entomological, and Microbial Material

3

MARGARET WALLACE

Contents

Introduction

"It is envisaged that DNA fingerprinting will revolutionize forensic biology" (Jeffreys, Gill, & Werrett, 1985a). In 1985 this was a very bold prediction; 25 years later it can be viewed as an understatement. DNA fingerprinting used the technique of restriction fragment length polymorphism (RFLP) to examine repetitive regions in the human genome. These variable number of tandem repeats (VNTRs) or minisatellites consist of blocks of 10–100 base pairs (bp) in length which are highly polymorphic. RFLP had excellent power of discrimination—approximately 1 in millions or greater with four or more markers (Butler, 2010). However, the limited sensitivity, lengthy processing time, statistical complications, and difficulties in interpretation were problematic. Since the technique required high molecular weight DNA, degraded samples could not be typed.

The polymerase chain reaction (PCR), a cyclic enzymatic amplification process, produces millions of copies of DNA from a single template (Saiki et al., 1985). At 100% efficiency, over 67 million copies of a targeted DNA region can be produced from a single copy of the template after 28 cycles. The first commercially (Cetus Corporation) available PCR-based method typed the Human Leukocyte Antigen (HLA) DQA1 gene on chromosome 6, via sequence polymorphisms (Comey et al., 1993). The technique successfully handled low molecular weight, degraded DNA. HLA/DQA1 typing was less discriminating than RFLP, but as additional markers were analyzed it became more powerful. The Polymarker (PM) kit (AmpliType PM+DQA1, Perkin Elmer) coamplified a portion of the DQA1 gene together with segments from five other genes (LDLR, GYPA, HBGG, D7S8, and GC) located on chromosomes 4, 7, 11, and 19. The AmpliType PM kit was rapid and had a relatively good—approximately 1 in 1,000—power of discrimination (Herrin, Fildes, & Reynolds, 1994).

Today, all modern forensic DNA laboratories rely on PCR-STR analysis for human identification. Microsatellites or short tandem repeats (STRs) are regions of DNA that have repetitive segments of 2–6 bp. The STR loci are moderately polymorphic. The analysis of STRs has several advantages for the forensic scientist. The use of PCR allows for a small amount of DNA to be amplified and examined. The fragment size required for PCR-STR is approximately 100–400 bp, making it useful for degraded DNA. Multiple loci can be typed simultaneously. The first PCR- STR multiplex systems, described in 1993 by Kimpton, Gill, and Walton, typed 14 different STR loci in three reactions. Currently it is not uncommon to analyze 16 loci in a single reaction. The Identifiler (Applied Biosystems) and PowerPlex 16 (Promega Corporation) kits each amplify 15 STR loci, and the gender identification locus, amelogenin. The advent of PCR-STR enabled forensic biologists to type a small-sized sample of questionable quality. The technique is sensitive and rapid and provides an excellent power of discrimination—approximately 1 in billions with 8–9 loci (Butler, 2010). In addition, multiplexing conserves samples and reduces the chance of contamination.

Molecular techniques that utilize DNA provide information that can be used to individualize many forms of biological evidence. While PCR-STR is currently the most widely used method for DNA typing in humans, its use with other species is limited due to the lack of sequence information coupled with the time and cost for the development and validation of multiplexes. Many forms of forensic evidence including botanical, entomological, and microbial contain DNA. To analyze these types of samples, forensic scientists have taken advantage of other molecular methods.

Forensic Botany

Classic Techniques

Forensic botany is the study of botanical evidence as it applies to criminal investigations. Botanical evidence has the potential to provide valuable information for the forensic scientist by establishing the time of death or linking a person to a location. Early techniques relied on morphological characteristics of botanical evidence as the source of information.

Plant systematics and plant anatomy attempt to classify or identify species based on morphological characteristics. Species identification by either method is not always possible, since it may be limited by the amount and/or condition of the evidence received, but if distinctive cells are present, determination of a genus or species can be achieved (Coyle et al., 2001; Hall, 1996). Species determination can be used to link a suspect with a specific location or to a broader geographic region. The specificity of the link is based on the distribution of the species in question; that is, the less dispersed the species, the more useful the information. In contrast, plant fragments present at a crime scene that are inconsistent with local vegetation may indicate a prior location of either the suspect or victim, which would provide information critical for accurate crime reconstruction (Hall, 1996).

Plant ecology provides information as to the succession patterns of plants in a particular location, as well as growth and decay information regarding particular species. Succession patterns are of particular interest to forensic scientists in areas where vegetation has been disturbed, as in the case of a buried body. Based on the type of plants growing and their stage of growth, plant ecologists can estimate a minimum time frame since the ground was disturbed, and from that, a possible time of death (Bock & Norris, 1997; Coyle et al., 2001; Hall, 1996).

Palynologists utilize microscopy to identify the genus or possibly even species of a plant based on the morphological characteristics of the pollen. Palynology is useful to forensic scientists because it can be utilized to link a person to a particular location, and it can aid in time of death estimations (Coyle et al., 2001). Pollen is dispersed by a number of means including insects, air, water, and animals (Hall, 1996). The method of dispersal, pollen size and shape, and environmental factors affect the range over which pollen is distributed and the amount that is deposited in a particular region (Coyle et al., 2001; Horrocks & Walsh, 1999; Randerson, 2002). The amounts and types of pollen present in a soil sample can be used to link a person with a crime scene. Time of death may be estimated from pollen present on victims based on the season that the pollen was released (Coyle et al., 2001).

Limnology is the study of freshwater ecology. Morphological identification of algae present in a freshwater sample is possible using microscopy. Limnology can be used to link a suspect with a location, prove that a drowning occurred in freshwater, and possibly determine the season in which a freshwater drowning occurred (Coyle et al., 2001; Hall, 1996). Algae will be present in the lungs of freshwater drowning victims, and the time that the algae were deposited may be determined, since the algae population varies seasonally (Coyle et al., 2001). This information can help determine, with greater precision, the location and time that a victim drowned. Algae can also be found in soil that has had contact with fresh water. This allows investigators to link a suspect to a body of water based on algae present in soil found on the suspect (Hall, 1996).

Plant systematics, anatomy, ecology, palynology, and limnology are fields that provide useful forensic information based on botanical evidence. Though invaluable, each relies primarily on morphological characteristics to determine genus and species and does not utilize recently developed molecular techniques to identify or individualize botanical evidence.

Molecular Techniques

Molecular techniques that utilize DNA provide information that can be used to individualize many forms of biological evidence. The genetic markers used for human identification have been well characterized. The STR loci used in forensics are widely distributed throughout the genome, are moderately polymorphic, exhibit low mutation rates, and are in Hardy-Weinberg and linkage equilibrium. While PCR-STR is currently the most widely used method for DNA typing in humans, its use with other species is limited. STRs can be isolated, and their primer sequences determined, but these processes can be lengthy, labor intensive, and inefficient, especially in species with low STR frequencies in the genome (Zane et al., 2002). However, in some instances, such as drug trafficking, where the need for an STR system offsets the time and expense for development, multiplex STR systems are being developed for forensic use (Howard et al., 2008).

Random Amplified Polymorphic DNA (RAPD; Jagadish et al., 1996) and Amplified Fragment Length Polymorphism (Vos et al., 1995) are techniques that permit one to type an organism when very little information is available about its genome. RAPD was used to link plant material from a source tree to a suspect in a homicide investigation (Yoon, 1993). However, the low stringency PCR conditions allow nonspecific binding of the primers and produce non-reproducible bands in the final product (Mueller & Wolfenbarger, 1999). Thus, results obtained with RAPD are not as reproducible and the resolution of genetic difference is not as high as the forensic community typically demands.

Amplified Fragment Length Polymorphism (AFLP) is a powerful method that combines techniques from classical hybridization-based (Jeffreys et al., 1985b) and PCR-based (Weber & May, 1989) genotyping strategies. AFLP can be used to genotype DNAs of any origin and complexity. The process involves three steps: restriction digestion of genomic DNA and ligation of oligonucleotide adapters, selective amplification (via two consecutive PCR reactions) of sets of restriction fragments, and electrophoretic analysis of the PCR fragments. Typically 50–100 restriction fragments are amplified and detected, making the AFLP technique a powerful genotyping method. The AFLP technique has several advantages: (1) reproducibility over a wide range of template concentrations due to the high stringency annealing conditions (Vos et al., 1995); (2) production of a large number of observable molecular markers due to the fact that the entire genome is subject to restriction digestion (Blears et al., 1998; Savelkoul et al., 1999); and (3) a high discriminative capacity since multiple combinations of selective nucleotides can be used to observe additional markers (Savelkoul et al., 1999). AFLP is currently being used in breeding studies, germplasm management, variety identification, backcross breeding in plants, animal genetics, as well as fungal and bacterial taxonomic identification and epidemiology (Savelkoul et al., 1999). Genetic mapping and linkage experiments have been performed using AFLP for a variety of plants (Meksem et al., 1995; Ridout & Donini, 1999; Saal & Wricke, 2002; Schondelmaier et al., 1996; Wang et al., 1997). In the fight against drugs, a national AFLP database was developed and evaluated for *Cannabis sativa* to determine the amount of genetic variation within and between plants seized by authorities (Coyle et al., 2001). In addition Coyle et al. (2003) developed an AFLP method for the individualization of marijuana samples. Bless et al. (2006) used AFLP for species identification and source attribution within a closed set of trees. AFLP profiles were obtained for 40 *Acer rubrum* (red maple) trees. Leaf material from five additional species was also typed. A number of *Acer rubrum* species-specific peaks were identified (Figure 3.1). In addition, within this closed set of samples, 15 of 16 (93.8%) blind samples tested were correctly identified (Figure 3.2).

Herbert et al. (2003) proposed a universal species identification system based on "DNA barcodes." Barcoding is the use of universal PCR primers to amplify and sequence an approximately 600-base-pair fragment of the cytochrome oxidase I (*COI*) gene in the mitochondrial genome. The resultant sequence is then compared to an existing database of "known" sequences from specimens previously identified by taxonomists. Although DNA barcoding has been used for identification in animals, fungi, and insects, it had not been successful in plants. The *COI* gene in plants is not discriminative since the locus exhibits limited variation and a low evolutionary rate (Wolfe, Li, & Sharp, 1987). No single variable barcoding gene, comparable to the *COI* locus, has been found for species identification in plants. Consequently, plant identification systems using a combination of morphological and molecular techniques have been proposed (De Ley et al., 2005). Ward et al. (2009) developed a molecular system for the identification (subfamily to species) of Australian grasses based on sequence polymorphisms at four chloroplast and two mitochondrial loci. Insertion-deletions (indels)

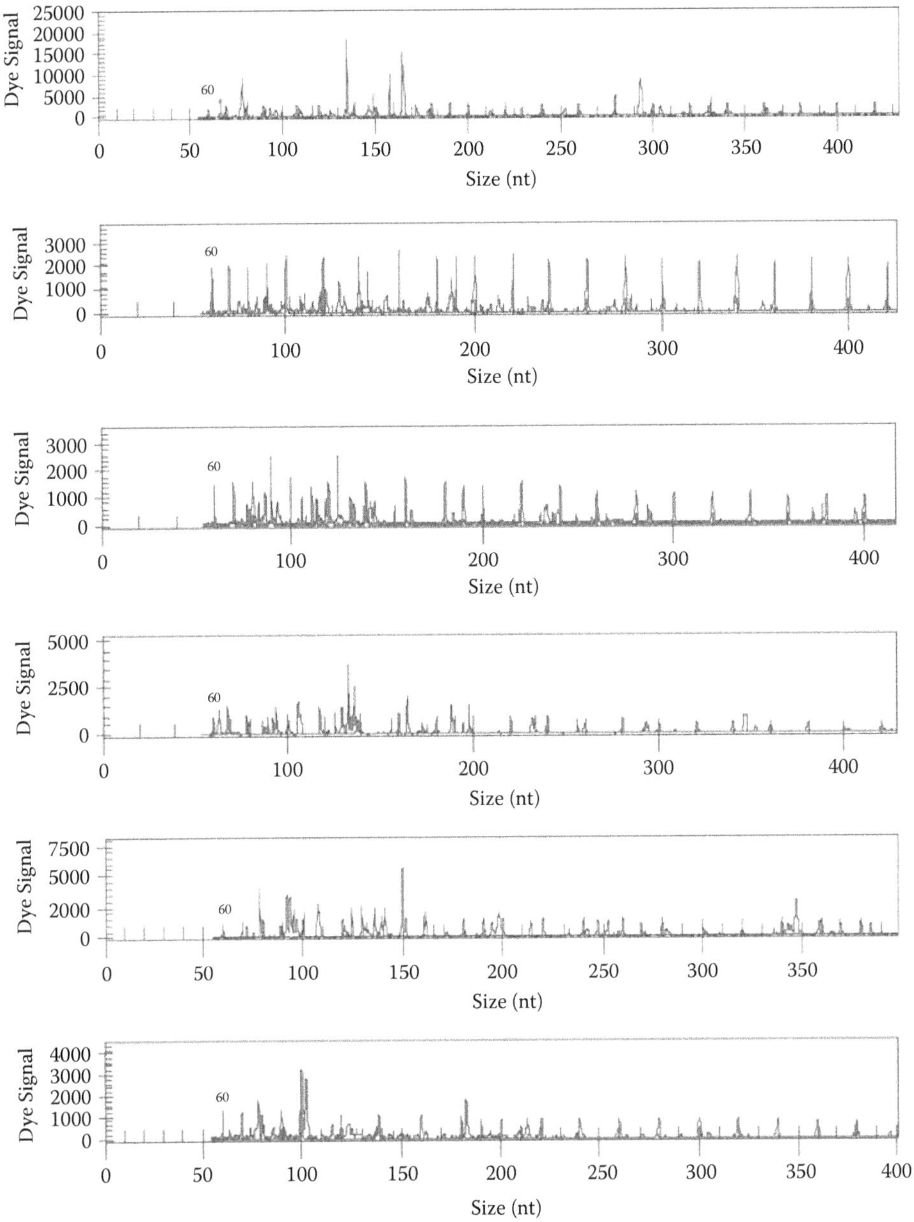

Figure 3.1 Species-specific AFLP profiles. From top: red Maple, oak, Japanese maple, Norway maple, sweet gum, and American elm. Reprinted with permission from Bless, C., Palmeter, H., and Wallace, M. (2006). Identification of *Acer rubrum* using Amplified Fragment Length Polymorphism. 2006. *J. Forensic Sci 51*, 31–38.

and single nucleotide polymorphisms (SNPs) were typed using PCR and allele specific (AS)-PCR, respectively.

Thus, DNA-based systems have been developed for identification of botanical evidence. These systems have been used successfully by forensic scientists. However, as with all novel techniques, challenges regarding admissibility of nonhuman DNA evidence in

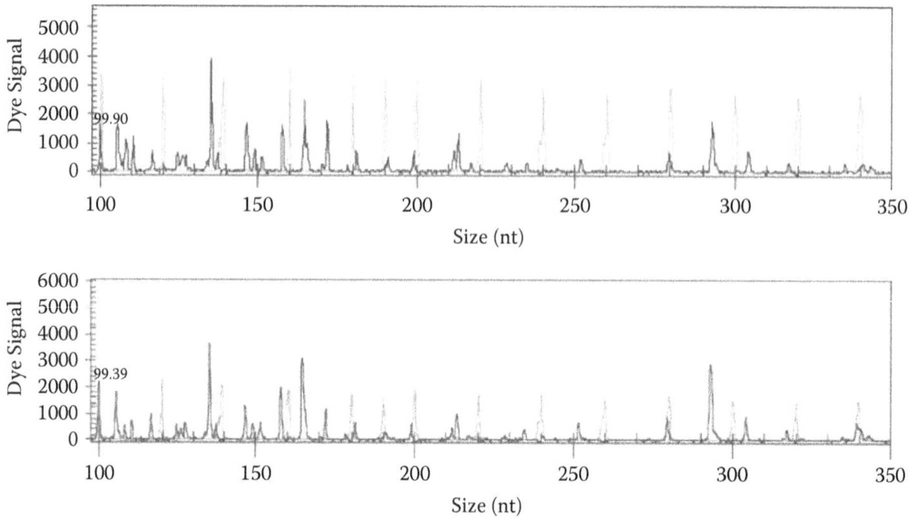

Figure 3.2 Blind sample profile (top) and database profile from same tree (below). Black peaks correspond to the AFLP profiles; gray peaks to the internal size standard. Reprinted with permission from Bless, C., Palmeter, H., and Wallace, M. (2006). Identification of *Acer rubrum* using Amplified Fragment Length Polymorphism. 2006. *J. Forensic Sci 51*, 31–38.

court, validity of the underlying scientific theory, validity of any statistical interpretations, and relevant scientific community will need to be addressed (Sensabaugh & Kaye, 1998).

Forensic Entomology

Classic Techniques

In forensics carrion-breeding insects are used primarily to estimate postmortem interval (PMI). Species identification is crucial if one intends to use larval developmental history as an index of time since death (Anderson, 1995). Particular species are attracted to specific states of decay and colonize a body for a limited period of time. Flies in the families Calliphoridae (blowflies) and Sarcophagidae (flesh-eating flies) are generally the first insects to be attracted to a body (Anderson, 1995; Tenorio, Oslon, & Coats, 2003). Immature flies take predictable amounts of time to pass through their developmental stages. This is a major key for forensic entomology since these developmental timelines are highly species specific and are subject to a host of variables including ambient temperature and humidity (Anderson, 2000). This insect faunal succession on cadavers (Bhaetu & Singh, 1995), together with knowledge of growth rates under specific environmental conditions (Anderson, 2000), can be used in criminal investigations to determine the PMI.

Forensic entomologists must correctly identify carrion-breeding species to associate a particular developmental pattern with succession. This is problematic since the morphology of larvae, particularly of closely related species, is very similar if not identical (Erzinçlio lu, 1985). Rearing the larvae to adulthood delays the determination of PMI and may compromise the specimens by exposing the larvae to contamination, parasitism, and predation (Erzinçlio lu, 1985).

The protocol cannot be applied when only dead insects or pieces of insects are found at a scene. In addition, the development of adults from larvae can take several weeks, especially when they are collected at the early stages of development (Anderson, 2000). It is often important for investigators to obtain an accurate PMI estimate early in their investigations, and waiting for insects to develop is not ideal. These problems demonstrate the need for an accurate and rapid means of performing species determination that could be applied to multiple sample types (live, dead, and fragmented larvae).

Molecular Techniques

In recent years the analysis of nonhuman DNA from organisms as diverse as viruses, bacteria, household pets, livestock, wild animals, plants, and insects has played an increasingly prominent role in the medicolegal field (Sensabaugh & Kaye, 1998). In forensics, DNA-based methods have been used for the identification of insect species (Wells & Stevens, 2008). Direct sequencing of mitochondrial genes encoding cytochrome oxidase subunits I and II (*COI* & *COII*) and tRNA-leucine genes has been used to identify blowfly species (Sperling, Anderson, & Hickey, 1994; Wells et al., 2001). The method, however, is time consuming and costly.

Tenorio et al. (2003) used mitochondrial DNA sequencing and PCR-RFLP to differentiate adults of the species *Cynomyopsis cadaverina*, *Calliphora livida*, *Calliphora vicina*, and *Phormia regina*. The researchers amplified a 348 bp fragment from the mitochondrial *COI* gene. The four species could be differentiated via three separate restriction digests using the enzymes *Dde*I, *Dra*I, and *Hinf*I. *C. cadaverina*, *C. livida*, and *C. vicina* could also be differentiated by sequencing the 348 bp fragment.

Ratcliff et al. (2003) devised an identification system using PCR-RFLP analysis of the 5.8S RNA gene and the flanking internal transcribed spacer regions (ITS 1 & ITS 2). Fragments from three restriction digests correctly identified 10 species in the Calliphoridae, Muscidae, and Sarcophagidae families. Although the method is relatively rapid (6 h), it is labor intensive.

RAPD and AFLP have also been used to differentiate insect species. RAPD profiles from maggots collected from a body bag clearly differentiated the three colonial species: *Lucilia spec.*, *Calliphora erythrocephala*, and *Qiceoptoma thoracicum* (Benecke, 1998). AFLP has been used to construct linkage maps (Hawthorne, 2001; Parsons & Shaw, 2002) and to study genetic relationships (Katiyar et al., 2000; Ravel et al., 2001; Salvato et al., 2002) and diversity (Kakouli-Duarte, Casey, & Burnell, 2001) among insects. The strength of the technique was demonstrated in a study conducted by Parsons and Shaw (2002) in which AFLP was used to differentiate morphologically cryptic species in the genus Laupala.

Species-specific AFLP profiles were developed using larval samples from *C. macellaria, S. bullata, and P. regina* (Beckert, Friedland, & Wallace, 2010). Peaks at 103, 107, 119, 127, 135, 151, 274 nucleotides (nt) were found in all the *C. macellaria* samples. The species specific profile for *S. bullata* contained peaks at 100, 102, 109, 113, 126, 128, 133, 137, 143, 165, 171, 183, 188, 242 nt. The electropherograms for the *P. regina* samples exhibited species-specific peaks at 113, 131, 138, 148, 178 nt. The results indicate that AFLP is a viable and valuable technique for identification of entomological material. The AFLP technique has several advantages for forensics. The method is rapid and robust, and many steps can be automated. Court challenges regarding admissibility of AFLP profiles from entomological material will need to be addressed (Sensabaugh & Kaye, 1998).

Microbial Forensics

On 9/11, as the Twin Towers crumbled, so did America's sense of security. The anthrax bioterrorism scare that followed in 2001 further eroded America's perception of safety. Since then, the subject of bioterrorism has become one of great concern.

Biological warfare is not a modern phenomenon. Two of the earliest instances in recorded history date back to the sixth century BC (Jacobs, 2004). The Assyrians reportedly poisoned the wells of their enemies with rye ergot, and during the siege of Cirrha, Solon of Athens poisoned the water supply with the herb purgative hellebore (skunk cabbage). Later, during the naval battle against King Eumenes of Pergamon in 184 BC, Hannibal's forces hurled earthen pots filled with serpents upon enemy decks (Ghosh et al., 2002). In medieval times, the development of the trebuchet led to the common practice of catapulting infected cadavers, animal carcasses, or human waste at enemies. In 1346, during the siege of Kaffa, the Tartar army hurled its plague-ridden dead over the walls of the city (Martin et al., 2007). At the battle of Carolstein, in 1422, bodies of plague-stricken soldiers plus 2,000 cartloads of excrement were hurled into the ranks of enemy troops (Jacobs, 2004). In the 1500s, the Spanish conquistadors presented the Native Americans gifts of clothing laden with smallpox (Jacobs, 2004). During the French and Indian War (1754–1763) the English captain, Ecuyer, gave blankets laced with smallpox to Indians loyal to the French (Christopher et al., 1997). During the Civil War (1860–1865), Confederate soldiers poisoned ponds by dumping the carcasses of dead animals into them (Robertson & Robertson, 1995).

The use of biological weapons became more prevalent in the 20th century. During World War I the Germans attempted to spread cholera in Italy, disperse plague in St. Petersburg, and drop biological bombs over Britain (Christopher et al., 1997; Robertson & Robertson, 1995). In 1915, a German-American, Dr. Anton Dilger, grew cultures of *Bacillus anthracis* and *Burkholderia (Pseudomonas) mallei* (glanders), supplied by the German government, in his Maryland laboratory (Jacobs, 2004). The agents and an inoculation device were given to Captain Frederick Hinsch, who used them to infect 3,000 head of horses, mules, and cattle in Baltimore before they were shipped to Allied troops in Europe.

In 1932, during the Japanese invasion of Manchuria, Shiro Ishii, a physician and army officer, began a biological weapons research program. In 1936 Ishii formed Unit 731, a bio-warfare unit masquerading as a water-purification unit. A 150-building complex just outside of Harbin, Manchuria, was constructed for experimental purposes (Jacobs, 2004). Another biological warfare site, Unit 100, near Changchun, Manchuria, field-tested biological agents such as *Bacillus anthracis*, *Clostridium botulinum*, *Clostridium perfringens*, *Neisseria meningitides*, *Shigella* spp., *Vibrio cholera*, and *Yersinia pestis* (Christopher et al., 1997; Geissler & van Courtland Moon, 1999; Jacobs, 2004) on Chinese soldiers. Between 1932 and 1945 at least 10,000 soldiers died as a result of plague, cholera, anthrax, and so on. In addition, tens of thousands of Chinese civilians died as a result of epidemics around the sites of Japanese biologic weapons facilities (Harris, 2002). During World War II the United States, Germany, France, Britain, Canada, and Russia all had limited biological weapons research programs (Jacobs, 2004).

The United States and the Soviet Union were two of the major forces behind biological weapons development during the Korean and Cold War eras. Many of these aggressive research programs were curtailed in 1975 when the United Nations proposed the Biological Weapons Convention, a treaty initially signed by 103 nations agreeing never to research, produce, or use biological weapons (Martin et al., 2007). Today, much of the threat of biological weapons stems from rogue nations and terrorist groups who do not honor the disarmament agreement and engage in what is known as *bioterrorism*—the use of biological agents to achieve a political or ideological objective (Martin et al., 2007).

The faces and the motives behind the release of biological agents have changed over time. The technology for the growth and dispersal of biological pathogens has also evolved, yet the outcome has remained the same: biological weapons have the potential to cause a devastating number of illnesses and/or fatalities.

In addition to the intentional spread of dangerous biological agents by terrorists, pandemics could also be caused by accidental release of such agents, as in the 2005 scare when a dangerous influenza strain was accidentally included in kits used by laboratories all over the world.

Identification of pathogenic agents is crucial for treatment as well as containment. In addition provenance is critical for determining the source—accidental or intentional—of the pathogenic organism.

Classic Techniques

Due to their characteristic morphological and metabolic profiles, pathogenic microorganisms have historically been identified by light microscopy and/or a battery of biochemical tests or staining procedures (Lim et al., 2005). Although such identifications may be somewhat accurate, they are tedious and time consuming. In addition, these methods offer nothing more than a presumptive identification because they cannot differentiate closely related strains. Identification of the microorganism's strain is of particular importance to microbial forensics, mainly because it enables possible source attribution.

Pathogens can also be identified by the enzyme-linked immunosorbent assay (ELISA). In ELISA, antigens from the unknown are immobilized on a solid support. Specific antibodies are then washed over the antigens. Antigen-antibody binding is typically detected via a fluorescent emission produced by an enzyme covalently attached to the antibody. ELISA is an inexpensive and rapid technique. However, the results are often less quantitative and the test itself is less sensitive than alternative analyses. The greatest disadvantage of ELISA is that it is a monoplex technology.

Instrumental Techniques

Several instrument-based methods of identification are currently available. Many of these instrumental methods are variations of mass spectroscopy (MS). A mass spectrometer uses an energy source to fragment an analyte into small fractions. These particles are then ionized and separated based on their mass-to-charge ratios. There are several ways to separate the ionized particles, but many researchers are currently using the time-of-flight (TOF) method. TOF is often paired with a variation of MS called matrix-assisted laser desorption and ionization (MALDI). In MALDI-TOF, a liquefied analyte is mixed with a liquid matrix compound. The analyte and the matrix co-crystallize as they dry on a plate. The plate is transferred to a mass spectrometer where a laser pulse initiates ionization. Ionization imparts a uniform charge on the analyte so that any differences in separation are due to mass alone (not charge). Pathogenic microorganisms can be identified using MALDI-TOF because each microorganism should have unique ionization and TOF profiles, which can be compared to known samples that have been previously analyzed.

MS-based approaches to pathogen identification such as the Ibis T5000™ Biosensor System have generated a great deal of attention from the research community (Ecker et al., 2008). The Ibis T5000™ Biosensor System combines PCR, high-performance electrospray mass spectrometry (ESI-MS) and base-composition analysis. The system identifies and quantifies pathogens providing information analogous to that obtained using microarray and DNA sequencing technologies.

MS-based technologies are rapid due to the vacuum environment in which the analysis occurs (Butler, 2010). However, although MS-based techniques do not require any specific knowledge of the analyte (e.g., nucleotide sequence), a mass spectra library of all possible analytes must be assembled prior to use. The resolution and sensitivity may be compromised if there is excess analyte and/or salt present (Butler, 2010). Lastly, as with many instrumental methods, the start-up and long-term costs are substantial.

Molecular Techniques

There are many methods available to identify pathogenic microorganisms. Techniques exist that yield identifications based on analytes as diverse as peptides, antigens, and other ligands. The primary disadvantage of many of these methods is that they lack the specificity needed to provide a positive identification. The genetic composition of an organism is unique. Therefore, it is likely that any viable technique for the identification of pathogenic microorganisms will have its foundation in genetics. In contrast to many of the more traditional methods of identification, most methods in development today focus on the use of genetic markers for detection and identification of biological pathogens. A genetic marker is any polymorphic region in an organism's genome that can be used for positive identification. Regions of the genome that are good candidates for markers are those that offer the ability to distinguish between very closely related (e.g., species and/or strains) microorganisms.

Polymorphisms are differences in the DNA from different organisms. Length polymorphisms represent differences in the size of the DNA upon fragmentation. Although several researchers have used techniques based on length polymorphisms (e.g., AFLP) to successfully differentiate several bacterial species (Radnedge et al., 2003), these techniques sometimes lack the specificity needed to distinguish very closely related microorganisms (Keim, et al., 2000; Valjevac et al., 2005).

Sequence polymorphisms are differences in the order of nucleotides in the DNA among different organisms. Quantitative PCR (Q-PCR, sometimes referred to as real-time PCR) uses the real-time accumulation of PCR products to identify and quantify target DNA using sequence-specific oligonucleotide probes. Q-PCR has been used to detect and identify pathogenic fungal (Hsu et al., 2003) and microbial (U'Ren et al., 2005) species. The main drawback of Q-PCR is limited multiplexing ability. Although Q-PCR is technically capable of multiplexing because of its use of the 5-dye chemistry, the method does not approach the multiplexing capabilities of other technologies such as DNA microarrays or bead-based assays.

The DNA microarray or "DNA chip" is probably the most formidable competitor of the bead-based technologies. DNA microarrays use a nonporous substrate, typically glass, imprinted with oligonucleotide probes (Saiki et al., 1989). The analyte (i.e., the unknown) usually consists of short segments of DNA that will hybridize with the immobilized probes, if complementarity exists. Hybridization between probe and target is typically detected by fluorescence emission from a fluororphore covalently attached to the target DNA. Microarrays are widely used because of their sensitivity, specificity, and multiplexing capabilities—a single chip can be imprinted with thousands of oligonucleotides. DNA chips have been used to identify and characterize pathogenic bacteria in the *Escherichia*, *Shigella*, *Salmonella*, *Aeromonas*, *Vibrio*, *Mycobacterium*, *Helicobacter*, *Proteus*, *Yersinia*, *Campylobacter*, and *Bacillus* genera (Kostić et al., 2007; Wang et al., 2004).

Microarrays require bioinformatics expertise for their design and analysis and are very expensive for routine use (Grate et al., 2003; Spiro et al., 2000; Summerbell et al., 2005). There are several problems associated with the immobilization of the probes on the chip. First, the probes may exhibit complementarity to their neighbors, so the position of the probes must be carefully chosen so as to avoid these undesirable interactions. Second, the glass substrate often precludes uniform hybridization throughout the probe molecule. For example, the bases closest to the end of the strand near the glass are more prone to steric hindrance, owing to the fact that they are sheltered by neighboring probes. Third, DNA microarrays are based on solid-phase two-dimensional chemistry. Since the probes are immobilized on a stationary glass chip, binding of the probe and target DNA depends solely on the motion of the target molecules. Ideally, neither the probe nor the target DNA should be stationary, thus maximizing the opportunities for collision and hybridization. In contrast to DNA microarrays, liquid phase assays such as the bead-based technologies are not as susceptible to the thermodynamic issues associated with the probe-target binding.

Liquid array analyses offer quantitative and multiplexing abilities, high specificity, and high sensitivity (Biagini et al., 2004; Dunbar & Jacobson, 2007a; Spiro et al., 2000). One of these platforms is a unique bead-based liquid array system, which represents a convergence of microsphere technology and flow cytometry. The Luminex® 100™ (Luminex, Austin, TX) multi-analyte profiling system with xMAP™ technology and MasterPlex Analysis (MiraiBio, San Francisco, CA) software is a bead-based liquid array system that relies on small (5.6 μm diameter) polystyrene microspheres internally labeled with a unique dye combination. The microspheres are coated with thousands of copies of a probe (oligonucleotides, peptides, antibodies, or other ligands) unique for a particular target (http://www.invitrogen.com/site/us/en/home/brands/BioSource.html). Hybridization between the probes and the target (DNA, RNA, or protein) is detected via fluorescent emission. The software classifies the microspheres by using a red diode laser (635 nm) to detect the fluorescence emitted by the internal dyes, and a green diode laser (532 nm) to detect and quantify the target analyte by measuring the intensity of the fluorescence emitted by a reporter. With this technology, up to 100 different analytes per sample can be rapidly and reproducibly detected in real time (Vignali, 2000).

Within the past decade, researchers have begun to use the Luminex liquid array technology for pathogen detection (Dunbar & Jacobson, 2007b; Wilson et al., 2005). Spiro, Lowe, and Brown (2000) used a multiplexed, bead-based method in which nucleic acid probes were employed to detect microorganisms in environmental samples (Spiro et al., 2000). Probes were designed to detect complementary PCR amplicons in both the microarray and Luminex platforms. Fluorescent signals in the microarray assay were often too weak to analyze and had higher cross-hybridization than those in the bead method (Spiro et al., 2000). In addition, since several hundred xMAP beads are examined in one assay, data from these replicates increase the statistical power.

The ELISA method is also very popular in pathogen detection. The greatest difference between the ELISA and Luminex assays is that the former is singleplexed and the latter is

Table 3.1 Net Mean Fluorescent Intensity

Sample**	BC Probe	EC Probe	SE Probe	SA Probe	MFI Ratio***
BC:EC 10:1	***1035***	***254***	−10	−2	4:1
BC:EC 5:1	***817***	***313***	21	9	2.5:1
BC:EC 2:1	***533***	***283***	−2	−6	2:1
BC:EC 1:1	***341***	***303***	−2	2	1:1
BC:EC 1:2	***315***	***470***	1	5	1:1.5
BC:EC 1:5	***331***	***907***	8	7	1:2.5
BC:EC 1:10	***303***	***1276***	18	23	1:4
BC:SE 10:1	***1074***	−3	*45*	−8	24:1
BC:SE 5:1	***901***	−10	***56***	−12	16:1
BC:SE 2:1	***560***	−8	*37*	−6	15:1
BC:SE 1:1	***383***	−4	***56***	−11	7:1
BC:SE 1:2	***420***	1	***97***	7	4.5:1
BC:SE 1:5	***275***	−5	***189***	−9	1.5:1
BC:SE 1:10	***291***	11	***340***	−5	1:1
BC:SA 10:1	***1169***	−6	1	***462***	2.5:1
BC:SA 5:1	***795***	−9	−11	***297***	2.5:1
BC:SA 2:1	***619***	−7	−2	***822***	1:1.5
BC:SA 1:1	***424***	−4	−1	***925***	1:2
BC:SA 1:2	***408***	0	2	***1332***	1:3.5
BC:SA 1:5	***335***	5	−9	***1815***	1:5.5
BC:SA 1:10	***242***	−4	5	***2075***	1:8.5
EC:SE 10:1	2	***1648***	***115***	33	14.5:1
EC:SE 5:1	0	***1036***	***64***	26	16:1
EC:SE 2:1	−4	***571***	*45*	9	12.5:1
EC:SE 1:1	−6	***380***	***49***	3	8:1
EC:SE 1:2	0	***292***	***89***	3	3.5:1
EC:SE 1:5	−6	***249***	***207***	1	1:1
EC:SE 1:10	−2	***232***	***374***	−1	1:1.5
EC:SA 10:1	−4	***1592***	43	***1226***	1.5:1
EC:SA 5:1	5	***1109***	3	***1009***	1:1
EC:SA 2:1	−13	***672***	−4	***1002***	1:1.5
EC:SA 1:1	1	***442***	6	***1050***	1:2.5
EC:SA 1:2	0	***472***	9	***190***	2.5:1
EC:SA 1:5	−2	***469***	10	***1987***	1:4
EC:SA 1:10	−4	***499***	−3	***2261***	1:4.5
SE:SA 10:1	6	10	***436***	***1012***	1:2.5
SE:SA 5:1	8	4	***252***	***983***	1:4
SE:SA 2:1	−2	6	***124***	***986***	1:8
SE:SA 1:1	1	0	***84***	***1028***	1:12
SE:SA 1:2	−5	14	***76***	***1386***	1:18
SE:SA 1:5	4	14	***103***	***1938***	1:19
SE:SA 1:10	5	15	***87***	***2398***	1:27.5

Source: Table 6 Reprinted with permission from Battaglia, A., Schweighardt, A. J., & Wallace, M. M. 2011. Pathogen Detection Using a Unique Liquid Array Technology. *J Forensic Sci* (DOI: 10.1111/j.1556-4029.2011.01708.x).

Note: MFI0 values* for the ratio mixture study. The combinations of designed complementarity are in italics. Values two times the average background (46) indicate a positive identification and are denoted in bold. False negative values are underlined.

*The net MFI values are equivalent to the raw MFI value less one background of the specific microsphere set.

**BC=*B. cereus*, EC=*E. coli*, SE=*S. enterica*, SA=*S. aureus*.

***An approximate ratio of MFI values was determined between the two organisms present in the sample by dividing the larger MFI value by the smaller one and rounding to the nearest 0.5.

multiplexed. One study analyzed confirmed anthrax samples by both methods and found accurate, directly proportional results between the two (Biagini et al., 2004). Both assays positively identified the *B. anthracis* in the samples and provided accurate quantifications. However, the Luminex proved to be more sensitive, with a minimum detectable concentration in whole serum to be half that with ELISA, 1.5 μg/mL versus 3.0 μg/mL (Biagini et al., 2004).

The small size of the Luminex instrument offers the possibility of constructing a field-deployable pathogen detection system. A portable system was comparable to a laboratory bench-top system in its ability to detect *B. anthracis* and *Yersinia pestis*, thereby demonstrating that field-deployable platforms need not suffer from an inferior performance (Hindson et al., 2004, 2005),

Dunbar and Jacobson (2007b) performed a quantitative, multiplexed nucleotide assay to detect 10 different microorganisms using the Luminex xMAP technology. They designed degenerate PCR primers that would amplify the 23S ribosomal RNA gene, *rrl*, of all the bacteria and species-specific capture probes for each. The authors found that the Luminex was capable of making a positive identification when at least 180 ng of PCR product was present (Dunbar and Jacobson, 2007b). Many of the probes differed by a few nucleotide bases, yet cross-hybridization was only observed between *Salmonella enterica* and *Shigella flexneri*. These probes differed by one nucleotide located early in the probe sequence (Dunbar and Jacobson, 2007b). Most recently Battaglia, Schweighardt, and Wallace (2011, in press) used the Luminex xMAP system to detect and identify microbial pathogens in pure and mixed samples. A 20-bp sequence in the 23S rRNA gene, *rrl*, was amplified in four microorganisms: *Bacillus cereus*, *Escherichia coli*, *Salmonella enterica*, and *Staphylococcus aureus*. PCR products were positively identified with the Luminex 100 system. The system could detect very low amounts of DNA and the instrument response was proportional to the input concentration. The lower limit of detection (LLD) was determined to be 0.5 ng for *B. cereus* and *E. coli* and 2 ng for *S. enterica*. The LLD for *S. aureus* was not determined as the instrument response was still above the threshold when quantities of DNA as low as 0.25 ng were used. The platform positively identified organisms present in mixed samples even when the minor component was overshadowed by a 10-fold excess of the major component (Table 3.1).

As is the case for human identification, emerging technologies for identification of non-human samples are DNA-based, automated, mutiplexed systems with high sensitivity. Future technological developments will incorporate real-time detection and field deployability.

References

Anderson, G.S.1995. The use of insects in death investigations: analysis of forensic entomology cases in British Columbia over a five-year period. *Can Soc Forensic Sci J* 28:277–92.

Anderson, G.S. 2000. Minimum and maximum development rates of some forensically important Calliphoridae (Diptera). *J Forensic Sci* 45:824–832.

Battaglia, A.J., Schweighardt, A.J., & Wallace, M.M. 2011. Pathogen detection using a unique liquid array technology. *J Forensic Sci* (in press).

Beckert, J., Friedland, D.E., & Wallace, M. 2010. Species differentiation of blowflies and flesh flies using Amplified Fragment Length Polymorphism. *Aust J Forensic Sci* 42:141–152.

Benecke, M. 1998. Random amplified polymorphic DNA (RAPD) typing of necrophageous insects (Diptera, Coleoptera) in criminal forensic studies: validation and use in practice. *Forensic Sci Int* 98:157–168.

Bhaetu, M., & Singh D. 1995. Insect faunal succession on decaying rabbit carcasses in Punjab, India. *J Forensic Sci* 48:1133–1143.

Biagini, R., Sammons, D., Smith, J. et al. 2004. Comparison of a multiplexed fluorescent covalent microsphere immunoassay and an enzyme-linked immunosorbent assay for measurement of human immunoglobulin G antibodies to anthrax toxins. *Clin Diagn Lab Immunol* 11(1):50–55.

Blears, M., De Grandis, S., Lee, H., & Trevors, J. 1998. Amplified fragment length polymorphism (AFLP): a review of the procedure and its applications. *J Ind Microbiol Biotechnol* 21 99–114.

Bless, C., Palmeter, H., & Wallace, M. 2006. Identification of *Acer rubrum* using Amplified Fragment Length Polymorphism. *J Forensic Sci* 51: 31–38.

Bock, J.M., & Norris, D.O. 1997. Forensic Botany: An underutilized resource. *J Forensic Sci* 42:364–367.

Butler, J.M. 2010. *Fundamentals of Forensic DNA typing.* New York: Elsevier Academic Press.

Christopher, G.W., Cieslak, T.J., Pavlin, J.A., & Eitzen, E.M. 1997. Biological warfare: a historical perspective. *JAMA* 278(5): 412–417.

Comey, C.T., Budowle, B., Adams, D.E., Baumstark, A.L., Lindsey, J.A., & Presley, LA. 1993. PCR amplification and typing of the HLA DQ alpha gene in forensic science samples, *J Forensic Sci* 38:69–70.

Coyle, H., Ladd, C., Palmbach, T., & Lee, H.C. 2001. The green revolution: Botanical contributions to forensics and drug enforcement. *Croat Med J* 42:340–345.

Coyle, H.M., Shutter, G., Abrams, S., et al. 2003. A simple DNA extraction method for marijuana samples using amplified fragment length polymorphism (AFLP) analysis. *J Forensic Sci* 48: 343–347.

De Ley, P., De Ley, I.T., Morris, K., et al. 2005. An integrated approach to fast and informative morphological vouchering of nematodes for applications in molecular barcoding. *Philos Trans R Soc Lond B Biol Sci* 360:1945–1958.

Dunbar, S., & Jacobson, J. 2007a. Parallel processing in microbiology: detection of infectious pathogens by Luminex xMAP multiplexed suspension array technology. *Clin Microbiol Newsl* 29(11):79–86.

Dunbar, S., & Jacobson, J. 2007b. Quantitative, multiplexed detection of *Salmonella* and other pathogens by Luminex® xMAP™ suspension array. *Methods Mol Biol* 394:1–19.

Ecker, D. J., Sampath, R., Massire, C., et al. 2008. Ibis T5000: a universal biosensor approach for microbiology. *Nat Rev Microbiol* 6: 553–558.

Erzinçlio lu, Y.Z. 1985. Immature stages of British *Calliphora* and *Cynomya*, with a re-evaluation of the taxonomic characters of larval Calliphoridae (Diptera). *J Nat Hist* 19: 69–96.

Geissler, E., & van Courtland Moon, J. (eds.). 1999. *Biological and Toxin Weapons: Research Development and Use from the Middle Ages to 1945.* Stockholm International Peace Research Institute, Chemical and Biological Warfare Studies. Oxford, UK: Oxford University Press.

Ghosh, T.K., Prelas, M.A., Viswanath, D.S., & Loyalka, S.K. (eds.). 2002. *Science and Technology of Terrorism and Counterterrorism.* New York: Marcel Dekker, Inc.

Grate, J., Bruckner-Lea, C., Jarrell, A., & Chandler, D. 2003. Automated sample preparation method for suspension arrays using renewable surface separations with multiplexed flow cytometry fluorescence detection. *Anal Chim Acta* 478: 85–98.

Hall, D. 1996. Forensic botany. In W. D. Haglund, & M. H. Sorg (eds.). *Forensic taphonomy: The postmortem fate of human remains* (pp. 353–363). Boca Raton: CRC Press LLC.

Harris, S. 2002. *Factories of death: Japanese biological warfare, 1932–1945, and the American Cover-up.* New York: Routledge.

Hawthorne, D.J. 2001. AFLP-based genetic linkage map of the Colorado potato beetle *Leptinotarsa decemlineata*: sex chromosomes and a pyrethroid-resistance candidate gene. *Genetics* 158:695–700.

Hebert, P. D. N., Cywinska A., Ball S. L., deWaard J. R. 2003. Biological identifications through DNA barcodes. *Proc R Soc Lond B* 270:313–321.

Herrin, G., Fildes, N., Reynolds, R. 1994. Evaluation of the AmpliType® PM DNA test system on forensic case samples. *J Forensic Sci* 39: 1247–1253.

Hindson, B., Brown, S., Marshall, G., et al. 2004. Development of an automated sample preparation module for environmental monitoring of biowarfare agents. *Anal Chem* 76(13):3492–3497.

Hindson, B., McBride, M., Makarewicz, A., et al. 2005. Autonomous detection of aerosolized biological agents by multiplexed immunoassay with polymerase chain reaction confirmation. *Anal Chem* 77(1):284–289.

Horrocks, M., & Walsh K. 1999. Fine resolution of pollen patterns in limited space: Differentiating a crime scene and alibi scene seven meters apart. *J Forensic Sci* 44:417–420.

Howard, C., Gilmore, S., Robertson, J., & Peakall, R. 2008. Developmental validation of a Cannabis sativa STR multiplex system for forensic analysis. *J Forensic Sci* 53:1061–1067.

Hsu, M-C., Chen, K-W., Lo, H-J., et al. 2003. Species identification of medically important fungi by the use of real-time LightCycler PCR. *J Med Microbiol* 52:1071–1076

Jacobs, M.K. 2004. The history of biologic warfare and bioterrorism. *Dermatol Clin* 22:231–246.

Jagadish, V., Robertson, J., & Gibbs, A. 1996. RAPD analysis distinguishes *Cannabis sativa* samples from different sources. *Forensic Sci Int* 79:113–121.

Jeffreys, A.J., Gill, P., & Werrett, D.J. 1985a. Forensic application of DNA "fingerprints." *Nature* 318: 577–579.

Jeffreys, A., Wilson, V., & Then, S.L. 1985b. Individual specific "fingerprints" of human DNA. *Nature* 316: 76–79.

Kakouli-Duarte, T., Casey, D.G., & Burnell, A.M. 2001. Development of a diagnostic DNA probe for the fruit flies *Ceratitis capitata* and *Ceratitis rosa* (Diptera: Tephritidae) using amplified fragment-length polymorphism. *J Econ Entomol* 94:989–97.

Katiyar, S.K., Chandel, G., Tan, Y., et al. 2000. Biodiversity of Asian rice gall midge (*Orseolia oryzae* Wood Mason) from five countries examined by AFLP analysis. *Genome* 43:322–32.

Keim, P., Price, L., Klevytska, A., et al. 2000. Multiple-locus variable-number tandem repeat analysis reveals genetic relationships within *Bacillus anthracis*. *J Bacteriol* 182(10): 2928–2936.

Kostić, T., Weilharter, A., Rubino, S., et al. 2007. A microbial diagnostic microarray technique for the sensitive detection and identification of pathogenic bacteria in a background of nonpathogens. *Anal Biochem* 360:244–254.

Kimpton, C.P., Gill, P., Walton, A., Urquhart, A., Millican, E.S. and Adams, M. 1993. Automated DNA profiling employing multiplex amplification of short tandem repeat loci. *PCR Meth* 3: 13–22.

Lim, D., Simpson, J., Kearns, E., & Kramer, M. 2005. Current and developing technologies for monitoring agents of bioterrorism and biowarfare. *Clin Microbiol Rev* 18: 583–607.

Martin, J.W., Christopher, G.W., & Eitzen, E.M. 2007. History of biological weapons: from poisoned darts to intentional epidemics, pp. 1–20 in: Dembek, Z.F. *Medical Aspects of Biological Warfare*. Washington DC: Borden Institute. Walter Reed Army Medical Center.

Meksem, K., Leister, D., Peleman, J., Zabeau, M., Salamini, F., & Gebhardt, C. 1995. A high-resolution map of the vicinity of the R1 locus of chromosome V of potato based on RFLP and AFLP markers. *Mol Gen Genet* 249:74–81.

Mueller, U.G., & Wolfenbarger, L.L. 1999. AFLP genotyping and fingerprinting. *Tree* 14:389–394.

National Institute on Drug Abuse (NIDA). 2009. Research Report Series. September, 2009. http://www.drugabuse.gov/infofacts/methamphetamine.html

Parsons, Y.M., & Shaw, K.L. 2002. Mapping unexplored genomes: a genetic linkage map of the Hawaiian cricket Laupala. *Genetics* 162:1275–82.

Radnedge, L., Agron, P., Hill, K., et al. 2003. Genome differences that distinguish *Bacillus anthracis* from *Bacillus cereus* and *Bacillus thuringiensis*. *Appl Environ Microbiol* 69(5): 2755–2764.

Randerson, J. 2002. Grassed up. *New Sci* 173: 32.

Ratcliffe, S.T., Webb, D.W., Weinzievr, R.A., & Robertson, H.M. 2003. PCR-RFLP identification of Diptera (Calliphoridae, Muscidae, and Sarcophagidae)—a generally applicable method. *J Forensic Sci* 48:783–785.

Ravel, S., Monteny, N., Velasco Olmos, D., Escalante Verdugo, J., & Cuny G. 2001. A preliminary study of the population genetics of *Aedes aegypti* (Diptera: Culicidae) form Mexico using microsatellite and AFLP markers. *Acta Trop* 78: 241–50.

Ridout, C.J., & Donini, P. 1999. Use of AFLP in cereals research. *Trends Plant Sci* 4:76–79.
Robertson, A.G., & Robertson, L.J. 1995. From asps to allegations: biological warfare in history. *Mil Med* 160:369–37.
Saal, B., & Wricke, G. 2002. Clustering of amplified fragment length polymorphism markers in a linkage map of rye. *Plant Breed* 121:117–123.
Saiki, R.K., Scharf, S., Faloona, F., et al. 1985. Enzymatic amplification of beta-globin genomic sequences and restriction site analysis for diagnosis of sickle cell anemia. *Science* 230: 1350–54.
Saiki, R.K, Walsh, P.S., Levenson, C.H., & Erlich, H.A. 1989. Genetic analysis of amplified DNA with immobilized sequence-specific oligonucleotide probes. *PNAS* 86: 6230–6234.
Salvato, P., Battisti, A., Concato, S., Masutti, L., Patarnello, T., & Zane, L. 2002. Genetic differentiation in the winter pine processionary moth (*Thaumetopoea pityocampa-wilkinsoni* complex), inferred by AFLP and mitochondrial DNA markers. *Mol Ecol* 11: 2435–2444.
Savelkoul, P., Aarts H, DeHaas, J., et al. 1999. Amplified-fragment length polymorphism analysis: the state of an art. *J Clin Microbiol* 37: 3083–3091.
Schondelmaier, J., Steinrucken, G., & Jung, C. 1996. Integration of AFLP markers into a linkage map of sugar beet (*Beta vulgaris* L.). *Plant Breed* 115:231–237.
Sensabaugh, G., & Kaye, D.H. 1998. Nonhuman DNA evidence. *Jurimetrics* 38:1–16.
Sperling, F.A.H., Anderson, G.S., & Hickey D.A. 1994. A DNA-based approach to the identification of insect species used for postmortem interval estimation. *J Forensic Sci* 39: 418–427.
Spiro, A., & Lowe, M. 2002. Quantitation of DNA sequences in environmental PCR products by a multiplexed, bead-based method. *Appl Environ Microbiol* 68(2):1010–1013.
Spiro, A., Lowe, M., & Brown, D. 2000. A bead-based method for multiplexed identification and quantitation of DNA sequences using flow cytometry. *Appl Environ Microbiol* 66:4258–4265.
Summerbell, R., Levesque, C., Seifert, K., et al. 2005. Microcoding: the second step in DNA barcoding. *Philos Trans R Soc Lond B 360*:1897–1903.
Tenorio, F.M., Oslon, J.K., & Coats, C.J. 2003. Decomposition studies with a catalog and descriptions of forensically important blow flies (Diptera: Calliphoridae) in central Texas. *Southwest Entomol* 28:37– 45.
U'Ren, J.M., Van Ert, M.N., Schupp, J.M., et al. 2005. Use of a real-time PCR TaqMan assay for rapid identification and differentiation of *Burkholderia pseudomallei* and *Burkholderia mallei*. *J Clin Microbiol* 43(11):5771–5774.
Valjevac, S., Hilaire, V., Lisanti, O., et al. 2005. Comparison of minisatellite polymorphisms in the *Bacillus cereus* complex: A simple assay for large-scale screening and identification of strains most closely related to *Bacillus anthracis*. *Appl Environ Microbiol* 71(11): 6613–6623.
Vignali, D. 2000. Multiplexed particle-based flow cytometric assays. *J Immunol Methods* 243(1–2):243–255.
Vos, P., Hogers, R., Bleeker, M., et al. 1995. AFLP: A new technique for DNA fingerprinting. *Nucleic Acids Res* 23:4407–4414.
Wang, S-H., Wen, J-K., Zhou, Y-F., et al. 2004. Identification and characterization of *Bacillus anthracis* by multiplex PCR on DNA chip. *Biosens Bioelectron 20*:807–813.
Wang, Y.H., Thomas, C.E., & Dean, R.A. 1997. A genetic map of melon (*Cucumis melo* L.) based on amplified fragment length polymorphism (AFLP) markers. *Theor Appl Genet* 95:791–798.
Ward, J., Gilmore, S.R., Robertson, J., & Peakall, R. 2009. A grass molecular identification system for forensic botany: a critical evaluation of the strengths and limitations. *J Forensic Sci* 54:1254–1260.
Weber, J.L., & May, P.E. 1989. Abundant class of DNA polymorphisms which can be typed using the polymerase chain reaction. *Am J Hum Genet* 44: 388–386.
Wells, J.D., Introna, F., Di Vella, G., Campobasso, C.P., Hayes, J., & Sperling, F.A.H. 2001. Human and insect mitochondrial DNA analysis from maggots. *J Forensic Sci* 46:685–687.
Wells J.D., & Stevens, J.R. 2008. Application of DNA-based methods in forensic entomology. *Annu Rev Entomol* 53:103–120.

Wilson, W., Erler, A., Nasarabadi, S., Skowronski, E., & Imbro, P. 2005. A multiplexed PCR-coupled liquid bead array for the simultaneous detection of four biothreat agents. *Mol Cell Probes* 19:137–144.

Wolfe, K.H., Li, W-H., & Sharp, P.M. 1987. Rates of nucleotide substitution vary greatly among plant mitochondrial, chloroplast, and nuclear DNAs. *PNAS* 84:9054–9058.

Yoon, C.K. 1993. Botanical witness for the prosecution. *Science* 260: 894–895.

Zane, L., Bargelloni, L., & Patarnello, T. 2002. Strategies for microsatellite isolation: A review. *Mol Ecol* 11:1–16.

Quantum Chemical Calculations Applied to Systems of Forensic Interest

4

ANNE-MARIE SAPSE

Contents

Introduction

Forensic science is continually developing into new areas and new methods of research. Other chapters discuss some of the new methods applied to the study of crime. This chapter describes the application of quantum chemistry to forensic science. One might be surprised that a purely theoretical method might prove useful to an area that is strictly concerned with experimental findings, such as those occurring at the scene of a crime. However, it has to be taken into consideration that the identification of various indices such as bloodstains, fingerprints, DNA, and others are based on chemical reactions involving different chemical reagents. To maximize the accuracy of these reactions, better and better reagents have to be found and one of the ways to proceed in this respect is to study the energetics of the given reactions. This is best accomplished by using quantum chemistry methods. Another domain in which quantum chemistry was proved to be useful is for the identification and characterization of presumed intermediates and by-products of reactions of interest in forensic science such as the illegal synthesis of drugs.

The Spartan suite of programs, the Titan program, the Gaussian suite of programs, and others provide possibilities to perform quantum chemical calculations on atoms and molecules, at different calculational levels, according to the method used. Starting with molecules as small as the hydrogen molecule and applying the methods to systems as large as DNA fragments and peptides, the calculations lead to the description of the systems, such as their energies, their optimum geometries (the geometries corresponding to the lowest energies, that is, to the most stable systems), their atomic charges, and other electrical properties, vibrational frequencies, NMR spectra, and thermodynamic properties.

The basis of quantum chemical calculations is the Schrödinger equation, which is a differential equation of the following form:

$$H\psi = E\psi$$

In this equation, ψ is the wave function characterizing the system. The square of this function represents the probability of finding the system in a given state. H is an operator representing the sum of the kinetic energy operator and potential energy operator, called the Hamiltonian operator, and E is the total energy of the system. The Schrödinger equation can be solved analytically only for simple systems, such as the free particle, the particle-in-the-box, and the hydrogen atom. Even for the hydrogen atom, the calculations are very elaborate, since the Hamiltonian operator has to be changed into spherical coordinates (r, θ, ϕ), from Cartesian coordinates (x, y, z). However, for systems containing more than one electron, where the electron-electron repulsion has to be introduced into the potential energy, no analytical solution is possible. Therefore, approximations have to be used to obtain E and ψ. These approximations are based on the Variational Theorem, which states that when a guess for the wave function is used, the resulting energy, obtained by the formula

$$E=\int\psi^{*}H\psi\, dv/\int\psi^{*}\psi\, dv$$

is always larger than the energy obtained by using the exact solution of the Schrödinger equation. Accordingly, to obtain the energy closest to the real energy of the system, it is sufficient to find the minimum in energy. The minimum can be obtained by setting the derivative of the energy with some parameter equal to zero and finding, thus, the optimum value of the parameter. However, since the setting of the first derivative of a function with a variable to zero represents both the minima and the maxima, to insure that the point obtained is a minimum indeed, the matrix of the second derivatives has to contain only positive values.

The methods of calculations of molecular properties comprise the semi-empirical methods and the ab initio methods. Semi-empirical calculations use a simplified molecular Hamiltonian operator. The name *semi-empirical* comes from the fact that the calculations make use of parameters adjusted to fit the experimental results. There are a large number of such methods, which differ from each other by the parameters used and by the degrees at which some less important terms are neglected. However, with the construction of better computers, these methods are somewhat obsolete and were replaced by ab initio methods.

Ab initio methods use the correct molecular Hamiltonian with all the parameters calculated theoretically. Among those, one of the methods currently used for the calculations of all molecular properties is the Hartree-Fock (self-consistent field) method. Indeed, the reason for which the Schrödinger equation for systems with more than one electron cannot be solved analytically is that the electron-electron interaction included in the potential energy operator involves r_{ij}, the interelectronic distance, which is extremely difficult to express in Cartesian or spherical electronic coordinates. The Hartree-Fock method, called the self-consistent field method, replaces these terms by the interaction of each electron with the electronic cloud of the other electrons. The spin terms are also introduced and an iteration procedure leads to the obtaining of the best possible wave functions and energies.

The orbitals used for the calculations are not the correct Slater orbitals that serve for the electron description, of the form exp $(-ar)$ where a is a combination of constants, and r is the distance between the electron and the nucleus. Indeed, such functions are difficult to integrate. They had been replaced by Gaussian functions, exp $(-ar^2)$ which facilitate the integrations. However, since the Gaussian functions do not represent the correct expressions, the Slater orbitals are expanded in sets of Gaussians. Some of the most used Gaussian basis sets are 6-31G* and 6-31G**. In both, two Slater orbitals are used for the description of valence electrons, one expanded in a set of three Gaussians and one approximated by one Gaussian. The core electrons are described by one Slater orbital, expanded in a series of six Gaussians. In addition, both 6-31G* and 6-31G** set d orbitals on the non-hydrogen atoms, while 6-31G** also sets p orbitals on the hydrogen atoms. Other Gaussian sets might also include f orbitals and/or describe the valence electrons by three Slater orbitals. These kinds of sets cannot be used for large systems, for computational reasons.

Another method implemented in the last few decades, also ab initio, uses the fact that the electronic density is a function of the wave functions. This method is called the Density Functional Theory (DFT). The Density Functional Theory attempts to calculate the ground state energy of a molecule as well as other molecular properties by using the ground-state electron density. Indeed, in 1964, Hohenberg and Kohn proved that the properties of a molecule in its ground state, including the energy, are uniquely determined by the electron probability density, which is a function of the electron's coordinates. The energy of the system becomes thus a function of a function, that is, a functional.

In addition to proving that the energy is a functional, Hohenberg and Kohn proved that the true ground-state electron density minimizes the energy functional, in the same way as the true wave function of a system minimizes the energy calculated by the variational integral.

The Spartan and Titan programs include density functional modules, which can be used for calculations of energies, wave functions, optimum geometries for the ground state and transitional states, as well as vibrational frequencies. The programs contain calculations using local density, BP, BLYP, EDF1, and B3LYP methods. The letters stand for initials of researchers in the domain. One of the most used methods is the B3LYP method, which is a hybrid functional and contains parameters chosen to give good fits to experimental atomization energies.

One of the issues of the molecular orbital method is the calculation of the correlation energy. In the self-consistent field method, the systems are characterized by a wave function, ψ, which represents the probability to find a system in a given state. Using this wave function, the energy of the system is calculated by solving the Schrödinger equation. The correlation energy represents the energy obtained by introducing the electron-electron repulsion in ψ itself. Since the Variational Theorem states that the calculated energy of a system is always higher than the experimental energy, the purpose of the calculations is to obtain the minimum energy possible. Introducing the correlation energy helps to lower the calculated energy. The calculation of the correlation energy is accomplished by different methods, such as the Moller-Plesset perturbation theory. However, using the DFT method at B3LYP level, the correlation function is introduced into the calculations via some empirical parameters.

The optimization of the geometry of a molecule is performed by setting the energy as a function of the geometrical parameters of the molecule, such as bond lengths, angles, and dihedral angles, and solving the equations for the derivatives of the energy with these variables set to zero. At the same time, the matrix of the second derivatives has to contain only positive values. A negative value of a second derivative would characterize the structure as a transition state and not a real minimum in energy. The infrared frequencies, being the square root of the second derivatives, are this way real. Imaginary frequencies are displayed by the programs as negative values.

The atomic charges on the system's atoms can be calculated by the Spartan and Titan programs by using either the Mulliken Population Analysis, natural bond orbital, or methods based on fits to the electrostatic potentials. In addition, the Spartan and Titan programs estimate solvation energies using the SM5.4 model of Cramer and Truhlar, based on semi-empirical methods. These values are then added to the gas-phase energies calculated at their respective level.

These methods are applied to the various systems of forensic or toxicological interest that will be described in the following sections.

Quantum Chemical Calculations Applied to the Study of Saxitoxin

Saxitoxin, also known as paralytic shellfish poison, produces death in humans due to the fact that respiratory paralysis occurs within 12 hours after the ingestion of the poison. The toxin is a small, water-soluble molecule naturally synthesized by the marine algal dinoflagellates *Gonyaulax catenella* and *G. excavate*. Its lethal activity is due to its ability to prevent sodium ions from passing through the membrane of nerve cells, thus interfering with the transmission of signals along the nerves. Saxitoxin was synthesized first by Kishi, Tanino, Nakata, and Kaneko, at Harvard in 1977, and later, in 1984, by Jacobi, Martinelli, and Polanc.

A particular interest of theoretical studies of saxitoxin and tetrodotoxin lies in the fact that the two toxins comprise guanidinium groups. Guanidinium ions are examples of the so-called Y aromaticity, discovered by Gund and coworkers. Indeed, as found by geometry-optimization, the three C-N bonds are equal in length, and they feature a length intermediary between single bond and double bond lengths. The Y aromaticity is mainly due to the delocalization of the π electrons on all three C-N bonds. The rotation energy of the H-N-H groups around the C-N bond is also intermediate between the barrier to rotation around a single bond and the one around a double bond.

In its neutral state, saxitoxin exhibits two guanidine groups, as shown in Figure 4.1. One of those is attached to a five-membered ring, and the second is attached to a six-membered ring. When one or both of these groups are protonated, the saxitoxin molecule becomes a positive ion or biion. The six-membered ring guanidine is almost entirely protonated. The five-membered ring guanidine can be protonated or non-protonated, depending on the pH of the medium. It has been shown by studies of the pH-dependent activity of saxitoxin that the protonated form of this guanidine group is directly involved in the blocking of the sodium channels. This interaction probably occurs between the guanidinium ion with carboxylate groups present in the ion channel walls, specifically Asp 384 and Glu 94. Another possible interaction is between the positive-charged sodium ions and the lone pair of electrons set on the exocyclic nitrogen of the guanidine group. To explore this possibility, the sodium affinity to the guanidine group was investigated with quantum chemical calculations. However, it has to be taken into consideration that

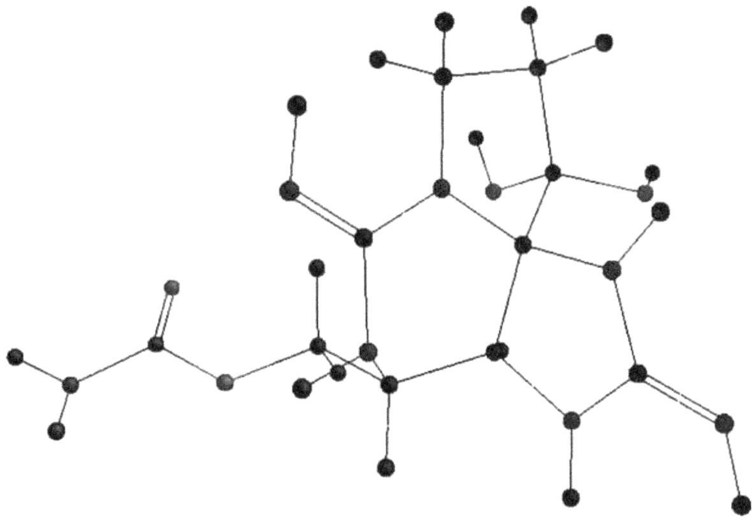

Figure 4.1 Optimized structure of saxitoxin.

the sodium ions are hydrated, making it harder for them to attach to the lone pair on the nitrogen.

Saxitoxin and the marine toxins tetrodotoxin and some of the analogs of tetrodotoxin have been investigated by various theoretical methods. Velmer et al. and Sapse et al. used sophisticated quantum chemical methods for the study of saxitoxin. Volmer used the Density Functional Theory (DFT) at B3LYP level.

The calculations of Volmer et al. served to obtain the protonation energy of the guanidine groups in saxitoxin. The results suggested that the protonation takes place at the pyrimidine group.

Sapse et al. performed Hartree-Fock calculations with the 6-31G* Gaussian basis set to obtain the proton affinities of neutral saxitoxin and, in addition, the sodium ion affinity for the guanidine groups. The rotational energies of the guanidinium groups in saxitoxin were computed, and, for comparison purposes, the rotational energies of the guanidinium groups attached to a five-membered ring and to a six-membered ring were also calculated. To perform the calculations, Sapse et al. (2006) used the Spartan ES 04 program. The geometry-optimized structure of neutral saxitoxin is shown in Figure 4.1.

Since calculations have shown that the structures of saxitoxin featuring different orientations of the guanidine exocyclic NH exhibit different energies, the lowest energy found is represented in Figure 4.1 and is used for all the calculations. To obtain the rotational energies for the guanidinium group attached to the five-membered ring, an angle α was defined, as the dihedral angle formed by one of the hydrogens of the guanidinium group, the nitrogen to which it is attached, the carbon, and a second (endocyclic) nitrogen. This angle was frozen at different values, as shown in Table 4.1, and the energy of the molecule was calculated by letting all the other parameters geometry-optimize. The procedure was repeated with the angle β, pertaining to the guanidinium group attached to the six-membered ring. Tables 4.1 and 4.2 show the results.

As expected, the lowest energy corresponds to the structures featuring the angles α and β around zero, since co-planarity insures the highest overlap of the p orbitals. Upon rotation, the p orbitals are not parallel anymore, so their overlap decreases. Indeed, the highest energies are obtained for α and β values around 90°.

The barriers to rotation as can be calculated from the tables are of 9.94 kcal/mol for the guanidinium ion attached to the five-membered ring, and of 10.92 kcal/mol for the guanidinium ion attached to the six-membered ring. In comparison, the barrier to rotation of the guanidinium group attached to a five-membered ring, by itself, without the rest of the molecule of saxitoxin is of 10.62 kcal/mol and the one attached to the six-membered ring alone is of 8.33 kcal/mol. All these values are similar to each other. It is interesting to notice how the geometry optimization shows the pyramidalization of the NH_2 groups for the rotated structures.

The proton affinities of the guanidine groups, calculated with the Hartree-Fock method, using the 6-31G* basis set, are 257.23 kcal/mol for the guanidine attached to the five-membered ring, and 263.72 kcal/mol for the guanidine attached to the six-membered ring. The values for the guanidine groups attached only to the rings are 256.87 kcal/mol and 262.90 kcal/mol, indicating that the rest of the saxitoxin molecule does not influence the proton affinities. The proton affinities calculated by the DFT method, at B3LYP level, with the 6-31G** basis set, show proton affinities of 257.69 kcal/mol for the guanidine attached to the five-membered ring in the saxitoxin molecule, and 258.31 kcal/mol for the guanidine attached to the six-membered ring, also in the saxitoxin molecules. All these values are quite similar, so it was deemed sufficient to calculate the sodium affinities of the guanidine attached to the five-membered ring and to the six-membered ring, with the DFT method, as shown above. These values are 56.63 kcal/mol and 53.41

Table 4.1 Energy as Dependent on the Angle α for Saxitoxin with the Guanidinium Group Attached to the Five-Membered Ring and Solvation Energies

Angle α	Energy (au)	Solvation Energy (kcal/mol)
0.69 (optimized)	−1069.61121	−69.59
20.57	−1069.61053	−69.08
40.57	−1069.60801	−68.21
60.57	−1069.60345	−67.38
90.38	−1069.59537	−68.80

Table 4.2 Dihedral Angle β-Dependent Energies and Solvation Energies of Saxitoxin Featuring the Guanidinium Group Attached to the Six-Membered Ring

Angle β	Energy (au)	Solvation Energy (kcal/mol)
6.15 (optimized structure)	−1069.62155	−63.62
19.85	−1069.61928	−64.04
39.85	−1069.61514	−65.02
59.85	−1069.61026	−63.96
89.85	−1069.60414	−61.73

kcal/mol, respectively. It can be seen that the sodium affinities are much lower than the proton affinities.

Sapse et al. concluded that the five-membered-ring guanidinium is more flexible to rotation, while the six-membered-ring-attached guanidine is more prone to protonation. The low values of the sodium affinities, together with the fact that the sodium ions are hydrated, suggest that they do show significant binding. Most likely, the inhibition of the sodium channels by saxitoxin is due to the binding of the guanidinium ions to carboxylate groups in the channel's walls.

Studies of Fingerprint Identification Reactions with the Use of Quantum Chemical Calculations

Fingerprint identification is one of the best ways to unequivocally determine the presence of an individual at a crime scene.

Fingerprinting dates from the second half of the 19th century, when Henry Faulds, in England, published three books on the subject of fingerprinting. Interestingly enough, at the beginning, Faulds did not study fingerprints for forensic purposes, but for anthropologic purposes, that is, to obtain information about the origin of mankind. He accumulated a collection of fingerprints of the people who surrounded him and, thus, discovered who was stealing some medical supplies and who tried to burglarize the hospital where Faulds was working. This way, he became aware of the value of fingerprints in criminalistics.

In France, toward the end of the 19th century, Alphonse Bertillon got the idea to identify suspects by measurements of different parts of their bodies. He identified this way a large number of criminals. Inspired by anthropometrics measurements, another English researcher, Galton, started to classify fingerprints to identify specific patterns. Once the forensic value of fingerprinting was recognized by the scientific community, researchers tried to improve the quality of the methods.

There are several types of fingerprints. Some of them are easily detected on certain surfaces. Others are harder to detect. The latter are called latent fingerprints. They are invisible prints, formed by the transfer of perspiration from the fingers to different objects. Unlike visible prints, latent prints require special techniques to be detected. One of these, making use of the chemical ninhydrin, has been used to develop latent fingerprints at crime scenes for over half a century. The activity of ninhydrin, in this respect, stems from the production of Ruhemann's Purple upon its reaction with the amino acids found in perspiration. Ninhydrin (2,2-dihydroxy-1,3-indanedione) was first synthesized by Ruhemann. After it was prepared, it was discovered that many substances turn blue when they are combined with ninhydrin. In 1954, it was found to be useful for identifying fingerprints, especially on some substances such as paper or wood where they cannot be seen otherwise. Indeed, Ruhemann's Purple is a brightly colored compound easily identified visually. In addition, it fluoresces slightly at the wavelengths 582 and 407 nm when treated with a zinc or cadmium salt. Some of the advantages of using ninhydrin for fingerprint identification are its low cost and lack of toxicity.

To obtain new methods for crime fighting, it would be beneficial to synthesize compounds that react with amino acids and feature activities superior to the ones of ninhydrin. Alternatives to ninhydrin were investigated in a large number of studies from the point of view of synthesis and characterization, but none has been found so far to surpass ninhydrin by offering significant advantages in color development. For example, 1,8-diaza-9-fluorenone (DFO) was synthesized in the late 1980s and was found to have superior sensitivity as compared to ninhydrin. However, the compound formed by its reaction with the amino acids found in the sweat from fingerprints is not as strongly colored as Ruhemann's Purple. To improve the chromogenic and fluorogenic properties of fingerprint detection agents, Petraco et al. applied quantum chemical calculations to obtain a better understanding of the mechanism of formation of Ruhemann's Purple. Indeed, this mechanism has not been completely understood, and a large number of studies undertaken since the discovery of ninhydrin as an indicator for the presence of amino acids, proteins, and peptides address this issue.

Petraco et al. applied quantum chemical calculations to the investigation of possible mechanisms of reaction of ninhydrin and amino acids, with the formation of Ruhemann's Purple. They calculated the energies of reactants, intermediates, and products, determining in this way the potential energy surface of the reactions. Alanine was chosen as a representative amino acid.

The mechanisms discussed in this work are the McCaldin, Lamothe, and Friedman mechanisms. Each molecule that is part of the reaction was geometry-optimized at the spin-restricted Hartree-Fock (self-consistent field) level, using the 6-31G* basis set. The Spartan suite of quantum chemistry computer programs was used. Cartesian coordinate gradients were optimized to less than 10^{-4} a.u. as convergence criteria. Vibrational frequencies were evaluated by numerical differences of analytical gradients. Since there were no imaginary frequencies, all the structures examined could be considered energetic minima. In addition, the DFT method, at B3LYP, with the 6-31G** basis set was used to perform calculations for obtaining structures of alanine, ninhydrin, and Ruhemann's Purple.

Figure 4.2 shows the optimized ninhydrin at DFT/B3LYP/6-31G** level. Figure 4.3 shows the optimized structure of an isomer of Ruhemann's Purple. The optimization was performed using the DFT/B3LYP/6-31G** method.

The McCaldin mechanism of reaction is shown in Figure 4.4, the Lamothe mechanism is shown in Figure 4.5, the Friedman mechanism is shown in Figure 4.6 and Figure 4.7 shows a mechanism proposed by Petraco.

These figures show three possible isomers of Ruhemann's Purple, labeled 1, 2, and 3. Experiments and theory seem to show that the most brightly colored isomer is an anion that does not feature a proton on the hydroxide group. Dietz et al. performed computations showing that isomer 1 might be the protonated species of the strongly colored

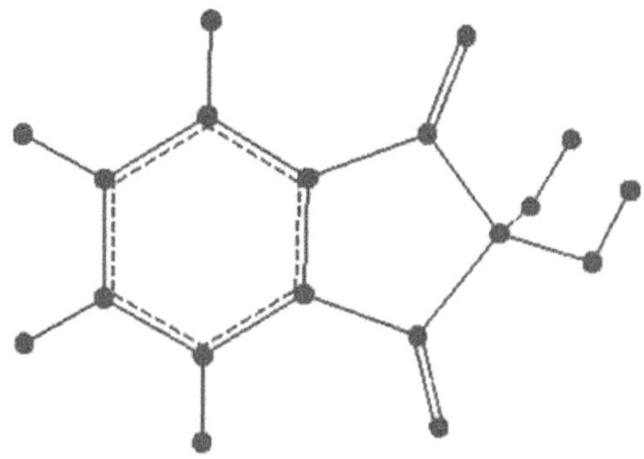

Figure 4.2 Optimized structure of ninhydrin, using the DFT/B3LYP/6-31G** method.

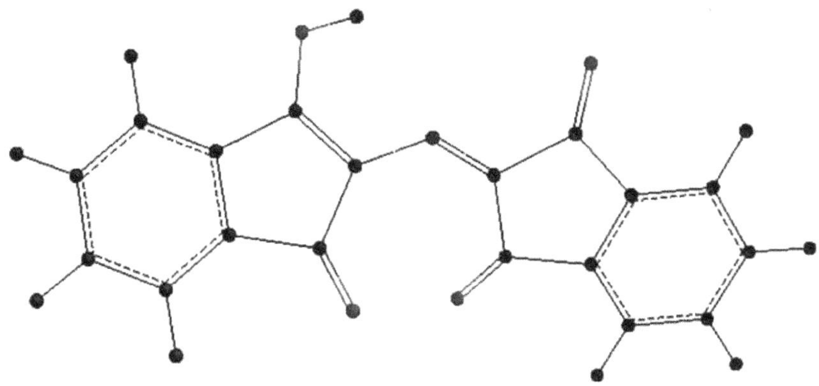

Figure 4.3 Optimized structure of an isomer of Ruhemann's Purple, using the DFT/B3LYP/6-31G** method.

version. However, Wigfield et al. surmised that isomer 2 is the protonated equivalent of the anion. The x-ray crystallographic studies of Grigg et al. seem to indicate that the protonated version is isomer 3. This hypothesis was confirmed by Elber et al. via semi-empirical calculations.

The energies of the basic reagents—ninhydrin, alanine, and Ruhemann's Purple—obtained with DFT/B3LYP/6-31G** and by HF/6-31G* calculations are displayed in Table 4.3. The isomer of Ruhemann's Purple chosen to be displayed in Table 4.3 and used in the discussion of the reaction energetics was the isomer 1, as it has a similar geometric and electronic structure to the brightly colored structure of the anion. The energies corresponding to the optimum geometries of isomers 2 and 3 differ from isomer 1 only by a few kilocalories per mole and, as such, they will not be discussed in the analysis of the mechanism of Ruhemann's Purple formation.

The focus on the protonated version of anionic Ruhemann's Purple is due to the fact that the reactions take place in an aquatic medium, and, therefore, the most abundant species is the protonated one. If the reaction takes place on paper, usually it is at a low pH so the same conclusion can be drawn.

Ruhemann formulated the hypothesis that the principal intermediate, 2-hydroxy-1,3-indanedione, exists in solution when ninhydrin reacts with amino acids and leads to the formation of hydrindantin. The latter combines with ammonium salts and forms Ruhemann's Purple. The subsequent mechanisms proposed agree that the reaction takes place in three general stages: the amino acid attacks ninhydrin (the rate-determining step, a special case of Strecker degradation), several intermediates are produced via dehydration, and, finally, some of the intermediates are involved in side reactions and some form Ruhemann's Purple.

Petraco et al.'s quantum chemical calculations found the reaction of attack of the lone pair of electrons on the nitrogen of the amino acid (alanine serving as model) on the tertiary carbon in the five-membered ring on ninhydrin, together with the loss of a water molecule, to be endothermic. The cost in energy is 7.08 kcal/mol. The intermediate thus formed loses carbon dioxide and water. This reaction is also endothermic but with an energy cost of only 2.22 kcal/mol. After this reaction, the McCaldin mechanism indicates the possibility of two paths: (1) the attachment of two protons, releasing −4.35 kcal/mol, followed by exothermical hydrolysis, with −5.20 kcal/mol; and (2) the formation of acetaldehyde and intermediate **3**, with a release of energy of −9.55 kcal/mol.

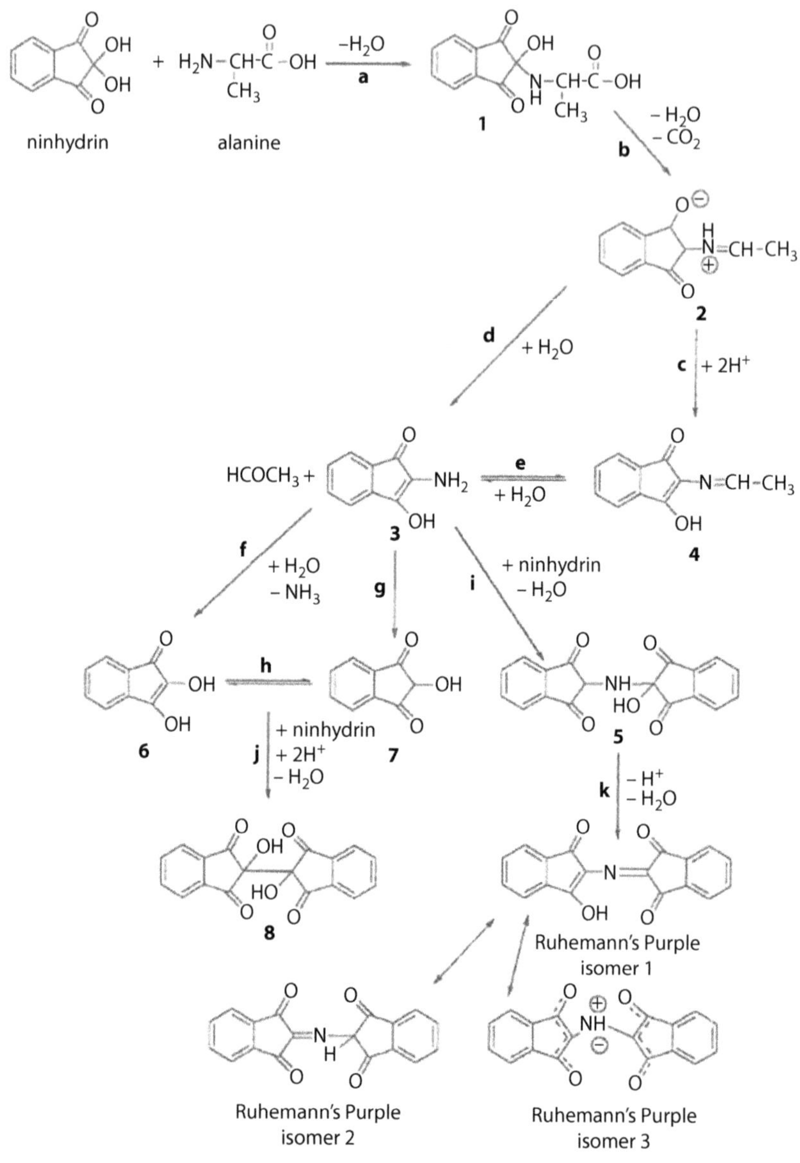

Figure 4.4 The reactions of the McCaldin mechanism.

The intermediate **3** in the McCaldin mechanism can proceed to the completion of the reaction via three routes: losing ammonia by hydrolysis to form intermediates **6** or **7** with an energy of reaction of 3.5 kcal/mol for 6 and –8.76 kcal/mol for 7. These reactions lead to the formation of **8**, by combining with ninhydrin and two protons and losing a molecule of water. Starting with 7, this reaction costs 1.36 kcal/mol. The third path is the combination with ninhydrin, with the formation of **5** and water. This reaction releases 8.42 kcal/mol, while the last reaction of the mechanism, which leads to the formation of Ruhemann's Purple, is endothermic by 28.94 kcal/mol.

Some researchers, such as Wittmann, Muller, and Ziegler, performed stoichiometric studies that supported the McCaldin mechanism. However, they stated that the formation of Ruhemann's Purple must occur with the participation of hydrindantin. Lamothe and

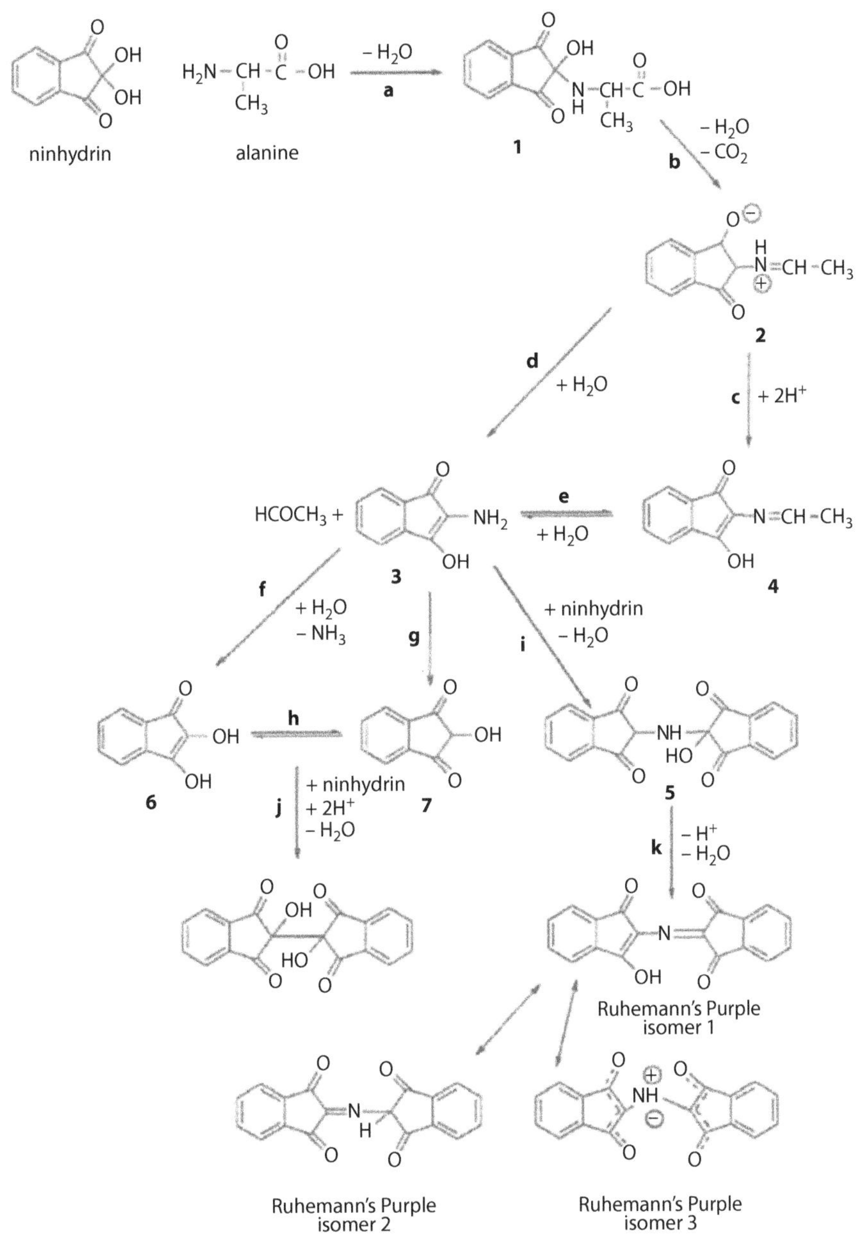

Figure 4.5 The reactions of the Lamothe mechanism.

McCormick used kinetic studies that led to the conclusion that intermediate **3** is unstable in the presence of ninhydrin and forms intermediates **9** and **6**. The latter dimerizes and forms Ruhemann's Purple either by reacting with **9**, or forming an equilibrium with **8** (hydrindantin). This way, hydrindantin participates more to the color formation.

The Lamothe mechanism is fairly similar to the McCaldin mechanism, but it lacks the step leading from entity **2** to entity **3**. The computations of Petraco et al. indicate that the reactions of intermediate **3** as suggested by the McCaldin mechanism should be taken into consideration because of the exothermicity of this path and the fact that the experimental conditions of the synthesis are acidic.

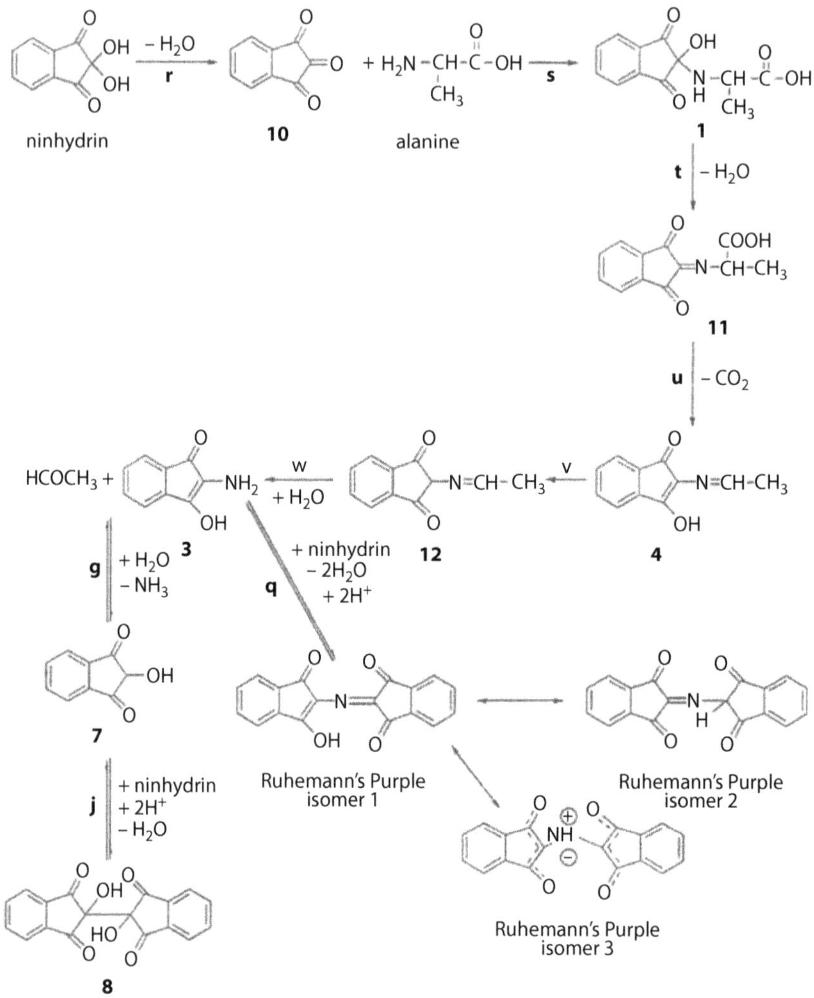

Figure 4.6 The reactions of the Friedman mechanism.

Table 4.3 Energies of the Reactants and Product

Compound	Energy (HF/6-31G*) (au)	Energy (DFT/B3LYP/6-31G**) (au)
Ninhydrin	-643.75680	-647.46062
Alanine	-321.85656	-323.74797
Ruhemann's Purple	-1040.75547	-1046.95747

As opposed to the McCaldin mechanism, the Lamothe mechanism proposes that **3** reacts with ninhydrin via dehydration and produces **6** and **9**. This reaction is high in energy cost, being endothermic by 22.68 kcal/mol. However, the reaction might lead to the formation of the intermediate **5'**, which is a tautomer of intermediate **5** of the McCaldin mechanism, higher in energy by 17.04 kcal/mol than the latter. In this case, either **5'** can dehydrate, or **6** and **9** can combine via dehydration and produce Ruhemann's Purple. Reaction **p** is also endothermic but by only 11.9 kcal/mol, which represents half of the cost in energy of the last step of the McCaldin mechanism. Reaction **o** is exothermic by

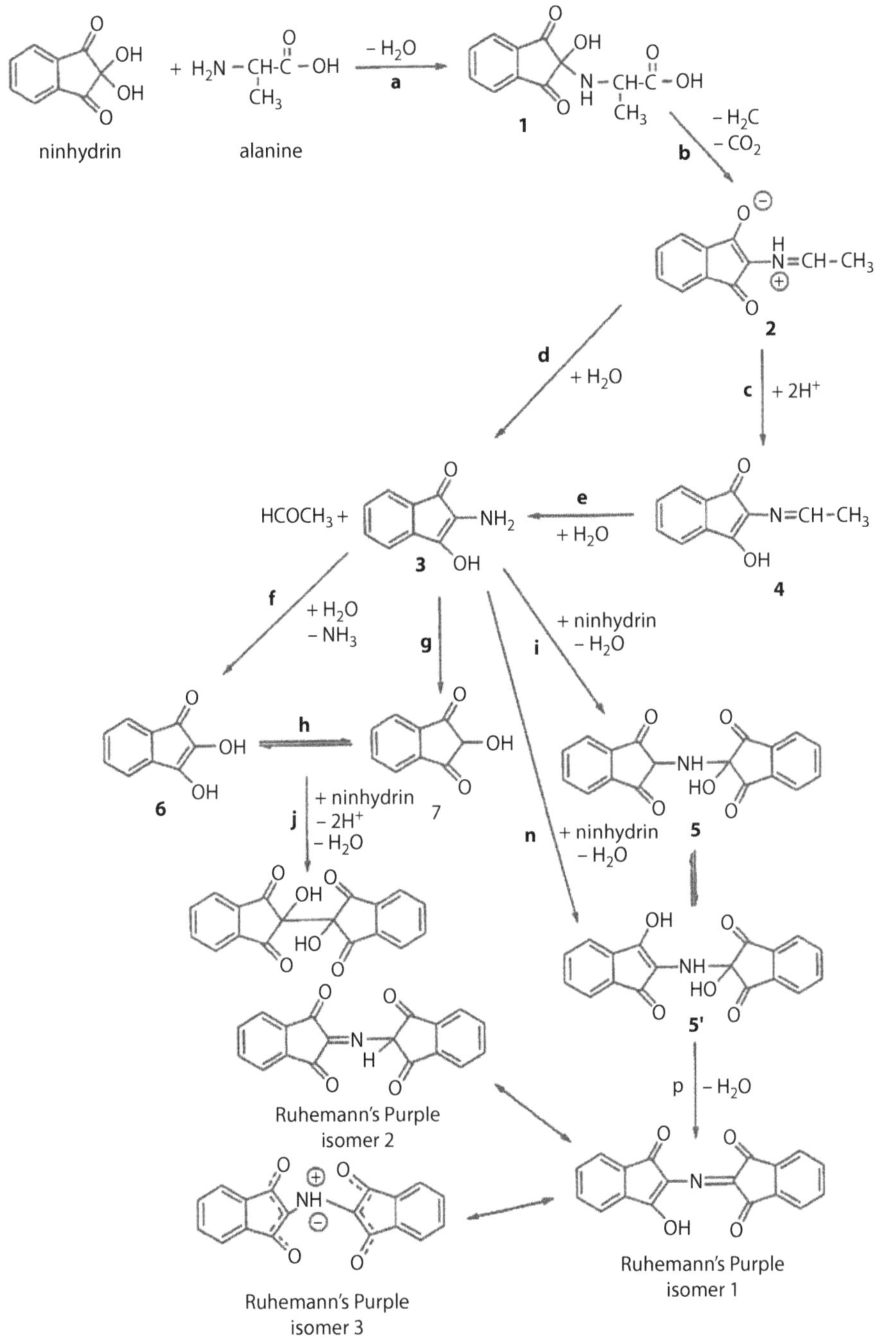

Figure 4.7 Petraco's suggested mechanism for the formation of Ruhemann's Purple.

–2.16 kcal/mol. The Lamothe mechanism suggests the participation of hydrindantin in reaction **m**, which is exothermic by –10.90 kcal/mol.

The stoichiometric studies of Friedman and Williams are quite different from the McCaldin mechanism. As seen in Figure 4.6, the reaction starts with the dehydration of ninhydrin. The dehydrated entity undergoes a Schiff base condensation reaction with alanine. Petraco et al.'s calculations showed this reaction to be exothermic by –10.87 kcal/mol. The dehydration reaction, though, is endothermic by 17.95 kcal/mol, bringing the total to about the same cost in energy as the first steps in the McCaldin and Lamothe mechanisms.

The Friedman mechanism continues with a water and carbon dioxide elimination avoiding this way the formation of an ylide present in the McCaldin and Lamothe mechanisms. The loss of water is endothermic by 9.21 kcal/mol, and the loss of carbon dioxide is exothermic by −11.34 kcal/mol. The intermediate **4** in the Friedman mechanism tautomerizes to intermediate **12** releasing −8.19 kcal/mol followed by an endothermic hydrolysis with a cost of 2.99 kcal/mol. Petraco et al. suggested that the formation of intermediate **3** directly is more probable since it is exothermic. However, according to the Friedman mechanism, **3** reacts with ninhydrin directly without passing through the intermediates suggested by the McCaldin and Lamothe mechanisms. This reaction is endothermic by 20.52 kcal/mol.

Jouille et al. indicated that when ninhydrin reacts with amino acids to form Ruhemann's Purple, the highest yield is obtained at a temperature of 100°C and at a pH of 5. Under these conditions, all three mechanisms could function from an energetic point of view. However, from a forensic point of view, it is important to have the reactions proceed at room temperature, that is, around 25°C. The computations of Petraco et al. suggest a mechanism for the formation of Ruhemann's Purple, shown in Figures 4.7. This mechanism can take place at relatively low temperatures. Indeed, by choosing the most exothermic and, thus, less endothermic reactions, the temperature of the reaction can be kept at low values. The calculations are performed in gas phase, while in reality the reactions take place on paper, but both media should lead to similar results because the relative mobility of the molecules are not examined, the aim of the calculations being the obtaining of the energetics of the reactions.

Table 4.4, obtained by Petraco et al.'s calculations, shows the energetics of the reactions of the three mechanisms. Using these results, a postulated mechanism is proposed, similar to the McCaldin mechanism, with the difference that the reactions **i** and **k** of the McCaldin mechanism are replaced by the reactions **n** and **p** of the Lamothe mechanism.

Petraco et al.'s work represents a significant example of the application of quantum chemistry to a basic area of forensic science. Indeed, as it will be shown later, a good understanding of the mechanism of formation of Ruhemann's Purple can lead to the design of better ninhydrin analogs.

Sapse and Petraco applied some of the above results to the design of ninhydrin analogs. They considered the following species:

Ninhydrin (1)
Fluoroninhydrin (2)
Fluoroninhydrin (3)
Aminoninhydrin (4)
Aminoninhydrin (5)
Methoxyninhydrin (6)
Methoxyninhydrin (7)
Hydroxyninhydrin (8)
Hydroxyninhydrin (9)

The structures labeled with even numbers feature the substituent on the C3 position on the six-membered ring of ninhydrin, while the odd numbered structures feature the substituent positioned at C2. The substituent is present in Ruhemann's Purple, at the same position on each six-membered ring.

Table 4.4 Energies of Reactions for the Mechanisms

	Reaction	Energy (kcal/mol)
	McCaldin Mechanism	
a	Ninhydrin+alanine→**1**+H_2O	7.08
b	**1**→**2**+H_2O+CO_2	2.22
c	**2**+2 H^+→**4**	-4.35
d	**2**+H_2O→**3**+acetaldehyde	-9.55
e	**4**+H_2O→**3**+acetaldehyde	-5.20
f	**3**+H_2O→**6**+NH_3	3.50
g	**3**+H_2O→**7**+NH_3	-8.76
h	**6**→**7**	-12.26
i	**3**+ninhydrin→**5**+H_2O	-8.42
j	**7**+ninhydrin+2H^+→**8**+H_2O	1.36
k	**5**→RP+H_2O+H^+	28.94
	Lamothe Mechanism	
l	**3**+ninhydrin→**6**+**9**+H_2O	22.68
m	**6**+ninhydrin→**8**+H_2O	-10.9
n	**3**+ninhydrin→**5'**+H_2O	8.62
o	**6**+**9**→RP+H_2O	-2.16
p	**5'**→RP+H_2O	11.9
	Friedman Mechanism	
q	Ninhydrin→**10**+H_2O	17.95
r	**10**+alanine→**1**	-10.9
s	**1**→**11**+H_2O	9.21
t	**11**→**4**+CO_2	-11.34
u	**4**→**12**	-8.19
v	**12**+H_2O→**3**+acetaldehyde	2.99
w	**3**+ninhydrin→RP+2 H_2O	20.52

The calculations performed on all the species employed the Hartree-Fock method, with the 6-31G** basis set as implemented by the Spartan programs. The total reactions considered are shown in Figure 4.8a. The first step of the reaction is seen in Figure 4.8b.

Table 4.5 shows the optimum energies of ninhydrin and its investigated analogs. Table 4.6 displays the optimum energies of Ruhemann's Purple and its analogs corresponding to the species shown in Table 4.5. Table 4.7 lists the energies corresponding to the reactions of formation of Ruhemann's Purple and its analogs from ninhydrin and its analogs and alanine. These energies are calculated as the energy of the products minus the sum of energies of the reactants. Table 4.8 refers to the first step of the McCaldin mechanism, that is, the formation of the intermediate **1**, as shown in Figure 4.3. These intermediates correspond to the given analog of ninhydrin.

The results displayed in Table 4.7, which refer to the net energies of the reactions of formation of Ruhemann's Purple and its analogs, do not depend on the mechanism considered. Indeed, the energies reported are not concerned with the details of the reactions but only with the reactants and the products. These are the same for all three mechanisms discussed above. As can be seen from Table 4.7 all the reactions are endothermic, absorbing energies. The energies of the substituted ninhydrin analogs increase the endothermicity of the

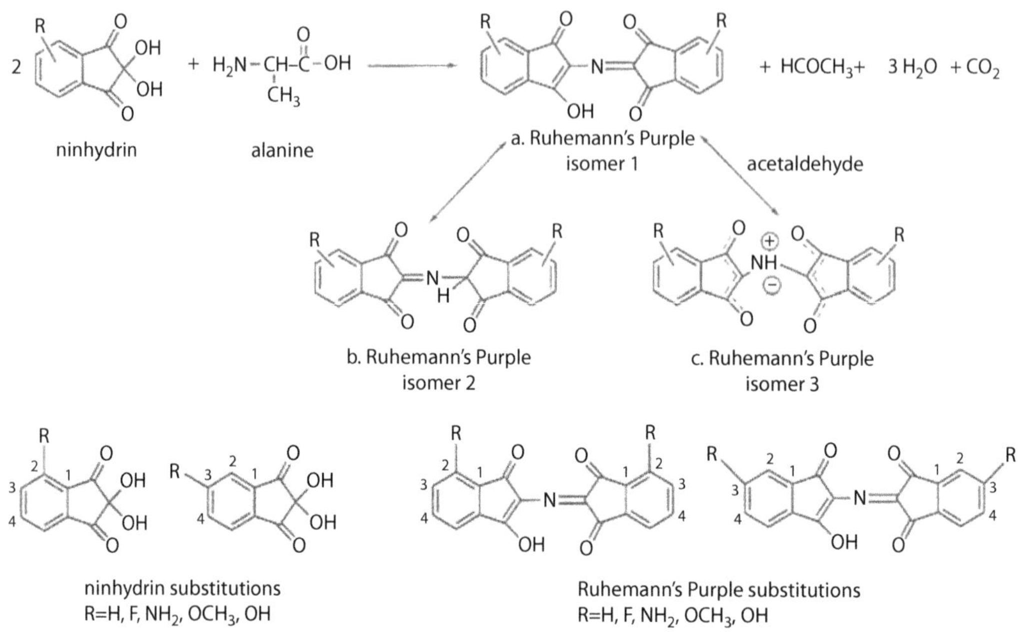

Figure 4.8a The reaction of formation of analogs of Ruhemann's Purple from the corresponding analogs of ninhydrin. The substitution patterns for ninhydrin and Ruhemann's Purple.

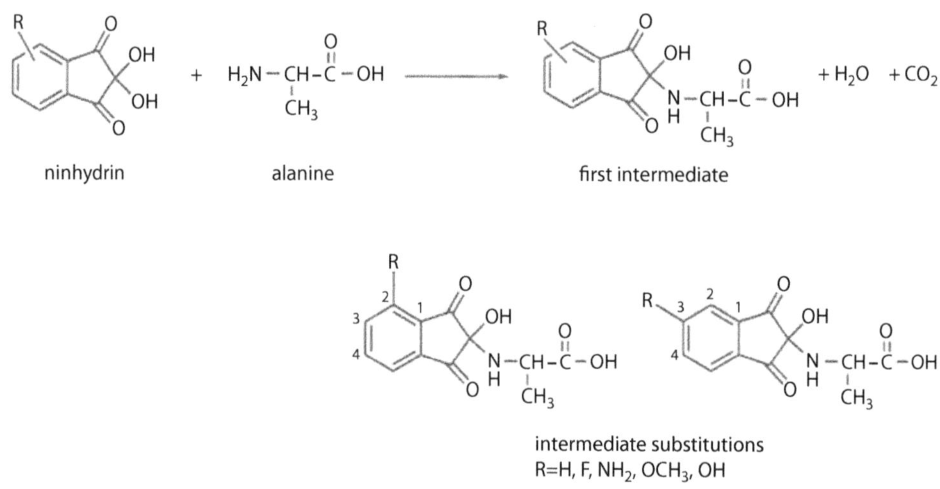

Figure 4.8b The first step of the reaction shown in Figure 4.8a.

reactions. The only exception is the fluoro-substituted ninhydrin, where the fluorine atom is positioned at the C2 carbon in the six-membered ring of ninhydrin. Indeed, it is found that this compound decreases the endothermicity of the reaction depicted in Figure 4.8 by 0.4 kcal/mol. As far as the other substituted species are concerned, the increase in endothermicity seems to be related to the bulk of the substituent. This fact suggests an effect of a steric nature. This suggestion is supported by the large increase in endothermicity, shown by the methoxy group positioned at the C3 carbon in the six-membered ring of ninhydrin. The endothermicity is proportional to the size of the substituent for both C2 and C3 substitutions. However, there is no clear difference between the C2 and C3 substitutions.

Table 4.5 Energy of Ninhydrin and Its Analogs

Compound	Energy (au)
Ninhydrin (1)	-643.77216
Fluoroninhydrin (2)	-742.61561
Fluoroninhydrin (3)	-742.62015
Aminoninhydrin (4)	-698.81878
Aminoninhydrin (5)	-698.81054
Methoxininhydrin (6)	-757.65593
Methoxininhydrin (7)	-757.66307
Hydroxyninhydrin (8)	-718.64468
Hydroxyninhydrin (9)	-718.63453

Table 4.6 Energies of Ruhemann Purple and Its Analogs

Compound	Energy (au)
Ruhemann Purple (10)	-1040.77428
Ruhemann Purple F (11)	-1238.46192
Ruhemann Purple F (12)	-1238.47031
Ruhemann Purple NH_2 (13)	-1150.85136
Ruhemann Purple NH_2 (14)	-1150.84773
Ruhemann Purple OCH_3 (15)	-1268.53424
Ruhemann Purple OCH_3 (16)	-1268.53907
Ruhemann Purple OH (17)	-1190.50446
Ruhemann Purple OH (18)	-1190.49527

Table 4.7 Reaction Energies of Ruhemann's Purple Substitutions

Substitution	Reaction Energy (kcal/mol) at HF/6-31G** Level
Unsubstituted	17.52
Ruhemann's Purple F (11)	17.12
Ruhemann's Purple F (12)	17.55
Ruhemann's Purple NH_2 (13)	27.72
Ruhemann's Purple NH_2 (14)	19.66
Ruhemann's Purple OCH_3 (15)	22.34
Ruhemann's Purple OCH_3 (16)	28.27
Ruhemann's Purple OH (17)	26.91
Ruhemann's Purple OH (18)	19.94

The same trends are observed in examining Table 4.8. An exception is the OH substituent which shows the highest endothermicity (8.24 kcal/mol) when substituted at C3 and the lowest (1.87 kcal/mol) when substituted at C2. It is interesting to note that the compound featuring the fluorine atom at the C3 position does not only decrease the endothermicity of the first step in the McCaldin mechanism, but makes this reaction exothermic, with an energy of –1.45 kcal/mol.

Table 4.8 Reaction Energies of Ruhemann's Purple Structures

Structure	Reaction Energy (kcal/mol) at HF/6-31G** Level
Unsubstituted intermediate (19)	3.14
Intermediate F (20)	−1.45
Intermediate F (21)	6.51
Intermediate NH_2 (22)	6.50
Intermediate NH_2 (23)	3.51
Intermediate OCH_3 (24)	6.94
Intermediate OCH_3 (25)	6.19
Intermediate OH (26)	8.24
Intermediate OH (27)	1.87

These results indicate the possibility of finding analogs of ninhydrin that would react better (with less endothermicity) to produce substituted analogs of Ruhemann's Purple. According to the theoretical results, experimentalists might synthesize fluorine-containing analogs of ninhydrin and investigate their usefulness as fingerprint identification agents.

AMPA and Kainic Acid Binding to Their Receptors: A Theoretical Study

Another domain, in which quantum chemistry calculations were applied to issues of forensic science interest, is related to forensic psychology. This area of study uses expertise with human motivation and pathology to analyze some aspects of criminal investigations. Indeed, disorders of the brain functions can lead to serious behavioral problems, in certain cases provoking criminal activity. Such personality disorders as schizophrenia, paranoia, obsessive-compulsive disorder, and others, can eventually lead to criminal behavior.

The work of Champeil et al. focuses on certain chemicals that play an important role in brain function, such as AMPA ((S)-2-amino-3-(3-hydroxy-5-methyl-4-isoxazolyl) propionic acid) and kainic acid (2S-(2α, 3β, 4β))-2-carboxy-4-(1-methylethenyl)-3-pyrrolidinacetic acid). Their malfunctions and those of their receptors can lead to mental disorders.

AMPA receptors, termed AMPARs, regulate fast excitatory synaptic transmissions. Accordingly, they play an essential role in the functioning of the mammalian brain. When additional AMPARs, which are glutamate-gated ion channels, are inserted into synapses after short periods of high frequency activity, a strengthening of some synaptic transmissions is produced. These transmissions are mainly related to the processes of learning and memory.

Other categories of ionotropic glutamate receptors feature N-methyl-D-Aspartic (NMDA) receptors and kainic acid (KA) receptors. These receptors play an important role in the neuronal degeneration that is associated with cerebral ischemia, Parkinson's disease, and Alzheimer's disease.

Pentikainen et al. showed that two sequence positions in the AMPA, NMDA, and kainic acid receptors, Arg485 and Glu705, are strongly involved in the binding of the ligand. A tyrosine and proline are also part of the receptors.

To investigate the binding of AMPA and kainic acid to their receptors, Champeil et al. applied ab initio (Hartree-Fock) quantum chemical calculations. The main purpose of the study was to establish the effects of mutations in the receptors upon the binding of AMPA and kainic acid to the mutated receptors in comparison to the wild-type receptors.

The energies of interaction between AMPA and tyrosine or proline were calculated by obtaining the energy of the complex and subtracting from it the sum of the energies of the subsystems. The same procedure was applied to complexes of kainic acid and tyrosine or proline. In addition, the complexes formed by tyrosine or proline and the anions of AMPA and kainic acid were also investigated.

Pentikainen et al. indicated that the AMPA receptor contains a Tyr-Ala-Pro sequence. The kainic acid receptor contains a Tyr-Ser-Ser sequence. Champeil et al. investigated the interactions between these sequences and their respective ligands, by applying the Hartree-Fock calculations with the 6-31G** basis set. They considered for the ligands two species: (1) the neutral AMPA and kainic acid, and (2) their anions. These species serve as ligands to three peptides: Tyr-Ala-Pro, Tyr-Ser-Pro, and Tyr-Ser-Ser. The first one represents the wild-type receptor for AMPA and a mutation for kainic acid. The reverse is true for the last one. The second one represents a mutation for both AMPA and kainic acid.

Figure 4.9 shows the optimized structures of AMPA and kainic acid. Figure 4.10 shows the complex formed by AMPA with proline, while Figure 4.11 shows the complex formed by AMPA with tyrosine. Figures 4.12 and 4.13 show the complexes between the AMPA anion with proline and tyrosine respectively.

Figures 4.14 and 4.15 show the complexes formed by kainic acid with proline and tyrosine respectively, while Figures 4.16 and 4.17 show the same complexes, only the neutral species are replaced by the anion of kainic acid. The interaction of the kainic acid dianion with proline and tyrosine are shown in Figures 4.18 and 4.19.

Figures 4.20, 4.21, and 4.22 show the complexes formed by AMPA with Tyr-Ala-Pro, Tyr-Ser-Pro, and Tyr-Ser-Ser, respectively. Figures 4.23, 4.24, and 4.25 show the same complexes where AMPA is replaced by its anion.

Figures 4.26, 4.27, and 4.28 show the complexes formed by kainic acid with the three peptides. Its anion complexes with the peptides are depicted in Figures 4.29, 4.30, and 4.31. Figures 4.32, 4.33, and 4.34 show the complexes formed by the three peptides and the dianion of kainic acid.

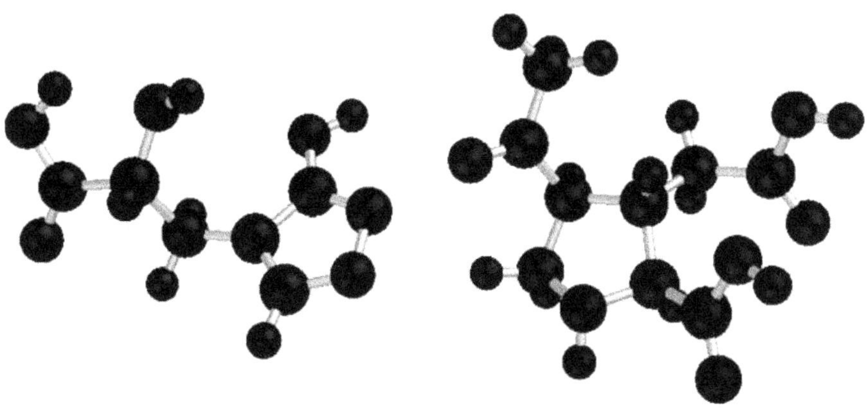

Figure 4.9 Optimized structures of AMPA and kainic acid.

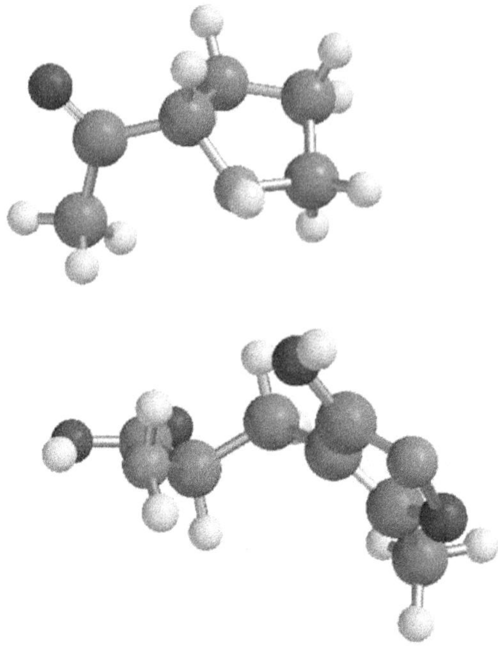

Figure 4.10 The optimized complex formed by AMPA with proline.

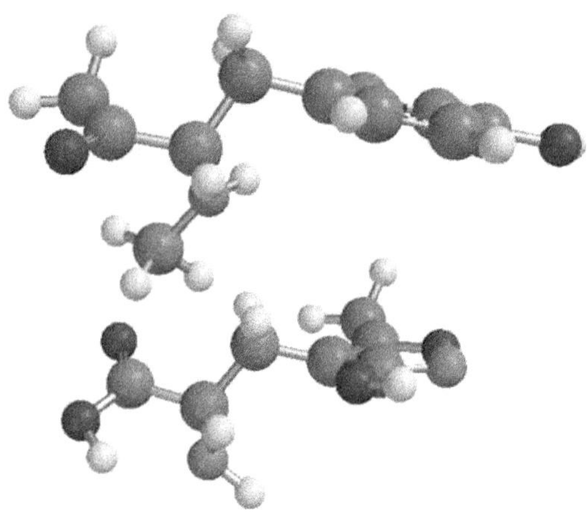

Figure 4.11 The optimized complex formed by AMPA with tyrosine.

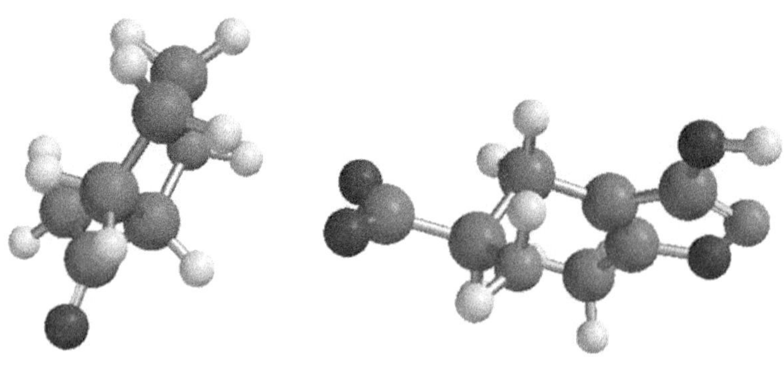

Figure 4.12 The optimized complex formed by the AMPA anion with proline.

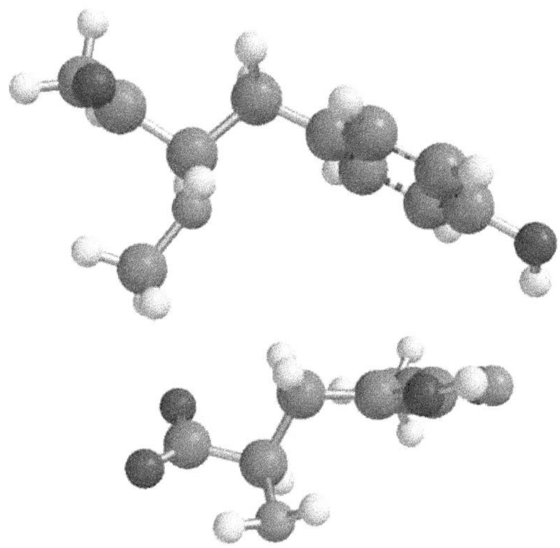

Figure 4.13 The optimized complex formed by the AMPA anion with tyrosine.

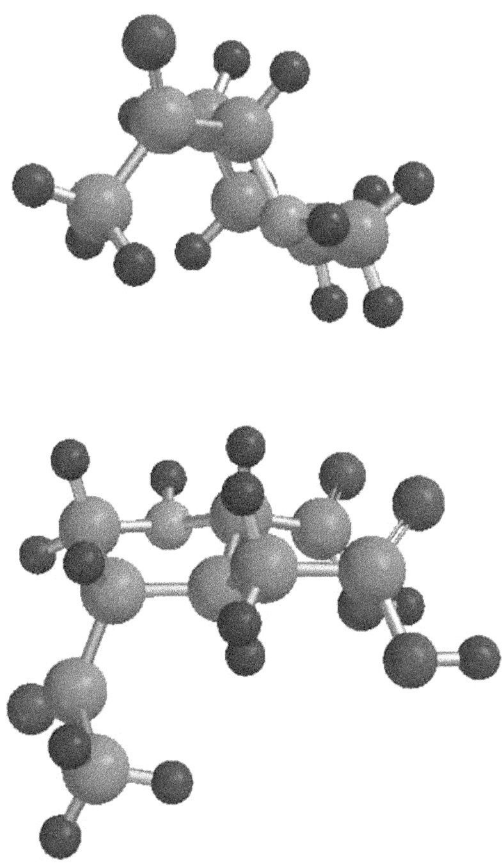

Figure 4.14 The optimized complex formed by kainic acid with proline.

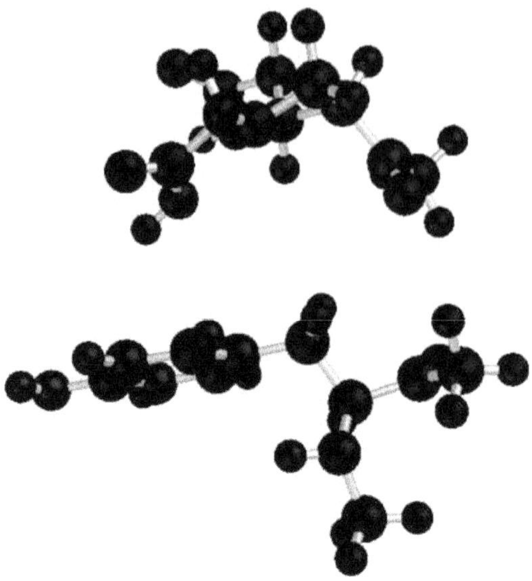

Figure 4.15 The optimized complex formed by kainic acid with tyrosine.

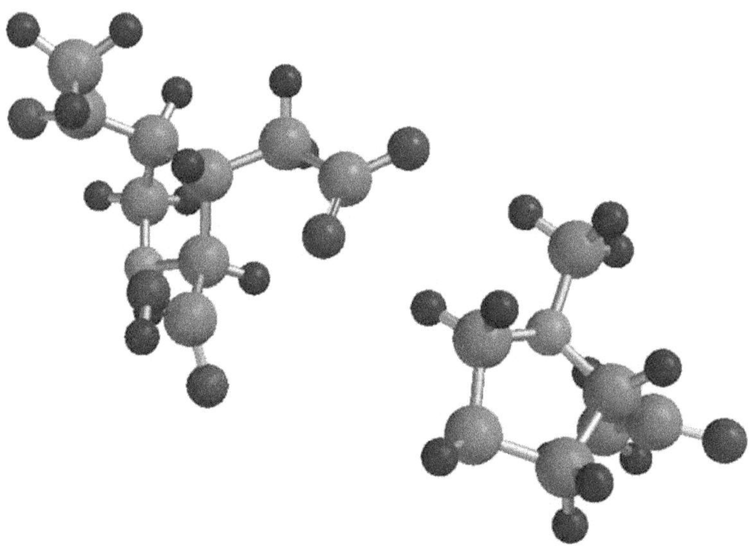

Figure 4.16 The optimized complex formed by kainic acid anion with proline.

In addition to the calculations of the total energies of the investigated species, Champeil et al. also calculated the solvation energies of the systems. Indeed, the interactions between receptors and ligands probably take place in an aquatic medium and the solvation energies might affect the binding. The aqueous solvation energies are estimated using the SM5.4 model of Cramer and Truhlar, and they can be added to the gas-phase energies obtained at the HF/6-31G** level of calculation.

Table 4.9 shows the binding energies of AMPA and kainic acid, as well as those of their anions, with proline and tyrosine. It also shows the binding solvation energies, calculated as the solvation energy of the complex, minus the sum of the solvation energies of the

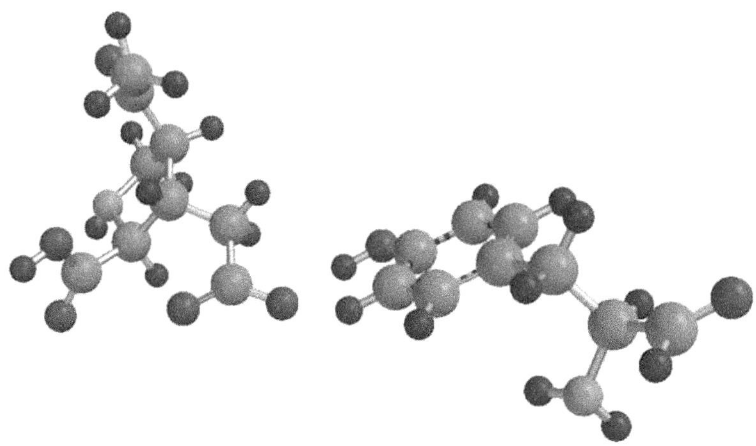

Figure 4.17 The optimized complex formed by kainic acid anion with tyrosine.

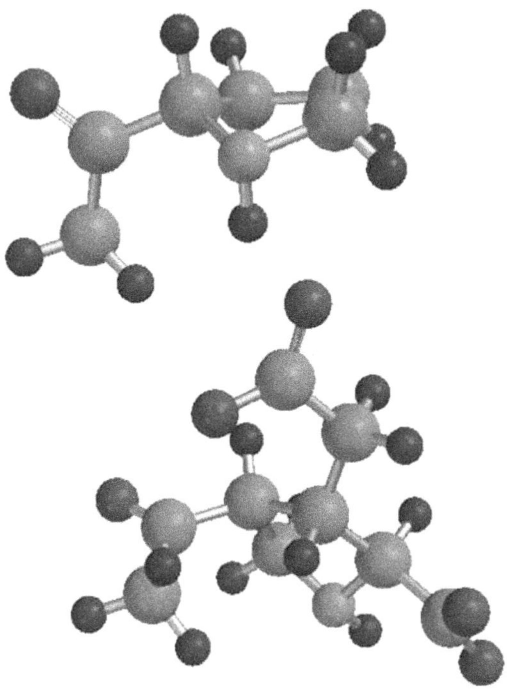

Figure 4.18 The optimized complex by kainic acid dianion with proline.

subsystems. Table 4.10 shows the binding total and solvation energies of AMPA, kainic acid, and their anions to the three peptides mentioned above.

As seen from Table 4.9, AMPA features stronger binding energies than kainic acid to both proline and tyrosine. The bonding to proline is weaker than the one to tyrosine, if no solvation energy is taken into account. However, including the solvation energy, the binding energies to proline and tyrosine are quite similar.

If at the pH of the medium, the acids are ionized and the species present are the anions, the binding energies become much higher. This is not at all unexpected, since this way, more electrostatic binding takes place. Since the binding in these complexes occurs mainly

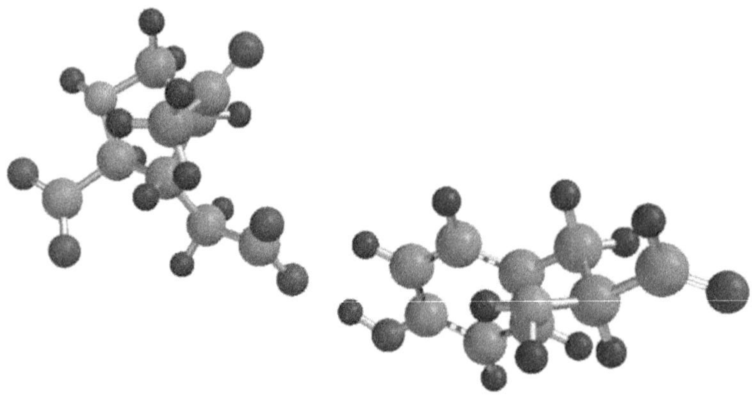

Figure 4.19 The optimized complex formed by kainic acid dianion with tyrosine.

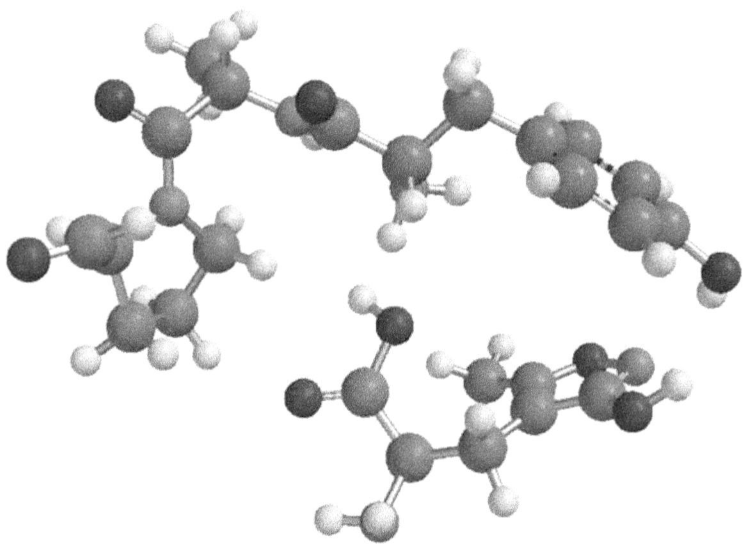

Figure 4.20 The optimized complex formed by AMPA with the tripeptide Tyr-ala-pro.

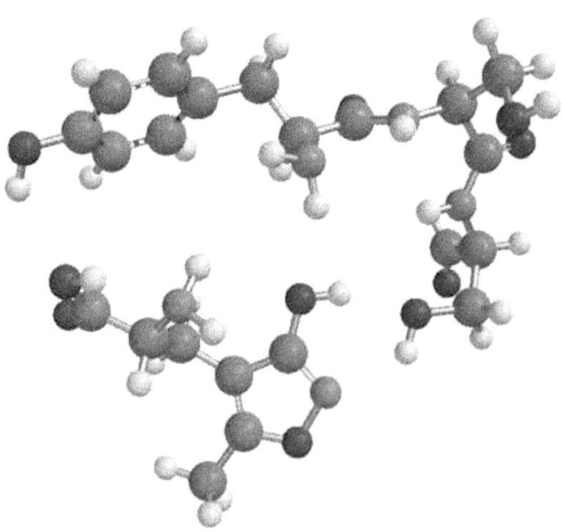

Figure 4.21 The optimized complex formed by AMPA with Tyr-ser-pro.

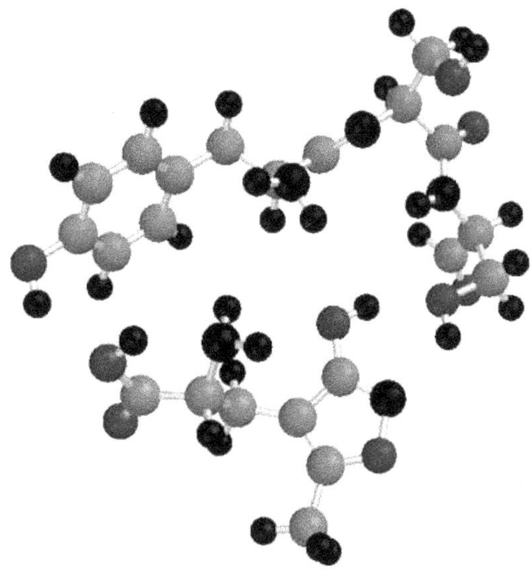

Figure 4.22 The optimized complex formed by AMPA with Tyr-ser-ser.

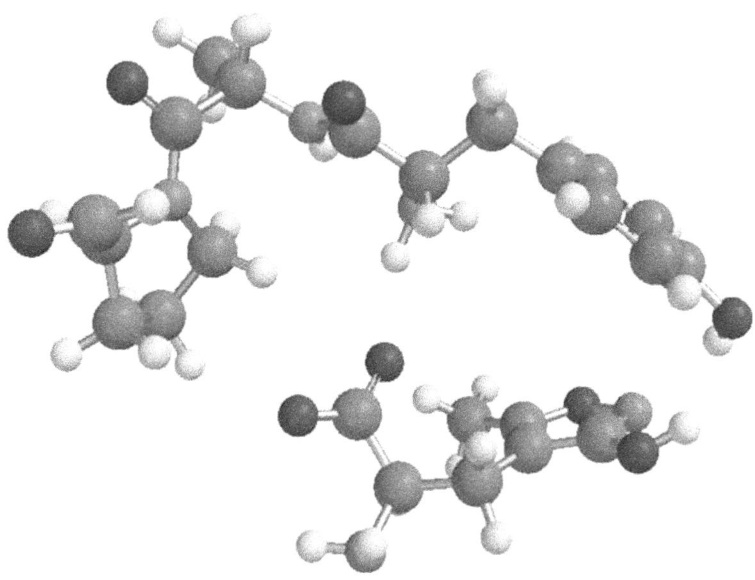

Figure 4.23 The optimized complex formed by the AMPA anion with Tyr-ala-pro.

via hydrogen bonding, when the ligand is an anion, the negative oxygen binds strongly to the positive hydrogens of the receptor. Indeed, the highest binding energy is featured by the dianion of kainic acid. Its binding energy to tyrosine is of –38.7 kcal/mol. Even if the positive binding solvation energy is added, still this system shows a strong binding, with a binding energy of –27.9 kcal/mol.

Atomic charges calculated using the Natural Population Analysis show hydrogen atoms in the receptors to feature from .5 to .8 positive electron charges, while the oxygen atoms of the carboxylate groups of the anion ligands feature –9 e.

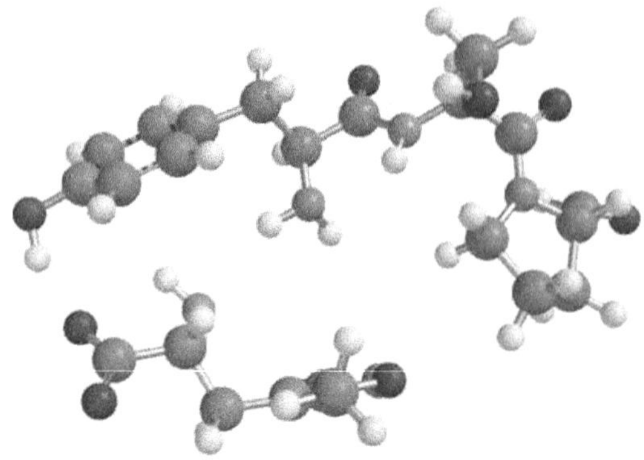

Figure 4.24 The optimized complex formed by the AMPA anion with Tyr-ser-pro.

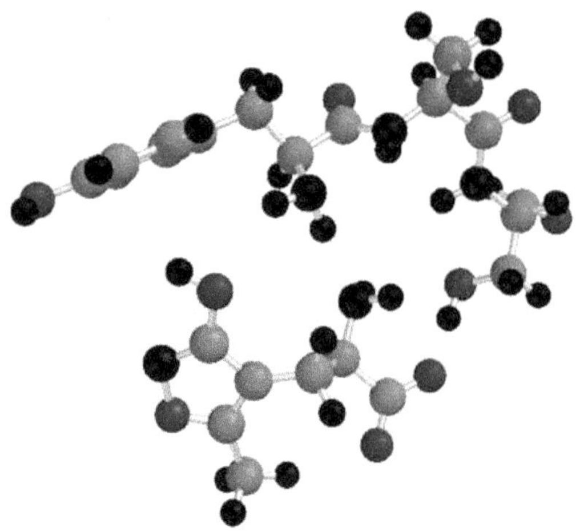

Figure 4.25 The optimized complex formed by the AMPA anion with Tyr-ser-ser.

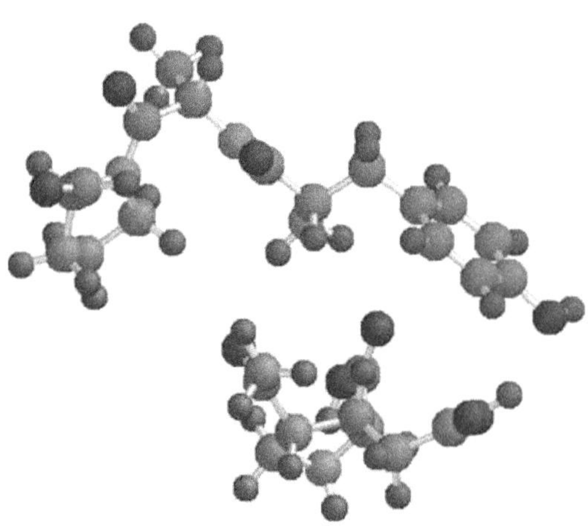

Figure 4.26 The optimized complex formed by kainic acid with Tyr-ala-pro.

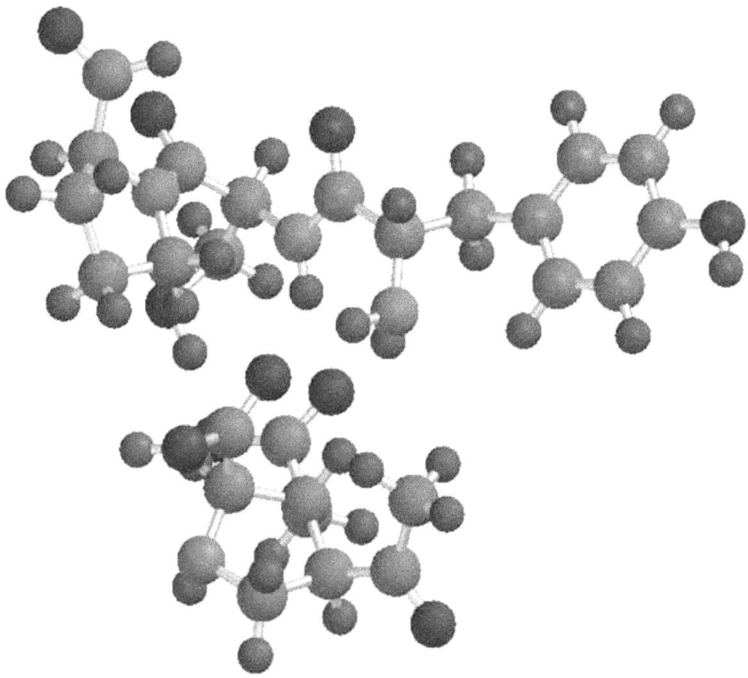

Figure 4.27 The optimized complex formed by kainic acid with Tyr-ser-pro.

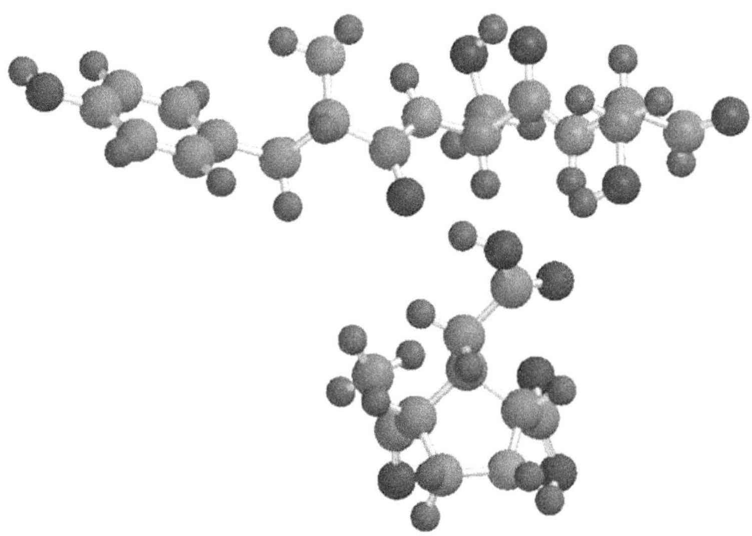

Figure 4.28 The optimized complex formed by kainic acid with Tyr-ser-ser.

Examining Table 4.10, one can see that kainic acid and its monoanion do not bind to the Tyr-Ser-Pro sequence. Even the dianion shows a small binding energy, of –15.2 kcal/mol, in contrast to its binding to the Tyr-Ala-Pro tripeptide, which features an energy of –58.4 kcal/mol, and to the Tyr-Ser-Ser sequence, which shows a binding energy of –50.9 kcal/mol. Neutral kainic acid and its monoanion are also bound to these tripetides, as seen in Table 4.10. If the binding solvation energy is taken into consideration, kainic acid does not bind to Tyr-Ser-Ser,

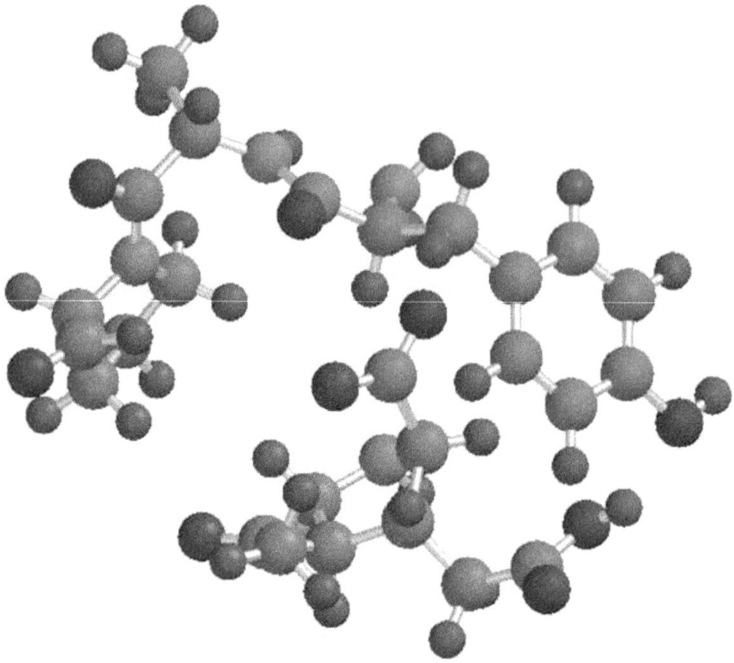

Figure 4.29 The optimized complex formed by kainic acid anion with Tyr-ala-pro.

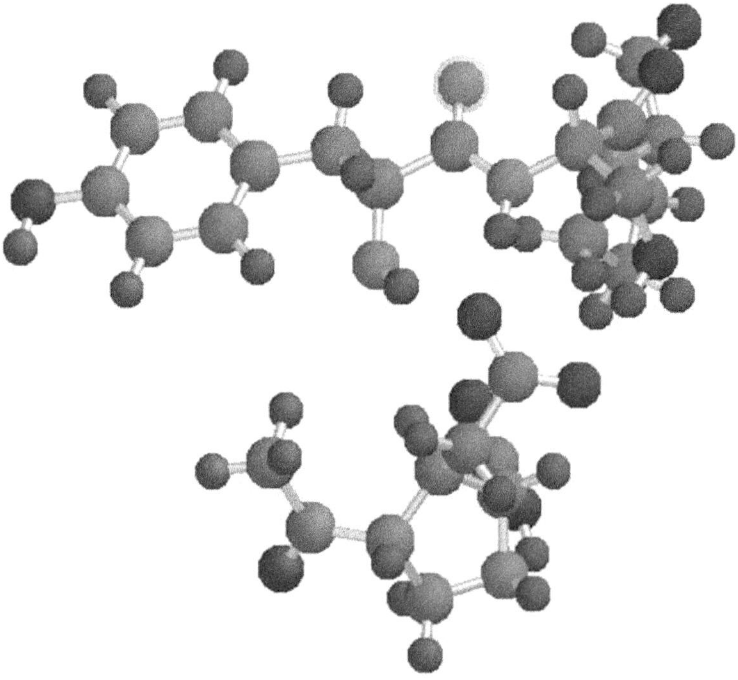

Figure 4.30 The optimized complex formed by kainic acid anion with Tyr-ser-pro.

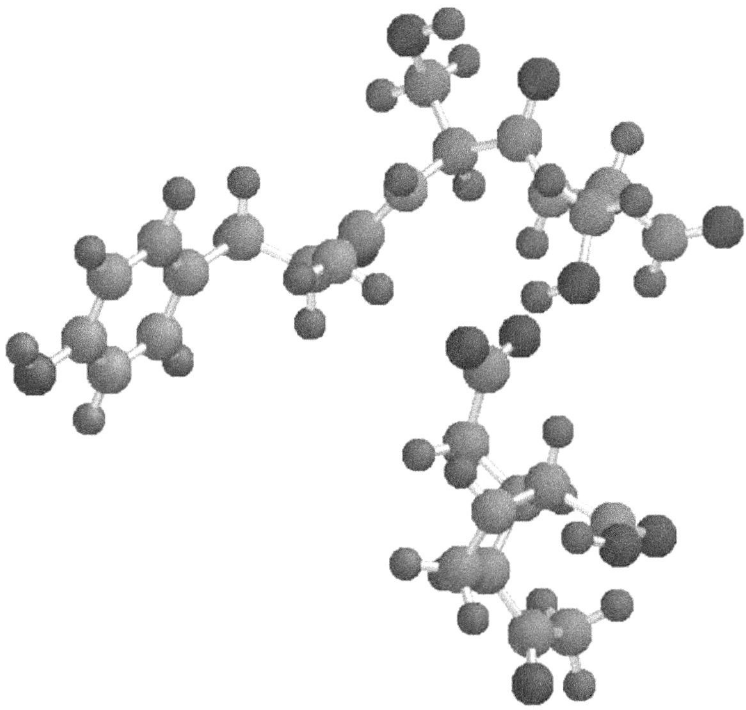

Figure 4.31 The optimized complex formed by kainic acid anion with Tyr-ser-ser.

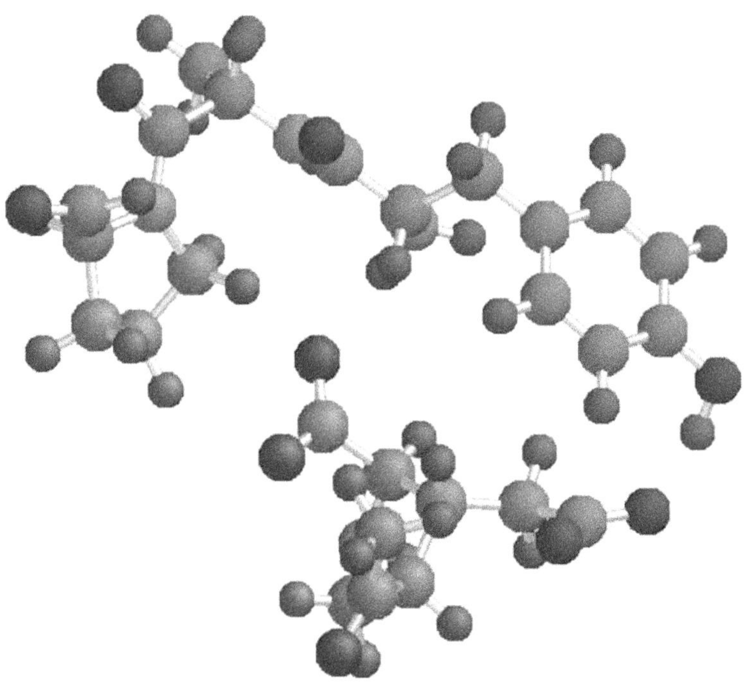

Figure 4.32 The optimized complex formed by kainic acid dianion with Tyr-ala-pro.

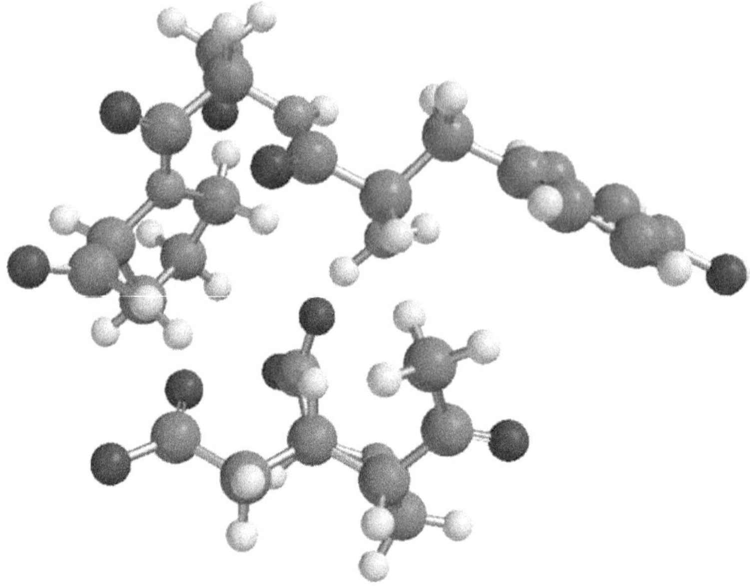

Figure 4.33 The optimized complex formed by kainic acid dianion with Tyr-ser-pro.

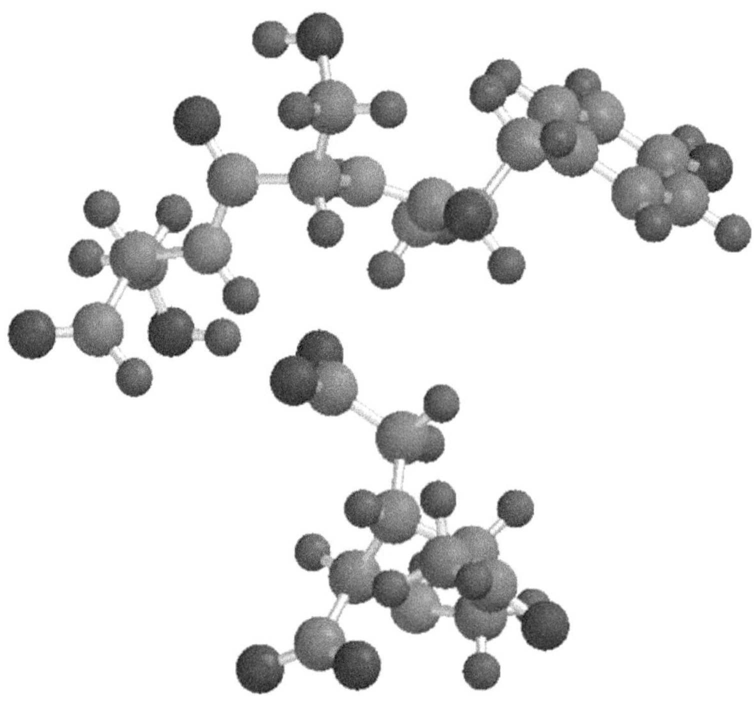

Figure 4.34 The optimized complex formed by kainic acid dianion with Tyr-ser-ser.

implying that the binding occurs either in a non-aqueous medium or the ligand species is the mono or dianion.

These results show that if mutations occur in the receptors, the binding of the substrates can be significantly affected. These changes in the binding, in turn, can affect some functions in the brain related to the learning process, to memory and, maybe, to criminal

Table 4.9 Binding Energies of AMPA and Kainic Acid Complexes with Proline and Tyrosine

Compound	Δ*E* (kcal/mol)	Δ*E* (solvation, kcal/mol)
1	-8.0	1.1
2	-10.2	2.9
3	-18.4	-3.7
4	-30.6	8.7
5	-2.3	2.1
6	-4.3	3.3
7	-11.4	1.3
8	-26.4	6.7
9	-23.0	18.0
10	-38.7	11.8

Table 4.10 Binding Energies of AMPA, Kainic Acid, and Their Anions with the Peptides

Compound	Δ*E* (kcal/mol)	Δ*E* (solvation, kcal/mol)
11	-7.3	3.9
12	-13.9	6.7
13	-11.3	16.0
14	-29.9	31.8
15	-26.2	22.3
16	-29.3	21.3
17	-9.8	8.9
18	—	11.3
19	-7.9	17.1
20	-26.5	7.4
21	—	5.1
22	-43.1	27.0
23	-58.4	5.4
24	-15.2	12.3
25	-50.9	21.5

behavior. Accordingly, from the point of view of forensic psychology, it might be beneficial to perform experiments that would investigate the possible correlation between mutations in the receptors and personality changes. For instance, aggressive behavior in animals upon mutations in the receptors could shed some light on these possibilities.

Quantum Chemical Calculations Applied to the Study of Methamphetamines

Methamphetamines are chemicals that are used recreationally in an illegal manner, but also for medical conditions and for weight loss. They are psycho stimulants and sympathomimetic drugs.

In the past few years, many laws were established to make it a crime to possess material and equipment suitable for methamphetamine synthesis. Accordingly, many illicit or clandestine laboratories were used to bypass these laws. In these laboratories, cold medications served as materials for the preparation of amphetamines. To circumvent these procedures, The Patriot Act includes a section called "The Combat Methamphetamine Epidemic Act of 2005." This section is a law that limits the quantities of nonprescription cold medicines that can be bought at a time.

Methamphetamines are produced in various ways and some of these involve a certain amount of danger. One of the dangerous aspects of methamphetamine production is the release of harmful chemicals, such as phosphine and methylamine. These chemicals are dangerous because they harm the skin, the eyes, and the respiratory tract. They are also harmful to the environment. Indeed, for every pound of methamphetamine produced, there are more than five pounds of toxic waste that pollute the rivers or go into the sewer system. Some of the chemicals used in methamphetamine production are highly explosive. About 15% of illegal methamphetamine laboratories were discovered because these chemicals produced dangerous explosions and fires.

In the United States, in 2006, 7,347 incidents involving illegal methamphetamine laboratories took place. Among these, the greatest numbers were in Missouri, Illinois, and Indiana. Other countries where methamphetamines are produced are, for instance, Belgium, the Netherlands, and Australia.

One of the illegal laboratories in Australia utilized the Wacker oxidation of safrole to 3, 4-methylenedioxyphenyl-2-propanone (MDP-2P) using palladium chloride, methanol, and p-benzoquinone. A number of studies described methods of synthesizing "ecstasy" or "XTC," a designer drug with the chemical formula 3',4'methylene dioxymethamphetamine (MDMA). These studies concentrated on identifying intermediates of the synthesis reaction, as well as by-products to facilitate recognition of MDMA synthesis in clandestine laboratories. They also shed light on the route employed for the synthesis.

A number of analytical methods have been reported for the detection of MDMA and its analogs. They include gas chromatography with mass spectrometry, liquid chromatography, thin-layer chromatography, and immunoassay. Sachs and Woo reported a detailed mechanistic fragmentation analysis of methamphetamines and select regioisomers by GC/MS. The importance of their methods for forensic purposes is exemplified in the BALCO case, where the main role was played by the interpretation of mass spectrometry studies on the synthetic steroid tetrahydrogenstrinone. Another case which illustrates the importance of the mass spectroscopy analysis featured ring-substituted amphetamine and p-methyl substituted methamphetamine, which were sold as amphetamine. This produced a harmful reaction in a seasoned amphetamine user.

Kato et al. described the layer chromatography fluorescence of MDMA and related compounds. They compared their thin-layer chromatography results with GC/MS studies. Some of the compounds they have tested were also investigated by Sapse et al. with quantum chemical calculations, as will be shown later. One of the routes of synthesis of MDMA described by Salouros et al., features the by-product N-Cyanomethyl-1- (3,4-methylenedioxyphenyl)-2-propylamine. For instance, Salouros et al. isolated the product proposed by Swist et al. as 2-(dimethylamino)-2-methyl-3-(3',4'-methylenedioxyphenyl)-2-propanenitrile. Salouros et al. applied NMR methods to this compound and elucidated its structure as N-cyanomethyl-N-methyl-1-(3',4'-methylenedioxyphenyl)-2-propylamine. Their experiments support the proposal of

Swist et al. that this compound plays the role of marker for the cyanoborohydride route of synthesis.

Sapse et al. applied quantum chemical calculations to the study of these reactions with the aim of confirming the structures proposed for by-products and intermediates. In addition, the work investigated the energetics of the different reactions of synthesis. The calculations include the infrared vibrational frequencies of the structures involved, which, when compared with the infrared spectra of the by-products or intermediates, can confirm or refute their putative structures.

Sapse et al. also investigated 3', 4'-methylenedioxymethamphetamines and related compounds, by applying quantum chemical calculations. The calculations of Sapse et al. used the Density Functional Theory (DFT), at B3LYP level, with the 6-31G** basis set, as implemented by the Titan computer program. They investigated the reaction of synthesis of MDMA and a number of analog amphetamines.

The reaction of synthesis of MDMA is:

$$\text{MDP-2P} + CH_3NH_2 - H_2O = \text{N-methyl-1-MDP-2-propylimine}$$

$$\text{N-methyl-1-1MDP-2-propylamine} + H_2 = \text{MDMA} \quad (1)$$

The components of this reaction are shown, in their optimum geometry, as follows: The MDP-2P is shown in Figure 4.35 (compound1), N-methyl-1-MDP-2-propylimine in Figure 4.36 (compound 2), and MDMA in Figure 4.37 (compound 3). The energetics of this reaction is calculated by geometry-optimization of the reactants, the intermediate, and

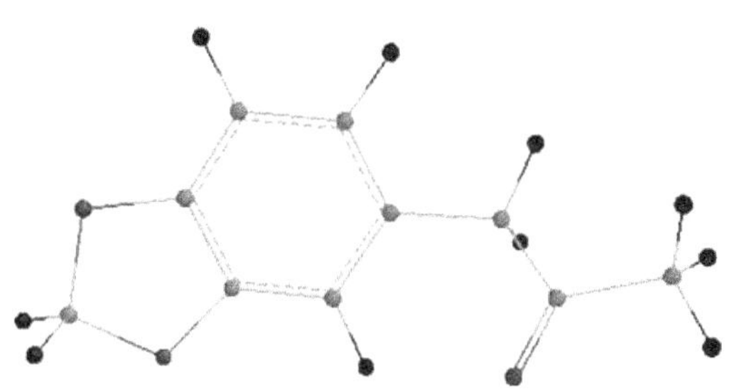

Figure 4.35 Optimized structure of MDP-2P (compound 1).

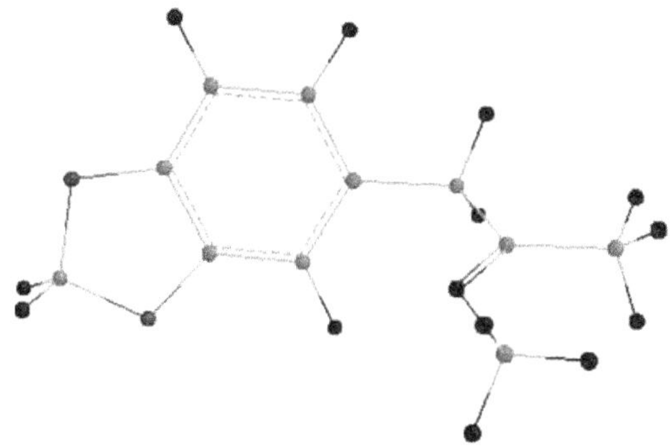

Figure 4.36 Optimized structure of N-methyl-1-MDP-2-propylimine (compound 2).

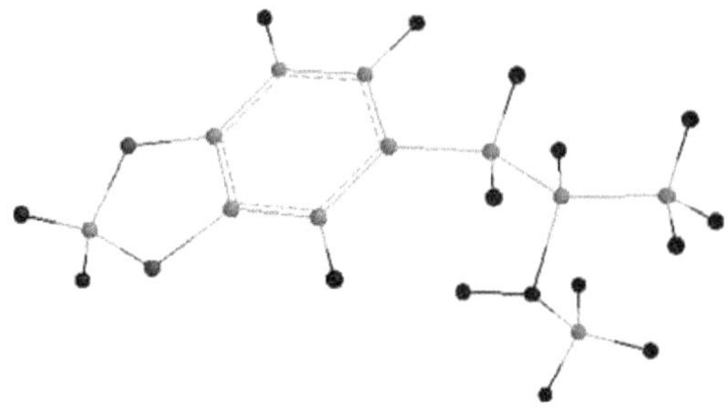

Figure 4.37 Optimized structure of MDMA (compound 3).

Table 4.11 Energies of Methamphetamine, Reactants, and Intermediates for Its Synthesis Reaction and By-Products

Compound	Energy (au)	Zero-Point Energy (kcal/mol)	Energy of Salvation (kcal/mol)
1	-612.74721	113.9	-8.8
2	-632.17683	139.1	-9.0
3	-633.39527	154.7	-6.0
4	-764.93053	171.5	-8.6
5	-764.93036	171.3	-7.9
CH_3NH_2	-95.86137	40.3	-6.3
H_2O	-76.42257	13.1	
H_2	-1.17850	6.4	
$ClCH_2CN$	-592.33926	23.18	-4.5

the products and calculation of the energy of all the species. Then, the sum of the energies of the reactants is subtracted from the sum of the energies of the intermediate and the hydrogen molecule, to obtain the energy of the first step of the reaction. The sum of the energies of the intermediate and of the hydrogen molecule is subtracted from the energy of MDMA to obtain the energy of the second step of the reaction. The energies of each entity are displayed in Table 4.11. This reaction also features some by-products shown in Figures 4.38 (compound 4), 4.39 (compound 5), 4.44 (compound 10), and 4.45 (compound 11). Compounds 4 and 11 can be synthesized according to the reactions:

$$\text{MDMA} + \text{ClCH}_2\text{CN} = \text{N-cyanomethyl-N-methyl-1-MDP-2-propylamine (Figure 4.38)} + \text{HCl} \quad (2)$$

and

$$\text{N-methyl-1-phenyl-2-propylamine (Figure 4.44)} + \text{ClCH}_2\text{CN} = \text{N-cyanomethyl-methyl-1-phenyl-2-propylamine (Figure 4.45)} + \text{HCl} \quad (3)$$

Some methamphetamine analogs are shown in Figures 4.40 (compound 6), 4.41 (compound 7), 4.42 (compound 8), and 4.43 (compound 9). These were also investigated by Sapse et al, using quantum chemical calculations, with the methods described above.

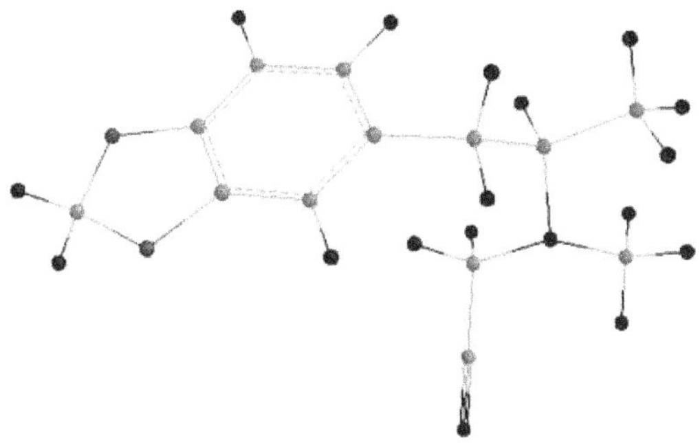

Figure 4.38 Optimized structure of N-cyanomethyl-N-methyl-1-MDP-2-propylimine (compound 4).

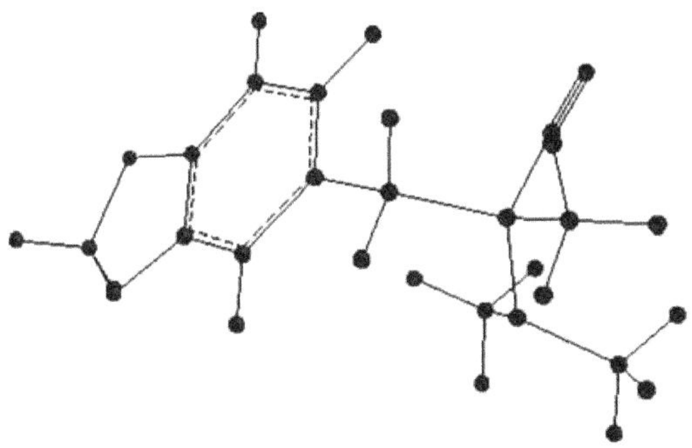

Figure 4.39 Optimized structure of N,N-dimethyl-1-MDP-2-cyano-2-propylamine (compound 5).

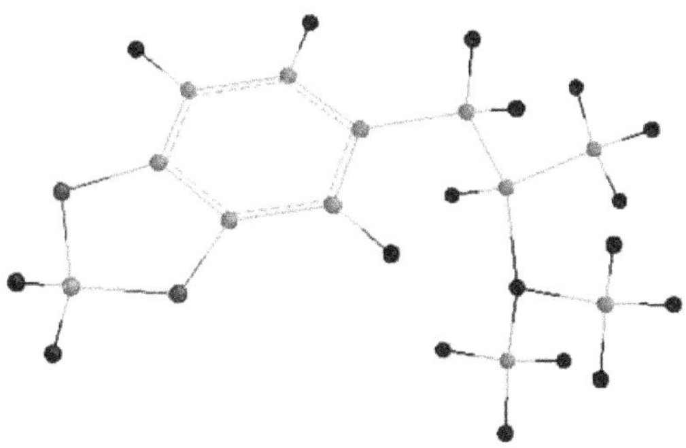

Figure 4.40 Optimized structure of 3,4-methylenedioxy-N,N-dimethylamphetamine (compound 6).

Their energies are displayed in Table 4.12, together with the energies of compounds shown in Figures 4.44 and 4.45. The energies of the compounds shown in Figures 4.38 and 4.39 are shown in Table 4.11. Tables 4.11 and 4.12 contain also zero-point energies and solvation energies.

As mentioned in the Introduction, infrared spectra can be calculated with the DFT (B3LYP) method. These results, as obtained by Sapse et al, are presented in Table 4.13 for the intermediate of the reaction of synthesis of MDMA. Tables 4.14 and 4.15 display the vibrational frequencies and intensities of the by-products featured in Figures 4.38 and 4.39.

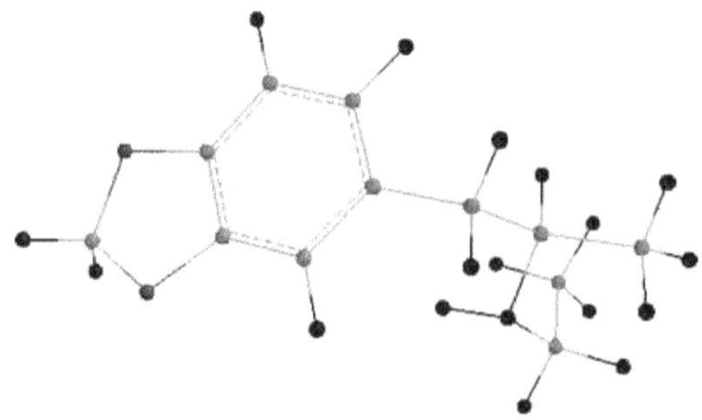

Figure 4.41 Optimized structure of 3,4-methylenedioxyethylamphetamine (compound 7).

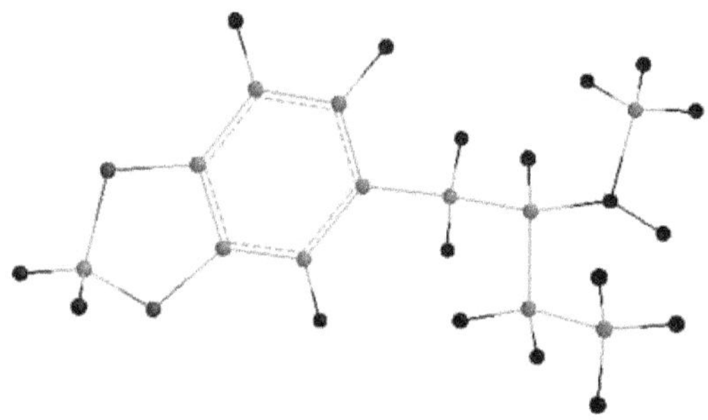

Figure 4.42 Optimized structure of N-methyl-1-(3,4-methylenedioxyphenyl-2-butanamine (compound 8).

Figure 4.43 Optimized structure of N-methyl-1-(3,4-methylenedioxyphenyl)-3-butanamine (compound 9).

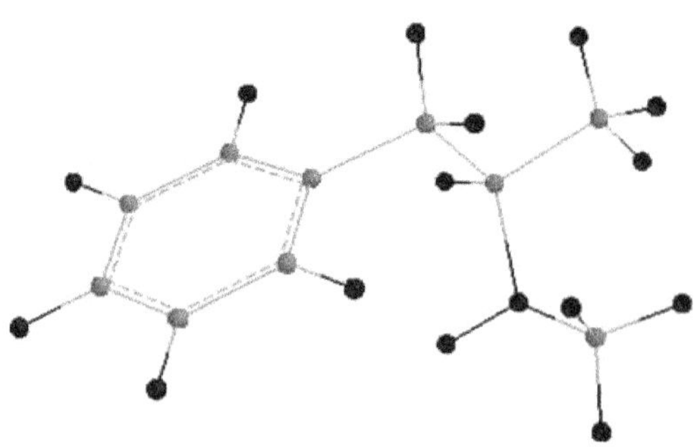

Figure 4.44 Optimized structure of N-methyl-1-phenyl-2-propylamine (compound 10).

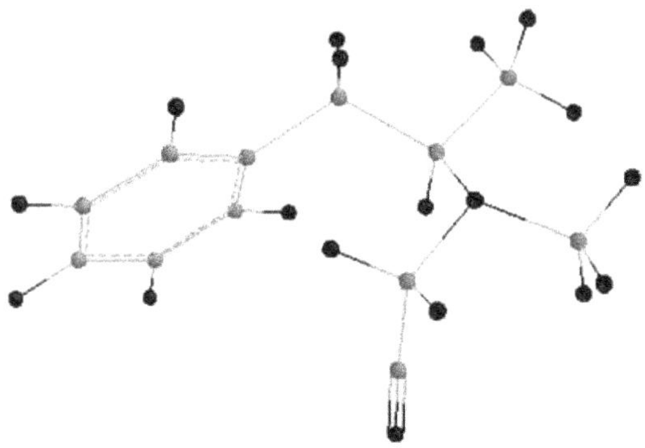

Figure 4.45 Optimized structure of N-cyanomethyl-methyl-1-phenyl-2-propylamine (compound 11).

Table 4.12 Energies of Some Analogs of Methamphetamine and By-Products

Compound	Energy (au)	Zero-Point Energy	Solvation Energy
6	−672.70090	172.2	−4.5
7	−672.71270	172.7	−5.1
8	−672.70880	165.3	−6.5
9	−672.70792	172.7	−6.5
10	−444.86572	145.1	−2.8
11	−576.40626	161.7	−3.4
HCl	−460.80080	4.2	−0.7

Table 4.13 Compound 2 (Figure 4.36)

Frequencies (cm^{-1})	Intensities
3106.2	54.3
3160.8	12.7
3088.2	21.5
3070.8	52.5
3008.2	139.8
2998.8	54.2
1754.6	92.7
1537.3	276.3
1487.1	40.0
1325.3	22.6
1294.0	235.3
1265.1	58.6
1193.0	23.3
1070.0	118.6
960.2	23.8
947.8	24.8

Table 4.14 Compound 4 (Figure 4.38)

Frequencies (cm^{-1})	Intensities
3114.8	34.4
3097.5	59.8
3010.8	136.1
2957.4	91.7
2945.8	43.9
2371.7	2.0
1538.7	229.0
1506.1	23.0
1487.5	55.6
1304.4	64.2
1296.7	207.1
1223.4	29.4
1154.9	24.7
1072.1	131.6
978.8	29.2
821.9	26.9

Table 4.15 Compound 5 (Figure 4.39)

Frequencies (cm^{-1})	Intensities
3152.3	32.8
3012.0	132.9
2983.8	58.6
2975.1	36.3
2335.0	2.7
1560.0	10.6
1519.8	15.2
1487.4	57.0
1261.5	26.4
1224.3	22.7
1138.8	42.9
1070.6	122.6
1000.4	35.4
956.5	31.6

The methamphetamine analogs shown in Figures 4.40 and 4.41, also in their optimum geometry, have been investigated and their energies are displayed in Table 4.12. Table 4.16 shows their infrared frequencies and intensities, while Table 4.17 shows the infrared frequencies and intensities of the compounds shown in Figures 4.42 and 4.43. Table 4.18 shows the frequencies and intensities of compound 11, shown in Figure 4.45.

As shown by Sapse et al., the reaction of synthesis of MDMA proceeds via an intermediate, as shown in reaction (**1**). The formation of the intermediate from MDP-2P and methylamine is found to proceed via an endothermic reaction with a cost in energy of 5.8 kcal/mol. The reaction of reduction of the intermediate by hydrogen is exothermic, with an energy of −25 kcal/mol. Therefore, the entire reaction (**1**) is exothermic, producing −19 kcal/mol.

Table 4.16 Compound 6 (Figure 4.40) and Compound 7 (Figure 4.41)

Compound 6		Compound 7	
Frequencies (cm^{-1})	Intensities	Frequencies (cm^{-1})	Intensities
3141.8	30.6	3136.2	30.0
3129	32.1	3123.7	32.1
3049	29.5	3108.6	43.8
3009	141.6	3100.2	53.4
2936.3	116.8	3008.4	151.3
2923.8	55.9	2925.5	112.4
2898.1	42	1539.4	236.5
1536	253.5	1487.1	67.0
1492	30.7	1304.4	70.3
1372.2	32.5	1210.0	36.8
1292.3	130.6	1164.2	40.9
1291.7	155.5	1086.1	43.2
1073.1	82.8	1069.9	101.8
1067.1	37.8	971.4	33.5
974.6	36.5		

Table 4.17 Compound 8 (Figure 4.42) and Compound 9 (Figure 4.43)

Compound 8		Compound 9	
Frequencies (cm^{-1})	Intensities	Frequencies (cm^{-1})	Intensities
3128.4	31.0	3134.0	27.8
3110.1	38.2	3117.9	35.2
3096.6	57.1	3105.4	41.9
3080.2	50.2	3102.0	57.5
3009.7	145.1	3095.5	37.2
2942.8	100.1	3077.9	38.7
2900.9	56.6	3040.8	36.6
1539.3	244.1	3004.9	142
1486.5	43.0	2945.3	97.3
1346.8	26.5	2896.4	62.5
1310.1	67.1	1537.8	245.8
1282.3	157.9	1486.4	49.5
1145.0	31.0	1402.8	28.0
1071.6	126.1	1298.8	59.8
971.0	39.3	1295.5	142.7
		1284.2	64.5
		1220.6	41.0
		1169.2	39.4
		1071.2	70.0
		1069.1	52.0
		973.6.0	31.2
		774.2	68.1

Table 4.18 Compound 11 (Figure 4.45)

Frequencies (cm^{-1})	Intensities
3047.7	35.9
2955.2	89.7
2929.7	49.4
1403.6	20.4
1172.4	30.0
1055.2	28.7
736.9	23.0

A by-product of this reaction, as proposed by Salouros et al., is N-cyanomethyl-N-methyl-1- (3',4'methylenedioxyphenyl)-2-propylamine. NMR studies showed this compound to have the structure shown in Figure 4.38. The infrared vibrational frequencies displayed in Table 4.14, obtained for the optimized geometry of this structure, might prove that this is indeed the structure of this by-product.

Swist et al. proposed as a by-product 2-(dimethylamino)-2-methyl-3- (3',4'-methylendioxyphenyl) propanenitrile. The geometry-optimized structure of this compound, as shown in Figure 4.39, has also been investigated by Sapse et al. and its infrared frequency had been calculated, as shown in Table 4.15. Eventual experiments which will obtain the infrared spectrum for the by-product can be compared to the theoretically found ones and confirm its structure.

Sapse et al. found the reaction of synthesis of compound 4 endothermic, with a cost in energy of 2.3 kcal/mol. On the contrary, the reaction of synthesis of compound 11 was found to be exothermic, releasing –1.32 kcal/mol.

All the structures geometry-optimized by Sapse et al. are real minima, since they do not exhibit imaginary infrared frequencies.

Conclusions

From all the studies described in the preceding sections, it can be seen that quantum chemical calculations applied to subjects of forensic or toxicological interest can shed light on many aspects of the problems. Among these are calculations of reaction energies, which can lead to the improvement of the reactions by designing analogs of useful agents, and structures of by-products of interest, as well as of intermediates of synthesis reactions. In addition, NMR and infrared vibrational frequencies can be calculated for putative structures and refute or confirm them. It is clear that the best use of quantum chemical calculations can be made in conjunction with experimental studies, using such methods as gas, liquid, and thin-layer chromatography, mass spectrometry, NMR and IR spectra, and others.

Bibliography

Beaven, C. *Fingerprints*. Hyperion, New York, 2001.

Chambers, C. C., Hawkins, G. D., Cramer, C. J., & Truhlar, D. J. 1996. Model for Aqueous Solvation Based on Class IV Atomic Charges and First Solvation Shell Effects. *J. Chem. Phys.* 100, 16385.

Champeil, E., Proni, G., & Sapse, D. 2009. Ab Initio Studies of Receptor Interaction with AMPA and Kainic Acid. J. *Mol. Model.* 15(9), 1109–1117.

Collins, M., Heagney, A., Condaro, F., Odgers, D., Tarrant, G., & Stewart S. 2007. Methyl 3-[3',4'-(methylenedioxy)phenyl]-2-methyl glycidate: An Ecstasy Precursor Seized in Sydney, Australia. *J. Forensic Sci.* 52, 898–903.

Colotta, V., Catarzi, D., Varano, F., Lenzi, O., Filacchioni, G., Costagli, C., Galli, A., Gherlandini, C., Galeotti, N., Gratteri, P., Sgrignani, J., Deflorian, F., & Moro S. 2006. Structural Investigation of the 7-chloro-3-hydroxy-1-*H*-quinazoline-2,4-diaone Scaffold to obtain AMPA and Kainate Receptor Selective Antagonists. Synthesis, Pharmacological, and Molecular Modeling Studies. *J. Med. Chem.* 49, 6015–6026.

Dietz, F., Rommel-Mohle, K., Schleitzer, A., Tyutyulkov, N. 1993, On the Chromophore of the Ninhydrin-aminoacid Colour Reactions, *Z.Naturforsch* 48b 1133–1137.

Elber, R., Frank, A., Almog, J. 2000, Chemical Developments of Latent Fingerprints : Computational Design of Ninhydrin Analogs. *J. Forensic* Sci. 45: 757–760.

Friedman, M., Williams, L.D. 1974, Stoichiometry of Formation of Ruhemann Purple in the Ninhydrin Reaction *Bioorg. Chem.* 1: 267–283.

Grigg, R. Malone, J.F. Mongkolaussavaratana, T. Thianpatanagul, S. 1989, X=Y-ZH compounds as potential 1,3-Dipoles. Part 23[1,2] mechanisms of the reactions of ninhydrin and phenalene trion with ∝-amino acids. X-ray crystal structure of protonated ruhemann's purple, a stable azomethine ylide, *Tetrahedron*, 45: 3849–3862.

Gaensslen, R. E., Harris, H. A., & Lee, H. *Introduction to Forensic Science & Criminalistics.* McGraw Hill, New York, 2008.

Gund, P. 1972. Guanidine, Trimethylenemethane, and Y-delocalization. Can Acyclic Compounds Have Aromatic Stability? *J. Chem. Ed.* 49, 100–103.

Hallett, P. J., & Standaert, D. G. 2004. Rational for and Use of NMDA Receptor Antagonist in Parkinson's Disease. *Pharmacol. Ther.* 102, 155–174.

Herzig, L., Massa, L. J., Santoro, A., & Sapse, A. M. 1981. An Ab Initio SCF Study of Guanidine and Substituted Guanidines. Rotational Barriers. *J. Org. Chem.* 46, 2330–2333.

Jacobi, P.A., Martinelli, M.J., Polanc, S. 1984, Total Synthesis of (.+-.)-Saxitoxin *J. Am. Chem. Soc* 106, 5594–5596.

Jouille, M.M., Thompson, T.R., Nemeroff, N.H. 1991, Ninhydrin and Ninhydrin Analogs, Syntheses and Applications. *Tetrahedron* 47: 8791–8882.

Kato, M., Fujita, S., Ohta, H., Fukuba, M., Toriba, A., & Hayakawa, K. 2008. Thin Layer Chromatography/Fluorescence Detection of 3.4-Methylenedixy-Methamphetamine and Related Compounds. *J. Forensic Sci.* 48, 1367–1371.

Kishi,Y., Tanino, H., Nakata, T., Kaneko,T. 1977, A Stereo Specific Total Synthesis of DL-Saxitoxin *J. Am. Chem. Soc.* 90, 2818–2819.

Lamothe , P.J., Mc Cormick, P.G., 1972, Influence of Acidity on the Reaction of Ninhydrin with Aninoacids. *Anal. Chem* 44: 821–845

Levine, I. N. *Quantum Chemistry* Prentice Hall, New Jersey, 5th edition, 2000.

Nilsen, A., & England, P. M. 2007. A Subtype-Selective, Use-Dependent Inhibitor of Native AMPA Receptors. *J. Am. Chem. Soc.* 128, 4902–4903.

Pentikainen, O. T., Settimo, L., Keinanen K., & Johnson, M. S. 2003. Selective Agonist Binding of AMPA and Kainate Receptors: A Molecular Modeling Study. *Biochem. Pharmacol.* 66, 2413–2425.

Petraco, N. D. K., Proni, G., Jackiw, J. J., & Sapse A. M. 2006. Amino Acid Alanine Reactivity with the Fingerprint Reagent Ninhydrin. A Detailed Ab Initio Computational Study. *J. Foren. Sci.* 51, 1267–1275, and references within.

Sachs, S.B., & Woo, F. 2007. A Detailed Mechanistic Fragmentation Analysis of Methamphetamine and Select Regioisomers by Gc/MS. *J. Forensic Sci.* 52, 308–319.

Salouros, H., Collins, M., Tarrant, G., & George, A. V. 2008. *N* –Cyanomethyl-*N*-methyl-1-(3',4'-methylenedixyphenyl) –2-propylamine: An MDMA Manufacturing By-Product. *J. Forensic Sci.* 53, 1083–1091.

Sapse, A. M., Herzig, L., & Snyder, G. 1981. A Self-Consistent Field Molecular Orbital Study of Hydroxyguanidine. *Cancer Res.* 41, 1824–1828.

Sapse, A. M., Rothchild, R., & Rhee, K. 2006. An Ab Initio Study of the Guanidinium Group in Saxitoxin. *J. Mol. Model.* 12, 140–145, and references within.

Sapse, D., Champeil, E., & Sapse, A. M. Theoretical Calculations Applied to the Study of the Energetics of the Reactions of Methamphetamine's Synthesis and to the Characterization of Reactants, Products, and By-products. To be published in 2011 in *Comptes Rendus de L'Academie Francaise.*

Sapse, D., & Petraco, N. D. K. 2007. A Step on the Path in the Discovery of New Latent Fingerprint Development Reagents: Substituted Ruhemann's Purples and Implications for the Law. *J. Mol. Model.* 13, 941–948, and references within.

Sellal, F., Nicoullon, A., Michel, G., Michel, B. F., Lacomblez, L., Geerts, H., Delini-Stula, A., Bordet, R., Bontue-Ferrer, D., & Allain, H. 2005. Pharmacology of Alzheimer's Disease: Appraisal and Prospects. *Dementia Geriatr. Cognit. Disord.* 19, 229–245.

Slemo, L., Volmer, D.A., Kovacevic, B., Maksic, Z.B., 2004, Gas-Phase Dissociations of Protonated Saxitoxin and Neosaxitoxin, *J. Am. Soc. Mass Spectrom.* 15, 462–477.

Spartan, Wavefunction Inc., California

Stuehr, D. J., Sapse, A. M., & Sapse, D. S. 1993. An Ab Initio Study of an Oxidative Mechanism that Forms Nitric Oxide from the N-Hydroxyguanidinium Ion. *Structural Chem.* 4, 3, 143–147.

Swist, M., Wilamowski, J., & Parczewski, A. 2005. Determination of Synthesis Method of Ecstasy Based on its Basic Impurities. *Forensic Sci. Int.* 152, 175.

Titan, Wavefunction Inc., California.

United Nations Office on Drugs and Crime. World drug report 2006.

Wahlgren, N. G. 1997. A Review of Earlier Clinical Studies on Neuroprotective Agents and Current Approaches. *Int. Rev. Neurobiol.* 40, 337–363.

Wigfield, D.C., Buchanan, G.W., Croteau, S.M. 1980 On Ruhemann Purple. *Can. J. Chem.* 58: 201–208.

Wittmann, H., Muller, A.K., Ziegler, E., 1969. Neue Reagentien zum papierchromatographischen Nachweis von Aminosäuren, 5. Mitt.: Reaktionen des 1, 2, 3-Trioxo-2, 3-dihydrophenalens mit primären Aminoverbindungen. *Monatsh Chem.* 100: 497–502.

DNA
Applications to Several Legal Cases and Quantum Chemical Calculations on Its Interaction with Methyllithium

5

DANIELLE SAPSE, ANNE-MARIE SAPSE, JACQUES MADDALUNO, AND CATHERINE FRESSIGNÉ

Contents

DNA (deoxyribonucleic acid) has become an essential tool of forensic science. Due to the fact that each individual body contains a specific DNA, evidence found at the scene of a crime containing human tissues of various natures can identify with a very high probability the presence of a suspected perpetrator or of an eventual victim whose body had been removed.

The existence of DNA in living organisms was discovered in the 19th century, and in the 20th century it became evident that it contains the blueprints of life. James Watson and Francis Crick, in collaboration with other scientists, discovered the double-helix model of DNA. All DNA molecules are polymers of entities called nucleotides, made out of a base (adenine, thymine, cytosine, or guanine), a sugar (deoxyribose), and a phosphate group. What distinguishes one DNA molecule from another is the order in which the bases in the nucleotides are positioned. The two strands that form the DNA molecule are kept together by hydrogen bonds between the bases of one strand and those of the second, according to the rule that adenine is bound to thymine and cytosine is bound to guanine.

Since every organism starts as a single cell with its specific DNA and the multiplication of the cells occurs via DNA replication, the DNA of that organism is conserved through all its life. The human DNA has approximately 3.5 billion base pairs, so applying combinatorial analysis, it becomes clear that the probability of two organisms having the same DNA is insignificant.

The replication of DNA is catalyzed by enzymes called DNA polymerases. The largest number of DNA molecules is found in the nuclei of the cells and this type of DNA is called nuclear DNA or genomic DNA. Another type of DNA, called mitochondrial DNA is found in the mitochondria, cells' power plants. These molecules of DNA also have forensic applications. The mitochondrial DNA, or mtDNA, has two regions called HV1 and HV2, where HV stands for hypervariable region. These regions in DNA sequences show a large variation between different individuals. Another very important property of mtDNA is its mode of heredity. Indeed, it is known that nuclear DNA is half inherited from the father, via the sperm and half from the mother via the ovules. The mtDNA is inherited only from the mother, without participation of the father. This fact allows the tracing of a certain DNA sequence for many maternal generations. The mtDNA also features a high copy number, implying that it can be identified even when it is taken from old remains.

To utilize fragments of DNA found in different tissues at the scene of a crime, DNA has to be typed. Except the DNA involved in protein synthesis and cell mitosis, organisms contain a large quantity of the so-called nonfunctional DNA, molecules whose role in the life process has not been determined. This type of DNA often contains tandemly repeated sequences, the number of which constitutes the polymorphism. The number of repeats of a sequence in a certain locus can be highly variable in different individuals, so these regions were given the name of VNTR (variable number of tandem repeat) loci.

Before the process of typing can be started, the DNA has to be extracted from the tissues found at the scene of the crime, such as blood, semen, saliva, and skin. The extraction takes place by digesting the materials with a protein-breaking enzyme (protease), and using organic solvents to isolate the DNA.

The first method of DNA typing, proposed in the 1980s is called RFLP (restriction fragment length polymorphism). This method, which is no longer used, consisted in cutting the DNA molecules into small pieces, using specific enzymes. These enzymes, called restriction endonucleases, acted at specific places in DNA and then using electrophoretic methods (the Southern blotting method), the fragments were separated and the specific alleles were detected by radioactivity or chemiluminescence methods.

Due to the results of Alec Jeffreys in 1985, in England, who reported that the RFLP method is very useful for shedding light on blood relationships, as well as individualizing people, the DNA typing methods were rapidly improved. A new technique, called polymerase chain reaction (PCR), addressed itself to the problem of finding quantities of DNA at the scene of a crime that were insufficient for typing by the RFLP method. The PCR method allowed the copying of a small DNA fragment into millions of copies. Besides this basic advantage, the PCR method is very rapid, a fact that enables forensic laboratories to handle the huge amount of DNA work necessary. The method is also more sensitive than the RFLP method and all these facts make it more appropriate for forensic work.

Another typing system was developed by the Cetus Corporation, for a locus called HLA-DQA1, using a technique called "reverse dot blotting" and based on PCR. In addition, Cetus developed a typing kit based on a repeat unit length of 15–20 base pairs, called DIS80.

More recently, the VNTR used for DNA typing have repeat units of 4–5 base pairs. These are found in large numbers in the human genome and out of them, 13 loci were investigated, since they seem to be sufficient to provide a high level of individualization. The names used for these loci are either microsatellites or short tandem repeats (STRs). A person's DNA typing leads to obtaining their profile, which can then be stored in a database. When DNA found at a crime scene is typed, it is then compared to the database to eventually find the individual to whom it belongs.

Jeffreys used the RFLP method shortly after its discovery. A boy returning from Ghana to England, declared himself to be the son of a woman who lived in England and he produced an English passport. The authorities suspected the document to be fake and refused to admit him in the country. Jeffreys used DNA typing on samples from the boy and his putative family and the results showed that the parental relation was real. The boy could, thus, enter the country.

This early application of the RFLP method was followed by a criminal investigation, in which a man called Richard Buckland was suspected of two rape-murder crimes, one in 1983 and the other in 1986. Upon DNA examination, it was proved that Buckland was innocent of both crimes and he was exonerated. He was the first person to be found innocent because of DNA analysis.

In the United States, a man called Tommy Lee Andrews was convicted of rape due to the fact that the DNA found at the scene of the crime was found to match his own with a probability of 1 in 10 billion. On the same basis, a higher court upheld the conviction upon appeal.

There are numerous examples of DNA-solved cases. They divide largely into two categories: those that exonerate a suspect and those that prove his culpability. In the second category, prosecutor and writer Harlan Levy describes some significant cases in his book *And the Blood Cried Out.*

The first case solved with the help of DNA analysis was handled by Dr. Jeffreys himself, for a crime committed in 1983 in England. Not far from Dr. Jeffreys's laboratory, a 15-year-old girl called Lynda Mann was found raped and murdered. Three years later, another girl, Dawn Ashworth, was found raped and murdered under similar circumstances. In both cases the mode of death was strangulation. Circumstantial evidence pointed to a 17-year-old boy, George Howard, who worked in a nearby psychiatric hospital. Probably under police pressure, Howard confessed to having raped and murdered Dawn but refused adamantly to admit to Lynda's rape and murder. Meanwhile, Jeffreys perfected the DNA analysis method and upon testing the semen found in Lynda, he concluded that it did not belong to Howard. When the same test was performed for Dawn, the result also indicated that that semen did not belong to Howard and furthermore, the semen found in Lynda and Dawn was identical, indicating that the same person committed both crimes and that person was not Howard. Therefore, he was released. The men of the near-by region were asked to provide blood samples, to be compared with the DNA found at the scenes of these two crimes. It was discovered that a man called Colin Pitchfork had bribed a friend to give a blood sample in his stead. He was thus obliged to provide a sample from his own blood, and it was found that his DNA corresponded with the DNA found in both victims. He was tried and sentenced to life in prison for each crime.

In the United States, DNA testing was developed and mainly used by two private companies: Cellmark (Maryland) and Lifecodes (New York State). One particular case brought ambivalent feelings about the reliability and admissibility of DNA-related evidence. This case concerned the murder of a young woman and her two-year-old daughter in their apartment in New York City. The suspect, Joseph Castro, had been seen in the apartment building where the murder took place and his watch had a bloodstain, possibly the blood of the victims. RFLP analysis, performed by the Lifecodes laboratory resulted in a match with the blood of the young woman killed presumably by Castro.

Indeed, the blood from the watch matched the victim's blood at three different chromosomes, which, according to Lifecodes, would be one in 100 million Hispanic people. One of the prosecution witnesses was Dr. Richard Roberts, a very prestigious researcher in DNA studies. His testimony agreed with the Lifecodes results. However, another scientist, Dr. Eric Lander, was troubled by the lack of controls of the results. He was approached by two lawyers, Peter Neufeld and Barry Scheck, whose aim was to use DNA testing more as a means to prove innocence than guilt, as will be shown later. Under these circumstances, a number of scientists concluded that the DNA results were not sufficient to determine if the blood on the watch belonged to the victim. As a consequence, the judge did not allow the DNA evidence to be presented to the jury. Other evidence was sufficient to convict

Castro who was offered and accepted a plea bargain of 20 years to life in prison. As he pleaded guilty, he recognized the fact that the blood on the watch belonged to the victim. However, this case showed that small technicalities could throw doubt on DNA results. Indeed, perpetrators convicted by DNA tests have tried to challenge the results under different pretexts. An example of such a case is *United States v. Shea*. In the late 1980s and early 1990s, when DNA tests started to be used in court, a number of arguments against the method were raised upon appeals. They concerned such issues as doubts about the RFLP method being reliable, about samples being degraded, about statistics of certain populations creating a too high matching probability, and other such concerns, some of them related to prejudice. In the Shea case, the defendant was suspected of robbery, by breaking into a bank in New Hampshire. There were two robbers and one of them cut himself and left traces of blood at the scene and in the getaway car. A forensic specialist performed PCR tests on Shea's blood and compared it to the DNA from the blood found in the bank. The two samples matched and the probability of finding another match was 1 in 200,000. At the appeal, Shea contested the reliability of the method employed for DNA testing and objected to the statistical projection. The court denied the objections to the reliability of the RFLP method and affirmed the statistics to be correct. The court also rejected Shea's complaint that presenting the statistics to the jury would influence their decision of a guilty verdict. On appeal, the conviction was affirmed.

Another kind of argument used by the defense against DNA evidence concerned population subgroups. The Chischilly case is an example. Daniel Chischilly, a Navajo man, was accused of rape and murder, and convicted on the basis of DNA tests. The DNA analysis was performed by using the FBI I-3 database, containing data of Native Americans. The defendant objected that his tribe (Navajo) was underrepresented in the database. The court ruled that the DNA experts' testimony has to be admitted and that the prosecution presented the case well.

There are a large number of cases where the DNA evidence could not be doubted or questioned.

In the 1990s, one of the cases where DNA evidence proved to be invaluable was the case of an Austrian killer, called Jack Unterweger. This man kidnapped and murdered a young woman, in 1974, when he was 24 years old. At his trial, in 1976, it was found that he had committed fifteen crimes and was sentenced to life imprisonment. In prison, he started writing and became an acclaimed writer, securing this way the support of writers' organizations. Due to the support of the literati and with the help of a psychiatrist, he was declared reformed and released from prison. When Unterweger was again a free man, he was 39 years old. About four months later, the killings started again, with the victims being prostitutes. In the 7–8 killings which occurred, no eyewitnesses were present, and no blood or fingerprints were found at the scene of the crimes. The crimes took place in Austria and Czechoslovakia.

In 1991, Unterweger took a trip to the United States, to Los Angeles, under the pretext that he was a journalist and wanted to write an exposé of the world of prostitution. To seemingly accomplish this goal, he secured the help of the LAPD who indicated to him the relevant locations. Soon after, three prostitutes were found murdered. They died by strangulation, with their own bras, similarly to some of the women killed in Vienna. After Unterweger's departure from the United States, the killings stopped.

The killer had returned to Austria, when the Austrian authorities established a link between the killings in their country, the one in Prague and the ones in Los Angeles.

It became quite clear that the pattern of the crime locations followed the pattern of Unterweger's trips in and out of Austria. He must have noticed that he was under police observation, so he departed for Switzerland and then Miami. There he was finally arrested in February 1991 and sent back to Austria where he stood trial.

An American Special Agent, Gregg McCrary, who worked for the Behavioral Science Unit, established that the eleven crimes committed in the three countries were all committed by the same person. The prosecution then had to prove the identity of that person, specifically that that person was Unterweger. The seats of the car driven by the suspect in Prague in 1990 were examined by the police. The examination resulted in the finding of a few head hairs, which were sent, together with hair from the Prague victim's scalp, to the police laboratory in Zurich. The laboratory ran PCR tests on the DNA extracted from the hairs and since the material was sufficient, they applied up to date methods which covered several genetic locations. The results indicated that the hair strands found on the car seat belonged indeed the Prague victim. The probability of the existence of another woman with the same DNA characteristics was one in 2.1 million.

Unterweger was tried in April 1994 for eleven murders and the main points of the prosecution were his travel pattern, the similarities in the modus operandi and the PCR results from the DNA analysis. Since in Austria a conviction can be obtained by the vote of the majority of the jury and unanimity is not necessary, the defendant was convicted for nine murders and sentenced to life in prison. He committed suicide in prison, by hanging himself with his shoelaces. This case is a clear example of the importance of DNA analysis, since the other pieces of evidence might not have been sufficient.

As mentioned before, Peter Neufeld and Barry Scheck decided to use DNA analysis to exonerate suspects wrongly convicted of crimes. To achieve this goal, they established the Innocence Project, which reopens old cases in which there was doubt about the guilt of the accused. Using the new tool of DNA analysis, some of these cases were found to have condemned innocent persons to years in prison.

One of these cases involved a man called Marion Coakley, a mentally disabled man, who was convicted of rape and sentenced to 15 years in prison. Due to his destructive behavior, he was transferred from one prison to another. A few years after Coakley was imprisoned, Scheck and Neufeld started working on the appeal.

Coakley had been recognized by his victims, undoubtedly due to his resemblance to the real culprit. Even though other factors seem to indicate that he was not the rapist, he was convicted. On appeal, fingerprints taken from a car involved in the crime proved not to belong to Coakley. To his great luck, both Coakley and the rapist proved to be secretors. A secretor is a person whose blood markers are found in other fluids of the body, such as semen and saliva. Coakley had blood type A, which did not correspond with the group found in the semen from the victim. Even though that fact should have proven the innocence of the defendant, the victims still insisted that he was the rapist and, as such, he was kept in prison, despite the evidence pointing to his innocence. By September 1987, he was paroled, and released while waiting for the case to be resolved. The end came a few months later when, in a new hearing, the Judge declared Coakley to be innocent.

Another case solved by DNA analysis was the trial of Walter Snyder. In 1985, in Alexandria, Virginia, a woman called Faye Treatser was raped in her apartment by a man dressed in red shorts. The man was a young African American, who smelled of cigarettes and alcohol. About two weeks after, Faye noticed a man in the vicinity and thought she recognized her assailant. The man she saw was called Walter Snyder, and he was a boiler mechanic. His police record consisted only in a trespassing conviction, in a school playground, to play basketball with some friends. He fit the description of the rapist and, upon identification by Faye, was arrested. Unfortunately for him, he had the same blood type as the perpetrator, as do 32% of the population. He also possessed a pair of red shorts. However, there were letters on them, a fact that the victim did not recall having seen. Finally, Walter Snyder was sentenced to 45 years in prison.

Edith Snyder, his mother, was convinced of his innocence and accumulated a file of information about the case. In 1993, she handed the file to Peter Neufeld, in New York. Indeed, she found out about the DNA analysis method and hoped that there was a possibility for this kind of test to exonerate her son. Walter's previous lawyer refused his demand to perform a DNA analysis. When Cellmark finally performed the test, it was found that the quantity of DNA was not sufficient to provide clear results.

A friend of Edith's suggested that they address themselves to a laboratory in Boston which used the PCR technique. As mentioned before, this method requires smaller amounts of DNA. This time the results were clear: the DNA found on Faye's underwear did not belong to Walter. After many efforts, with the help of Peter Neufeld and the Innocence Project, Walter Snyder was finally released and could restart a normal life and work.

When a crime is committed and bodily fluids or tissues are found at the scene, they can be examined and analyzed for their DNA content. However, there are situations when DNA-containing material was found at the scene of a presumed crime and there is no information about the date and time when the crime was committed. Therefore, the age of the DNA is hard to determine. To shed light on this issue, Sapse et al. have applied quantum chemistry calculations to the interaction of DNA fragments with lithium compounds, such as methyllithium. The purpose of utilizing organic lithium compounds is the following: when either a negative charge or an electron-rich atom is present in the investigated molecule, the lithium atom present in organolithium compounds, featuring normally a strong positive charge, will form a lithium bond with the negative atom, similar to hydrogen bonds. Therefore, the molecule studied and the lithium-containing reagent will form complexes featuring a certain binding energy.

The DNA-containing material found at a crime scene should be purified and dried to eliminate the presence of water. Indeed, water would cause lithium compounds to hydrolyze and prevent thus their reaction with the DNA fragment. It is known that the RLi compounds, where R is an organic radical, are highly sensitive to water.

In general, the interaction of organolithium with such very important biomolecules as DNA bases, nucleosides, or nucleotides has not been studied enough and a rigorous theoretical investigation would be of high value. The presence of different sites on the ligand where the lithium compound can be attached leads to a number of isomers of the complexes, with energies determined by the calculations. This way, their relative stability can be established.

A number of studies have investigated the interaction of isolated lithium ion with the oxygen or nitrogen atoms in the DNA bases. For instance, Burda et al. have applied Hartree-Fock calculations to the study of guanine and adenine interactions with monovalent (among which lithium ion) and divalent cations.

Another study, performed by Lee, employing the DFT-B3LYP method, addressed itself to the interaction between DNA bases and the lithium cation and concluded that the lithium cation features a stronger interaction with the oxygen atoms than with the nitrogen atoms. The DFT-B3LYP method was applied also by Meyer and Suhnel to the investigation of cyclic base tetrads interaction with Li, Na, and K cations. The same method, with the larger 6-311+G(2df,2p) basis set was used by Russo et al. to describe the lithium ion binding to the most stable isomers of the DNA bases. This basis set uses three Slater orbitals for the valence electrons, one expanded in a series of three Gaussians, and the other two approximated by one Gaussian each, diffuse functions, two d orbitals and f orbitals on the non-hydrogen atoms, and two p orbitals on the hydrogen atoms.

The attraction of alkaline and alkaline earth metal cations to the DNA bases was studied by Zhu et al. The B3LYP method, with the smaller basis set 6-31+G* was used by Sun and Bu to show that the complexation between the lithium ion and the guanine-cytosine pair can strengthen the interaction between the two bases. The binding of a number of metal ions, including lithium, to guanine-cytosine pairs was studied by Reynisson and Steenken with DFT calculations.

Calculations of NMR parameters of complexes formed by monovalent cations and guanine quartets were performed by Mourik and Dingley. Plaush and Sharp investigated the NMR parameters of lithium ion complexes with nucleosides.

Sapse et al. applied Hartree-Fock and DFT-B3LYP calculations to describe the interaction of the lithium ion with the DNA bases, but, in addition, the study investigated the interaction of methyllithium with the DNA bases, nucleosides, and nucleotide pairs. They studied thus a number of DNA fragments which could represent experimental situations. In the investigated complexes, the binding can occur in different ways, such as the following:

- The binding of an oxygen or nitrogen atom from the DNA base to the lithium atom from the methyllithium, via the formation of a lithium bond
- The deprotonation of the base by the methyllithium leading to the formation of a lithium enolate and methane
- The positioning of the lithium atom from the methyllithium at the phosphate group which binds two adjacent nucleotides, resulting in the formation of a lithium bond between methyllithium and the oxygen of the phosphate group
- The interaction between an A-T nucleoside pair (as representing a double strand) and a methyllithium molecule positioned between the two bases

Sapse et al.'s study is not kinetics-oriented; it does not aim to evaluate the speed of the reactions but investigates them only from a thermodynamic point of view.

They used the Spartan and Titan programs, with the Hartree-Fock and DFT-B3LYP methods. The basis set used for both methods is the 6-31G** basis set. (The description of the methods and of the basis set can be found in Chapter 4.) To evaluate the eventual changes in the results obtained by the addition to diffuse basis sets, the 6-31G+* basis set was used for calculating the energy of the Adenine-Li^+ complex. The results were different from those obtained without diffuse functions by only 2%. Indeed, diffuse functions are more appropriate for anions, where the electronic cloud is further from the nucleus. These complexes involve cations and neutral bases.

The initial geometries of the complexes studied were obtained by positioning the lithium ion in the vicinity of the nitrogen or oxygen atoms from the DNA bases. Three isomers of the adenine-lithium complex were investigated. They are represented in Figures 5.1, 5.2, and 5.3. Cytosine and guanine-lithium complexes are represented in Figures 5.4 and 5.5, respectively, while Figures 5.6 and 5.7 show two isomers of thymine-lithium complexes.

The structures presented are global minima. There are no negative eigenvalues and all the infrared frequencies are real. To evaluate the binding energies of the systems, Sapse et al.

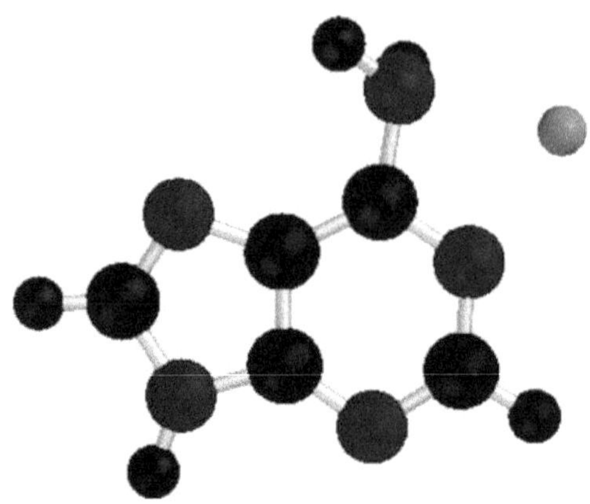

Figure 5.1 A complex of adenine with the lithium ion.

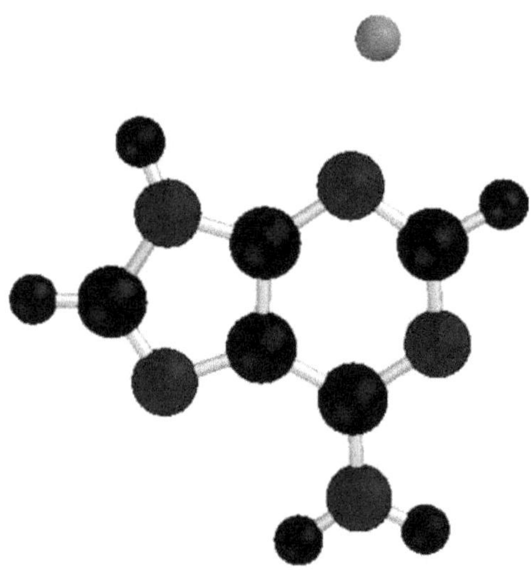

Figure 5.2 A complex of adenine with the lithium ion.

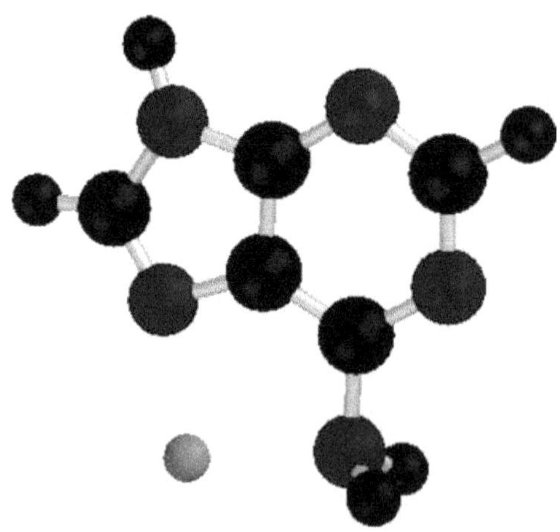

Figure 5.3 A complex of adenine with the lithium ion.

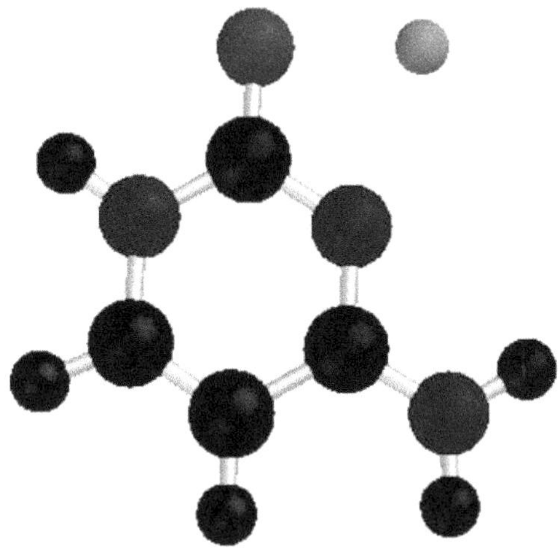

Figure 5.4 Complex of cytosine with the lithium ion.

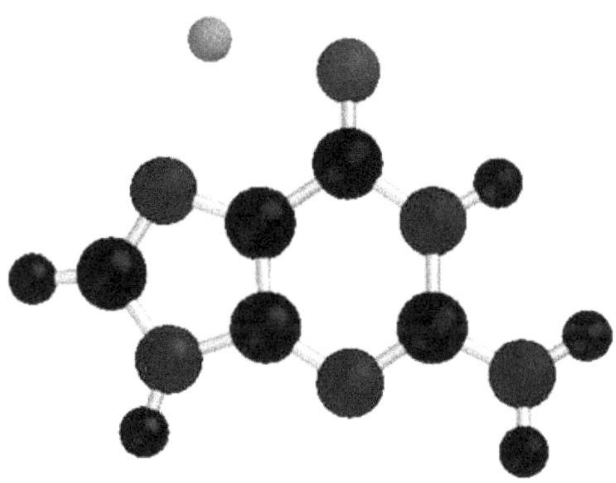

Figure 5.5 Complex of guanine with the lithium ion.

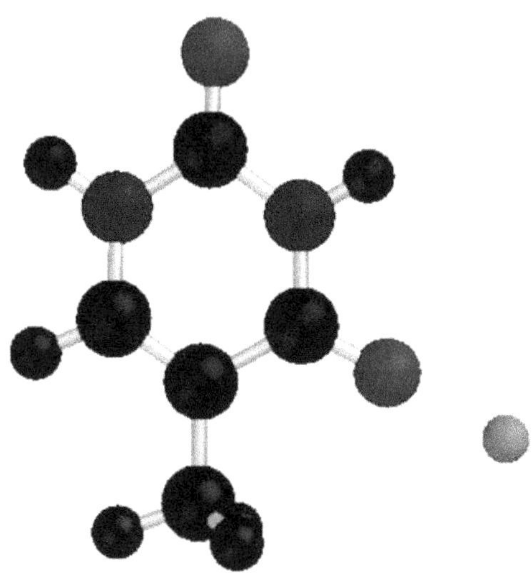

Figure 5.6 A complex of thymine with the lithium ion.

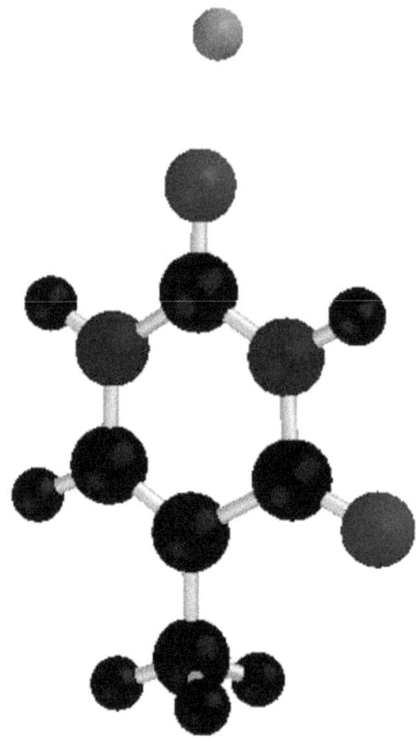

Figure 5.7 A complex of thymine with the lithium ion.

calculated the zero-point vibrational energy differences between the complexes and the subsystems. They found it to be in the vicinity of 1 kcal/mol, therefore small enough to be neglected.

The complexes shown in the figures were optimized with the HF/6-31G** method. The sum of the energies of each base and of the lithium ion was subtracted from the energy of the complex, to obtain the binding energies. These results are shown in Table 5.1. It was found that the complex of cytosine and the lithium ion which features the ion positioned between the nitrogen of the amino group and a nitrogen of the ring does not represent a minimum. On the contrary, the guanine complex featuring the lithium ion positioned between the two nitrogen atoms was found to represent a minimum but its binding energy was higher by 40 kcal/mol.

The next set of complexes investigated by Sapse et al. were formed by each nucleoside with methyllithium. Figures 5.8, 5.9, and 5.10 show isomers of the complexes of adenosine with methyllithium. Figures 5.11 and 5.12 show the complexes formed by cytidine and guanosine with methyllithium, Figures 5.13 and 5.14 show two isomers of the complexes of thymidine with methyllithium. Table 5.2 displays the binding energies of these complexes. However, these complexes, as mentioned by Sapse et al., are probably transient entities, in a reaction ending by the deprotonation of the base. This reaction is:

$$\text{Base} + CH_3Li = \text{BaseLi} + CH_4$$

As shown by Sapse et al., the deprotonation of the cyclic NH group in adenine and guanine leads to the corresponding lithium amides, while the proton removal on the

Table 5.1 The Binding Energies of the DNA Bases with the Lithium Ion

Compound	Binding Energy (kcal/mol)
1	-51.9
2	-46.5
3	-54.3
4	-76.0
5	-78.4
6	-50.1
7	-51.8

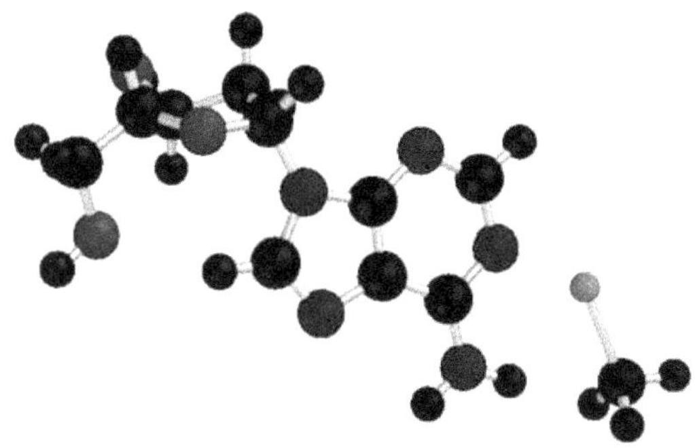

Figure 5.8 A complex of adenosine with methyllithium.

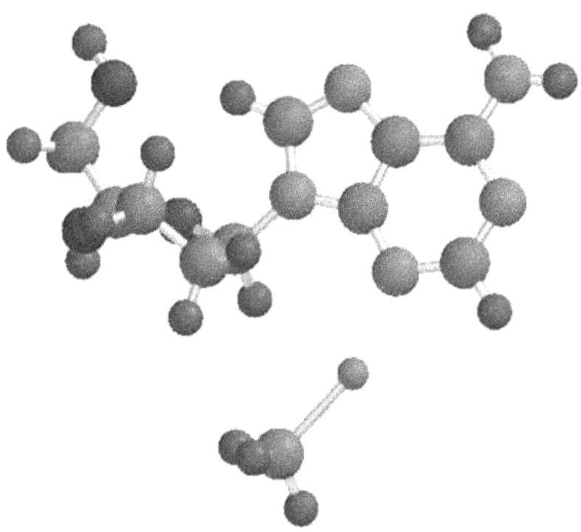

Figure 5.9 A complex of adenosine with methyllithium.

NH group of the pyrimidone in cytosine and thymine leads to the formation of lithium 4-aminopyrimidin-2-oxide. In the case of thymine, only two regioisomers are possible, since the imide NH is much more acidic than the amide one. The deprotonation of the amino group, with the formation of the NHLi amide, was also investigated by Sapse et al., with both the HF/6-31G** method and the DFT-B3LYP/6-31G** method, but these structures were found to exhibit higher energies. Figure 5.15 displays the optimized structures

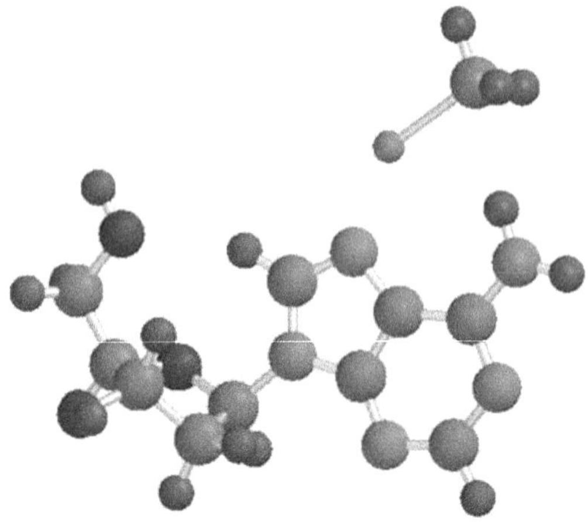

Figure 5.10 A complex of adenosine with methyllithium.

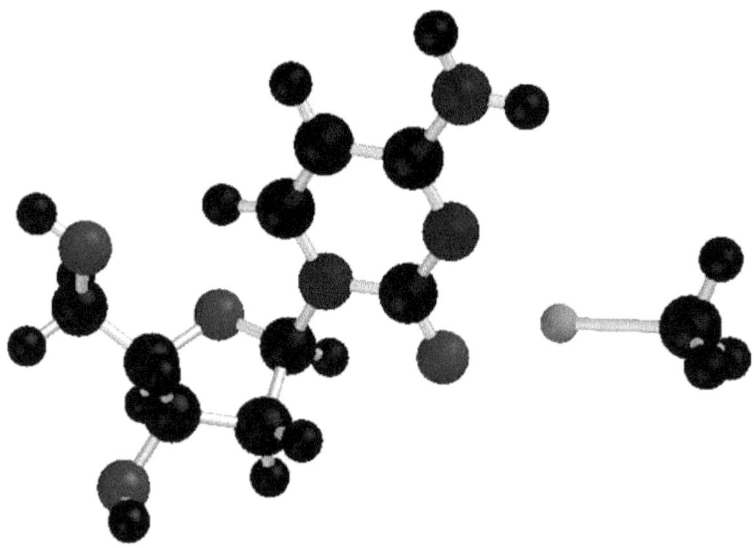

Figure 5.11 Complex of cytidine with methyllithium.

of the BaseLi complexes. Table 5.3 shows the reaction energies of the above shown set of reactions.

Sapse et al. also reported the calculations on single-strand nucleosides pair complexes with methyllithium, in which the methyllithium is positioned near the phosphate group. Mulliken population analysis, using the HF/6-31G** method, shows the presence of strong negative charges on the oxygens of the phosphate group, making them prone to the lithium binding. These complexes are formed from methyllithium and the A-G, A-T, and T-C pairs. They are shown in Figures 5.16, 5.17, and 5.18 and their binding energies are shown in Table 5.4.

Figure 5.19 shows the complex formed by the binding of methyllithium to the double strand pair A-T. Its binding energy is also shown in Table 5.4.

It is clear from examining Table 5.1, that all the DNA bases have strong affinities for the lithium ion. The highest binding energy is shown by guanine and cytosine. This is due

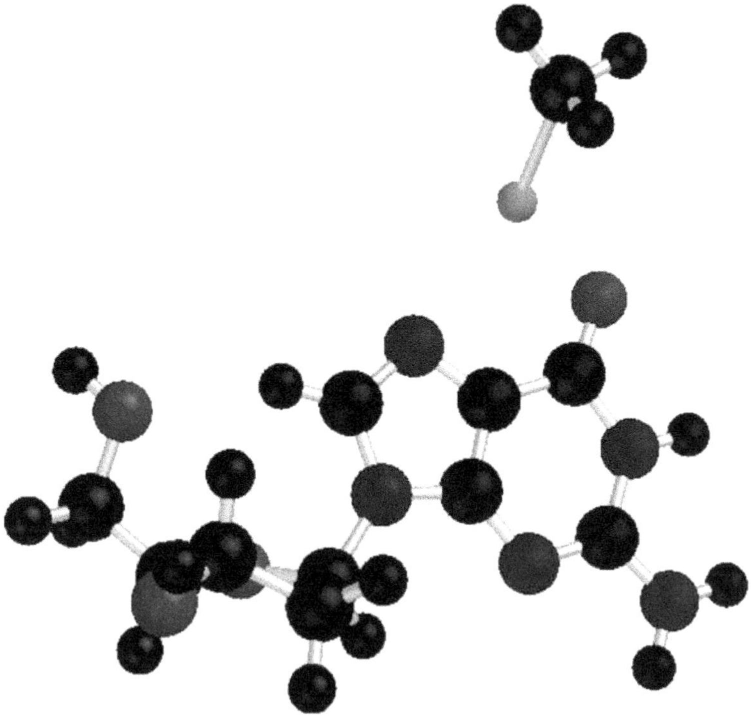

Figure 5.12 Complex of guanosine with methyllithium.

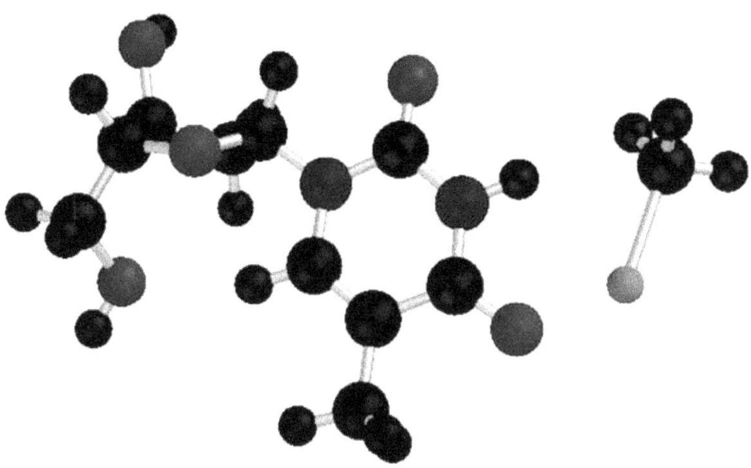

Figure 5.13 A complex of thymidine with methyllithium.

to the fact that the lithium ion, being positioned between the oxygen and the nitrogen atoms, binds to both. Among the isomers of adenine, the strongest binding is obtained in the structure featuring the lithium ion between the nitrogen of the five-membered ring and the amine nitrogen, as shown in Figure 5.3. As can be seen from Figure 5.3, the binding results in a deformation of the amine group. The latter is not conjugated anymore with the aromatic ring, being no longer planar. The distance between the amino nitrogen and the lithium ion is of 2.1 A, and the distance between the ring nitrogen and the lithium ion is of 1.97 A. In the thymine complex, the lithium ion can bind to either of the two oxygen atoms.

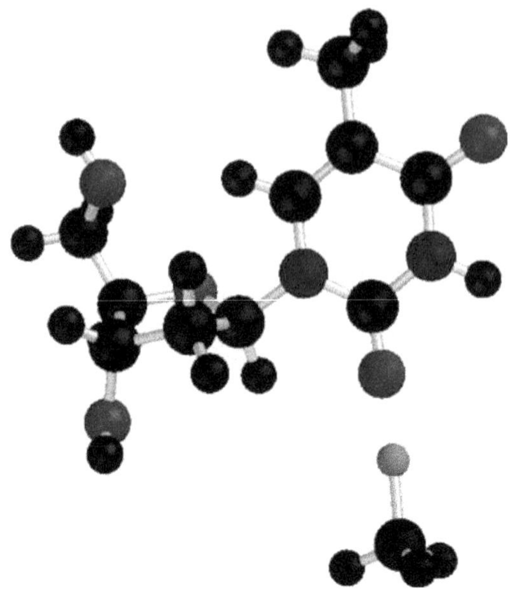

Figure 5.14 A complex of thymidine with methyllithium.

Table 5.2 The Binding Energies of the Nucleosides with Methyllithium

	Binding Energy (kcal/mol)	
Compound	HF/6-31G**	DFT-B3LYP/6-31G**
8	−25.8	−29.6
9	−21.6	−25.5
10	−27.9	−31.6
11	−32.6	−32.8
12	−29.3	−30.1
13	−27.1	−26.9
14	−25.8	−25.3

The structure featuring the lithium ion bound to the oxygen remote from the methyl group is more stable by 1.7 kcal/mol than the other structure.

Examining Table 5.2, one can see, as expected, that the strongest binding occurs between the lithium atom in methyllithium and the oxygen of a carbonyl group or an aromatic nitrogen atom. Indeed, the lithium ion features a strong positive charge (around 0.8 eu), so, as it was mentioned before, it is prone to the formation of a lithium bond, highly electrostatic in nature.

Sapse et al. performed the calculations at both HF/6-31G** and DFT-B3LYP/6-31G** levels. It was found that the order of stability for isomers of the same complex is the same. However, the formation of the adenosine-MeLi complex is the more exothermic as calculated with the DFT method, while HF calculations indicate the formation of the guanosine-MeLi complex to be more exothermic. At DFT level, cytidine shows the strongest binding. In general, the size of the binding energies as calculated by the DFT and HF methods are quite similar.

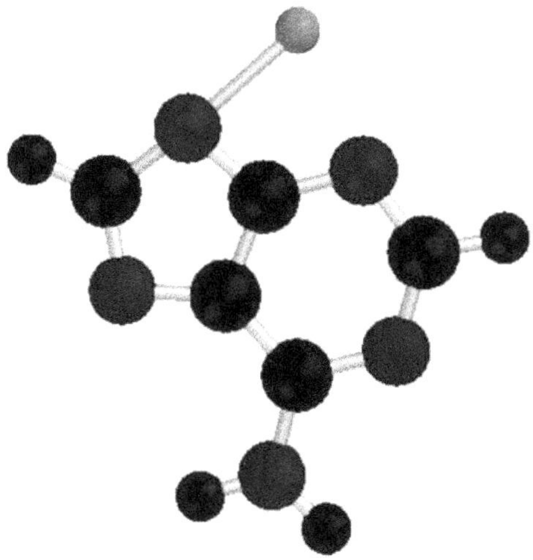

Figure 5.15a Lithium-containing adenine.

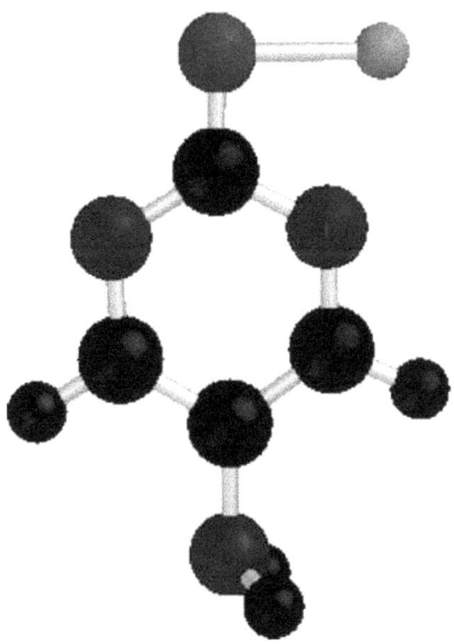

Figure 5.15b Lithium-containing cytosine.

Lithium can also be incorporated in the DNA bases following deprotonation. In this situation, a N-Li bond is formed, which can rearrange into an isomer featuring an O-Li bond. This can occur in guanine, cytosine, and thymine. Table 5.3 shows that these reactions are exothermic, with the largest energy released by guanine, followed by cytosine. The latter produces lithium 4-aminopyrimidin-2-oxy upon N-H deprotonation. The cytosine reaction is followed by those of thymine, with adenine at a very small difference. The thymine reaction which is more exothermic occurs with the lithium atom attached to the oxygen closer to the methyl group. The HF/6-31G** method shows an energy bigger by 1.4 kcal/mol for this isomer, while the DFT-B3LYP/6-31G** method shows a 2.1 kcal/mol difference between the two isomers. In adenine, the deprotonation occurs in the five-member-ring nitrogen.

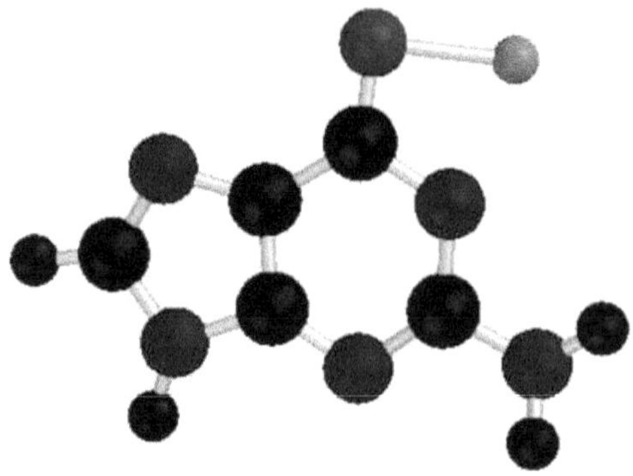

Figure 5.15c Lithium-containing guanine.

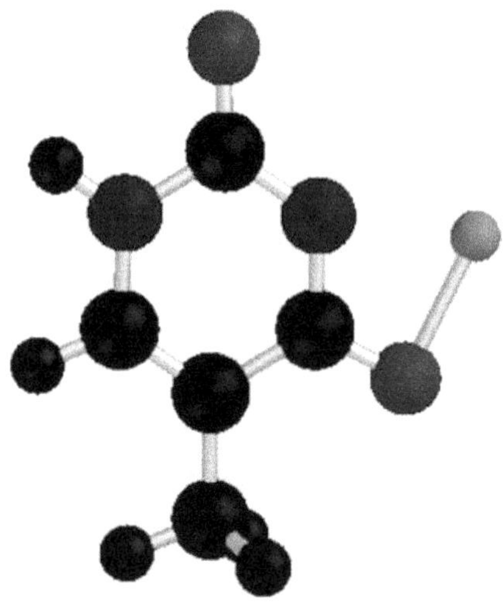

Figure 5.15d An isomer of lithium-containing thymine.

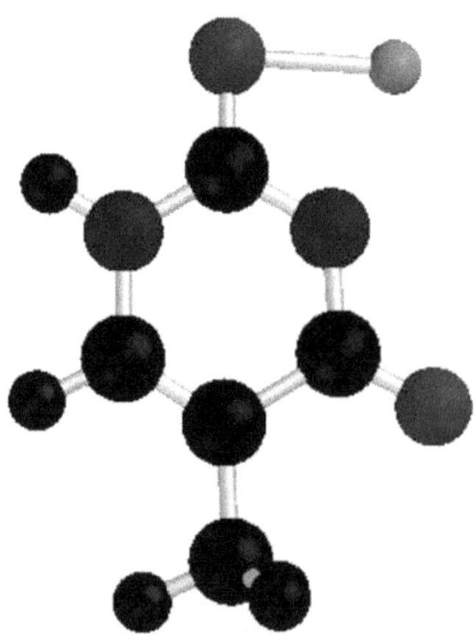

Figure 5.15e An isomer of lithium-containing thymine.

Table 5.3 Energies of Deprotonation of the DNA Bases

	Energy (kcal/mol)	
Compound	HF/6-31G**	DFT-B3LYP/6-31G**
15a	-61.6	-61.6
15b	-72.8	-70.6
15c	-65.3	-64.3
15d	-63.9	-62.2
15e	-72.0	-70.3

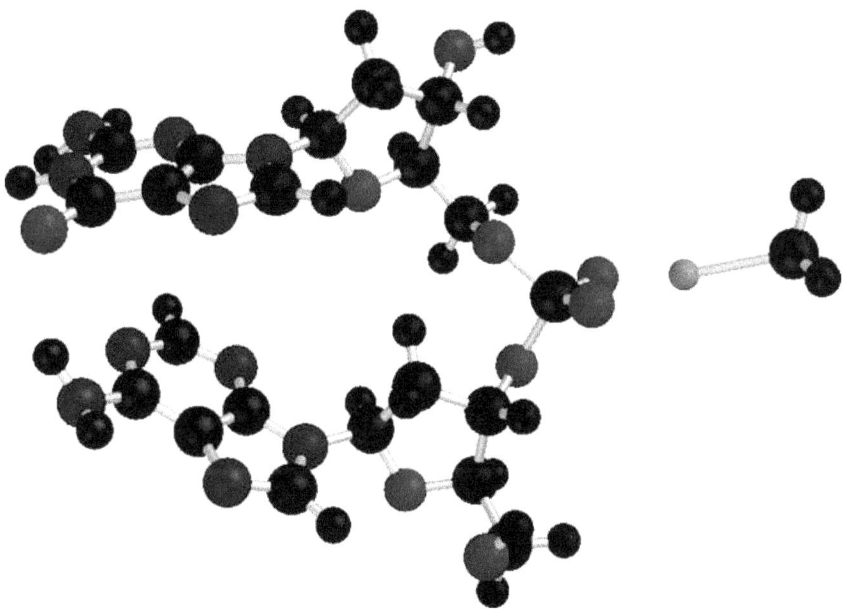

Figure 5.16 Complex of the A-G pair with methyllithium.

The O-Li bond lengths are found to be between 1.8 A and 1.89 A, upon geometry optimization. The N-Li bonds are between 1.93 A and 2.00 A.

These results suggest that upon reaction with methyllithium, the DNA bases and their derivatives form metastable complexes, that is, local minima that can act as intermediates in the reaction of deprotonation of an NH group. It is probable that the global minima will follow the formation of a C-O-Li or C-N-Li group. It might be concluded that the lithium atom is incorporated into the bases following deprotonation.

In the single strand base pairs, the methyllithium binds to the phosphate group, as can be seen from the figures. The T-C sequence features the highest binding energy. The A-G sequence is next, followed by the A-T sequence. Upon complexation, the Li-C bond in methyllithium is elongated by .1 A. The distances between Li and the closest oxygen atom in the phosphate group are between 1.7 A and 2.1 A.

All the structures examined are true minima since the eigenvalues of the second derivative matrices are positive and there are no imaginary frequencies.

These biomolecules become more and more important in crime scene investigations. The theoretical results obtained in the above studies might help the characterization of DNA fragments through, for instance, ^{6}Li or ^{7}Li NMR studies of the resulting products.

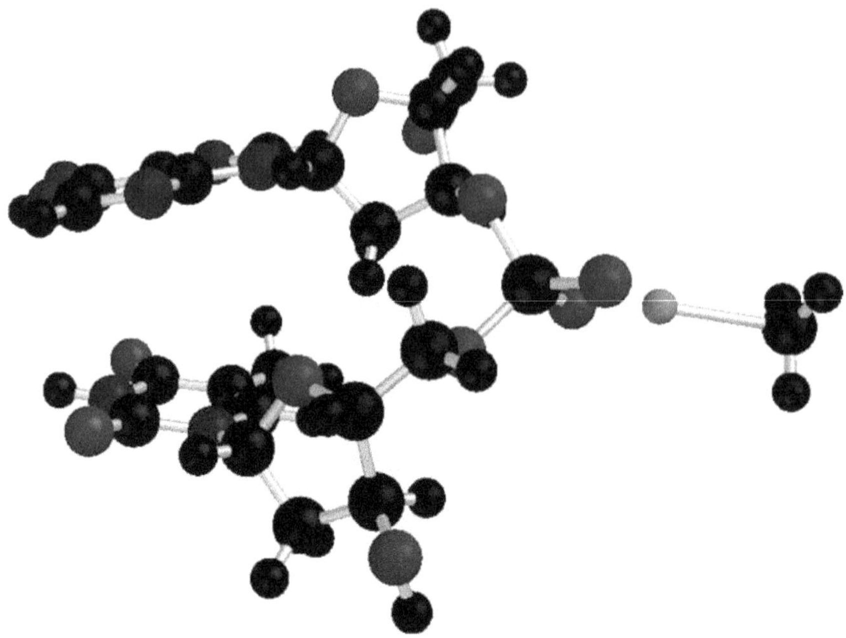

Figure 5.17 Complex of the A-T pair with methyllithium.

Figure 5.18 Complex of the T-C pair with methyllithium.

Table 5.4 Binding Energies of the Complexes Formed by MeLi and the Nucleoside Pairs

	Energy (kcal/mol)
Complex	HF/6-31G**
A-G (single strand)	−41.9
A-T (single strand)	−41.5
T-C (single strand)	−45.7
A-T (double strand)	−31.4

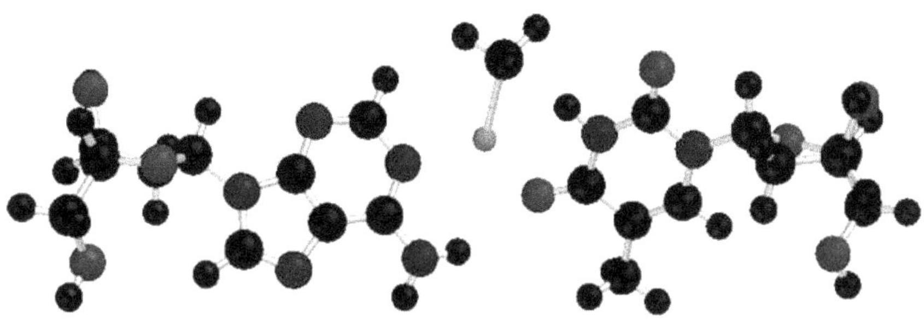

Figure 5.19 Complex of the A-T pair (double strand) with methyllithium.

Thus, the degradation of DNA fragments with time could be analyzed via complexation with, for instance, lithium compounds. Such analysis performed on fragments found at the scene of a crime can be of help for the elucidation of the time elapsed between the crime perpetration and the finding of the DNA fragments. Experiments, such as NMR, could characterize the change in the nature of the complexes obtained as dependent upon the time elapsed. These experiments would have to be performed in a non-aqueous medium; otherwise, the lithium compounds could not be used.

Bibliography

Beck Lissitzyn, C. *Forensic Evidence in Court.* Carolina Academic Press, Durham Carolina, 2008.

Burda J. V., Sponer, J., & Hobza, P. 1996. Ab Initio Studies of the Interaction of Guanine and Adenine with Various Mono- and Bivalent Metal Cations. *Journal of Physical Chemistry* 100, 7250–7255.

Gaensslen, R. E., Harris, H. A., & Lee, H. *Introduction to Forensic Science & Criminalistics*, McGraw Hill, New York, 2008.

Lee, G. B. 2002. DFT Studies of the Lithium Complexes of DNA Bases. *Bulletin of the Korean Chemical Society* 23(7), 1023–1026.

Levy, H. *and the blood cried out.* Basic Books, a division of HarperCollins publishers, New York, 1996.

Meyer, M., & Suhnel, J. 2003. *Journal of Biomolecular Structure and Dynamics* 20(4): 507–517.

Mourik, T., & Dingley, A. J. 2005. Characterization of the Monovalent Ion Position and Hydrogen Bond Network in Guanine Quartets by DFT Calculations of NMR Parameters. *Chem. European Journal* 11: 6064–6079.

Plaush A. C., & Sharp R. R. 1976. Ion Binding to Nucleosides. A Chorine-35 and Lithium-7 NMR Studies. *Journal of American Chemical Society* 98(25), 7973–7980.

Reynisson, J., & Steenken, S. 2003. The Calculated Base-Pairing Energies of 8-Oxoguanine in Syn-Anti Conformation with Cytosine, Thymine, Adenine, and Guanine. *Journal of Molecular Structure* 635, 133–139.

Russo, N., Toscano, M., Grand, A. 2001, Lithium Affinity for DNA and RNA Nucleobases. The Role of Theoretical Information in the Elucidation of the Mass Spectroscopy Data. *J. Phys Chem. B* 105 : 4735–4741.

Sapse, D. S., Champeil, E., Maddaluno, J., Fressigne, C., & Sapse A. M. 2008. An Ab Initio Study of the Interaction of DNA Fragments with Methyllithium. *Comptes Rendus des Seances de L'Academie Francaise, Chemistry,* 11, 1262–1270.

Scheck, B., Neufeld, P., & Dwyer, J. *Actual Innocence.* Doubleday, New York, 2000.

Sun, L. Bu, Y. 2005, Marked Variations of Dissociation Energy and H-Bond Character of the Guanine-Cytosine Base Pair Induced by One-Electron Oxidation and Li^+ Cation Coupling. *J. Phys. Chem.* 109: 593–600.

Zhu, W., Luo, X., Puah, C.M., Tan, X., Shen, J., Gu, J., The Multiplicity, Strength, and Nature of the Interaction of Nucleobases with Alkaline and Alkaline Earth Metal Cations: A Density Functional Theory Investigation. Chen, K, Jiang, H. 2004. *J. Phys. Chem. A, 108* (18), 4008–4018.

Magnetic Resonance Spectroscopy

A Powerful Tool for the Identification and Quantitation of Drugs and Drugs of Abuse in Biofluids

6

ELISE CHAMPEIL

Contents

Introduction

Testing for substances of abuse in biofluids has great forensic relevance. The need for testing arises in many different situations: identifying drugs of abuse, supporting or denying a person's statement that they have or have not taken drugs, or determining what drug may have caused an overdose. Many methods, notably commercially produced immunoassays that may be used in workplace testing, or gas chromatography–mass spectrometry (GC-MS), which is commonly used in forensic laboratories, have already been well researched and accepted in the scientific community. However, these methods are prone to certain downfalls. Immunoassays are presumptive tests that are not definitive and are subject to high rates of false negatives or false positives due to cross-reactivity or adulterants in the samples tested [1]. Chromatographic methods require sample preparation such as extraction and derivatization of the compounds and extensive operator training; they are also time consuming. In addition, GC-MS instrumentation may not be readily available when it is necessary to determine the cause of an overdose in a timely manner for proper medical treatment [2]. Nuclear magnetic resonance (NMR) spectroscopy has many advantages. It allows positive identifications, very little sample preparation or operator training is needed, and a spectrum can be gathered in only a few minutes. NMR spectroscopy also shows signals from all NMR-active materials, and therefore is not limited to screening for specific drugs. It is widely used in the field of metabonomics for studying metabolites in biological samples [3]. NMR spectroscopy has also been used to identify compounds in urine from intentional and unintentional overdoses [2] [4] [5] [6] [7]. This chapter focuses on the use of magnetic resonance spectroscopy as a tool for the identification and quantitation of drugs in biofluids.

NMR

Theory

The current, most common type of NMR spectroscopy, Fourier transform NMR (which will be referred to in the rest of this chapter as NMR, which is the current convention, instead of the more precise acronym FT-NMR) was developed in the late 1960s. It has been commercially available since the 1970s. The introduction of superconducting magnets (also in the 1970s), and the consequent sensitivity increases resulted in the first applications of NMR spectroscopy drug analysis in biofluids. Explanations of NMR spectroscopy may be found in most instrumental textbooks [8]. A short overview of one-dimensional proton NMR spectroscopy follows here.

Hydrogen nuclei (protons) have either a +1/2 or −1/2 spin. In the absence of a magnetic field, these two states have the same energy, which means that the population of nuclei is divided evenly between positive and negative spins. When a magnetic field is introduced, an energy difference arises, with spins aligned with the field (+1/2) having a lower energy, and spins against the field (−1/2) having a higher energy. This energy difference means that the population distribution changes in a magnetic field, with lower energies being slightly preferred, as seen in Figure 6.1.

Using a scanning, second electromagnetic field, protons with lower energy (β spin state) will flip to an α spin state when the electromagnetic field is equal to the change in energy between the states, known as the resonance energy or frequency. The energy difference is dependent upon the electronic environment around the proton nuclei. The electronegativity of nearby atoms, as well as induced local magnetic fields from circulating π electrons will either shield or deshield protons. For instance, a hydrogen atom bonded to a carbon atom will have a different chemical environment than a hydrogen atom bonded to an oxygen atom. Because of this environmental dependence, each compound will have a unique spectrum, with signals arising at the resonance frequencies (chemical shifts) of each proton. An appreciation of the concepts of electronegativity (inductive effects) and

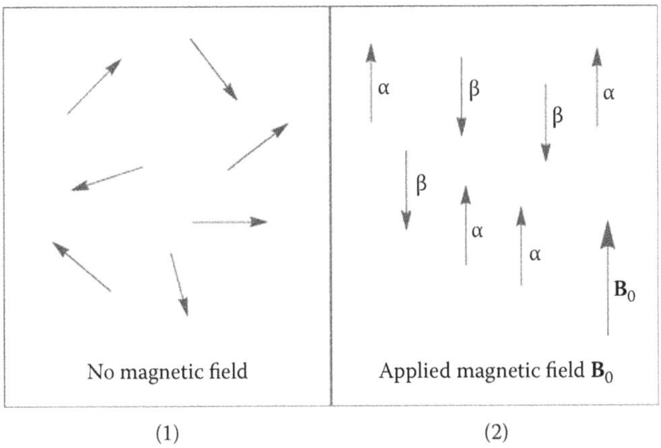

Figure 6.1 (1) Random orientation of the magnetic moments of protons (represented by arrows) in the absence of a magnetic field. (2) The protons align themselves either with the applied external magnetic field B_0 (α spin state) or against (β spin state).

of electron delocalization (combined with an understanding of diamagnetic anisotropy) permits the prediction of chemical shifts. A spectrum can give information about a compound's structure, and can also be used to identify the compound. The resonance frequency, also known as the chemical shift, can be expressed in hertz (Hz) or in parts per million (ppm). The signal of a particular hydrogen atom will also be "affected" by the presence of vicinal hydrogens. Multiplicity of a signal arises from the interaction between vicinal protons. A particular proton (A) will be affected by one of its vicinal protons (B) since the latter has two energy states (+1/2 and −1/2). Each energy state creates a different environment for A such that part of the population of A is in one type of environment and the other part is in another environment. Therefore, the signal arising from proton A will be split into two peaks. The difference, or split, between the peaks gives the parameter of the *J* coupling constant. Finally, each peak can be integrated to determine quantitative information about the molecular makeup.

NMR spectroscopy scans a large range of chemical shifts, such that all NMR active compounds in a solution will have peaks in the range scanned. As each compound has characteristic peaks, compounds in the solution do not have to be physically separated to be analyzed using NMR spectroscopy. In the cases of indistinguishable overlapping of peaks, two-dimensional NMR techniques may be used to determine which peaks originates from the same compound.

Isotope Used in the Study of Drugs by NMR

Proton NMR spectroscopy is the most common NMR technique used. The ^1H nucleus is present in all drugs and has the highest sensitivity of any stable nucleus. Moreover, it is the most abundant (99.98% natural abundance) of the two natural isotopes (^1H and ^2H or deuterium) of the hydrogen atom. However, the small chemical shift range and the extensive multiplicity due to homonuclear *J*-coupling sometimes make the observation and quantification of drug metabolites difficult. Moreover, ^1H NMR spectra of biological fluids contain an intense resonance from water that must be reduced or eliminated.

Lithium-7 (^7Li), the major lithium isotope, has a high NMR sensitivity. Since it is not a spin $I = 1/2$ but a spin $I = 3/2$ nucleus, it possesses a quadrupole moment which gives rise to broad spectral lines. ^{7}Li NMR is not hampered by interference with endogenous signals. One study using lithium-7 involved the *in vivo* determination of the pharmacokinetic profile of lithium salts in brain and calf muscle of healthy volunteers or patients with depression [9].

Although carbon atoms are found in all drugs, the magnetically active isotope carbon-13 (^{13}C) is neither abundant nor particularly sensitive. These drawbacks, combined with the low concentrations of drugs and their metabolites in biological systems make this nucleus in its natural abundance rather hard to detect. However, improved sensitivity can be attained with polarization transfer experiments.

The majority of studies on the metabolism of clinical drugs [10] in the literature concern fluorine-19 (^{19}F) NMR mainly because of the favorable NMR characteristics of this nucleus (100% natural abundance, high NMR sensitivity, large chemical shift range). Moreover, the negligible level of endogenous fluorine eliminates interfering background signals and dynamic range problems.

The phosphorus-31 (^{31}P) nucleus is readily detected as it has a 100% natural abundance and is relatively sensitive. The presence of endogenous phosphates and derivatives (phosphomonoesters, phosphodiesters, etc.) may interfere with signals from phosphorated drugs and their metabolites. In practice, this is not a large obstacle as there are relatively few endogenous compounds producing detectable signals. However, as there are few phosphorated drugs in current use, only a few ^{31}P NMR studies have so far been carried out [11].

Solvent Suppression Techniques

Because the main component of human fluids is water, it is necessary to use solvent suppression techniques to suppress the water signal from the biofluids which would otherwise override any other signal and interfere with the spectroscopic analysis. These solvent suppression techniques are commonly used in modern NMR. The following paragraphs review some of the different solvent suppression techniques used for the analysis of drugs in human fluids.

Classical Presaturation Experiments

Presaturation [12] [13] is a simple two-pulse experiment that utilizes a relatively long, low-power radio frequency pulse to selectively saturate a specific frequency, typically water, and a nonselective 45–90° pulse to excite the desired resonances. This pulse sequence is particularly useful for aqueous samples or those with a single large solvent signal. With proper optimization, the resulting spectrum can be mostly free of the solvent signal and lead to improved signal-to-noise (S/N) for solute resonances due to the reduction in dynamic range and subsequent increase in available gain. Classical presaturation, however, has numerous drawbacks, which can include poor phase properties and lack of suppression in comparison to more recent gradient based solvent suppression approaches.

WET (Water Suppression Enhanced through T_1 Effects)

Among the many solvent suppression schemes, the WET sequence has become very popular, especially in the field of hyphenated techniques such as HPLC-NMR although it was originally introduced for localized *in vivo* spectroscopy. The WET method uses selective pulses to excite the solvent resonances and pulsed field gradients to dephase residual solvent magnetization. A subsequent hard radio frequency pulse excites only the resonances of the solutes, because no longitudinal magnetization of the solvent remains. The WET method is preferred for continuous-flow NMR [14] [15]. The technique provides solvent-resonance suppression factors in excess of 10,000 in a single scan, and can deal with multiple non-deuterated solvent mixtures. The suppression requires only 50–100 msec, in contrast to conventional presaturation which typically takes 1–2 sec and a very high level of solvent suppression is achieved without time intensive techniques.

*WATERGATE (*WATER *Suppression through* GrA*dient* T*ailored* E*xcitation)*

This method for water suppression employs pulsed field gradient spin-echoes to destroy the unwanted solvent resonance but retain all others. The WATERGATE technique is claimed to be independent of line-shape, yielding better suppression compared to other methods. Exchangeable protons are not affected and there is no phase jump at the water resonance, although signals very close to the water resonance are also suppressed. The sequence is a spin-echo experiment in which the 180° pulse is embedded between two pulsed field gradients. After excitation by the first pulse, a gradient is applied which defocuses all the spins. This is followed by a pulse sequence (binomial sequence) which leaves the water magnetization unchanged but flips the rest of the spins by 180°. A second field gradient pulse refocuses the spins that have been subjected to 180° flip and dephases the water signal even further. (Alternatively, the binomial sequence can be replaced by a hard pulse and a selective 180° pulse, which leaves the water resonance unchanged.) Watergate is not necessary for samples that require residual water suppression and is best utilized on 90% of water samples. This method allows for a fast solvent suppression (solvent is suppressed in milliseconds, compared to 1 to 2 sec for classical presaturation) [16].

Excitation Sculpting

This method can be used for the selective excitation (or removal) of a resonance or resonances in a spectrum based on the use of a sequence of pulsed field gradient spin echoes, the best known example being the "double pulsed field gradient spin-echo" sequence, also called excitation sculpting. The WATERGATE technique described earlier provides a rather good suppression of the water signal but has problems with base-line roll and signal phasing. The excitation sculpting solves this problem by applying the WATERGATE sequence twice. This method provides very clean excitation (or removal) of the target resonance(s) and is used in selective 1D experiments as well as in solvent suppression methods [17].

*PURGE (*P*resaturation* U*tilizing* R*elaxation* G*radients and* E*choes)*

During the PURGE experiment, the initial presaturation period is analogous to that in the classic presaturation experiments. It is followed by a 90° pulse which flips the magnetization into the XY plane. The magnetization is then inverted by a 180° pulse. This helps suppress exchangeable solvent signals based on a T_2 relaxation process. Next, a 90° pulse inverts the magnetization onto the *z* axis, and the following spoil gradient destroys any residual transverse magnetization. Subsequently, another very short presaturation period follows. It partially tips some of the main solvent resonance from the *z* axis so it is dephased by the next gradient. During this period, the bulk remains aligned along the *z* axis. Depending on the phase, the magnetization will have undergone either a 0° or a 180° rotation. At this point it is possible to terminate the sequence with an appropriate read pulse. However, repeating the sequences leads to increased solvent suppression [18].

NMR Probe Improvement

As the role of NMR has evolved, an ever-increasing range of application has opened, enabled by the developing technology. The advent of high field NMR impacted significantly on the biological applications area as the much greater sensitivity that this afforded has significantly extended the NMR boundaries of detection. The availability of a 1 GHz magnet is imminent from manufacturers such as Bruker and Varian with 800, 900, and 950 MHz magnets now being widely available with cryoprobe platform capabilities.

The most significant advance in NMR probe development is the introduction of CryoProbes. In these NMR probes, the electronic components are cryogenically cooled to −20K. By operating the electronic components at this low temperature, while the sample remains at ambient temperature, the electronic noise is greatly reduced [19]. On average, CryoProbes enable a three- to four-fold enhancement of the sensitivity in high-resolution NMR compared to conventional probes. These new probes dramatically increase ^{13}C sensitivity and reduce acquisition time 100-fold compared to a room temperature (RT) Dual Broadband (DB) probe. They also offer a significantly improved ^{1}H sensitivity, reducing acquisition time for ^{1}H detected experiments 75-fold compared to a RT DB probe. A novel cryoflow probe was recently built and evaluated for its potential to advance the NMR sensitivity for LC-NMR-MS in the determination of acetaminophen urinary metabolites [20]. The signal/noise ratio was improved more than three times compared to conventional NMR probes, and this enabled the NMR analysis of lower concentrations of metabolites than was previously possible for untreated samples.

Another recent advancement in NMR probes is the possibility to record several NMR spectra in parallel rather than in series. This cuts down on instrument time and ensures that any changes to the sample composition register in all spectra. It works by combining established protocols for acquiring data called pulse sequences into one “super sequence.” This new scheme is called PANACEA (**P**arallel **A**cquisition **N**MR, an **A**ll-in-one **C**ombination of **E**xperimental **A**pplications). PANACEA takes advantage of recent advances in NMR instrumentation that made possible the parallel acquisition of signals from up to four nuclei [21].

Furthermore, as automated NMR technologies are continually developed and updated, large sample cohorts such as those from epidemiological or population studies have become feasible as high-throughput, operator independent spectral acquisition is achievable. Such automated systems involve the use of 96-well plates, robotic sample handling and transfer to NMR flow probes; typically up to 250 ^{1}H NMR profiles can be acquired per day, but there is potential for running at much higher rates.

NMR Studies on Human Urine

Commonly Abused Types of Drugs in Urine and Current Methodologies for Testing

Current methodologies in use for the analysis of drugs of abuse in human urine include immunoassay tests and GC-MS. The concentration of a drug or a metabolite is dependent on how the drug was ingested, how much drug was ingested, the time span over when the drug was taken, how much time elapsed between intake and excretion, the physiological makeup of the person taking the drug, and other factors such as how much food or water was ingested while the drug was in the body. Every measurement system is constrained by its limit of detection (LOD), and, if a quantitative measurement is desired, by the limit of quantitation (LOQ). LOD is generally defined as three times the standard deviation of the background noise of the blank, while LOQ is ten times the standard deviation of the background noise of a blank [8c] [22]. Even if a substance can be detected at a very low level, this does not necessarily make it a relevant amount in forensic analysis. Even though drugs may be present and measurable below the cutoff limit, it is not automatically documented as a positive result. For the testing of opioids in urine for instance, a cutoff limit is chosen, whereby a concentration of drugs in urine above the limit is a positive result. In forensic casework or federal workplace testing, if a presumptive immunoassay test is done first, it must be later confirmed by GC or GC-MS in order for the result to be reported positive. However, a confirmatory test is generally done only if the immunoassay test is positive.

Tables 6.1 and 6.2 are compiled from public-domain information in the Mandatory Guidelines for Federal Workplace Drug Testing Programs. They are for urine analysis of the commonly abused types of drugs known as the SAMHSA Five [23] (Mandatory Guidelines for Federal Workplace Drug Testing, 2004). These guidelines were first instituted on December 1, 1998.

The guidelines listed are only mandated for federal workplace drug testing programs. Private companies may develop their own method of drug testing, but as most immunoassay tests are manufactured based on SAMHSA cutoff levels, many companies adopt these same standards. Immunoassay tests for screening for substances of abuse in urine are generally calibrated to show if a sample is above or below a cutoff level for a particular drug. If the substance is found to be present above the cutoff level, the sample is then confirmed and quantitated using a different method, such as chromatography.

Range of Detectable Drugs in Urine

NMR spectroscopy is well suited to a direct analysis of drugs in urine samples without change to the matrix. Compounds present normally in urine are easily identified and are generally small molecules with only a few resonance peaks. This is seen in work done by Zuppi et al. [24], wherein the chemical shifts and quantitative ranges of metabolites in normal urine were identified. Other researchers have also identified the same peaks to differentiate peaks of endogenous compounds from those arising from xenobiotics [4] [25] [26]. The similarity of the spectra gathered by these different groups indicate that barring

Table 6.1 Initial Drug Cutoff Levels

Drug	Nanograms per Milliliter (ng/mL)
Marijuana metabolites	50
Cocaine metabolites	150
Opiate metabolites[1]	2000
Phencyclidine (PCP)	25
Amphetamines[2]	500

[1] Labs are permitted to initially test all specimens for 6-acetylmorphine at a 10 ng/mL cutoff.

[2] Target analyte must be *d*-methamphetamine and the test must significantly cross-react with 3,4-Methylenedioxymethamphetamine (MDMA), 3,4-Methylenedioxyamphetamine (MDA), and *N*-methyl-diethanolamine (MDEA).

Table 6.2 Confirmatory Drug Cutoff Levels

Drug	Nanograms per Milliliter (ng/mL)
Marijuana metabolite[1]	15
Cocaine metabolite[2]	100
Opiates	
Morphine	2000
Codeine	2000
6-acetylmorphine[4]	10
Phencyclidine (PCP)	25
Amphetamines	
Amphetamine	250
Methamphetamine[3]	250
MDMA	250
MDA	250
MDEA	250

[1] Delta-9-tetrahydrocannabinol-9-carboxylic acid.
[2] Benzoylecgonine.
[3] Specimen must also contain *d*-amphetamine at a concentration >100 ng/mL.
[4] Labs test for 6-acetylmorphine when the morphine concentration exceeds 2,000 ng/mL.

specific metabolic diseases or ingestion of xenobiotics, human urine is qualitatively similar interpersonally. An example of such a spectrum can be seen in Figure 6.2.

Nuclear magnetic resonance (NMR) spectroscopy has been used to identify and quantitate low molecular weight organic compounds that accumulate in urine. Those organic detectable organic compounds can be classified in three groups: pharmaceutical drugs or their metabolites (taken therapeutically or in overdose), drugs of abuse or their metabolites (Ethanol, *gamma*-hydroxybutyric acid (GHB), 3,4-methylenedioxymethamphetamine (MDMA, ecstasy), and other miscellaneous compounds ingested by accident or to attempt suicide.

NMR spectroscopy studies of drugs in urine have generally focused on cases involving toxic amounts of drugs, such as in accidental overdoses, intentional overdoses, and poisoning attempts. This is due to the fact that NMR spectroscopy has a higher limit of detection than other methods currently in use. One exception is the study done by Holmes et al. [25], which analyzed urine from subjects and looked for peaks from acetaminophen or ibuprofen metabolites, presumed to be from normal, self-administered dosages.

The Lhermitte laboratory has published a large number of papers relating to the study of xenobiotics found in urine. These include cases of poisonings by salicylic acid, valproic acid, paraquat, tetrohydrofuran (THF), and *gamma*-hydroxybutyric acid (GHB) [27] [4]. They also include studies of poisonings by methanol, ethylene glycol [7], *alpha*-chloralose [6], adulterated soda [28], and chloroquine [29]. The supplementation of creatine has been examined in a similar fashion. Creatine is found normally in urine, but additional supplementation is considered doping in some countries [30]. This illustrates the ability of NMR spectroscopy to be used for the identification and the quantitation of xenobiotics in urine.

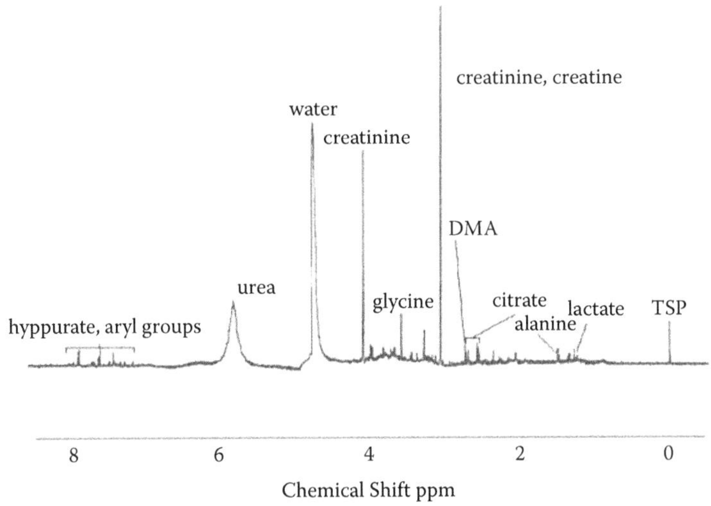

Figure 6.2 Labeled spectra of blank urine sample recorded on a Bruker 500 MHz NMR spectrometer (16 scans) using the PURGE water suppression method. DMA = dimethlyamine, TMAO = trimethylamine *N*-oxide, TSP = 3-(trimethylsilyl)-2,2′,3,3′-tetradeuteropropionic acid sodium salt (standard).

Other labs have done similar work for the detection of xenobiotics. One common compound seen in urine is propylene glycol, which is used as a nonactive ingredient in drug formulations but can lead to intoxication itself [2] [5]. Metabolites of ibuprofen, aspirin, acetaminophen, carbamazepine and erythromycin have also been detected in intoxication cases [2]. Komoroski et al. [2] indicated that NMR spectroscopy was found to be entirely insensitive to tricyclic antidepressants and antipsychotics, as these were not detected in urine from cases of known intoxication with those drug classes. In addition to erythromycin, two other antibiotics, levofloxacin and rifampicin, have been studied in detail [31].

Besides xenobiotics, NMR spectroscopy can also analyze urine for metabolic disorders, and has many clinical and medical applications. A meta-review of metabonomics in toxicology has been done by Robertson [32].

All of the prior examples are of drugs either taken normally, such as the analgesics mentioned, or very rarely ingested; that is, only ingested accidentally, or taken with the intent of a lethal or toxic outcome. Drugs of abuse (taken recreationally, prescribed legally, or overdosed upon) are common in forensic toxicology, but very few have been studied in urine samples using NMR spectroscopy.

One example includes *gamma*-hydroxybutyric acid, which has been identified in urine samples [4] and analyzed along with the corresponding lactone, *gamma*-hydroxybutyrolactone [33]. Another one is 3,4-methylenedioxymethamphetamine (MDMA, ecstasy) which has been detected in the urine of five cases of intoxication [34]. The ^{1}H NMR spectrum of the urine of a user of MDMA recorded on a Bruker 500 MHz NMR spectrometer can be seen in Figure 6.3.

Methanol intoxication has also been studied by Janus et al. [35] and the same group has done work with metabolic differences in urine after chronic use of opiates and amphetamines [36].

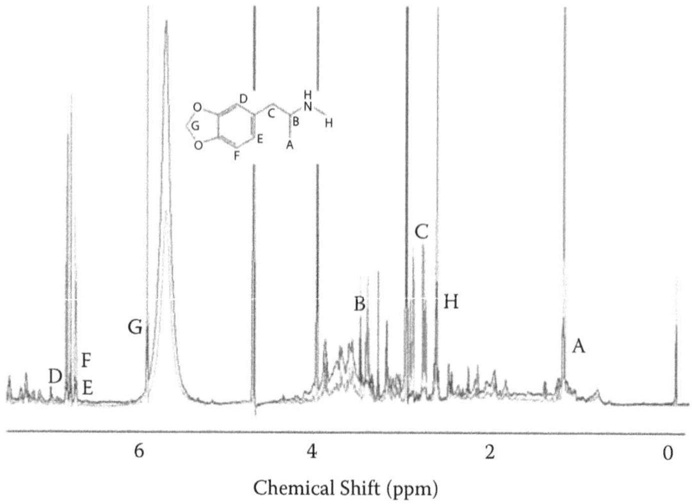

Figure 6.3 Labeled spectra of a urine sample from a user of 3,4-Methylenedioxymethamphetamine (MDMA) recorded on a Bruker 500 MHz NMR spectrometer (256 scans) using the PURGE water suppression method. All signals due to MDMA are visible and labeled as A, B, C, D, E, F, G. Superimposed in gray is the spectrum of MDMA spiked urine (0.50 mg/mL; 16 scans).

NMR Studies on Other Biofluids

Blood plasma and saliva are among other biofluids which have been studied by ^{1}H NMR spectroscopy. ^{1}H NMR has been used to quantify lipoprotein subclasses directly from serum or plasma. The applications of ^{1}H NMR metabonomics of serum in biomedicine have been discussed in details in a review by Mika Ala-Korpela. Experimental and data analysis methodologies were discussed together with the biochemical rationale [37]. Particular emphasis is placed on the concepts of *risk assessment* and *diagnostics* in relation to the potential clinical role of ^{1}H NMR metabonomics; recent applications in the area of coronary heart diseases and diabetes are addressed in more detail.

Concerning the detection of drugs of abuse, high-resolution ^{1}H NMR spectroscopy has been employed to investigate the detection and quantitation of the illicit date-rape drug *gamma*-hydroxybutyrate (GHB) in both human saliva [38] and in plasma [33].

Quantitation Studies

For NMR spectroscopy, quantitation can be done using peak heights or peak areas (integrals). However, most quantitation analyses are done using peak areas. One feature of the proton NMR is that the intensity of the absorbance of a given class of nuclei (with a certain chemical shift) is proportional to the number of protons giving rise to the signal; that is, the area under a given peak (the *integration*) is directly proportional to the number of protons of the same type in the molecule. This can have forensic use as it allows quantitation of the amount of drug present in a sample. This technique does not affect the problems associated with the other techniques. For instance, the GC quantitation method is relatively labor intensive. In addition, most methods rely on sample comparison with a known external standard which can be problematic. With regard to the drugs that have been studied in urine using NMR spectroscopy, a variety of concentrations have been found. In general, a spectrum from ^1H NMR can be obtained with at least 1 μg of analyte [8a].

For quantitative measurements, a number of NMR criteria have to be considered [8d], [8e]:

1. The entire spectral width (SW) must be uniformly excited by the RF pulse.
2. The data processing must be optimized to enhance results:
   - The acquired data can be manipulated prior to Fourier transformation (FT) by mathematical functions known as window functions to reduce the noise amplitude and to increase sensitivity.
   - A careful correction of the phase as well as of the baseline distortions of the spectrum is essential for an accurate quantitation of the resonances.
   - Peak areas are integrated using manufacturer's standard software. Typically, spectra are integrated five times sequentially and the mean integral value is considered. With lower signal-to-noise (S/N) values or when the resonance signals are not well resolved, the best results are obtained by the reliable, if somewhat time-consuming, method of cutting out the peaks of interest and weighing [39].
3. A reference signal of known concentration must be detected to provide a calibration standard. One can use an internal reference or an external reference contained in a coaxial capillary put into the larger NMR tube. Both of them must have some common specifications (i.e., high purity, chemical inertness, low volatility, and a resonance signal well resolved from the analyte signals). Moreover, the internal reference must present an easy solubility in aqueous media. For quantitative proton NMR analysis, 3-(trimethylsilyl)-2,2′,3,3′-tetradeuteropropionic acid sodium salt (TSP) is a very common standard [40]. However, to provide a field/frequency lock for the spectrometer, deuterium nuclei must also be present in the sample analyzed. For this purpose, usually 10% (sometimes 5%) of deuterated water (D_2O) is added to the biofluid analyzed. Although the external reference contained in a coaxial capillary needs to be previously calibrated against solutions of known concentration (i.e., a calibration curve is established by linear regression analysis using the peak integral of the substance and its nominal concentration [41] or using the ratio [peak area of the substance/peak area of the internal standard] and the concentration of the pure substance [42]). This method of quantitation has several advantages: (1) one single calibrated capillary can serve for any number of samples; (2) the external reference is dissolved in a deuterated solvent, which can be not only water, but any organic solvent. The deuterated solvent provides the field/frequency lock for the spectrometer. There is no contamination of the sample, which is available for analysis by a subsequent alternative technique; (3) the external reference can be used for analysis of any biofluid without problems of protein-binding or chemical-exchange phenomena.
4. Normally in quantitative NMR, one waits for complete relaxation (the term *relaxation* describes processes by which nuclear magnetization prepared in a non-equilibrium state return to the equilibrium distribution. In other words, relaxation describes how fast spins "forget" the direction in which they are oriented), or 5 * T_1, of the slowest relaxing protons to restore the thermal equilibrium magnetization along the *z* axis before repeating a pulse sequence. Uniform

excitation for both analytes and standards is also used. Integrals then reflect the number of moles of protons present in the sample regardless of a particular proton's T_1. That is, one mole of an analyte proton gives the same integral as one mole of an added standard proton.

T. N. Kolokolova et al. have recently optimized the experimental NMR conditions to achieve maximal accuracy in the quantitative analysis of identified urinary metabolites [43]. Below are several examples of direct quantitation of drugs in biofluids samples using NMR spectroscopy.

Chew et al. [44] have successfully measured the concentration of *gamma*-hydroxybutyrate (GHB) using NMR spectroscopy. The concentration of GHB was determined by comparing integrated signal intensities of the internal standard (1,4-dioxane, represented by eight protons with a single resonance signal at 3.75 ppm) and the NaGHB protons. The experiments demonstrated a high level of reproducibility as well as accurate quantitative measurements of the GHB sample based on NMR theory. The amount of *gamma*-hydroxybutyrate (GHB) and *gamma*-hydroxybutyrolactone (GBL) has also been successfully quantified both in human serum and urine using spiked samples. Quantitation was achieved using calibration curves. The researchers used a 300 MHz instrument. [33]. In another study done by Meshitsuka et al. [5], the amount of propylene glycol in the urine of an infant patient was determined using NMR spectroscopy by integrating the methyl signal of the drug. For quantitation of creatine or creatinine in urine, Cartigny et al. [30] have used an internal standard made with a titrated solution of 3-trimethylsilyl 2,2',3,3'-tetradeuteropropionic acid sodiumsalt (TSP) in deuterium. A titrated solution of TSP in deuterium oxide was added to a capillary tube which was coaxially inserted into the NMR tube. Creatine and creatinine were spiked in control urine by known amounts in the range 1–20 mmol/L. All quantitation processes were run on the methyl groups of creatine and creatinine by using the ratio [peak area of the substance/peak area of the internal standard (TSP)]. The researchers have used the same method to quantify the amount of tetrahydrofuran in the urine and serum of a patient in a case of acute tetrahydrofuran poisoning [27] and the amount of methanol or ethylene glycol in the serum and urine of three patients in a metabolic acidotic state [7]. In addition, Lee et al. have also developed an alternative method of quantitation to determine the amount of methylamine metabolites in urine. Quantification was performed using an internal standard of acetonitrile (5 mM). Peak integrals related to the compound were measured and expressed as a ratio of the acetonitrile integral. The authors used acetonitrile as an internal standard because its resonance is removed from the spectral region of interest [45].

Advantages and Limitations of NMR

NMR has several advantages over the conventional chromatographic methods for the analysis of drugs in urine although it also has a few drawbacks. First, insome cases it enables direct study of the urine sample without resort to treatment. Problems of extraction, recovery, and chemical derivatization and those that may be encountered with pH sensitive compounds are consequently avoided. The method is nonspecific and unexpected substances are not overlooked during the investigation since all compounds are detected simultaneously in a single analysis. This contrasts with chromatography which usually requires some prior knowledge of the structure of drugs or metabolites to optimize sample preparation and/or detection. Novel entities may therefore be missed. It also avoids the use of a number of different chromatographic techniques, which is sometimes necessary. Furthermore, NMR provides uniquely rich structural information. Indeed, chemical shifts, multiplicity, integrals, as well as homo- and heteronuclear two-dimensional (2D) experiments make up a powerful toolkit to probe the molecular structure. In addition, it is easy to obtain quantitative data and NMR can be used routinely in the same way as HPLC. Given a good signal-to-noise ratio, NMR can quantify substances accurately and reproducibly. Set against these advantages, however, are a number of disadvantages that need to be taken into account. NMR spectrometers are expensive instruments with the cost rising steeply with the field strength of the magnet used. Higher field strengths provide greater chemical shift dispersion and increase the sensitivity. Nonetheless, currently, the price of a routine NMR spectrometer (corresponding to a proton resonance frequency of 300 MHz) does not exceed that of a sophisticated liquid chromatography–mass spectrometry (LC–MS) machine. Moreover, the magnets have long useful lifetimes (≈15–20 years) and the advances in computer technology may be incorporated continuously in NMR spectrometers at a reasonable cost.

Although there is little or no interference from endogenous molecules in ^{31}P, ^{7}Li, ^{19}F, ^{13}C NMR, the problem of peak overlap is critical in ^{1}H NMR since the signals of a large number of endogenous compounds are present in a relatively narrow chemical shift range. Suppression of the intense signal from water is a prerequisite for ^{1}H NMR spectroscopy of biological fluids. In most biofluids, the region of the spectrum deshielded from the water signal is relatively low in interfering resonances so that aromatic or heterocyclic drugs can be studied with relative ease.

The total volume of sample required for NMR analysis ranges between 0.3–0.7 and 2.0–3.0 mL with 5 and 10 mm tubes, respectively, depending if a coaxial capillary is or not employed. The volume needed for an experiment may be reduced without having to redesign the radio-frequency (RF) coil, using several approaches: utilization of smaller tubes (for example 3 mm microtubes requiring 130–150 μL) or tubes fitted with plastic plugs matched to the susceptibility of the solvent or spherical microcells. In the two last cases, the volume sample (60–80 μL under favorable circumstances, or 18μL, respectively) is placed within the active region of the RF coil [46] [47].

In addition, NMR probe manufacturers now offer probes with "saddle-type" coils smaller than those used in standard high-resolution NMR spectrometers, as well as solenoidal coils oriented at the magic angle (54.7°) with respect to the static magnetic field. These probes accommodate a total sample volume in the 140–25 μL range for the "saddle-shaped" coils and from 6 μL to a maximum of 40 μL for the solenoidal coils rapidly spinning at the magic angle [46][48][49].

Submillimeter coils have been also designed for static analyses. They require 0.4–1.4 μL [50] or 200 nL sample volumes [47] with solenoidal microcoils and 30, 120, or 470 nL with planar microcoils [51].

NMR spectroscopy avoids false positive and negative identifications which are common with immunoassay tests due to cross-reactivity with other compounds or adulterants that may disrupt the mechanism of the tests [52][1]. Most opiate immunoassays test for morphine or codeine, but will commonly have some cross-reactivity with other opioids or opioid metabolites [53].

However, compared with most chromatographic and other spectroscopic techniques, NMR is relatively insensitive, which represents the principal drawback of the technique. Indeed the limit of detection (LOD) of NMR ranges between 10^{-9} and 10^{-11} mol whereas

UV–vis absorbance reaches 10^{-13} to 10^{-16} mol, radiochemical 10^{-14} to 10^{-19} mol, mass spectrometry 10^{-13} to 10^{-21} mol and fluorescence 10^{-18} to 10^{-23} mol [54].

With the development of microliter- and nanoliter-volume static probes, it is possible to achieve NMR structural elucidation of mass-limited products. Indeed, LOD (defined as the analyte amount that yields a S/N of 3) of 44 pmol was calculated from a proton NMR spectrum of an 82.6 mM menthol solution acquired in 9 min in an observed volume (*V*obs) of 31 nL, the total sample volume used being 200 nL [48]. Similarly, from 10 min acquisition time of ^{1}H NMR, spectra of three sucrose solutions (5 mM for the first two and 500 mM for the third solution) in *V*obs of 131, 88, and 5 nL (sample volume considered as infinite since a flow probe configuration was used), LODs of 17.6, 34.1, and 18.8 pmol were found, respectively [50] [55].

Twenty years ago, Nicholson and Wilson [56] considered that the detection limit for ^{1}H NMR in biological matrices was theoretically about 10 μM for 500 MHz (or above) spectrometers using a 5 mm probe. Even after suppression of the intense signal from water with adequate strategies, the "chemical noise" of the sample caused by the presence of hundreds of compounds near the limit of detection whose signals sum to give an irregular baseline, as well as the line broadening due to macromolecules binding and chemical-exchange phenomena, (especially severe in plasma and bile), make that it was often difficult to quantify accurately compounds present at concentrations lower than 100 μM.

Today, the sensitivity limit for low molecular weight metabolites in body fluids is in the low micromolar range depending on the number of hydrogens that contribute to a signal, the multiplicity of the resonance, and the difficulty to quantitate the metabolites of interest due to chemical noise caused by considerable signal overlaps in some regions of the spectrum, especially between 3.5 and 4.1 ppm [57].

Accuracy and reproducibility decrease with lower concentrations and depend on the measurement time and the resulting signal-to-noise ratio in the spectra. Finally, another drawback of NMR spectroscopy is its inability to detect NMR "silent" function groups having poor or non-existent magnetic properties (as for SO_4).

Coupled Techniques: LC-NMR and LC-NMR-MS

The direct linking of high resolution NMR and Liquid Chromatography (LC) increases the NMR capability of solving structural problems of complex structures. During the past decade LC-NMR has been successfully applied to the analysis of mixtures of drugs [58] and drug metabolites [59]. However, an inherent drawback of LC-NMR is the difficulty of observing analyte signals in the presence of the large resonance of the LC mobile phases, typically when reverse phase LC separations with multiple protonated solvents are employed and when solvent gradients are used. Thereby, the capability of the determination of an unknown structure by LC-NMR alone is limited. However, with recent technical advances in high resolution NMR and probe development, on-line LC-NMR hyphenation has become technically applicable.

Using LC-MS and LC-NMR in a synergistic way for rapid and unequivocal identification of unknowns has shown great promise. MS rapid screening and preliminary structure investigation, followed by supplementary NMR structure determination, has become a typical structure elucidation protocol in clinical, biological, and natural product research. However, data correlation based on independent LC-MS and LC-NMR results of the same sample is sometimes difficult, due to possible different chromatograms obtained by the two systems. In addition, NMR itself is not sufficient for the structure elucidation of compounds containing NMR non-detectable nuclei such as sulfate. To avoid this ambiguity, MS and NMR are combined with one LC to operate as LC-NMR-MS, and this combination has attracted considerable investigation interest.

LC-NMR-MS allows for the acquisition of MS and NMR data simultaneously in a single LC run, which provides inclusive analysis of a complex matrix through the real-time comparison and complementation of NMR and MS data. Because MS analysis can provide the number of exchangeable protons of a compound by comparing the MS data in deuterated and non-deuterated solvents [60], it helps for the determination of, for example, the number of hydroxyls in an unknown. On the other hand, the acidic proton exchange also complicates MS data interpretation. The first online-coupled LC-NMR-MS system [61] appeared in the middle 1990s. A year later, a second application, based on an iron trap MS, was developed for rapid identification of some expected acetaminophen glucoronide and sulfate containing metabolites in human urine [62]. In addition, a number of unknown endogenous metabolites that are normally observed by other techniques were detected by this hyphenated system. This study clearly demonstrated the value of LC-NMR-MS in the comprehensive analysis of drug metabolites. Over the past years, LC-NMR-MS has been applied to speed up the process of screening active fractions in biomedical and pharmaceutical materials [63], drug metabolites in biological specimens [64], and bioactive constituents in nature products [65].

Stimulated by the promising potential of LC-NMR-MS, researchers have fruitfully used this technique for a variety of applications. The targeted analytes of interest include ibuprofen metabolites in an extract of human urine [66], the urinary metabolic fate of 2-chloro-4-trifluoromethylaniline [67] and 2-bromo-4-trifluoromethylaniline [68] in rat and metabolites of the HIV-1 reverse-transcriptase inhibitor BW935U83 [69] GW420867 and GI265080 [70].

Online LC-NMR-MS has been shown to be a powerful tool for solving identification and structure related problems that an LC-MS or LC-NMR alone cannot handle, without the necessity of laborious fractionation and purification. Numerous obstacles to coupling both MS and NMR to LC have been overcome during its years of development, especially the improvement of NMR on-flow detection sensitivity.

The high-level analytical excellence achieved may trigger the development of dedicated instruments to further improve the performance of this technique for routine use in the analysis of drugs in biofluids.

References

1. Smith, M. 2006. Part II. Methodologies: Immunoassay. In *Principles of Forensic Toxicology*, ed. B. Levine, 119–139. Washington, D.C.: AACC Press.
2. Komoroski, E. M., Komoroski, R. A., Valentine, J. L., Pearce, J. M., Kearns, G. L. 2000. The use of nuclear magnetic resonance spectroscopy in the detection of drug intoxication. *J. Anal. Toxicol.* 24: 180–187.
3. (a) Coen, M., Kuchel, P. W. 2004. Metabonomics based on NMR spectroscopy. *Chemistry in Australia, magazine of The Royal Australian Chemical Institute, July*: 13–17; (b) Coen M., Holmes E., Lindon J. C., Nicholson J. K. 2008. NMR-based metabolic profiling and metabonomic approaches to problems in molecular toxicology. *Chem. Res. Toxicol.* 21: 9–27.

4. Imbenotte, M., Azaroual, N., Cartigny, B., Vermeersch, G., Lhermitte, M. 2003. Identification and quantitation of xenobiotics by ^{1}H NMR spectroscopy in poisoning cases. *Forensic Sci. Int.* 133: 132–135.
5. Meshitsuka, S., Inoue, M., Seki, A., Koeda, T., Takeshita, K. 1999. Screening of urine by one-dimensional and pulsed-field gradient two-dimensional ^{1}H NMR spectroscopy: intoxication by propylene glycol in an infant patient. *Clin. Chim. Acta* 279: 47–54.
6. Savin, S., Cartigny, B., Azaroual, N., Humbert, L., Imbenotte, M., Tsouria, D. 2003. ^{1}H NMR spectroscopy and GC-MS analysis of alpha-chloralose. Application to two poisoning cases. *J. Anal. Toxicol.* 27: 156–161.
7. Wahl, A., Azaroual, N., Imbenotte, M., Mathieu, D., Forzy, G., Cartigny, B., Vermeersch, G., Lhermitte, M. 1998. Poisoning with methanol and ethylene glycol: ^{1}H NMR spectroscopy as an effective clinical tool for diagnosis and quantification. *Toxicology* 128: 73–81.
8. (a) Lambert, J., Shurvell, H., Lightner, D., Cooks, R. 1998. *Organic Structural Spectroscopy.* Upper Saddle River, NJ: Prentice Hall. (b) Silverstein, R., Bassler, G. 1967. *Spectrometric Identification of Organic Compounds* (2nd ed.). New York: John Wiley & Sons, Inc. (c) Skoog, D., Holler, F., Nieman, T. 1998. *Principles of Instrumental Analysis* (5th ed.): Brooks Cole. (d) Friebolin, H. 1998. *Basic One- and Two-dimensional NMR Spectroscopy.* Weinheim: Wiley-VCH (3rd revised ed.). (e) Claridge, T. D W. 1999. *High-resolution NMR Techniques in Organic Chemistry.* Amsterdam: Pergamon Press.
9. Gyulai, L., Wicklund, S.W., Greenstein, R., Bauer, M. S., Ciccione, P., Whybrow, P. C., Zimmerman, J., Kovachich, G., Alves, W. 1991. Measurement of tissue lithium concentration by lithium magnetic resonance spectroscopy in patients with bipolar disorder. *Biol. Psychiatry* 29: 1161–1170. Komoroski, R.A., Newton, J. E. O., Walker, E., Cardwell, D., Jagannathan N. R., Ramaprasad, S., Sprigg, J. 1990. In vivo NMR spectroscopy of lithium-7 in humans. *Magn. Reson. Med.* 15: 347–356. Renshaw, P. F., Wicklund, S. 1988. In vivo measurement of lithium in humans by nuclear magnetic resonance spectroscopy. *Biol. Psychiatry* 23: 465–475.
10. Everett, J. R., Jennings, K., Woodnutt, G. 1985. ^{19}F NMR spectroscopy study of the metabolites of flucloxacilin in rat urine. *J. Pharm. Pharmacol.* 37: 869–873. Wade, K. E., Wilson, I. D., Troke, J. A., Nicholson J. K. 1990. ^{19}F and ^{1}H magnetic resonance strategies for metabolic studies on fluorinated xenobiotics: application to flurbiprofen [2-(2-fluoro-4-biphenylyl)propionic acid]. *J. Pharm. Biomed. Anal.* 8: 401–410.
11. Cartigny, B., Azaroual, N., Imbenotte, M., Mathieu, D., Vermeersch, G., Goullé, J., Lhermitte, M. 2004. Determination of glyphosate in biological fluids by ^{1}H and ^{31}P NMR spectroscopy. *Forensic Sci. Int.* 143: 141–145; Martino, R., Gilard, V., Desmoulin, F., Malet-Martino, M. 2005. Fluorine-19 or phosphorus-31 NMR spectroscopy: a suitable analytical technique for quantitative in vitro metabolic studies of fluorinated or phosphorylated drugs. *J. Pharm. Biomed. Anal.* 38: 871–891.
12. Hoult, D. I. 1976. Solvent peak saturation with single phase and quadrature Fourier transformation. *J. Magn. Reson.* 21: 337–347.
13. Altieri, A.S., Byrd, R. A. 1995. Randomization approach to water suppression in multidimensional NMR using pulsed field gradients. *J. Magn. Reson. B* 107: 260–266.
14. Ogg, R. J., Kingsley, P. B., Taylor, J. S. 1994. WET, a T1- and B1-insensitive water-suppression method for in vivo localized ^{1}H NMR spectroscopy. *J. Magn. Reson. B* 104: 1–10.
15. Smallcombe, S. H., Patt, S. L., Keifer, P. A. 1995. WET solvent suppression and its applications to LC NMR and high-resolution NMR spectroscopy. *J. Magn. Reson. A* 117: 295–303.
16. Piotto, M., Saudek, V., Sklenar, V. 1992. Gradient-tailored excitation for single-quantum NMR-spectroscopy of aqueous solutions. *J. Biomol. NMR* 2: 661–665.
17. Hwang, T. L., Shaka, A. J. 1995. Water suppression that works-excitation sculpting using arbitrary wave forms and pulsed-field gradients. *J. Magn. Reson. A* 112: 275–279.
18. Simpson, A. J., Brown, S. A. 2005. Purge NMR: Effective and easy solvent suppression. *J. Magn. Reson.* 175: 340–346.

19. Serber, Z., Richter, C., Moskau, D., Bohlen, J. M., Gerfin, F., Marek, D., Haberli, M., Baselgia, L. Laukien, F., Stern, A. S., Hoch, J. C., Dotsch, V. New carbon-detected protein NMR experiments using cryoProbes. *J. Am. Chem. Soc.* 122: 3554–3555.
20. Spraul, M., Freund, A. S., Nast, R. E., Withers, R. S., Maas, W. E., Corcoran, O. 2003. Advancing NMR sensitivity for LC-NMR-MS using a cryoflow probe: application to the analysis of acetaminophen metabolites in urine. *Anal. Chem.* 75: 1536–1541.
21. Kupče, É., Freeman, R. Molecular structure from a single NMR Experiment. 2008. *J. Am. Chem. Soc.*, 130 (32): 10788–10792.
22. Armbruster, D. A., Tillman, M. D., Hubbs, L. M. 1994. Limit of detection (LOD)/limit of quantitation (LOQ): comparison of the empirical and the statistical methods exemplified with GC-MS assays of abused drugs. *Clin. Chem.* 40: 1233–1238.
23. Mandatory guidelines for federal workplace drug testing, 69 F. Register. 19644 (April 13, 2004)
24. Zuppi, C., Messana, I., Forni, F., Rossi, C., Pennacchietti, L., Ferrari, F., Giardina, B. 1997. ^{1}H NMR spectra of normal urines: reference ranges of the major metabolites. *Clin. Chim. Acta* 265: 85–97.
25. Holmes, E., Loo, R. L., Cloarec, O., Coen, M., Tang, H., Maibaum, E., Bruce, S., Chan, Q., Elliot, P., Stamler, J., Wilson, I. D., Lindon, J. C., Nicholson, J. K. 2007. Detection of urinary drug metabolite (xenometabolome) signatures in molecular epidemiology studies via statistical total correlation (NMR) spectroscopy. *Anal. Chem.* 79: 2629–2640.
26. Lenz, E. M., Bright, J., Wilson, I. D., Morgan, S. R., Nash, A. F. 2003. A ^{1}H NMR-based metabonomic study of urine and plasma samples obtained from healthy human subjects. *J. Pharm. Biomed. Anal.* 33: 1103–1115.
27. Cartigny, B., Azaroual, N., Imbenotte, M., Sadeg, N., Testart, F., Richecoeur, J., Vermeersch, G., Lhermitte, M. 2001. ^{1}H NMR spectroscopic investigation of serum and urine in a case of acute tetrahydrofuran poisoning. *J. Anal. Toxicol.* 25: 270–274.
28. Cartigny, B., Azaroual, N., Bochu, C., Vinner, E., Imbenotte, M., Vermeersch, G., Lhermitte, M. 2006. Analysis of ingested material and urine by GC-MS and ^{1}H NMR spectroscopy: poisoning of an adult with adulterated soda. *J. Anal. Toxicol.* 30: 86–90.
29. Maschke, S., Azaroual, N., Wieruszeski, J. M., Lippens, G., Imbenotte, M., Mathieu, D., Vermeersch, G., Lhermitte, M. 1997. Detection by ^{1}H-NMR spectroscopy of chloroquine in urine from acutely poisoned patient. *Clin. Chem.* 43: 698–699.
30. Cartigny, B., Azaroual, N., Mille-Hamard, L., Imbenotte, M., Kintz, P., Vermeersch, G., Lhermitte, M. 2002. ^{1}H NMR urine analysis as an effective tool to detect creatine supplementation. *J. Anal. Toxicol.* 26: 355–359.
31. Salem, A. A., Mossa, H. A., Barsoum, B. N. 2005. Quantitative determinations of levofloxacin and rifampicin in pharmaceutical and urine samples using nuclear magnetic resonance spectroscopy. *Spectrochim. Acta A Mol. Biomol. Spectrosc.* 62: 466–472.
32. Robertson, D. G. 2005. Metabonomics in toxicology: a review. *Toxicol. Sci.* 85: 809–822.
33. Del Signore, A. G., McGregor, M., Cho, B. P. 2005. ^{1}H NMR analysis of GHB and GBL: further findings on the interconversion and a preliminary report on the analysis of GHB in serum and urine. *J. Forensic Sci.* 50: 81–86.
34. Liu, J., Decatur, J., Proni, G., Champeil, E. 2009 Identification and quantitation of 3,4-methylenedioxy-*N*-methylamphetamine (MDMA, ecstasy) in human urine by ^{1}H NMR spectroscopy. Application to five cases of intoxication. *Forensic Sci. Int.* 194(1): 103–107.
35. Janus, T., Borowiak, K. S., Pabisiak, K., Machoy-Mokrzynska, A., Swiniarski, A., Rozwadowski, Z. 2005. ^{1}H nuclear magnetic resonance spectroscopic investigation of urine for diagnostic and clinical assessment of methanol intoxication. *Basic Clin. Pharmacol. Toxicol.* 97: 257–260.
36. Janus, T., Borowiak, K. S., Rozwadowski, Z., Machoy-Mokrzynska, A., Suchocka, J. 2006. Changes in urine metabolic profiles in patients with chronic intake of amphetamine and opiates revealed using ^{1}H NMR spectroscopy with pattern recognition technique. *Acta Toxicologica* 14: 111–116.

37. Ala-Korpela M. 2008. Critical evaluation of ^{1}H NMR metabonomics of serum as a methodology for disease risk assessment and diagnostics. *Clin. Chem. Lab. Med.* 46: 27–42.
38. Grootveld, M., Algeo, D., Silwood, C. J. L., Blackburn, J. C., Clark, A. D. 2006. Determination of the illicit drug *gamma*-hydroxybutyrate (GHB) in human saliva and beverages by ^{1}H NMR analysis. *Biofactors* 27: 121–136.
39. Wilson, I. D., Wade, K. E., Nicholson, J. K. 1989. Analysis of biological fluids by high-field nuclear magnetic resonance spectroscopy. *Trends Anal. Chem.* 8: 368–74.
40. a) Wevers, R. A., Engelke, U. D. F., Moolenaar, S. H., Brautigam, C., de Jong, J. G. N., Duran, R., de Abreu, R. A., van Gennip, A. H. 1999. ^{1}H-NMR spectroscopy of body fluids: Inborn errors of purine and pyrimidine Metabolism. *Clin. Chem.* 45: 539–548. b) Moolenaar, S. H. Gohlich-Ratmann, G., Engelke, U. F. H., Spraul, M., Humpfer, E., Dvortsak, P., Voit, T., Hoffmann, G. H., Brautigam, C., van Kuilenburg, A. B., van Gennip, A., Vreken, P., Wevers, R. A. 2001. Beta-ureidopropionase deficiency: a novel inborn error of metabolism discovered using NMR spectroscopy on urine. *Magn. Reson. Med.* 46: 1014–1017.
41. Monté, S. Y., Ismail, I. , Mallett, D. N., Matthews, C., Tanner, R. J. N. 1994. The minimal metabolism of inhaled 1,1,1,2-tetrafluoroethane to trifluoroacetic acid in man as determined by high sensitivity 19F nuclear magnetic resonance spectroscopy of urine samples, *J. Pharm. Biomed. Anal.* 12: 1489–1493.
42. Busse, D., Busch, F. W., Bohnenstengel, F., Eichelbaum, M., Fischer, P., Opalinska, J., Schumacher, K., Schweizer, E., Kroemer, H. K. 1997. Dose escalation of cyclophosphamide in patients with breast cancer: consequences for pharmacokinetics and metabolism *J. Clin. Oncol.* 15: 1885–1896.
43. Kolokolova, T. N., Sergeev, N. M., Korol'kov, A. Yu. 2008. Quantitative determination of metabolites in human urine by ^{1}H NMR spectroscopy. *Clinical Studies* 2: 418–425.
44. Chew, S. L., Meyers, J. A. 2003. Identification and quantitation of *gamma*-hydroxybutyrate (GHB) by Nuclear Magnetic Resonance Spectroscopy. *J. Forensic Sci.* 48: 292–298.
45. Lee, M. B., Storer, M. K., Blunt, J. W., Lever, M. 2006. Validation of ^{1}H NMR spectroscopy as an analytical tool for methylamine metabolites in urine. *Clin. Chim. Acta* 365: 264–269.
46. Lacey, M. E., Subramanian, R., Olson, D. L., Webb, A. G., Sweedler, J. V. 1999. High resolution NMR spectroscopy of sample volumes from 1 nL to 10 μL. *Chemical Reviews*: 133–3152, 1999.
47. Reynolds, W. F., Yu, M., Enriquez, R. G. 1997. Investigating the sensitivity limits of ^{13}C-detected ^{1}H–^{13}C chemical shift correlation sequences with modern microprobe and microtube technology, *Magn. Reson. Chem.* 35: 614–618.
48. Olson, D. L., Lacey, M. E., Sweedler, J. V. 1998. High-resolution microcoil NMR for analysis of mass-limited, nanoliter samples. *Anal. Chem.* 70: 645–650.
49. Martin, G. E., Crouch, R. C., Zens, A. P. 1998. Gradient submicro inverse detection: rapid acquisition of inverse-detected heteronuclear chemical shift correlation data on submicromole quantities of material. *Magn. Reson. Chem.* 36: 551–557.
50. Subramanian, R., Lam, M., Webb, A. G. 1998. RF microcoil design for practical NMR of mass-limited samples. *J. Magn. Reson.* 133: 227–231.
51. Massin, C., Vincent, F., Homsy, A., Ehrmann, K., Boero, G., Besse, P. A., Daridon, A., Verpoorte, E., de Rooij, N. F., Popovic, R. S. 2003. Planar microcoil-based microfluidic NMR probes. *J. Magn. Reson.* 164: 242–255.
52. Jenkins, A. 2006. Part I. Introduction: Forensic Drug Testing. In *Principles of Forensic Toxicology*, ed. B. Levine (2nd ed.), 31–45. Washington, D.C.: AACC Press.
53. Kerrigan, S., Goldberger, B. 2006. Part III: Analytes: Opioids. *Principles of Forensic Toxicology*, ed. Levine (2nd ed.), 219–237. Washington, D.C.: AACC Press.
54. Lacey, M. E., Subramanian, R., Olson, D. L., Webb, A. G., Sweedler, J. V. 1999. High resolution NMR spectroscopy of sample volumes from 1 nL to 10 μL. *Chem. Rev.* 99: 3133–3152.
55. Olson, D. L., Peck, T. L., Webb, A. G., Magin, R. L., Sweedler, J. V. 1995. High-resolution microcoil ^{1}H-NMR for mass-limited, nanoliter-volume samples. *Science* 270: 1967–1970.

56. Nicholson, J. K., Wilson, I. D. 1989. High resolution proton *NMR spectroscopy* of biological fluids. *Prog. NMR Spectrosc.* 21: 449–501.
57. Wilson, I. D., Fromson, J., Ismail, I. M., Nicholson, J. K. 1987. Proton magnetic resonance spectroscopy of human urine: excretion of 1-(3′-carboxypropyl)-3,7-dimethylxanthine by man after dosing with oxpentifylline. *J. Pharm. Biomed. Anal.* 5: 157–163.
58. Albert, K., Dachtler, M., Glaser, T., Händel, H., Lacker, T., Schlotterbeck, G., Strohschein, S., Tseng, L. H., Braumann, U. 1999. On-line coupling of separation techniques to NMR. *J. High Resolut. Chromatogr.* 22:135–143.
59. Lindon, J. C., Nicholson, J. K., Wilson, I. D. 2000. Directly coupled HPLC-NMR and HPLC-NMR-MS in pharmaceutical research and development. *J. Chromatogr. B.* 748: 233–258.
60. Holt, R. M., Newman, M. J., Pullen, F. S., Richards, D. S., Swanson, A. G. 1997. High-performance liquid chromatography/NMR spectrometry/mass spectrometry: further advances in hyphenated technology. *J. Mass. Spectrom.* 32: 64–70.
61. Pullen, F. S., Swanson, A. G., Newman, M. J., Richards, D. S. 1995. "On-line" liquid chromatography/nuclear magnetic resonance mass spectrometry. A powerful spectroscopic tool for the analysis of mixtures of pharmaceutical interest. *Rapid Commun. Mass Spectrom.* 32: 1003–1006.
62. Shockcor, J. P., Unger, S. E., Wilson, I. D., Foxall, P. J. D., Nicholson, J. K., Lindon, J. C. 1996. Combined HPLC, NMR spectroscopy and ion trap mass spectrometry with application to the detection and characterization of xenobiotic and endogenous metabolites in human urine. *Anal. Chem.*, 68: 4431–4435.
63. Sandvoss, M., Pham, L. H., Levsen, K., Preiss, A., Miigge, C., Wiinsch, G. 2000. Isolation and structural elucidation of steroid oligoglycosides from the starfish *Asterias rubens* by means of direct online LC-NMR-MS hyphenation and one- and two-dimensional NMR investigations. *Eur. J. Org. Chem.* 1253–1262.
64. Farrant, R. D., Cupid, B. C., Nicholson, J. K., Lindon, J. C. 1997 Investigation of the feasibility of directly-coupled HPLC-NMR with ^2H detection with application to the metabolism of *N*-dimethylformamide-d_7. *J. Pharm. Biomed. Anal.* 16: 1–5.
65. Wison, I. D., Morgan, E. D., Lafont, R., Shockcor, J. P., Lindon, J. C., Nicholson, J. K., Wright, B. 1999. High performance liquid chromatography coupled to nuclear magnetic resonance spectroscopy and mass spectrometry applied to plant products: identification of ecdysteroids from *Silene otites*. *Chromatographia*. 49: 374–378.
66. Clayton, E., Taylor, S., Wright, B., Wilson, I. D. 1998. The application of high-performance liquid chromatography, coupled to nuclear magnetic resonance spectroscopy and mass spectrometry (HPLC-NMR-MS), to the characterisation of ibuprofen metabolites from human urine. *Chromatographia* 47: 264–270.
67. Scarfe G. B., Wright, B., Clayton, E., Taylor, S., Wilson, I. D., Lindon, J. C., Nicholson, J. K. 1999. Quantitative studies on the urinary metabolic fate of 2-chloro-4-trifluoromethylaniline in the rat using ^{19}F NMR spectroscopy and directly coupled HPLC-NMR-MS. *Xenobiotica* 29:77–91.
68. Scarfe, G. B., Wright, E., Clayton, E., Taylor, S., Wilson, I. D., Lindon, J. C., Nicholson, J. K. 1998. ^{19}F NMR and directly coupled HPLC-NMR-MS investigations into the metabolism of 2-bromo-4-(trifluoromethyl)aniline in rat: a urinary excretion balance study without the use of radiolabelling. *Xenobiotica*. 28: 373–378.
69. Shockcor, J. P., Unger, S. E., Savina, P., Nicholson, J. K., Lindon, J. C. 2000. Application of directly coupled LC-NMR-MS to the structural elucidation of metabolites of the HIV-1 reverse-transcriptase inhibitor BW935U83. *J. Chromatogr. B* 748: 269–279.
70. Dear, G. J., Plumb, R. S., Sweatman, B. C., Ayrton, J., Lindon, J. C., Nicholson, J. K., Ismail, I. M. 2000. Mass directed peak selection, an efficient method of drug metabolite identification using directly coupled liquid chromatography-mass spectrometry-nuclear magnetic resonance spectroscopy. *J. Chromatogr. B* 748: 281–293.

Role of Pharmacogenetics in Forensic Toxicology

7

DELPHINE ALLORGE AND GILLES TOURNEL

Contents

Introduction

Forensic toxicology is a branch of modern-day forensic medicine used in cases of fatality where some form of poisoning is suspected or implied. Today, the potential applications of forensic toxicology are even broader and can concern criminal and civil matters involving drug use or abuse, road and workplace safety, sport doping, and so on.

Death through poisoning, either deliberate or accidental, has been recorded since ancient times. For example, in Greece and Egypt, components of common herbs, plants, and even food were used as poisons, and, in Europe during the Middle Ages, opium, arsenic, and hydrocyanic acid were often used for poisoning. During this time, the philosopher Paracelsus (1493–1541) observed, "All things are poisons; there is none which is not a poison. Solely the dose determines that a thing is not a poison and the right dose differentiates a poison from a remedy." This observation that any substance could be a poison depending on its dose still applies today (Ferrer-Dufol & Menao-Guillen, 2009).

In cases of suspected poisoning, toxicological analyses are essential to identify the drug(s) involved, and, furthermore, to determine death-related fatal drug concentrations. Today, the drugs most commonly targeted include amphetamines, benzodiazepines, cannabis, cocaine, opiates, and, more generally, any drug that can be used illegally as a recreational drug. Their identification and quantification in biological fluids such as blood or urines requires the expertise of a well-equipped toxicology laboratory with modern analytical techniques such as specific immunoassays, mass spectrometry coupled with high-performance liquid chromatography (LC-MS) or gas chromatography (GC-MS) (Levine, 2003; Drummer, 2010), and extensive chemical libraries. Furnished with this information, it is possible for the forensic toxicologist to determine and differentiate therapeutic, toxic, and fatal concentrations of various drugs in postmortem material.

To determine accurately the cause surrounding a death through poisoning, a number of variables must be taken into consideration. These include the circumstances and context of death, which could have a significant impact on drug concentrations in body fluids and tissues, such as severe trauma resulting in stomach/diaphragm rupture in cases of motor vehicle accidents, resuscitation attempts, and post-accident medication (Pounder, Fuke, Cox, Smith, & Kuroda, 1996; Pounder, Adams, Fuke, & Langford, 1996). In addition, modification of drug concentrations in cadavers can arise from redistribution and/or anaerobic metabolism phenomena (Gilliland & Bost, 1993; O'Neal & Poklis, 1996; Pélissier-Alicot, Gaulier, Champsaur, & Marquet, 2003; Pélissier-Alicot, Fornaris, Bartoli, Piercecchi-Marti, Sanvoisin, et al., 2005; Pélissier-Alicot, Coste, Bartoli, Piercecchi-Marti, Sanvoisin, et al., 2006; Butzbach, 2010). Finally, sensitivity and specificity of the analytical methods, quality of the samples and of their storage, inherent drug stability, and knowledge of the drug(s) disposition are additional essential co-variables to be considered when interpreting drug toxicological data (Drummer, 2010). Another factor more recently recognized as beneficial to circumvent interpretative hurdles in forensic toxicology is the knowledge that the toxicity of drugs can show large variability within and/or between individuals. This is due to environmental and individual factors such as diet, smoking, age, disease, and so on, and, more importantly, due to genetic factors that affect the pharmacokinetic and pharmacodynamic properties of the drug(s) such as polymorphisms in drug transporters, drug metabolizing enzymes, and drug receptors. Collectively, these latter factors represent the discipline of pharmacogenetics and will be described in detail in the following sections in relation to forensic toxicology.

Genetic Variability of Drug Disposition and Response

Drug Disposition

Drug disposition deals with the interactions of therapeutic molecules with proteins on the surface of cell membranes, as well as intracellular proteins, leading to the protection of normal cellular functions, but, on some occasions, to toxic events. Various proteins are involved in the overall process of drug disposition, but the two main systems that synergistically interplay are composed of transporter proteins and drug-metabolizing enzymes (DMEs). Another important class of proteins that are involved in drug response is composed of target proteins, such as receptors or enzymes. Figure 7.1 summarizes the four

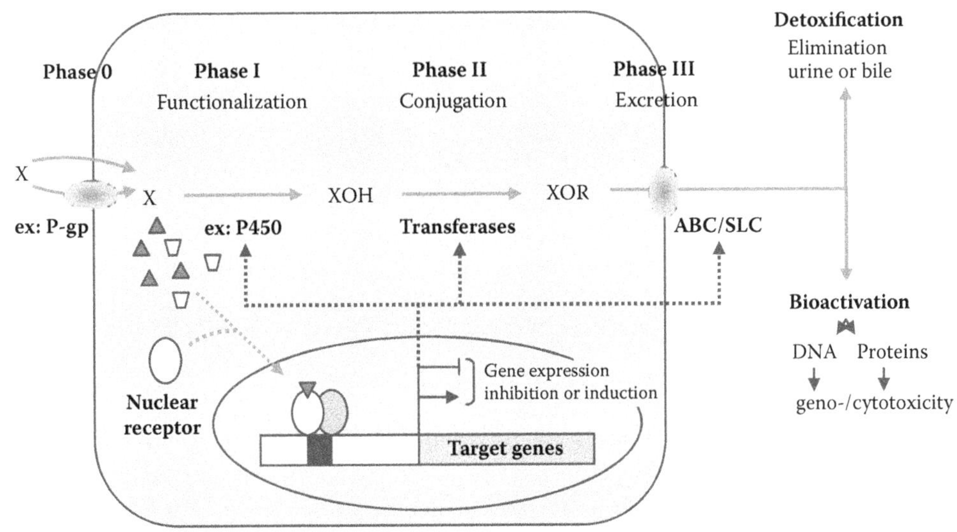

Figure 7.1 Schematic representation of the cellular metabolism and transport of drugs. X, drug; XOH and XOR, more polar metabolites; P-gp, glycoprotein-P; P450, cytochromes P450; ABC, ATP-binding cassette proteins; SLC, solute carrier proteins.

main phases involved in the cellular processing of drugs which mainly takes place in mammals in hepatic cells, but also in the cells of extra-hepatic tissues such as intestine, kidney, lung, and others.

As most drugs are hydrophobic in nature, to enter the cell, they must first pass through membranes via transporters, which either facilitate or prevent uptake. This first phase is sometimes referred to as Phase 0. Drug transporters are generally classified into the SLC (solute carrier) and ABC (ATP-binding cassette) superfamilies and are targeted into appropriate membrane regions in polarized and non-polarized cells, thereby involved both in the influx and efflux of substrates. Transporter proteins are expressed in various tissues with excretory and protective functions, such as the intestine, liver, kidney, and the blood-brain barrier. For instance, one of the best-characterized proteins involved in drug transport is the P-glycoprotein or MDR-1 (multidrug resistance protein-1), which is encoded by the ABCB1 gene and participates in the transport of many compounds into the intestinal lumen. Once in the cell, drugs undergo metabolism by the so-called Phase I and Phase II enzymes. The Phase I enzymes, mainly represented by the cytochrome P450 superfamily, modify functional moieties on chemicals via hydrolysis, oxidation, reduction, or hydroxylation. The Phase II enzymes facilitate excretion in the bile and/or the urine through conjugation of polar groups, such as glutathione, sulfate, glycine, or glucuronic acid, to the parent molecule or to the Phase I–generated metabolites. These reactions are catalyzed by a large group of broad-specificity transferases, such as glutathion S-transferases (GSTs), sulfotransferases, or UDP-glucuronosyltransferases (UGTs). The final metabolites can then be actively excreted out of cells by Phase III proteins consisting of SLC and ABC transporters. An additional group of proteins, that is now regarded as an essential part of the xenobiotic/drug disposition process, is represented by xenosensors that are involved in the transcriptional control of expression and activity of the Phase 0 to III partners. Numerous nuclear receptors, such as the pregnane X receptor (PXR) and the constitutive androstane receptor (CAR), have been characterized and coordinate regulation of Phase I and II XMEs and Phase 0 and III transporters through interaction with responsive element sequences in the regulatory region of target genes (Nakata, Tanaka, Nakano, Adachi, Tanaka, et al., 2006).

In total, although these processes generally act in concert to detoxify drugs and remove them from cells, they can also give rise to the production and/or the accumulation of reactive metabolites which form the chemical basis of cytotoxicity or carcinogenicity (Figure 7.1). Importantly, drug disposition can be altered in an individual and is sometimes highly variable between individuals due to various exogenous and endogenous factors which have to be taken into account to fully understand the overall response of the body toward drug exposure (Lazarou, Pomeranz, & Corey, 1998).

Variability of Drug Disposition and Response

Drug disposition and response can be altered in an individual (intraindividual variability) and is sometimes highly variable between individuals (interindividual variability) due to various exogenous and endogenous factors, which must be taken into account to fully understand and interpret the overall response of the body toward drug exposure. In the field of forensic toxicology, and specifically in the context of fatal drug poisoning, it is important for the toxicologist to interpret postmortem drug levels in light of potential variables that can affect kinetics and dynamics of drugs (Ingelman-Sundberg, Johansson, Dahl, Bertilsson, Yue, et al., 1992; Allorge & Loriot, 2004).

Environmental factors such as diet, alcohol consumption, and smoking, as well as physio-pathological factors such as age, gender, pregnancy, obesity, inflammation, and hepatic and renal functions, are all recognized factors that can alter drug disposition and response since they can affect to various degrees the systems that control absorption, distribution, metabolism, and excretion of drugs (Nicolas, Espie, & Molimard, 2009; Morgan, Goralski, Piquette-Miller, Renton, Robertson, et al., 2008; Nekvindova & Anzenbacher, 2007; Smeraldi, Zanardi, Benedetti, Di Bella, Perez, et al., 1998; Ferrer-Dufol & Menao-Guillen, 2009). Drug-drug interactions are also a major source of variation in the pharmacokinetic and pharmacodynamic properties of drugs. Inhibition and induction of drug transporters and metabolizing-enzymes by environmental compounds or co-administered drugs are two major mechanisms that contribute to drug disposition variability (Liu, Hao, Liu, Wang, & Xie, 2007; Xu, Li, & Kong, 2005). However, it is now well established that genetic factors participate to a significant extent to the overall interindividual variability in drug disposition and response. Depending on the drugs or classes of drugs, around 20 to 95% of the interindividual differences in drug metabolism and response have been proven or are highly suspected to be of genetic origin (Kalow, 1998; Ingelmann-Sundberg, Daly, Oscarson, & Nebert, 2000; Ingelman-Sundberg & Evans, 2001). Furthermore, nearly 60% of drugs that are frequently involved in adverse drug reactions are metabolized at least by one enzyme that is known to have a genetic variant for a poor metabolism phenotype (Phillips, Veenstra, Oren, Lee, & Sadee, 2001). It is also noteworthy that environmental factors cause transient changes in an individual's response to drug therapy, whereas genetic factors are permanent in nature. Since the first descriptions of inherited differences in drug metabolism in the 1950s, the identification of an increasing number of genetic variations affecting genes that encode drug-metabolizing enzymes, drug transporters, and drug targets has contributed to the development of the field of pharmacogenetics and to its gradual translation from a research area into a promising medical tool for personalized pharmacotherapy.

Molecular Mechanisms and Methods of Investigation of Pharmacogenetic Traits

The best-characterized and most extensively studied area in pharmacogenetics is drug metabolism, also referred to as biotransformation. Much Phase I metabolism is performed by polymorphic enzymes, especially members of the cytochrome P450 superfamily. Out of the known 57 P450 human genes, those from families CYP1, CYP2, and CYP3 are collectively responsible for most of Phase I biotransformations of drugs and other xenobiotics. CYP2C9, CYP2C19, and CYP2D6 are involved in the hepatic metabolism of approximately half of the 200 drugs most often prescribed in the United States (Zanger, Turpeinen, Klein, & Schwab, 2008), and their genetic polymorphisms affect the metabolism of 20%–30% of all clinically used drugs (Kirchheiner & Brockmöller, 2005; Ingelman-Sundberg & Rodriguez-Antona, 2005). In addition to cytochromes P450, genetic polymorphisms of numerous Phase II enzymes, such as UDP-glucuronosyltransferases, *N*-acetyltransferases, sulfotransferases, or methyltransferases, also contribute to individual variability in drug metabolism. Pharmacogenetic-related molecular mechanisms, as well as applicable methods of investigation in living or even dead subjects, will be depicted and illustrated in this section using data collected from studies on DMEs.

Molecular Mechanisms and Phenotype Classification

Genetic variability in drug disposition and response occurs as a result of molecular alterations that affect genes encoding drug-metabolizing enzymes, drug transport proteins, as well as drug targets/receptors. These molecular alterations can affect drug dependency phenotypes by altering the function of a gene product or by altering gene expression. Genetic variation in the human genome is a common phenomenon and two main forms of genetic variation have been described in genes of pharmacogenetic interest, namely single nucleotide polymorphisms (SNPs) and complex genomic rearrangements. SNPs are single-base pair changes at a unique site that are present in the human genome with a frequency of approximately 1 per 1,000 base pairs. Whereas the vast majority of SNPs are biologically silent, some occur in functionally important regions of genes, such as coding or regulatory regions, and, consequently, may impact protein function by altering the amino acid sequence of the encoded proteins, RNA splicing, or even gene transcription. Among complex genomic rearrangements, partial or complete gene deletions and gene amplifications (duplication being the most frequent type of gene amplification) have been described for genes of pharmacogenetic interest, especially for those encoding DMEs. These copy number variations (CNVs), which have been found to alter approximately 12% of the human genome, can result in gene dosage imbalance, coding sequence disruption, or gene regulation alteration. Overall, when these genetic variations (i.e., SNPs or CNVs) occur in genes encoding DMEs, they can abolish, reduce, or even increase the expression and/or the activity of these enzymes (Figure 7.2) and, consequently, give rise to various metabolic phenotypes within the general population (Figure 7.3). As most of the genes encoding DMEs are autosomal genes, metabolic phenotypes are inherited as autosomal recessive or (co)-dominant traits. Accordingly, whereas individuals with two "normal" functional alleles are termed rapid or extensive (EM) metabolizers, those with two variant alleles resulting in inactive or absent enzyme are of the limited or poor metabolizer (PM) phenotype. Two additional phenotypes, the so-called intermediate metabolizer (IM) and ultra-rapid metabolizer (UM) phenotypes,

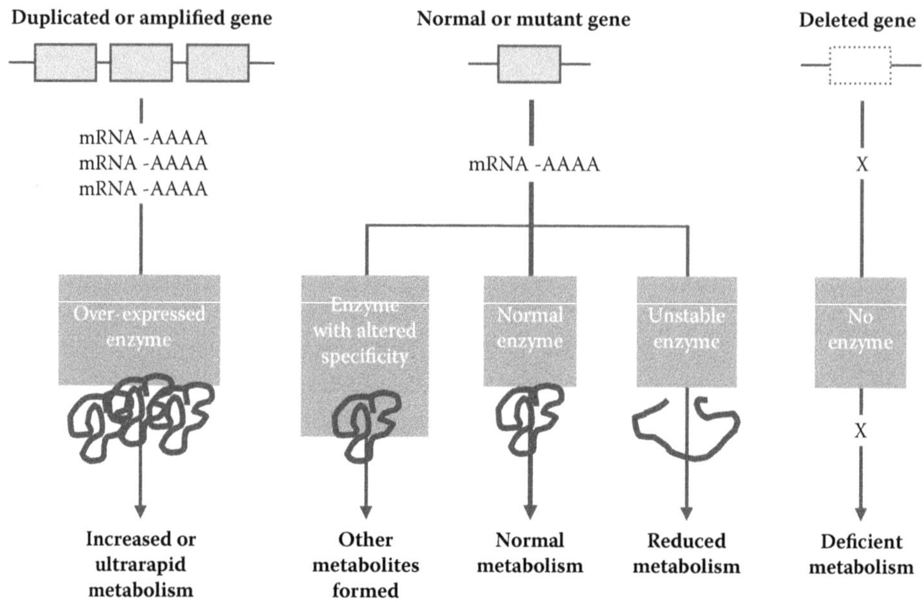

Figure 7.2 Molecular mechanisms of the variability of drug-metabolizing enzyme expression and/or activity.

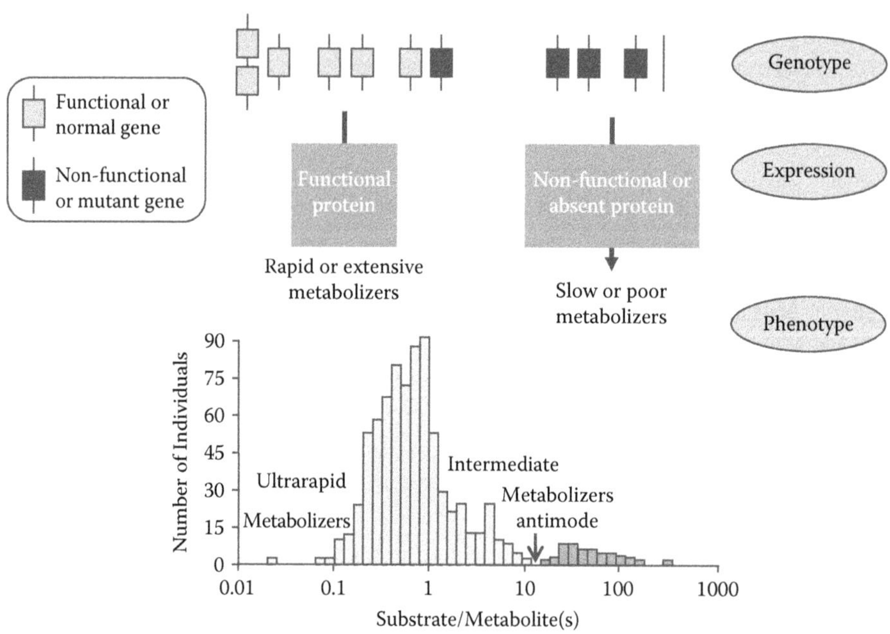

Figure 7.3 Phenotypic expression of a genetic polymorphism affecting a drug-metabolizing enzyme in the general population.

can arise from the expression of one nonfunctional allele and one partially functional allele or two partially active alleles for IMs, and from the expression of gene (multi) duplication for UMs. The incidence of each metabolizer phenotype for a given enzyme can vary significantly between populations of various ethnic origins. This results from differences in the nature and frequency of the genetic polymorphisms that occur within a particular population that is characterized not only by racial background but also by exposures to different environments exerting selection pressure.

One of the best examples to illustrate all these concepts is the genetic polymorphism of the cytochrome P450 2D6 (CYP2D6), an enzyme involved in the metabolism of around 25% of all drugs on the market (Evans & Relling, 1999; Eichelbaum, Ingelman-Sundberg, & Evans 2006). More than 80 distinct variant alleles, summarized at the Human CYP Allele Nomenclature Committee home page (http://www.cypalleles.ki.se), have been described for the CYP2D6 gene and are divided into alleles causing abolished, decreased, normal, and ultrarapid enzyme activity, according to *in vitro* and/or *in vivo* data. The most frequent null alleles are the *CYP2D6*4*-type alleles (*CYP2D6*4A* to *CYP2D6*4N*), characterized by a point mutation causing a splice defect. The *CYP2D6*10*, **17*, and **41* are among the most common alleles with decreased activity. Many CNVs have been described for *CYP2D6*, in particular a complete deletion (*CYP2D6*5*) and gene amplifications (*CYP2D6*XN*) consisting in 2 to 13 tandem repeats of a functional or a non-functional allele. Important interethnic differences exist for CYP2D6 polymorphism and phenotypes. PMs are mainly found in Caucasian populations, with reported frequencies of 5 to 10%, and are nearly absent in Asian populations (<1%). UMs and IMs are the most frequently observed phenotypes in Africans and Asians, respectively. This interethnic variability has to be taken into account when genotyping strategies are developed and used to predict individual phenotypes.

Methods of Investigation

Two main methods can be used for the analysis of pharmacogenetic polymorphisms (Daly, 2004). The first method, referred as to the "phenotyping" method, is concerned with phenotype determination either by measurement of enzyme activities or by monitoring levels of a metabolite in blood or urine. This method is sometimes seen by some authors as the "gold standard" method as it permits real-time measurement of enzyme activity that takes into account not only genetic but also environmental and physiological factors and, consequently, reflects directly the metabolic capacity of an individual. The second one, referred to as the "genotyping" method, consists of the direct analysis of DNA for the occurrence of one or several specific genetic polymorphism(s). To be adequately and routinely used, genotyping requires that a clear concordance between genotype and phenotype has been previously demonstrated. However, genotyping offers the advantage that it can be applicable to any polymorphic gene that encodes a protein of pharmacogenetic interest including enzymes, transporters, and receptors, whereas phenotyping is mainly applicable to metabolizing enzymes. Furthermore, in case of postmortem analyses, the phenotype determination by phenotyping can be difficult, or even impossible, depending on the type of samples available and on their quality (delay between death and sampling, sample storage conditions, etc.). Genotyping can circumvent these drawbacks.

Phenotyping Measurement of levels of enzyme activity or protein in an accessible tissue, such as red blood cells (RBC) or leukocytes, is the most convenient phenotyping approach. For instance, this method is the one used routinely to determine the enzymatic activity of the thiopurine *S*-methyltransferase (TPMT), a Phase II enzyme involved in the detoxification of the thiopurine drugs, azathioprine, and 6-mercaptopurine. It consists of the incubation of a RBC lysate with a probe substrate, in general 6-mercaptopurine, followed by the dosage of the corresponding metabolite formed by TPMT (i.e., 6-methylmercaptopurine).

The TPMT activity is then expressed as the number of nmol of 6-methylmercaptopurine formed per hour per milliliter of RBC (or sometimes pmol/h/mg of hemoglobin) and, based on the observed value, subjects are categorized as low, intermediate, or high methylators by comparison to reference values.

Unfortunately, many enzymes of pharmacogenetic interest are not expressed in RBC or leukocytes. This is particularly true for cytochromes P450, which are mainly expressed at high levels in the liver. Consequently, numerous *in vivo* phenotyping tests have been developed to characterize P450 activities in humans. They are based on the administration, generally *per os*, of a sub-therapeutic dose of a selective probe drug, followed by the collection of an appropriate biological sample (blood or urine) and the calculation of a pharmacokinetic parameter, such as clearance or area under the plasma concentration versus time curve (AUC), or of a molar ratio (MR) of the parent compound to the metabolite. For instance, in the most commonly used phenotyping method for CYP2D6 determination, subjects are administered a single oral dose of 15–50 mg of dextromethorphan (DM), that is *O*-demethylated by CYP2D6 into dextrorphan (DX), and the urine is collected over a period of 8–12 hours. The DM/DX ratio is then measured in urine by HPLC-based methods and subjects with a MR higher than 0.3 are considered to be PMs, whereas those with MR lower than 0.3 are considered to be EMs. Various "cocktail" approaches using mixtures of several selective probe drugs have also been developed to simultaneously study several enzymes and transporters pathways in a single experiment. Moreover, some single probe substrates allow the simultaneous assessment of the phenotypes of various DMEs, like caffeine, which is extensively metabolized in humans and can serve to phenotype *in vivo* CYP1A2, CYP2A6, *N*-acetyltransferase-2, and xanthine oxidase (Hakooz, 2009).

However, although phenotyping reveals the activity of a DME at a particular time and indicates the metabolic capacity of the individual, the result may not be reproducible over time and can be altered by various confounding factors, such as concomitant medication or concurrent diseases. This "phenocopy" phenomenon, which generally gives rise to the erroneous classification of an EM individual as a PM, can be circumvented by genotyping methods.

Genotyping As the molecular basis of most pharmacogenetic polymorphisms is now known, genotyping assays can be used to accurately predict a metabolic phenotype. However, a prerequisite for pharmacogenetics to be applied in clinical or forensic practice is the development of fast, reliable, and cost-effective techniques for routine genotyping. Most of the currently used genotyping techniques are based on a first step of DNA amplification of part of the gene of interest by PCR, followed by a specific detection step of the studied polymorphism(s). The choice of the method will be determined by a number of factors including equipment available in the laboratory, the number of samples to be analyzed, as well as the number of polymorphisms to be identified to predict the phenotype with the highest level of accuracy. This latter point, which will ensure the prediction of a particular phenotype with a detection rate close to 100%, requires that the frequency of each genetic variant has been previously determined in large populations of known ethnic origin, as it is now well established that significant differences in allele frequencies exist between ethnically distinct populations.

As the evolution of SNP detection technologies has been tremendously intensive over the past decades, numerous SNP genotyping methods are now available (Shi, 2001; Kwok & Chen, 2003). Some of them correspond to genotyping assays of targeted SNP and are relatively simple but low-throughput methods, mainly well adapted when dealing with a small number of samples. For instance, they are based on digestion of a PCR product with a restriction enzyme that distinguishes between the wild-type and mutant sequences (namely, restriction fragment length polymorphism-PCR (RFLP-PCR) analysis) or on specific amplification of individual alleles using allele-specific primers (namely, allele-specific-PCR (AS-PCR) analysis), both followed by electrophoresis-based discrimination. More recently developed methods for targeted SNP genotyping are non-gel-based high-throughput technologies that include a fluorescent dye-based procedure, such as the TaqMan® Allelic Discrimination assay (Shi, 2001). This latter assay uses the 5′-nuclease activity of *Taq* polymerase to detect a fluorescent reporter signal generated during or after PCR amplification and requires one pair of PCR primers to specifically amplify the targeted sequence and one pair of TaqMan® probes to discriminate between wild-type and mutated alleles. In addition to detecting targeted SNPs, this method allows the identification of small gene deletions and insertions (Shi, 2001). DNA microarray molecular tests have also emerged recently and the AmpliChip CYP450, approved by the Food and Drug Administration (FDA), is now available to identify functional polymorphisms in two major polymorphic DMEs, CYP2D6, and CYP2C19 (Jain, 2005).

More global SNP detection technologies can be used to screen genes of interest for pharmacogenetic variants (Kwok & Chen, 2003). They generally offer the advantage of combining identification of known SNPs with detection of new polymorphisms. Single-strand conformation polymorphism (SSCP) analysis and denaturing HPLC (DHPLC) are among the most commonly used mutation screening methods and are based on detection of the modification of the conformational profile of single-stranded DNA and of the melting characteristics of double-stranded DNA, respectively, when a mutation is present. With these methods, the use of positive controls of known genotypes, previously checked by sequencing, allows an accurate genotype designation. However, any new polymorphism that is detected by these screening methods will need to be precisely identified further by sequencing of the corresponding region. As DNA sequencing technologies have been remarkably improved in terms of both ease of use and cost, direct DNA sequencing using automated sequencers has been increasingly applied to identify pharmacogenetic polymorphisms. An important issue of these global SNP detection technologies is the need of additional experimentation, such as *in vitro* functional analyses, when an unknown polymorphism with no obvious functional consequences is characterized.

Different technologies are also available to detect or identify large structural gene alterations, such as CNVs. Although Southern blotting-RFLP was the first technique applied to detect gene deletions or duplications, such as for the CYP2D6 gene (Gonzalez, Skoda, Kimura, Umeno, Zanger, et al., 1988; Johansson, Lundqvist, Bertilsson, Dahl, Sjöqvist, et al., 1993), it is a poorly applicable technique for routine genotyping and is no longer used. Long-template PCR methods have been used extensively to detect the presence of deletion or duplication in pharmacogenetic genes, but these cumbersome and technically demanding methods have been progressively replaced by newer techniques, such as real-time PCR or pyrosequencing, that are able to discriminate between gene deletions, duplications, and multiplications (Meijerman, Sanderson, Smits, Beijnen, & Schellens, 2007; Ingelman-Sundberg, Sim, Gomez, & Rodriguez-Antona, 2007), and are now widely used for routine genotyping of pharmacogenetic CNVs.

Medically Relevant Pharmacogenetic Markers

Despite the plethora of genetic information that has been released over the past decades, especially in the field of pharmacogenetics, the number of medically relevant pharmacogenetic markers is still somewhat small and their testing is rarely used in clinical practice (Manolopoulos, 2007). However, as guidelines for pharmacogenetics/genomics in drug development have been published in 2005 by the FDA and should soon be released by the European Medicines Agency (EMEA), it can be expected that pharmacogenetic testing will be extensively implemented in clinical practice in the near future. Currently, information regarding the use of certain pharmacogenetic biomarkers is already available to clinicians through drug labels approved by the FDA (Frueh, Amur, Mummaneni, Epstein, Aubert, et al., 2008). A list of valid genomic biomarkers that were approved by the FDA is available (see the website: http://www.fda.gov/Drugs/ScienceResearch/ResearchAreas/Pharmacogenetics) and provides pharmacogenomic information either without immediate recommendation for genetic testing or with recommended or required genetic testing. The genetic polymorphism that affects the thiopurine *S*-methyltransferase (TPMT) enzyme is one of the best examples of a validated pharmacogenetic biomarker, as it is the first test that has crossed from research to routine use (Ford & Berg, 2010) and its cost-effectiveness has been proven (Winter, Walker, Shapiro, Gaffney, Spooner, et al., 2004). TPMT is involved in the detoxification pathway of the thiopurine molecules, azathioprine (Aza) and 6-mercaptopurine (6-MP), which are widely used as antineoplasic or immunosuppressant agents. TPMT activity is controlled by a genetic polymorphism (Weinshilboum, 2001) and around 90% of Caucasians inherit high TPMT activity, 10% intermediate TPMT activity, and less than 1% low TPMT activity (Weinshilboum & Sladek, 1980). Three major variants, *TPMT*2* (c.238G>C), *TPMT*3A* (c.460G>A, c.719A>G), and *TPMT*3C* (c.719A>G), represent the most prevalent mutant alleles in Caucasian and African American populations and account for 80–95% of intermediate and deficient methylator phenotypes. Patients with low or absent TPMT activity, who carry two deficient *TPMT* allelic variants, are at an increased risk of developing severe, life-threatening myelotoxicity if receiving conventional doses of Aza or 6-MP (Krynetski & Evans, 2003). Individuals with intermediate TPMT activity, who carry one *TPMT* variant allele, also have an increased risk of developing thiopurine-induced myelosuppression, compared with individuals with normal activity (Higgs, 2010). It is now well recognized that TPMT genotyping or phenotyping should be performed prior to thiopurine administration to predict the risk for patients to develop severe hematotoxicity and to individualize the drug treatment by adapting the thiopurine dosage or by choosing an alternative therapy.

Pharmacogenetics in Forensic Medicine

As stated earlier, most pharmaceutical drugs are metabolized by enzymes belonging to the cytochrome P450 superfamily (Table 7.1; Kupiec, Raj, & Vu, 2006). Furthermore, the activities of the major P450 enzymes involved in drug metabolism are influenced by genetic polymorphisms. Consequently, it is not surprising that the currently available examples of the beneficial use of pharmacogenetics in the interpretation of forensic toxicology data predominantly concern drugs that are extensively metabolized by P450s. Many cases of poisoning causing serious intoxication or even death can be attributed to genetic polymorphisms in drug-metabolizing enzymes resulting in toxic concentrations of either the

Table 7.1 Selected List of CYP Enzymes and Substrates

P450 Isoform	Drug Substrates
CYP1A2	Amitriptyline, Caffeine, Clomipramine, Clozapine, Erythromycin, Fluvoxamine, Haloperidol, Imipramine, Naproxen, Paracetamol, Propranolol, Theophyline, Verapamil, Warfarin
CYP2C9	Dextromethorphan, Diclofenac, Fluoxetine, Ibuprofen, Naproxen, Phenytoin, S-Warfarin, Tolbutamide
CYP2C19	Aminopyrine, Citalopram, Clomipramine, Diazepam, Imipramine, Mephenytoin, Omeprazole, Phenytoin, Progesterone, Sertraline
CYP2D6	Beta-blockers, Debrisoquine, Fentanyl, Haloperidol, Flecainide, Mexilitine, Meperidine, Paroxetine, Procainamide, Risperidone, SSRIs, Pro-drug activation of Tramadol, Codeine, Venlafaxine, Oxycodone, and Doxepin
CYP2E1	Acetaminophen, Ethanol, Halothane, Pentobarbitone, Rifampicin, Tolbutamide
CYP3A4	Alfentanil, Alprazolam, Clonazepam, Cocaine, Dexamethasone, Lidocaine, Methadone, Testosterone, Triazolam

parent drug or metabolite(s) in the body. The following are examples of such poisoning and are categorized according to the class of drug.

Opioids

Therapeutic opioids, such as codeine, tramadol, oxycodone, hydrocodone, ethylmorphine, and methadone, used for acute and chronic pain and dependency, are commonly implicated in severe adverse effects, as well as drug-related deaths (Sachdeva & Stadnyk, 2005; Manchikanti & Singh, 2008; Ferreiros, Dresen, Hermanns-Clausen, Auwaerter, Thierauf, et al., 2009; Helland, Isaksen, & Slørdal, 2010; Modesto-Lowe, Brooks, & Petry, 2010). Most opioid drugs are partly or extensively metabolized by the highly polymorphic CYP2D6 enzyme to more potent antinociceptive metabolites, leading to CYP2D6 PMs being more prone to therapeutic inefficiency in contrast to CYP2D6 UMs who can experience life-threatening toxicity (Somogyi, Barratt, & Coller, 2007). Moreover, many drugs are inhibitors of CYP2D6 resulting in the possibility of opioid intoxication due to drug-drug interactions (Druid, Holmgren, Carlsson, & Ahlner, 1999; Samer, Daali, Wagner, Hopfgartner, Eap, Rebsamen, Rossier, Hochstrasser, Dayer, & Desmeules, 2010; Samer, Daali, Wagner, Hopfgartner, Eap, Rebsamen, Rossier, Hochstrasser, Dayer, & Desmeules, 2010).

Codeine

Codeine is a weak narcotic analgesic used to treat mild to moderate pain and is classified as a second step analgesic on the three step analgesic ladder as defined by the World Health Organization (Cunliffe, 2001). Codeine is well absorbed via the oral route and metabolized partly via *O*-demethylation by CYP2D6 to form morphine, the active analgesic metabolite (Williams, Hatch, & Howard, 2001, Williams, Patel, & Howard, 2002). The metabolism of codeine to morphine by CYP2D6 is a minor pathway (around 10%) of codeine metabolism, but this bioactivation pathway is essential for codeine to exert its analgesic effect. Accordingly, codeine can be ineffective at normal therapeutic doses in 5–10% of Caucasians who are CYP2D6 PMs (Desmeules, Gascon, Dayer, & Magistris, 1991), whereas, conversely, codeine intake can result in a morphine overdose in 1–10% of Caucasians who are

CYP2D6 UMs (Gasche, Daali, Fathi, Chiappe, Cottini, et al., 2004; Voronov, Przybylo, & Jagannathan, 2007). Furthermore, codeine toxicity via morphine overdose can be increased in CYP2D6 UM individuals when co-administered with drugs like macrolides and/or azole derivatives, these latter drugs being inhibitors of CYP3A4, another enzyme involved in codeine metabolism (Gasche, Daali, Fathi, Chiappe, Cottini, et al., 2004).

Codeine is commonly used in the postpartum period for pain associated with episiotomy or caesarean section. Several cases of codeine toxicity in breastfed neonates and infants have been reported. Koren et al. (2006) reported a fatal morphine poisoning in a breastfed neonate of a codeine-prescribed mother who was a CYP2D6 UM (Koren, Cairns, Chitayat, Gaedigk, & Leeder, 2006). Whereas the mother had been taking a conventional dose of 30 mg of codeine twice a day for 2 weeks, the morphine concentration of a milk sample, stored at day 10 by the mother, was found to be as high as 87 ng/mL (expected milk concentrations are 1.9 to 20 ng/mL at doses of 60 mg every 6 h) and the morphine concentration in the neonate blood was measured at 70 ng/mL (expected concentrations <2 ng/mL). This severe case was further investigated using additional pharmacogenetic testing and showed that both the mother and the infant were carriers of a *UGT2B7*2/*2* genotype, which is associated with an increased production of morphine-6-glucuronide, a highly active metabolite of morphine (Madadi, Koren, Cairns, Chitayat, Gaedigk, et al., 2007). A case-control study confirmed that a combined CYP2D6 and UGT2B7 UM phenotype is a risk factor of life-threatening CNS depression in breastfed newborns of mothers who are prescribed codeine for obstetrical pain relief (Madadi, Ross, Hayden, Carleton, Gaedigk, et al., 2009). A further recent investigation of the risk of codeine poisoning through breastfeeding even revealed that newborns of mothers with a CYP2D6 EM phenotype have comparable risks to those of mothers with a CYP2D6 UM phenotype (Willmann, Edginton, Coboeken, Ahr, & Lippert, 2009).

Tramadol

Tramadol is a centrally acting analgesic used in the treatment of moderate to severe pain and has a wide range of applications, including treatment for acid reflux and fibromyalgia. Tramadol possesses weak agonist actions at the μ-opioid receptor and displays additional antinociceptive actions via the inhibition of the neuronal reuptake of norepinephrine and serotonin (Grond & Sablotzki, 2004). The main metabolic pathways of tramadol are *O*- and *N*-demethylation, catalyzed by CYP2D6 and CYP2B6, respectively (Grond & Sablotzki, 2004). *O*-desmethyltramadol (ODT) is considered as the major analgesic metabolite, with about 300-fold higher affinity than the parent compound for μ opioid receptors. Consequently, tramadol therapeutic efficiency and toxicity are expected to vary extensively between individuals depending on their CYP2D6 genotypes. In particular, the use of tramadol can be expected to be more problematic in CYP2D6 UMs than PMs, because of the possibility of an ODT overdose. Stamer et al. reported the case of an opioid-related respiratory depression in a patient receiving tramadol for analgesia (Stamer, Stüber, Muders, & Musshoff, 2008). Analysis of the patient's genotype revealed a CYP2D6 gene duplication resulting in ultra-rapid metabolism of tramadol to its active metabolite ODT. Moreover, concomitant renal impairment resulting in decreased metabolite clearance further enhanced opioid toxicity in this patient. Other studies suggested that the alternative *N*-demethylation route of tramadol metabolism could prevent the accumulation of the parent drug in CYP2D6 PMs (Jackson, Tucker, Lennard, & Woods, 1986; Subrahmanyam, Renwick, Walters, Young, Price, et al., 2001).

Interestingly, Levo et al. (2003) demonstrated that the value of the metabolite ratio tramadol/*O*-desmethyltramadol is still highly correlated with the CYP2D6 genotype in postmortem blood samples, the value of this metabolic ratio decreasing as the number of functional alleles increases (Levo, Koski, Ojanperä, Vuori, & Sajantila, 2003). This observation confirms that analysis of genetic variation of DMEs using postmortem blood is both feasible and relevant for the evaluation of adverse drug effects.

Oxycodone

Oxycodone (14-hydroxy-7,8-dihydrocodeinone) is a semi-synthetic opioid agonist frequently prescribed for the relief of moderate to severe pain. Like codeine, oxycodone is *O*-demethylated by CYP2D6, the resulting active metabolite being oxymorphone (Tyndale, Droll, & Sellers, 1997). Jannetto et al. (2002) showed that the abuse of oxycodone can result in toxicity in case of CYP2D6 metabolism deficiency. Accordingly, the author stated that postmortem drug concentrations of oxycodone should be interpreted in conjunction with the medical history, death scene investigation, autopsy findings, and postmortem interval as well as pharmacogenetics. Because CYP2D6 is highly polymorphic, the optimization of pain management therapy with oxycodone may be enhanced by genotyping patients. Patients with a CYP2D6 deficiency would require dose reduction or be placed on an alternative drug not metabolized by CYP2D6 (Linder & Valdes, 1999).

Methadone

Methadone is a synthetic opioid used medically as a chronic-pain-alleviating drug and as a maintenance anti-addictive drug in heroin addiction. Methadone has been implicated in numerous fatal poisoning cases over the past decade. Interindividual variation in the pharmacokinetics and pharmacodynamics of methadone can be explained by polymorphisms in genes encoding methadone-metabolizing enzymes, transporter proteins, and μ-opioid receptors (Li, Kantelip, Gerritsen-van Schieveen, & Davani, 2008; Bunten, Liang, Pounder, Seneviratne, & Osselton, 2010). CYP1A2, CYP2D6, CYP3A4, and CYP2B6 have been identified as the main P450 isoforms involved in methadone metabolism, all exhibiting genetic polymorphisms. Methadone is also a P-gp substrate and, consequently, P-gp genetic polymorphisms can contribute to the interindividual variability of methadone kinetics and influence dose requirements. To avoid methadone overdose and consequent fatality, clinicians must be aware of the pharmacokinetic properties and pharmacological interactions of methadone to personalize methadone administration (Li, Kantelip, Gerritsen-van Schieveen, & Davani, 2008).

Wong et al. (2003) reported that methadone toxicity may be partially due to *CYP2D6*3*, **4*, and **5* variant alleles, that result in poor drug metabolism (Wong, Wagner, Jentzen, Schur, Bjerke, et al., 2003). A retrospective analysis was performed on co-variables and risk factors of 21 methadone overdose cases from the Milwaukee County Medical Examiner's Office (1998–2000). Wong et al. (2003) showed that this limited number of cases had a higher prevalence of CYP2D6 PMs, but not significantly different from that of a control group, suggesting that pharmacogenetics, in this particular patient sample at least, is insufficient to explain methadone toxicity. A more conclusive explanation is that *CYP2D6* polymorphism has a minor or absent impact on methadone pharmacokinetics/dynamics and, accordingly, it is now recognized and well established that CYP2B6 genetic polymorphism is the major source of methadone toxicity (Kupiec, Raj, & Vu, 2006). Methadone metabolism by CYP2B6 is stereoselective toward (S)-methadone, a potentially highly toxic enantiomer due to its cardiac potassium channel inhibition property (Eap, Crettol, Rougier, Schläpfer, & Sintra Grilo, 2007). As a consequence, CYP2B6 PMs present a higher risk than CYP2B6 EMs of increased (S)-methadone plasma concentration with a greater risk of severe cardiac side effects and death (Eap, Crettol, Rougier, Schläpfer, & Sintra Grilo, 2007).

Psychotropic Agents

Psychotropic drugs are frequently involved in drug-related suicides and suicide attempts (Lardeur, Compain, Baudier, & Baudier, 2001). Numerous survey studies worldwide have reported a significant contribution of antidepressants and antipsychotics in drug-related deaths (Jönsson, Holmgren, & Ahlner, 2000; Flanagan, 2008; Bjornaas, Teige, Hovda, Ekeberg, Heyerdahl, et al., 2010). Several genetic polymorphisms affecting DMEs, neurotransmitter receptors, and monoamine transporters have been identified and recognized as major determinants of interindividual variability of psychotropic drug response and toxicity (Vandel, Talon, Haffen, & Sechter, 2007). Among these pharmacogenetic factors, P450 genes play a major role since they are involved in the metabolism of most psychotropics (Schosser & Kasper, 2009). Regarding antidepressants and antipsychotics, dosing of 50–60% of the drugs used is dependent, to a large extent, on the CYP2D6 and CYP2C19 enzymes (van der Weide & Hinrichs, 2006). For these reasons, CYP2D6 and CYP2C19 genotyping tests have been one of the first pharmacogenetic tests to be included in clinical guidelines available for psychiatrists (de Leon, Armstrong, & Cozza, 2006).

Tricyclic Antidepressants

Tricyclic antidepressant overdose can be lethal due to severe cardiotoxicity. The tricyclic antidepressants amitriptyline and nortriptyline are metabolized by several cytochromes P450. The isozyme CYP2C19 is of major importance in *N*-demethylation of these drugs, whereas CYP2D6 has been shown to participate in trans-hydroxylation of the benzylic C-10 in both amitriptyline and nortriptyline (Breyer-Pfaff, Pfandl, Nill, Nusser, Monney, et al., 1992; Olesen & Linnet, 1997; Venkatakrishnan, Greenblatt, von Moltke, Schmider, Harmatz, et al., 1998; Shimoda, Someya, Yokono, Morita, Hirokane, et al., 2002). Both amitriptyline and nortriptyline show large interindividual metabolic variations due to genetic polymorphisms of the enzymes involved in their biotransformation (Brosen, 2004; Grasmäder, Verwohlt, Rietschel, Dragicevic, Müller, et al., 2004; van der Weide, van Baalen-Benedeck, & Kootstra-Ros, 2005; Thieme, Rolf, Sachs, & Schmid, 2008). Koski et al. (2006) studied a series of 202 postmortem toxicological cases and performed genotyping of CYP2D6 and CYP2C19, as well as blood determination of amitriptyline and metabolite concentrations (Koski, Sistonen, Ojanperä, Gergov, Vuori, et al., 2006). CYP2D6 and CYP2C19 genotypes were shown to be correlated with amitriptyline metabolite patterns in postmortem materials, with amitriptyline metabolism being more dependent on CYP2D6 than on CYP2C19 genotype. Furthermore, the authors reported an unusually high peripheral blood concentration of amitriptyline in one suicidal case with a CYP2D6 PM genotype. Doxepin is another psychotropic agent with tricyclic antidepressant and anxiolytic properties. Koski et al. (2007) reported a case of fatal doxepin poisoning coinciding with a CYP2D6 PM phenotype due to a completely nonfunctional CYP2D6 genotype (Koski, Ojanperä, Sistonen, Vuori, & Sajantila, 2007).

Selective Serotonin Reuptake Inhibitors

The selective serotonin reuptake inhibitors (SSRIs), fluoxetine, fluvoxamine, paroxetine, sertraline, and citalopram, have similar antidepressant efficacy and side effect profile. They are extensively metabolized by P450s and some of them are potent P450 inhibitors, with subsequent high interindividual variability in pharmacokinetic properties (Hiemke & Härtter, 2000; Charlier, Broly, Lhermitte, Pinto, Ansseau, et al., 2003).

Fluoxetine (Prozac®) is approved for the treatment of major depression (including pediatric depression), obsessive-compulsive disorder (in both adult and pediatric populations), bulimia nervosa, panic disorder, and premenstrual dysphoric disorder. In 2000, Sallee et al. described the first report of a fluoxetine-related death in a child with a confirmed genetic polymorphism of the CYP2D6 gene that results in impaired drug metabolism (Sallee, DeVane, & Ferrell, 2000). The 9-year-old boy was diagnosed with attention-deficit hyperactivity disorder, obsessive-compulsive disorder, and Tourette's disorder and was treated with a combination of methylphenidate, clonidine, and fluoxetine. Signs and symptoms suggestive of metabolic toxicity marked by bouts of gastrointestinal distress, low-grade fever, incoordination, and disorientation were observed over a 10-month period. He went into status epilepticus followed by cardiac arrest and subsequently expired. At autopsy, blood, brain, and other tissue concentrations of fluoxetine were several-fold higher than expected based on literature reports for overdose situations. The death was caused by fluoxetine toxicity. As the child's adoptive parents controlled medication access, they were suspected and investigated by social welfare agencies and their other adoptive children were taken away from home. Further genetic testing of autopsy tissue revealed the presence of a completely defective CYP2D6 genotype, which results in poor metabolism of fluoxetine. Finally, the criminal proceedings of the adoptive parents were quashed (Sallee, DeVane, & Ferrell, 2000).

Example of Drug-Drug Interaction with Antiretrovirals

Drug-drug interactions also play a role in toxicological outcomes associated with genetic polymorphisms. Interactions between P450 enzymes and, in general, between any DMEs, are relevant only among extensive metabolizers, as the PM phenotype do not produce an active enzyme at all. One study examined the use of *CYP2D6* genotyping on postmortem blood samples as a supplementary tool for the interpretation of forensic toxicology data in cases with high metabolic ratios. This study concluded that the PM phenotype was not very frequent and that drug-drug interaction in EMs constituted a more frequent and important finding (Druid, Holmgren, Carlsson, & Ahlner, 1999).

In 2002, Antoniou evoked the influence and the interaction between recreational drugs and antiretroviral agents. Indeed, all protease inhibitors and nonnucleoside reverse transcriptase inhibitors are substrates and potent inhibitors or inducers of the cytochrome P450 system. Many classes of recreational drugs, including benzodiazepines, amphetamines, and opioids, are also metabolized by the liver and can potentially interact with antiretrovirals. Overdoses secondary to interactions between the "rave" drugs methylenedioxymethamphetamine (MDMA) or gamma-hydroxybutyrate (GHB) and protease inhibitors have been reported. Protease inhibitors, particularly ritonavir, may also inhibit metabolism of amphetamines, ketamine, lysergic acid diethylmide (LSD), and phencyclidine (PCP). Some pharmacokinetic studies suggest that nevirapine and efavirenz induce methadone metabolism, which may lead to symptoms of opiate withdrawal. A similar interaction may exist between methadone and the protease inhibitors ritonavir and nelfinavir.

Opiate metabolism can be inhibited or induced by concomitant protease inhibitors, and patients should be monitored for signs of toxicity and/or loss of analgesia. Protease inhibitors should not be coadministered with midazolam and triazolam, since prolonged sedation may occur (Antoniou & Tseng, 2002).

Conclusion

The interpretation of toxicological data is often difficult in forensic toxicology even though drug toxicity levels may be well defined. It is important for the forensic pathologist and for the forensic toxicologist to define as accurately as possible the cause and manner of death, taking into account numerous elements such as autopsy findings, medical history, and crime scene investigation for the forensic pathologist and, for the forensic toxicologist, co-variables that can affect the identified drug(s) pharmacokinetics and pharmacodynamics. All these variables are compared and juxtaposed to provide the best diagnosis. In certain cases, pharmacogenetics can play an important role in the diagnosis, particularly if, for example, a poor metabolizer phenotype for the detected drug(s) is identified, leading to the accumulation of toxic levels. Thus, pharmacogenetic factors should be considered in the interpretation of postmortem drug levels and can be an important new tool in the determination of the cause and manner of death.

For this reason, Jannetto et al. (2002) proposed an algorithm for the best use of pharmacogenetic data in forensic toxicology (Jannetto, Wong, Gock, Laleli-Sahin, Schur, et al., 2002). Their model takes into account various co-variables such as acute or chronic toxicity, autopsy findings, site of sample collection, postmortem interval, concomitant drug use, case/medical history, death scene investigation, and intent. If the toxicologist finds, by a comprehensive drug screen, an elevated drug(s) or metabolite(s) concentration, the findings are compared with reference toxicological cases and additional co-variables, such as toxic drug concentration, high metabolic ratio, drug-drug interactions, and polymorphic drug metabolism, would need to be investigated. On occasion, the analysis of the above co-variables is insufficient to explain the cause of death, and it is possible that postmortem redistribution of the drug(s) may have caused the toxic levels. In such cases, it is necessary to perform drug analyses on different tissues and/or alternative blood sources, to clarify the cause and manner of death.

Bibliography

Allorge, D., M.A. Loriot. 2004. Pharmacogenetics or the promise of a personalized medicine: variability in drug metabolism and transport. *Ann Biol Clin* 62:499–511.

Antoniou, T., and Tseng, A.L. 2002. Interactions between recreational drugs and antiretroviral agents. *The Annals of Pharmacotherapy* 36(10):1598–1613.

Bjornaas, M.A., B. Teige, K.E. Hovda, O. Ekeberg, F. Heyerdahl, D. Jacobsen. 2010. Fatal poisonings in Oslo: a one-year observational study. *BMC Emerg Med* 10:13.

Breyer-Pfaff, U., B. Pfandl, K. Nill, E. Nusser, C. Monney, M. Jonzier-Perey, D. Baettig, P. Baumann. 1992. Enantioselective amitriptyline metabolism in patients phenotyped for two cytochrome P450 isozymes. *Clin Pharmacol Ther* 52(4):350–358.

Brosen, K. 2004. Some aspects of genetic polymorphism in the biotransformation of antidepressants. *Therapie* 59:5–12.

Bunten, H., W.J. Liang, D.J. Pounder, C. Seneviratne, D. Osselton. 2010. OPRM1 and CYP2B6 gene variants as risk factors in methadone-related deaths. *Clin Pharmacol Ther* 88(3):383–389.

Butzbach, D.M. 2010. The influence of putrefaction and sample storage on post-mortem toxicology results. *Forensic Sci Med Pathol* 6(1):35–45.

Charlier, C., F. Broly, M. Lhermitte, E. Pinto, M. Ansseau, G. Plomteux. 2003. Polymorphisms in the CYP 2D6 gene: association with plasma concentrations of fluoxetine and paroxetine. *Ther Drug Monit* 25(6):738–742.

Cunliffe, M. 2001. Codeine phosphate in children: time for re-evaluation? *Br J Anaesth* 86:329–331.

Daly, A.K. 2004. Development of analytical technology in pharmacogenetic research. *Naunyn Schmiedebergs Arch Pharmacol* 369(1):133–40.

de Leon, J., S.C. Armstrong, K.L. Cozza. 2006. Clinical guidelines for psychiatrists for the use of pharmacogenetic testing for CYP450 2D6 and CYP450 2C19. *Psychosomatics* 47(1):75–85.

Desmeules, J., M.P. Gascon, P. Dayer, M. Magistris. 1991. Impact of environmental and genetic factors on codeine analgesia. *Eur J Clin Pharmacol* 41(1):23–26.

Druid, H., P. Holmgren, B. Carlsson, J. Ahlner. 1999. Cytochrome P450 2D6 (CYP2D6) genotyping on post-mortem blood as a supplementary tool for interpretation of forensic toxicological results. *Forensic Sci Int* 99(1):25–34.

Drummer, O.H. 2010. Forensic Toxicology. *EXS* 100:579–603.

Eap, C.B., S. Crettol, J.S. Rougier, J. Schläpfer, L. Sintra Grilo, J.J. Déglon, J. Besson, M. Croquette-Kroka, P.A. Carrupt, H. Abriel. 2007. Stereoselective block of hERG channel by (S)-methadone and QT interval prolongation in CYP2B6 slow metabolizers. *Clin Pharmacol Ther* 81(5):719–728.

Eichelbaum, M., M. Ingelman-Sundberg, W.E. Evans. 2006. Pharmacogenomics and individualized drug therapy. *Annu Rev Med* 57:119–137.

Evans, W.E., M.V. Relling. 1999. Pharmacogenomics: translating functional genomics into rational therapeutics. *Science* 286(5439):487–491.

Ferreiros, N., S. Dresen, M. Hermanns-Clausen, V. Auwaerter, A. Thierauf, C. Müller, R. Hentschel, R. Trittler, G. Skopp, W. Weinmann. 2009. Fatal and severe codeine intoxication in 3-year-old twins-interpretation of drug and metabolite concentrations. *Int J Legal Med* 123(5):387–394.

Ferrer-Dufol A., S. Menao-Guillen. 2009. Toxicogenomics and clinical toxicology: an example of the connection between basic and applied sciences. *Toxicology Letters* 186:2–8.

Flanagan, R.J. 2008. Fatal toxicity of drugs used in psychiatry. *Hum Psychopharmacol* 23 Suppl 1: 43–51.

Ford, L.T., J.D. Berg. 2010. Thiopurine S-methyltransferase (TPMT) assessment prior to starting thiopurine drug treatment: a pharmacogenomic test whose time has come. *J Clin Pathol* 63(4):288–295.

Frueh, F.W., S. Amur, P. Mummaneni, R.S. Epstein, R.E. Aubert, T.M. DeLuca, R.R. Verbrugge, G.J. Burckart, L.J. Lesko. 2008. Pharmacogenomic biomarker information in drug labels approved by the United States food and drug administration: prevalence of related drug use. *Pharmacotherapy* 28(8):992–998.

Gasche, Y., Y. Daali, M. Fathi, A. Chiappe, S. Cottini, P. Dayer, J. Desmeules. 2004. Codeine intoxication associated with ultrarapid CYP2D6 metabolism. *N Engl J Med* 351(27):2827–2831.

Gilliland, M.G.F., R.O. Bost. 1993. Alcohol in decomposed bodies: post-mortem synthesis and distribution. *J.F.S.C.A.* 38:1266–1274.

Gonzalez, F.J., R.C. Skoda, S. Kimura, M. Umeno, U.M. Zanger, D.W. Nebert, H.V. Gelboin, J.P. Hardwick, U.A. Meyer. 1988. Characterization of the common genetic defect in humans deficient in debrisoquine metabolism. *Nature* 331(6155):442–446.

Grasmäder, K., P.L. Verwohlt, M. Rietschel, A. Dragicevic, M. Müller, C. Hiemke, N. Freymann, A. Zobel, W. Maier, M.L. Rao. 2004. Impact of polymorphisms of cytochrome-P450 isoenzymes 2C9, 2C19, and 2D6 on plasma concentrations and clinical effects of antidepressants in a naturalistic clinical setting. *Eur J Clin Pharmacol* 60:329–336.

Guengerich, F.P. 1990. Mechanism-based inactivation of human liver microsomal cytochrome P450IIIA4 by gestodene. *Chem. Res Toxicol* 3:363–371.

Grond, S., A. Sablotzki. 2004. Clinical pharmacology of tramadol. *Clin Pharmacokinet* 43(13): 879–923.

Hakooz, N.M. 2009. Caffeine metabolic ratios for the in vivo evaluation of CYP1A2, N-acetyltransferase 2, xanthine oxidase, and CYP2A6 enzymatic activities. *Curr Drug Metab* 10(4):329–338.

Helland, A., C.V. Isaksen, L. Slørdal. 2010. Death of a 10-month-old boy after exposure to ethylmorphine. *J Forensic Sci* 55(2):551–553.

Hiemke, C., S. Härtter. 2000. Pharmacokinetics of selective serotonin reuptake inhibitors. *Pharmacol Ther* 85(1):11–28.

Higgs, J.E., K. Payne, C. Roberts, W.G. Newman. 2010. Are patients with intermediate TPMT activity at increased risk of myelosuppression when taking thiopurine medications? *Pharmacogenomics* 11(2):177–188.

Ingelman-Sundberg, M., I. Johansson, M.L. Dahl, L. Bertilsson, Y.Q. Yue, F. Sjöqvist. 1992. Genotyping predicts the phenotype for drug metabolism. *Läkartidningen* 89(19):1675–1678.

Ingelmann-Sundberg, M., A.K. Daly, M. Oscarson, D.W. Nebert. 2000. Human cytochrome P450 (CYP) genes: recommendations for the nomenclature alleles. *Pharmacogenetics* 10:91–93.

Ingelman-Sundberg, M. and W.E. Evans. 2001. Unravelling the functional genomics of the human CYP2D6 gene locus. *Pharmacogenetics* 11:553–554.

Ingelman-Sundberg, M. and C. Rodriguez-Antona. 2005. Pharmacogenetics of drug-metabolizing enzymes: implications for a safer and more effective drug therapy. *Philos Trans R Soc Lond B Biol Sci* 360(1460):1563–1570.

Ingelman-Sundberg, M., S.C. Sim, A. Gomez, C. Rodriguez-Antona. 2007. Influence of cytochrome P450 polymorphisms on drug therapies: pharmacogenetic, pharmacoepigenetic and clinical aspects. *Pharmacol Ther* 116(3):496–526.

Jackson, P.R., G.T. Tucker, M.S. Lennard, H.F. Woods. 1986. Polymorphic drug oxidation: pharmacokinetic basis and comparison of experimental indices. *Br J Clin Pharmacol* 22(5):541–550.

Jain, K.K. 2005. Applications of AmpliChip CYP450. *Mol Diagn* 9(3):119–127.

Jannetto, P.J., S.H. Wong, S.B. Gock, E. Laleli-Sahin, B.C. Schur, J.M. Jentzen. 2002. Pharmacogenomics as molecular autopsy for post-mortem forensic toxicology: genotyping cytochrome P450 2D6 for oxycodone cases. *J Anal Toxicol* 26(7):438–447.

Johansson, I., E. Lundqvist, L. Bertilsson, M.L. Dahl, F. Sjöqvist, M. Ingelman-Sundberg. 1993. Inherited amplification of an active gene in the cytochrome P450 CYP2D locus as a cause of ultrarapid metabolism of debrisoquine. *PNAS USA* 90(24):11825–11829.

Jönsson, A., P. Holmgren, J. Ahlner. 2000. Fatal intoxications in a Swedish forensic autopsy material during 1992-2002. *Forensic Sci Int* 143(1):53–59.

Kalow, W. 1998. Pharmacogenetics in perspective. *Drug Metabol and Dispos* 29(4):468–470.

Kim, D.K., S.W. Lim, S. Lee, S.E. Sohn, S. Kim, C.G. Hahn, BJ Carroll. 2000. Serotonin transporter gene polymorphism and antidepressant response. *NeuroReport* 11(1):215–219.

Kirchheiner, J., J. Brockmöller. 2005. Clinical consequences of cytochrome P450 2C9 polymorphisms. *Clin Pharmacol Ther* 77(1):1–16.

Koren, G., J. Cairns, D. Chitayat, A. Gaedigk, S.J. Leeder. 2006. Pharmacogenetics of morphine poisoning in a breastfed neonate of a codeine-prescribed mother. *Lancet* 368:704.

Koski, A., J. Sistonen, I. Ojanperä, M. Gergov, E. Vuori, A. Sajantila. 2006. CYP2D6 and CYP2C19 genotypes and amitriptyline metabolite ratios in a series of medicolegal autopsies. *Forensic Sci Int* 158:177–183.

Koski, A., I. Ojanperä, J. Sistonen, E. Vuori, Sajantila A. 2007. A fatal doxepin poisoning associated with a defective CYP2D6 genotype. *Am J Forensic Med Pathol* 28(3):259–261.

Krynetski, E., W.E. Evans. 2003. Drug methylation in cancer therapy: lessons from the TPMT polymorphism. *Oncogene* 22(47):7403–7413.

Kupiec, T.C., V. Raj, N. Vu. 2006. Pharmacogenomics for the forensic toxicologist. *Journal Anal Toxicology* 30:65–72.

Kwok, P.Y., X. Chen. 2003. Detection of single nucleotide polymorphisms. *Curr Issues Mol Biol* 5(2):43–60.

Lardeur, J.Y., C. Compain, B. Baudier, A. Baudier. 2001. Management of self poisoning at an emergency medical center. *Presse Med* 30(13):626–630.

Lazarou, J., B. Pomeranz, P. Corey. 1998. Incidence of adverse drug reactions in hospitalized patients: a meta-analysis of prospective studies. *J Am Med Assoc* 279:1200–1205.

Leinonen E., H.J. Koponen, U. Lepola. 2004. Paroxetine increases serum trimipramine concentration: a report of two cases. *Human Psychopharmacol Clin Exp* 10:345–347.

Levine, B. 2003. Principles in forensic toxicology. Second Edition 385 p. ed. Washington, DC AACC.

Levo, A., A. Koski, I. Ojanperä, E. Vuori, A. Sajantila. 2003. Post-mortem SNP analysis of CYP2D6 gene reveals correlation between genotype and opioid drug (tramadol) metabolite ratios in blood. *Forensic Sci Int* 135:9–15.

Li, Y., J.P. Kantelip, P. Gerritsen-van Schieveen, S. Davani. 2008. Interindividual variability of methadone response: impact of genetic polymorphism. *Mol Diagn Ther* 12(2):109–124.

Linder, M.W., R. Valdes Jr. 1999. Pharmacogenetics in the practice of laboratory medicine. *Mol Diagn* 4:365–379.

Liu, Y.T., H.P. Hao, C.X. Liu, G.J. Wang, H.G. Xie. 2007. Drugs as CYP3A probes, inducers, and inhibitors. *Drug Metab Rev* 39(4):699–671.

Madadi, P., G. Koren, J. Cairns, D. Chitayat, A. Gaedigk, J.S. Leeder, R. Teitelbaum, T. Karaskov, K. Aleksa. 2007. Safety of codeine during breastfeeding: fatal morphine poisoning in the breastfed neonate of a mother prescribed codeine. *Can Fam Physician* 53:33–35.

Madadi, P., C.J. Ross, M.R. Hayden, B.C. Carleton, A. Gaedigk, J.S. Leeder, G. Koren. 2009. Pharmacogenetics of neonatal opioid toxicity following maternal use of codeine during breastfeeding: a case-control study. *Clin Pharmacol Ther* 85(1):31–35.

Manchikanti, L., A. Singh. 2008. Therapeutic opioids: a ten-year perspective on the complexities and complications of the escalating use, abuse, and nonmedical use of opioids. *Pain Physician* 11(2Suppl):63–88.

Manolopoulos, V.G. 2007. Pharmacogenomics and adverse drug reactions in diagnostic and clinical practice. *Clin Chem Lab Med* 45(7):801–814.

Meijerman, I., L.M. Sanderson, P.H. Smits, J.H. Beijnen, J.H. Schellens. 2007. Pharmacogenetic screening of the gene deletion and duplications of CYP2D6. *Drug Metab Rev* 39(1):45–60.

Modesto-Lowe, V., D. Brooks, N. Petry. 2010. Methadone deaths: risk factors in pain and addicted populations. *J Gen Int Med* 25(4):305–309.

Moffat, A.C., M.D. Osselton, B. Widdop. Clarke's Analysis of drugs and poisons. Third Edition. Pharmaceutical Press 2004.

Morgan, E., K. Goralski, M. Piquette-Miller, K. Renton, G. Robertson, M. Chaluvadi, K. Charles, S.J. Clark, M. Kacevska, C. Liddle, T. Richardson, R. Sharma, C. Sinal. 2008. Regulation of drug-metabolizing enzymes and transporters in infection, inflammation, and cancer. *Drug Metab Dispos* 36(2):205–216.

Musshoff, F., P. Scmidt, B. Madea. 1999. Fatality caused by a combined trimipramine-citalopram intoxication. *Forensic Science International* 106:125–131.

Nakata, K., Y. Tanaka, T. Nakano, T. Adachi, H. Tanaka, T. Kaminuma, T. Ishikawa. 2006. Nuclear receptor-mediated transcriptional regulation in Phase I, II, and III xenobiotic metabolizing systems. *Drug Metab Pharmacokinet* 21(6):437–457.

Nekvindova, J., P. Anzenbacher. 2007. Interactions of food and dietary supplements with drug metabolising cytochrome P450 enzymes. *Ceska Slov Farm* 56(4):165–173.

Nicolas, J.M., P. Espie, M. Molimard. 2009. Gender and interindividual variability in pharmacokinetics. *Drug Metab Rev* 41(3):408–421.

Olesen, O.V. and K. Linnet. 1997. Metabolism of the tricyclic antidepressant amitriptyline by cDNA-expressed human cytochrome P450 enzymes. *Pharmacology* 55(5):235–243.

O'Neal, C.L., A. Poklis. 1996. Postmortem production of ethanol and factors that influence interpretation: a critical review. *Am J Forensic Med Pathol* 17:8–20.

Pélissier-Alicot, A.L., J.M. Gaulier, P. Champsaur, P. Marquet. 2003. Mechanisms underlying postmortem redistribution of drugs: a review. *J Anal Toxicol* 27(8):533–544.

Pélissier-Alicot, A.L., M. Fornaris, C. Bartoli, M.D. Piercecchi-Marti, A. Sanvoisin, G. Leonetti. 2005. An unusual case of post-mortem redistribution of ethanol. *Forensic Sci Int* 150:81–83.

Pélissier-Alicot, A.L., N. Coste, C. Bartoli, M.D. Piercecchi-Marti, A. Sanvoisin, J. Gouvernet, G. Leonetti. 2006. Comparison of ethanol concentrations in right cardiac blood, left cardiac blood, and peripheral blood in a series of 30 cases. *Forensic Sci Int* 156:35–39.

Philips, K.A., D.L. Veenstra, E. Oren, J.K. Lee, W. Sadee. 2001. Potential role of pharmacogenomics in reducing adverse drug reactions: a systematic review. *JAMA* 286(18):2270–2279.

Pounder, D.J., C. Fuke, D.E. Cox, D. Smith, N. Kuroda. 1996. Postmortem diffusion of drugs from gastric residue: an experimental study. *Am J Forensic Med Pathol* 17(1):1–7.

Pounder, D.J., E. Adams, C. Fuke, A.M. Langford. 1996. Site to site variability of post-mortem drug concentrations in liver and lung. *J Forensic Sci* 41(6):927–932.

Sachdeva, D.K, J.M. Stadnyk. 2005. Are one or two dangerous? Opioid exposure in toddlers. *J Emerg Med* 29(1):77–84.

Sallee, F.R., C.L. DeVane, R.E. Ferrell. 2000. Fluoxetine-related death in a child with cytochrome P-450 2D6 genetic deficiency. *J Child Adolesc Psychopharmacol* 10 (1):27–34.

Samer, C.F., Y. Daali, M. Wagner, G. Hopfgartner, C.B. Eap, M.C. Rebsamen, M.F. Rossier, D. Hochstrasser, P. Dayer, J.A. Desmeules. 2010. The effects of CYP2D6 and CYP3A activities on the pharmacokinetics of immediate release oxycodone. *Br J Pharmacol* 160(4):907–918.

Samer, C.F., Y. Daali, M. Wagner, G. Hopfgartner, C.B. Eap, M.C. Rebsamen, M.F. Rossier, D. Hochstrasser, P. Dayer, J.A. Desmeules. 2010. Genetic polymorphisms and drug interactions modulating CYP2D6 and CYP3A activities have a major effect on oxycodone analgesic efficacy and safety. *Br J Pharmacol* 160(4):919–930.

Schosser, A., S. Kasper. 2009. The role of pharmacogenetics in the treatment of depression and anxiety disorders. *Int Clin Psychopharmacol* 24(6):277–288.

Seifritz, E., E. Holsboer-trachsler, U. Hemmeter, C.B. Eap, P. Baumann. 1994. Increased trimipramine plasma levels during fluvoxamine comedication. *Eur. Neuropsychopharmacology* 4:15–20.

Shi, M.M. 2001. Enabling large-scale pharmacogenetic studies by high-throughput mutation detection and genotyping technologies. *Clin Chem* 47(2):164–172.

Shimoda, K., T. Someya, A. Yokono, S. Morita, G. Hirokane, S. Takahashi, M. Okawa. 2002. The impact of CYP2C19 and CYP2D6 genotypes on metabolism of amitriptyline in Japanese psychiatric patients. *J Clin Psychopharmacol* 22(4):371–378.

Smeraldi, E., R. Zanardi, F. Benedetti, D. Di Bella, J. Perez, M. Catalona. 1998. Polymorphism with the promoter of the serotonin transporter gene and antidepressant efficacy of fluvoxamine. *Mol Psychiatry* 3:508–511.

Somogyi, A.A., D.T. Barratt, J.K. Coller. 2007. Pharmacogenetics of opioids. *Clin Pharmacol Ther* 80(6):682–690.

Stamer U.M., F. Stüber, T. Muders, F. Musshoff. 2008. Respiratory depression with tramadol in a patient with renal impairment and CYP2D6 gene duplication. *Anesthesia Analgesia* 107(3):926–929.

Subrahmanyam, V., A.B. Renwick, D.G. Walters, P.J. Young, R.J. Price, A.P. Tonelli, B.G. Lake. 2001. Identification of cytochrome P-450 isoforms responsible for *cis*-tramadol metabolism in human liver microsomes. *Drug Metab Dispos* 29(8):1146–1155.

Thieme, D., B. Rolf, H. Sachs, D. Schmid. 2008. Correlation of inter-individual variations of amitriptyline metabolism examined in hairs with CYP2C19 and CYP2D6 polymorphisms. *Int J Leg Med* 122:149–155.

Tyndale, R.F., K.P. Droll, E.M. Sellers. 1997. Genetically deficient *CYP2D6* metabolism provides protection against oral opiate dependence. *Pharmacogenetics* 7(5):375–379.

Vandel, P., J.M. Talon, E. Haffen, D. Sechter. 2007. Pharmacogenetics and drug therapy in psychiatry—the role of the CYP2D6 polymorphism. *Curr Pharm Des* 13(2):241–250.

van der Weide, J., E.H. van Baalen-Benedeck, J.E. Kootstra-Ros. 2005. Metabolic ratios of psychotropics as indication of cytochrome P450 2D6/2C19 genotype. *Ther Drug Monit* 27:478–483.

van der Weide, J., J.W. Hinrichs. 2006. The influence of cytochrome P450 pharmacogenetics on disposition of common antidepressant and antipsychotic medications. *Clin Biochem Rev* 27(1):17–25.

Venkatakrishnan, K., D.J. Greenblatt, L.L. von Moltke, J. Schmider, J.S. Harmatz, R.I. Shader. 1998. Five distinct human cytochromes mediate amitriptyline N-demethylation in vitro: dominance of CYP 2C19 and 3A4. *J Clin Pharmacol* 38(2):112–121.

Voronov, P., H.J. Przybylo, N. Jagannathan. 2007. Apnea in a child after oral codeine: a genetic variant—an ultra-rapid metabolizer. *Pediatric Anesthesia* 17:684–687.

Weinshilboum, R.M., S.L. Sladek. 1980. Mercaptopurine pharmacogenetics: monogenic inheritance of erythrocyte thiopurine methyltransferase activity. *Am J Hum Genet* 32:651–662.

Weinshilboum, R. 2001. Thiopurine pharmacogenetics: clinical and molecular studies of thiopurine methyltransferase. *Drug Metab Dispos* 29(4):601–605.

Williams, D.G., D.J. Hatch, R.F. Howard. 2001. Codeine phosphate in paediatric medicine. *Br J Anesth* 86:413–421.

Williams, D.G., A. Patel, R.F. Howard. 2002. Pharmacogenetics of codeine metabolism in an urban population of children and its implications for analgesic reliability. *Br J Anesth* 89:839–845.

Willmann, S., A.N. Edginton, K. Coboeken, G. Ahr, J. Lippert. 2009. Risk to the breast-fed neonate from codeine treatment to the mother: a quantitative mechanistic modeling study. *Clin Pharmacol Ther* 86(6):634–643.

Winter, J., A. Walker, D. Shapiro, D. Gaffney, R.J. Spooner, P.R. Mills. 2004. Cost-effectiveness of thiopurine methyltransferase genotype screening in patients about to commence azathioprine therapy for treatment of inflammatory bowel disease. *Aliment Pharmacol Ther* 20:593–599.

Wong, S.H.Y., M.A. Wagner, J.M. Jentzen, C. Schur, J. Bjerke, S.B. Gock, C.J. Chang. 2003. Pharmacogenomics as an adjunct of molecular autopsy for forensic pathology/toxicology: does genotyping CYP 2D6 serve as an adjunct for certifying methadone toxicology. *J Forensic Sci* 48:1406–1415.

Xu, C., C.Y. Li, A.N. Kong. 2005. Induction of phase I, II, and III drug metabolism/transport by xenobiotics. *Arch Pharm Res* 28(3):249–268.

Zanger, U.M., M. Turpeinen, K. Klein, M. Schwab. 2008. Functional pharmacogenetics/genomics of human cytochromes P450 involved in drug biotransformation. *Anal Bioanal Chem* 392(6):1093–1108.

Virtual Autopsy
Modern Cross-Sectional Imaging

8

FABRICE DEDOUIT, MARIE FARUCH, NORBERT TELMON, PHILIPPE OTAL, HERVÉ ROUSSEAU, FRANCIS JOFFRE, AND DANIEL ROUGÉ

Contents

Introduction

The word *autopsy* is of ancient Greek origin, being the combination of *autos* (self) and *opsomei* (see) and can be translated as "a seeing for oneself" (Di Maio and Di Maio 2001; Knight et al. 2004). In forensic imaging literature, nowadays most authors use the term *virtopsy*, a combination of virtual and autopsy (Thali et al. 2003e, 2009). Medicolegal autopsy has many aims: reconstitution of the events and circumstances that preceded and led to death, including premortem diseases, determination of cause of death, its judicial classification (homicide, suicide, natural death), precise time of death, and identification of the deceased (Knight et al. 2004).

Autopsy techniques have been aided and improved by new advances in pathology, molecular biology, toxicology, and imaging. However, autopsy may be limited for demonstration of intra- or extravascular gas and some skeletal lesions (Thali et al. 2009). Some diagnoses can indeed be made but may require specific technical protocols that can sometimes be difficult to apply. This is the case for example for demonstration of intra- or extravascular gas (such as pneumothorax, pneumomediastinum, rupture of emphysematous bullae, gaseous embolism, pneumoperitoneum), various skeletal trauma (cervical spine fractures, such as transverse or spinous process fractures or pedicular fractures), complex and multiple fractures of the face or limbs, bone marrow injuries, and ballistic wounds in putrefied or carbonized corpses (Di Maio and Di Maio 2001; Thali et al. 2009). The performance of autopsy may also be restricted for religious or cultural reasons.

For a long time, radiology in routine forensic medicine was limited to plain x-rays, which converted the original three-dimensional data into two-dimensional data; this has always been a problem (Brogdon 1998). Thanks to the advent in 1988 of clinical multislice computed tomography (MSCT), for the first time it was possible to obtain isotropic voxels, which are the basis of high-quality multiplanar reconstructions (Haaga et al. 2003). Although MSCT and magnetic resonance imaging are widely used in clinical medicine, the routine diffusion of these techniques in forensic medicine seems unfortunately to be limited on a worldwide scale (Brogdon 1998).

In this chapter we shall address only documentation of internal lesions, which can easily be performed in routine forensic radiology. We will deal first with the technical aspects of radiology and then with normal postmortem appearances. Aspects of postmortem pathology will be developed, including the value of postmortem imaging in deaths from specific causes and in sudden natural deaths. Finally, identification of individuals through postmortem imaging will be discussed.

Forensic Applications: Technical Aspects of Radiology

Overall, the virtual autopsy approach leads to increased quality and added value in the fields of forensic medicine and science. Basically, modern slice imaging techniques have two applications in forensic pathology: in **thanatology** and **anthropology** (Dedouit et al. 2007b, 2007c).

In thanatology, virtual autopsy contributes to the documentation of judicial evidence. The advantages of this technique are numerous: it enables objective data archiving, is nondestructive, yields actual-size documentation, provides three-dimensional information, is an additional examination tool, and can be transmitted by teleradiology and the Internet (Thali et al. 2009). The postmortem images obtained are of real value as evidence. Of course, virtual autopsy also has drawbacks, namely cost, limited tissue resolution, and lack of color visualization.

External Body Documentation

This requires particularly advanced technology combining MSCT, photogrammetry, and photography and enables photogrammetric 3D documentation (Figure 8.1) (Thali et al. 2003a, 2003b, 2003c). The technique is based on the fusion of body surface scan data and radiological data. Optical 3D surface scanning is also possible.

Internal Body Documentation

MSCT and MRI are currently used for this purpose.

MSCT

3D visualization of radiological MSCT data is possible for isotropic documentation, with no loss of spatial resolution (Haaga et al. 2003). Five main rendering techniques are used in reconstruction of CT data:

- Two-dimensional reconstructions by multiplanar reconstruction (MPR) are easily obtained not only for the orthogonal planes used in clinical radiology (axial, frontal, and sagittal), but also oblique and curved slices (Figure 8.2; Haaga et al. 2003).
- Three-dimensional reconstructions:
  - Maximum intensity projection (MIP) which corresponds to the evaluation of a volume by drawing a virtual light ray from the observer's eye through the data volume and selecting the voxel with the highest attenuation (Figure 8.3A). This voxel is then used as a displayed pixel of the rendered picture (Haaga et al. 2003).
  - Minimum intensity projection (MinIP) is quite similar to MIP, but the voxel with the least attenuation along a virtual light ray is visualized (Figure 8.3B; Haaga et al. 2003).
  - Shaded surface display (SSD): the drawback of this method is that the surface is derived from only a small percentage of the available data (Figure 8.4). This technique is not indicated for structures which do not

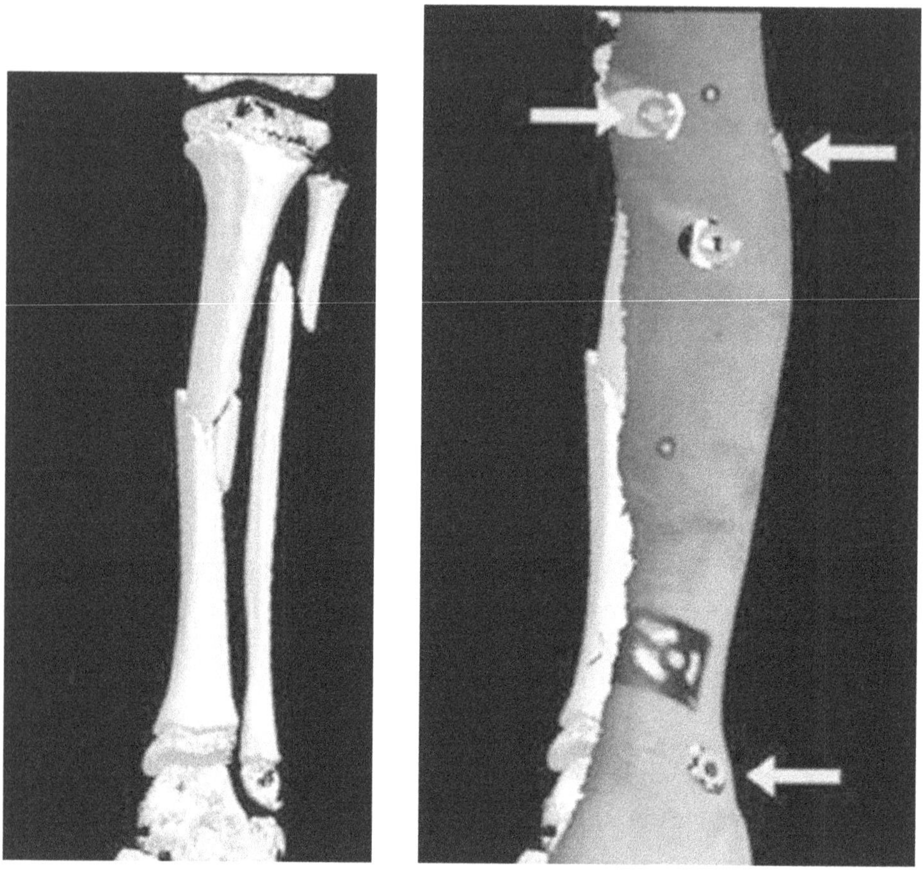

Figure 8.1 Examples of external body documentation: visualization of impact injuries of the left lower leg of a child. A. The wedge fracture of the tibia is clearly visible in the CT model. B. The colored surface model displays the impact injury (hematoma). For the fusion of surface data of the external injuries and CT data of the internal body, the surface model is transformed into the radiological coordinate system (multimodality markers (arrows) serve as reference targets). From Buck et al., 2007. Application of 3D documentation and geometric reconstruction methods in traffic accident analysis: With high resolution surface scanning, radiological MSCT/MRI scanning and real data based animation. *Forensic Sci Int* 170: 20–28, with permission.

have well-differentiated surfaces: subtle bony fissures will not be visible because of the smoothing artifacts of the extracted surface (Haaga et al. 2003).

- Volume-rendering technique (VRT) renders the whole volume and not only surfaces defined by threshold values (Figure 8.5; Haaga et al. 2003). VRT takes the entire volume data and sums the contribution of each voxel along a line from the viewer's eye through the 3D dataset. The resulting composite of each voxel is then displayed on the screen. With a 3D workstation, it is possible to modify opacity, brightness and color. Special uses for VRT are virtual bronchioscopy and colonoscopy, permitting endoscopic views inside air-filled body cavities.

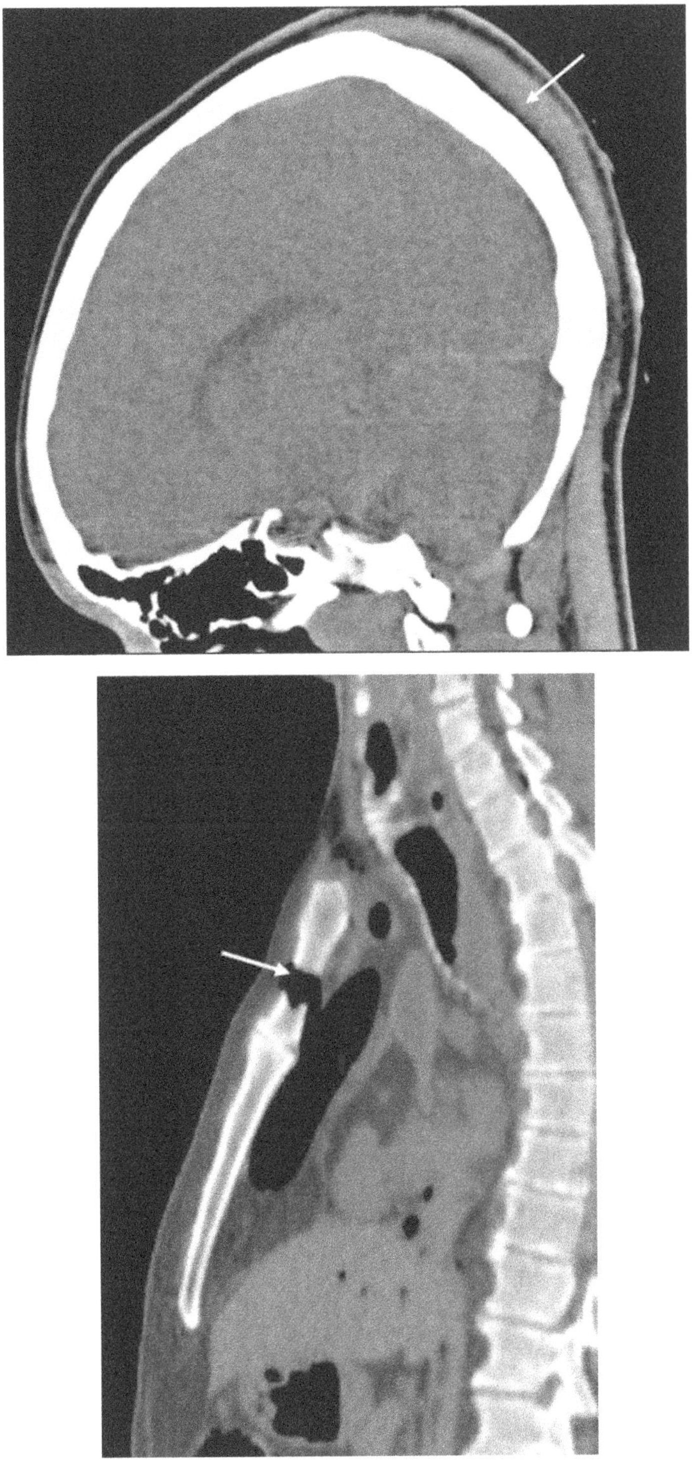

Figure 8.2 Examples of sagittal MPR reconstructions. Classically, MPR may be useful in clinical applications for examination of the spine. A. Head: large subcutaneous hematoma (arrow). B. Chest: sternal fracture (arrow).

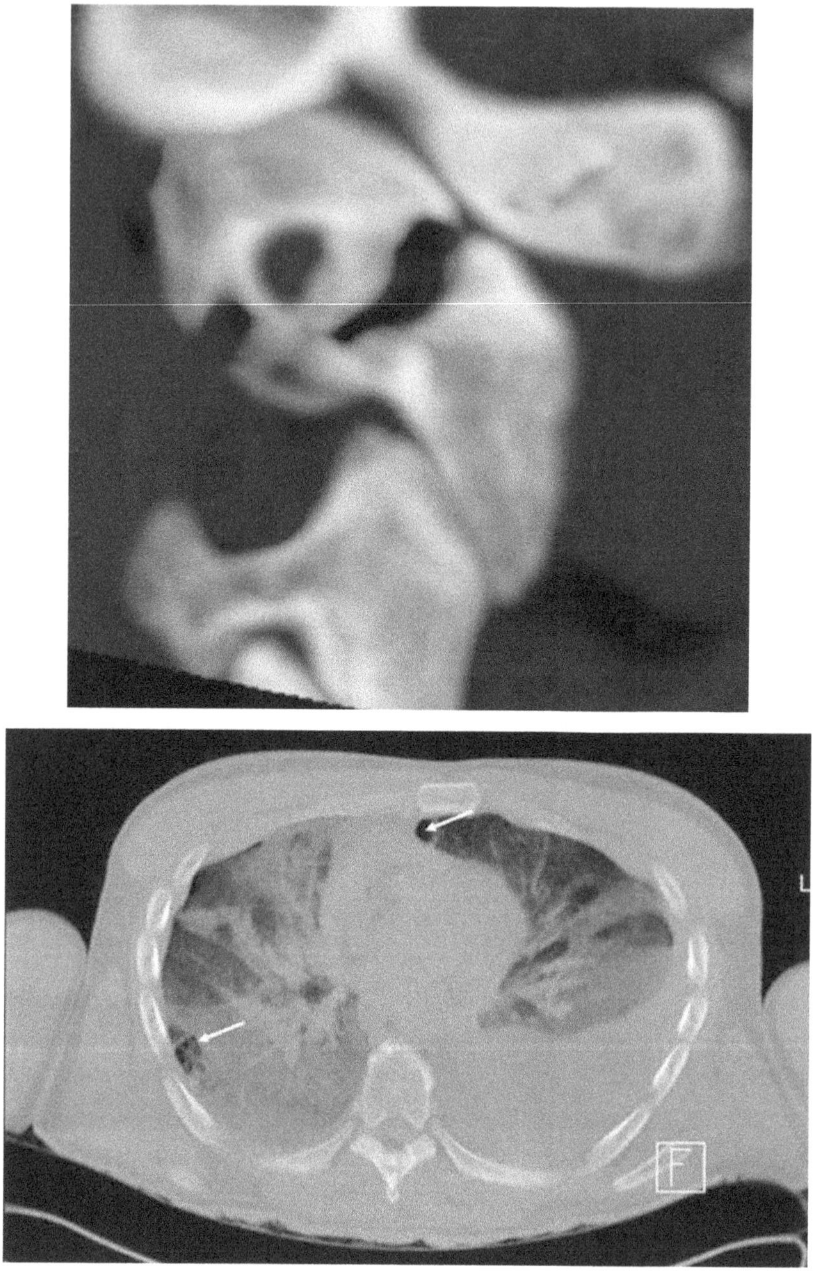

Figure 8.3 A. MIP is classically useful in clinical imaging for creation of angiographic pictures. Example of MIP image: lateral view of the cervical spine after a fall from a high height, showing a right pedicle fracture. B. MinIP is classically the clinical method of choice for visualizing very low x-ray attenuation such as air or other gases, pneumothorax, air embolism, lung injuries. Example of MIP image: lung axial CT image, left pleural effusion with bilateral pulmonary condensations accompanied with trapping areas (hypodense hyperaerated subpleural areas, arrows).

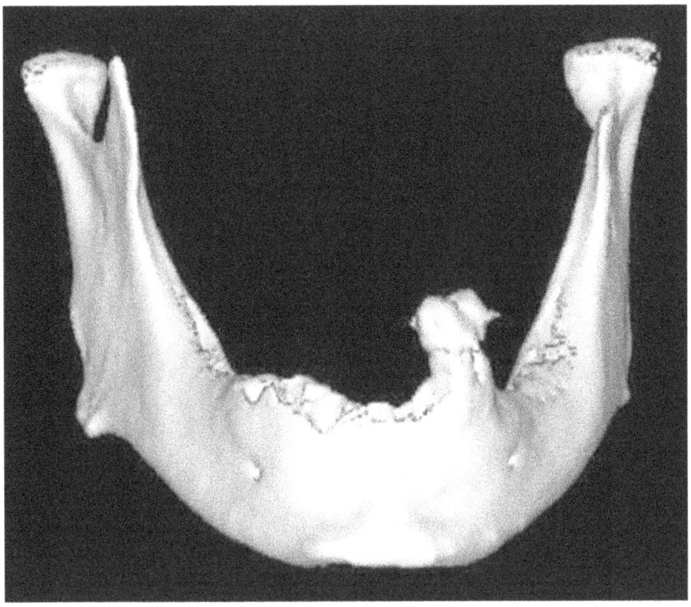

Figure 8.4 SSD mode of a human mandible. Although providing 3D information, the quality of the reconstructions is inferior to the VRT mode (see Figure 8.41B).

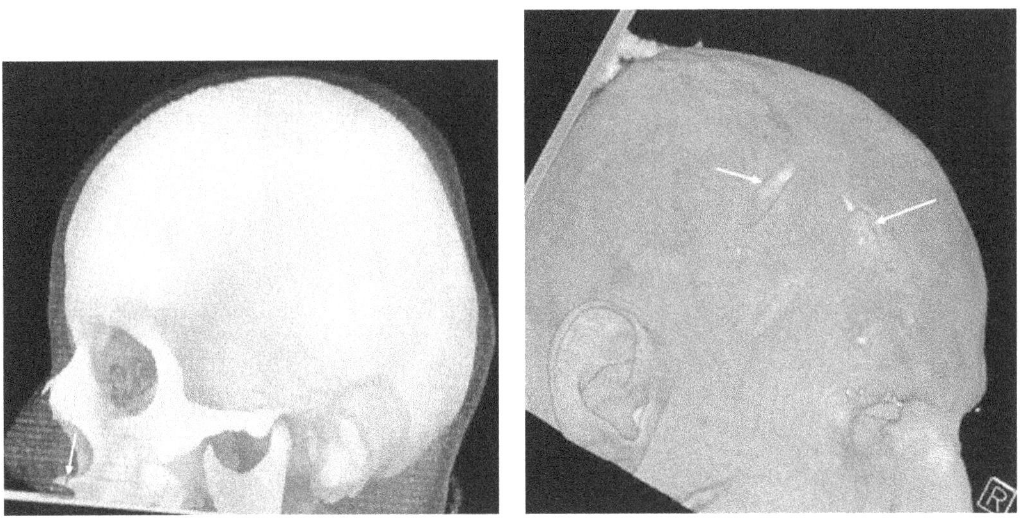

Figure 8.5 VRT mode is the most efficient method for three-dimensional documentation at the present time. A. Bone filter reconstruction: fracture of the anterior nasal spine (arrow). B. Soft tissue filter reconstruction: deep skin wounds of the cephalic extremity can be seen (arrows).

All these post-processing techniques need reconstruction workstations with advanced commodity graphics cards and a high memory capacity.

MRI

The temperature of the body influences the MR relaxation times of tissues (Doyon 2001). Consequently, T1-weighted sequences, T2-weighted sequences, and proton density sequences, which are the classical sequences used in clinical exploration, will not have the same appearance (Figure 8.6; Thali et al. 2009). However, intertissular contrast persists

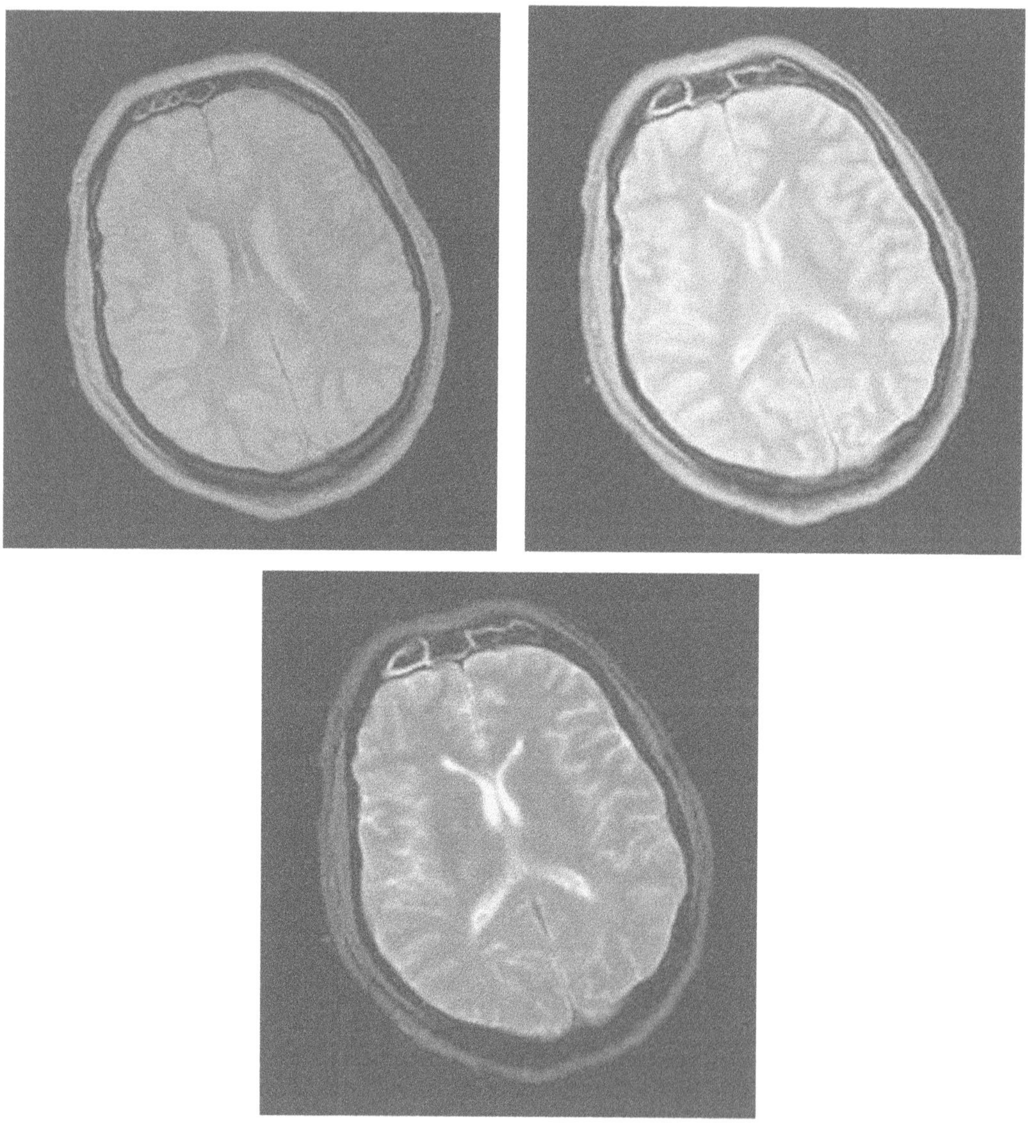

Figure 8.6 Postmortem MRI: normal appearance of the brain parenchyma. A. Axial MRI T1-weighted appearance. B. Axial MRI Proton density appearance. C. Axial MRI T2-weighted appearance.

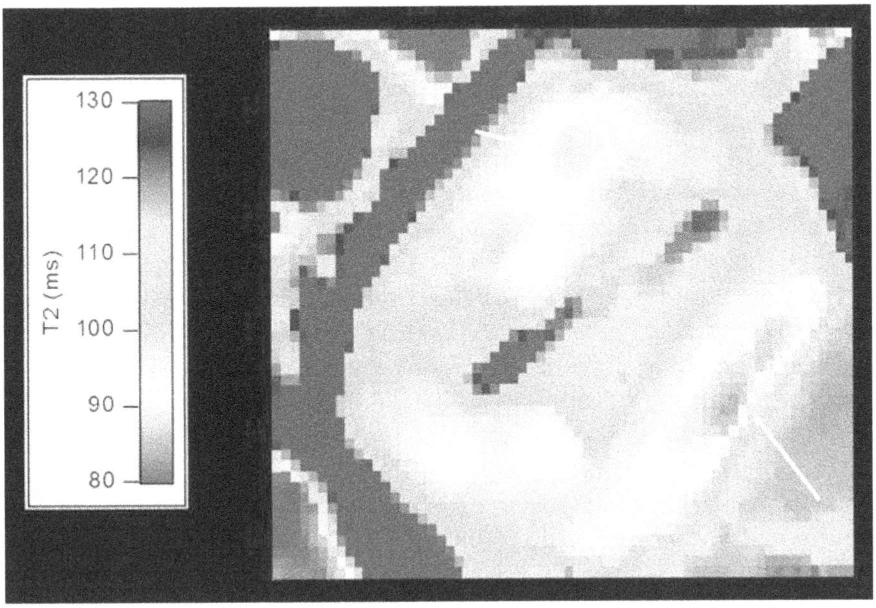

Figure 8.7 Quantitative MRI, T2-weighted image, porcine heart, short axial slice of the left ventricle: hypo-T2 signals within the myocardium secondary to myocardial infarction (arrows).

longer than on CT images. Some authors recommend use of MRI quantification methods but these are still not routinely applicable (Figure 8.7; Thali et al. 2009).

Early and Late Postmortem Changes

The **semiology** of postmortem imaging is calqued on that of clinical imaging, but has to take into account early postmortem changes that occur as soon as the person dies. In postmortem imaging, among the various early changes, the radiologist has to be familiar with livor mortis and postmortem tissue desiccation.

Livor mortis is the purple-red discoloration that results from the settling of blood to the dependent portions of the body. It begins to develop after the heart stops beating and becomes more intense with time, so that if livor is perceptible after 3 to 4 hours, it will be even more readily seen at 6 to 8 hours (Dix 2000; Di Maio and Di Maio 2001; Knight et al. 2004). Livor becomes fully developed after around 10 to 12 hours. Blood is pushed out of the areas of the body that are lying on the ground or on other objects, resulting in patches of contact pallor. Livor mortis by definition requires blood in the vascular tree and so it may be difficult to see in cases of hemorrhagic shock or exsanguination, or in an anemic individual. Lividity is seen not only externally, but is also apparent internally. The lungs are among the best organs to demonstrate internal lividity.

Drying of the tissues is a postmortem artifact (Dix 2000; Di Maio and Di Maio 2001; Knight et al. 2004). Drying of the mucous membranes results in a dark red to black discoloration. This may be misinterpreted as injury or cyanosis. When postmortem imaging is done, this will change the normal tissular contrast on MRI sequences but will not change the quality of spontaneous intertissular contrast.

Putrefactive decomposition corresponds to decomposition of organic components under the action of autolysis and microorganisms (Dix 2000; Di Maio and Di Maio 2001; Knight et al. 2004). Putrefactive decomposition results from postmortem bacterial proliferation with gas formation. The gas production causes bloating of the tissues externally and internally. This gas contains CH_4, NH_3, H_2S, CO_2, H_2, N_2, cadaverin, and putrescin, and is a result of protein catabolism by anaerobic bacteria such as *Proteus* and *Escherichia* species and *Bacillus subtilis* (Haglund and Sorg 1997). As a component of the physiological flora of the intestine, the putrefaction bacteria reach the organs mainly via the vessels after death. Decomposition processes cause characteristic time- and temperature-dependent alterations of the intracranial tissues such as liquefying and gas intrusion.

We summarize in the following sections the postmortem appearance of the principal organs.

Brain

The appearance of the cerebral parenchyma is similar to that of patients in a brain-dead state, with poor differentiation between white and gray matter (loss of cortico-medullary differentiation) and parenchymal edema and brain swelling (Figure 8.8) (Dedouit et al. 2006). The parenchyma is, however, homogeneous. Cortico-medullary differentiation

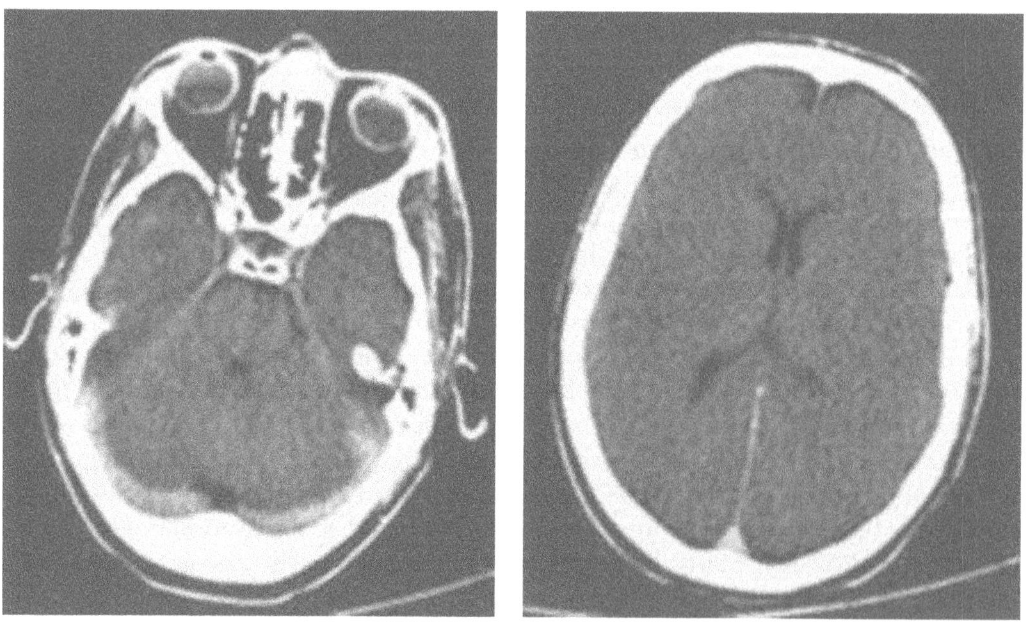

Figure 8.8 Normal postmortem cerebral axial CT images. A-B. Cortico-subcortical dedifferentiation, small pericerebral spaces, no supra- or infra-tentorial herniation is present. From Dedouit, F., et al. 2006. Role of modern cross-sectional imaging in thanatology: a pictorial essay. *J Radiol* 87: 619–38, with permission.

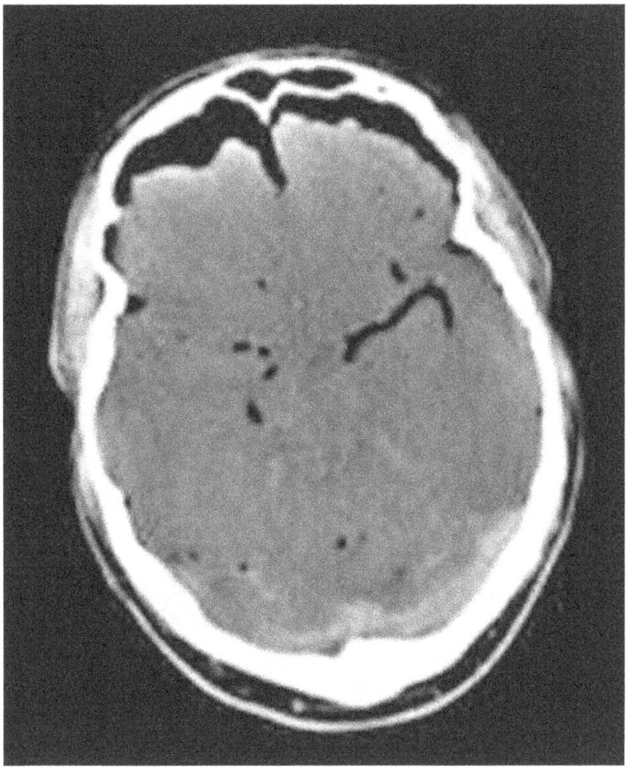

Figure 8.9 Putrefaction and the brain: cerebral axial CT image showing gas within the brain parenchyma and cerebral vessels (arteries and veins). From Dedouit, F., et al. 2006. Role of modern cross-sectional imaging in thanatology: a pictorial essay. *J Radiol* 87: 619–38, with permission.

persists longer on MRI images than on MSCT images. Vessels are spontaneously hyperdense. Pericerebral space and ventricular structures are reduced because of brain edema. No meningeal hemorrhage is seen. Putrefactive changes consist of the production of gas, first within and later outside vessels (Figure 8.9).

Cervical Spine

The various components of the cartilaginous and osseous larynx are clearly seen (Figure 8.10A, B; Dedouit et al. 2006). Intra- and perispinal postmortem modifications may occur, such as gas within the epidural veins, resembling pneumorachis; gas may also be present in the carotid arteries and jugular veins (Figure 8.10C).

The observer needs to be aware of certain pitfalls which must not be misinterpreted as fractures (Dedouit et al. 2006). These are, for example, a heterogeneous appearance of the laminae of the thyroid cartilage, heterogeneous calcification of the extremities of the tubercles of the greater horns of the hyoid bone, the joint (synchondrosis) between the body and the greater horns of the hyoid bone, presence of triticeal cartilage, and medialized superior horns of the thyroid cartilage (Figure 8.11; Dedouit et al. 2006).

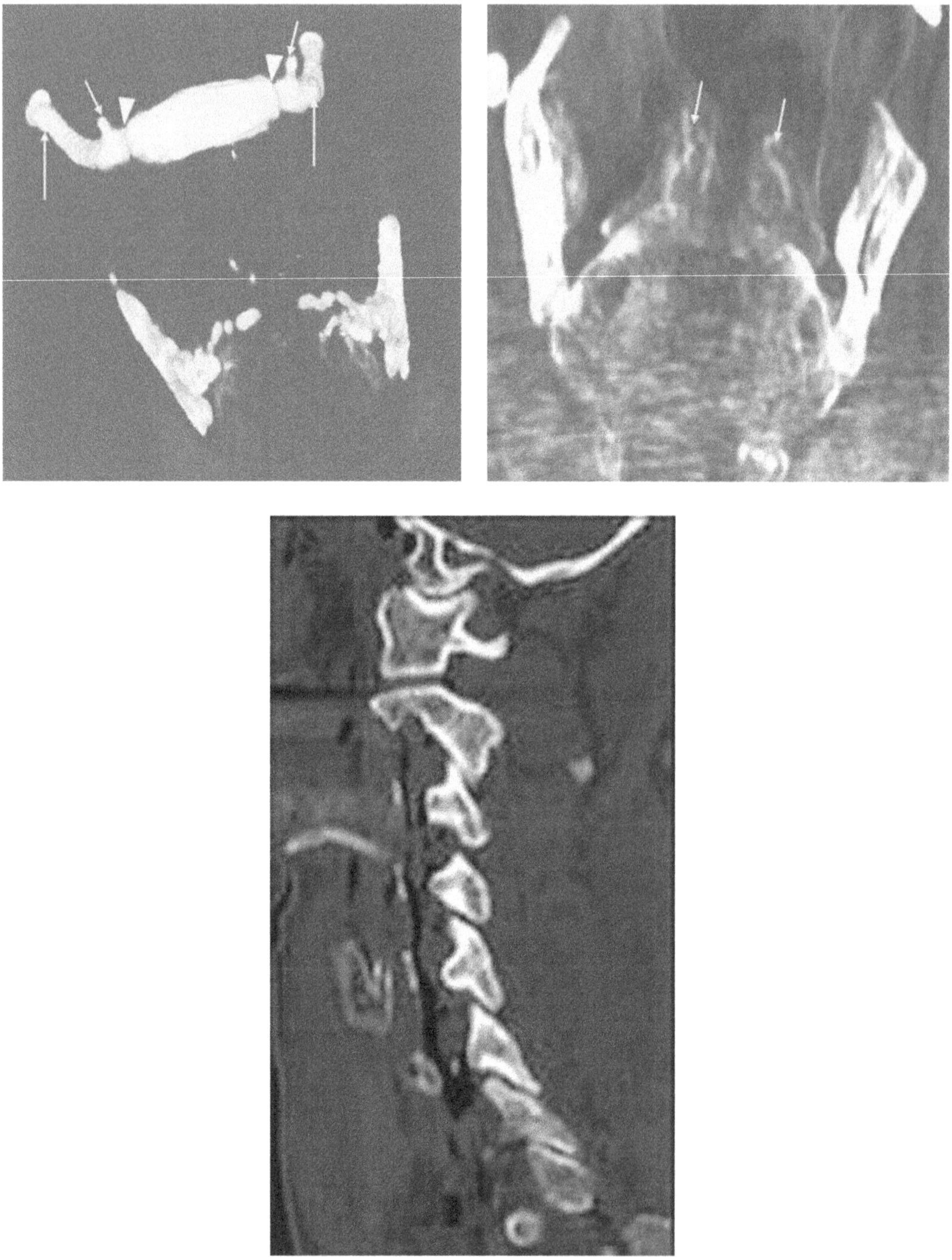

Figure 8.10 Normal postmortem appearance of the laryngeal tract. A. Laryngeal VRT CT reconstruction, anterior view: visualization of the greater hyoid horns (long arrows), lesser hyoid horns (short arrows), both joints (arrowheads), superior horns of the thyroid cartilage and both laminae with a heterogeneous calcified appearance in a young person. B. Laryngeal VRT CT reconstruction, posterior view: visualization of the cricoid and arythenoid cartilages (arrows). C. Cervical CT reconstruction, MPR mode, sagittal slice: gas within vertebral artery. From Dedouit, F., et al. 2006. Role of modern cross-sectional imaging in thanatology: a pictorial essay. *J Radiol* 87: 619–38, with permission.

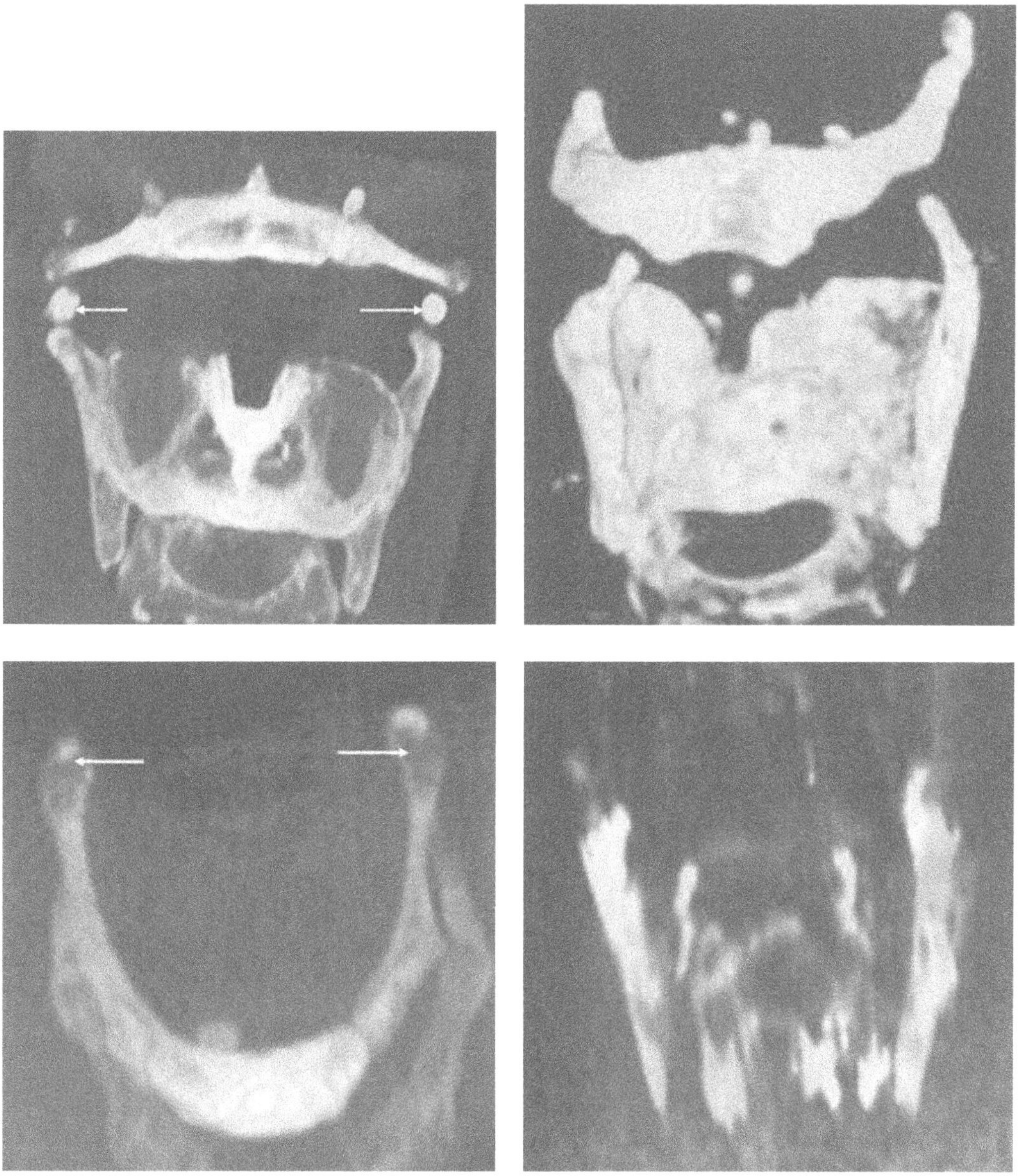

Figure 8.11 Larynx and CT pitfalls. A. Laryngeal VRT CT reconstruction, anterior view: bilateral triticeal cartilage (arrows). B. Laryngeal VRT CT reconstruction, posterior view: medial deviation of the superior horns of the thyroid cartilage. C. Laryngeal VRT CT reconstruction, superior view: heterogeneous calcification of the extremities of the greater horns of the hyoid cartilage (arrows). D. Laryngeal VRT CT reconstruction, anterior view: heterogeneous calcification of both laminae of the thyroid cartilage in a young man. From Dedouit, F., et al. 2006. Role of modern cross-sectional imaging in thanatology: a pictorial essay. *J Radiol* 87: 619–38, with permission.

Chest

Mediastinum

The aortic wall generally appears hyperdense (Figure 8.12A; Dedouit et al. 2006). The thoracic aorta may also appear to be trifoliate or often to have a withered structure (the aorta seems to be vanishing), which must not be confused with an aortic dissection (Figures 8.12B, C).

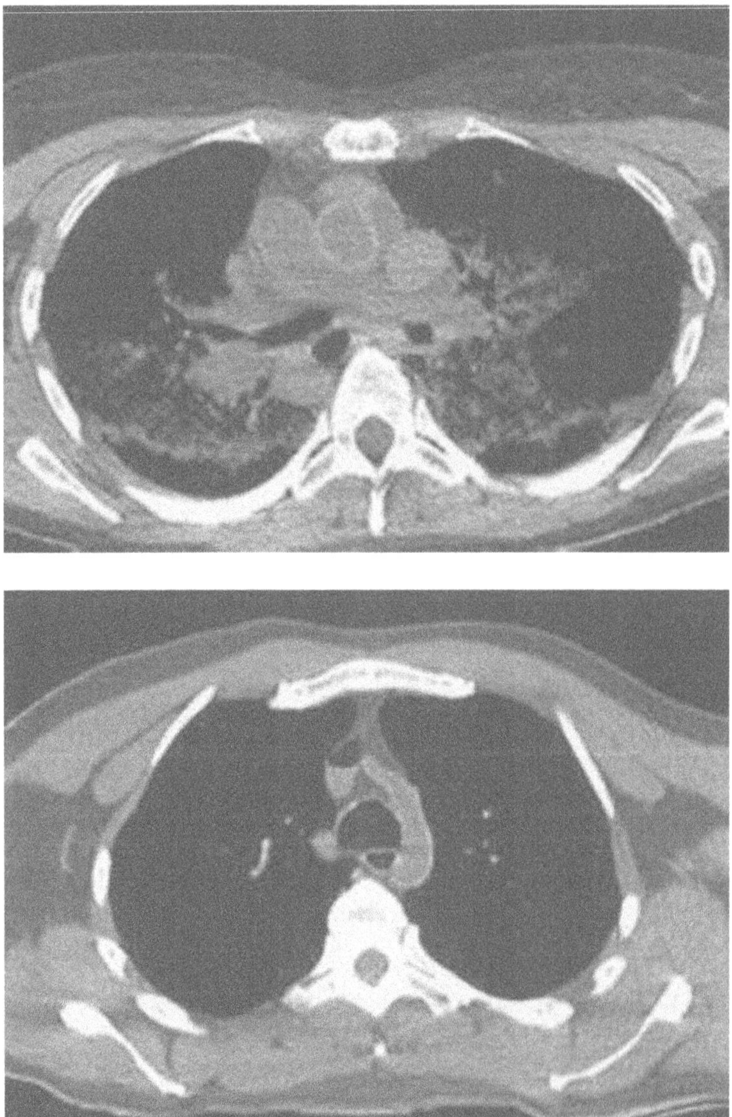

Figure 8.12 Normal postmortem CT appearance of the thoracic aorta and heart. A. Axial thoracic CT image: spontaneous hyperdense aortic wall. B. Axial thoracic CT image: "faded" or "vanishing" appearance of the aorta. C. Axial thoracic CT image: trifoliate appearance of the aorta. D. Axial thoracic CT image: presence of fluid-fluid levels within the cardiac cavities. From Dedouit, F., et al. 2006. Role of modern cross-sectional imaging in thanatology: a pictorial essay. *J Radiol* 87: 619–38, with permission.

Calcified coronary vessels are visible. Within the cardiac cavities, different densities may be seen, due to sedimentation of the cellular components (predominantly erythrocytes of the blood after the stagnation of circulation (Jackowski et al. 2005). In this case, a fluid-fluid level may be seen within the cavities (Figure 8.12D). Normally, no pericardial effusion is visible. Bubbles may be seen within the cardiac cavities due to putrefaction. In such cases, bubbles will be present in both the left and right cavities. This differs from gas embolism, which is seen as bubbles exclusively or predominantly within the right cavities. Normally, no pneumomediastinum is visible.

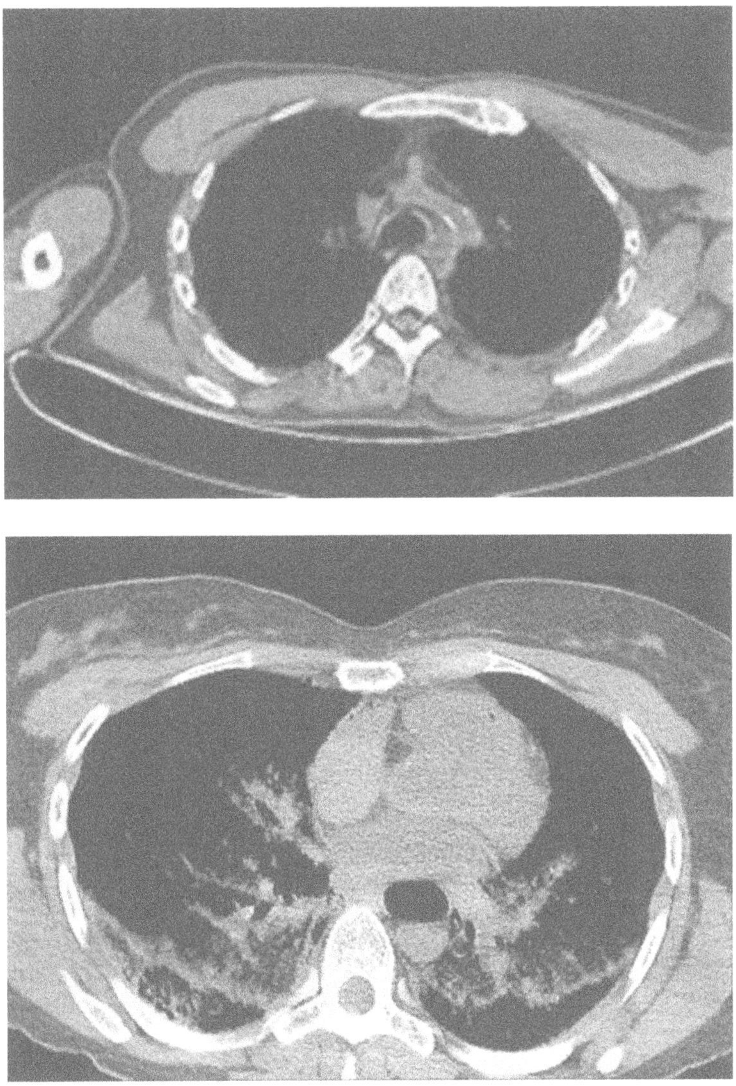

Figure 8.12 (Continued) Normal postmortem CT appearance of the thoracic aorta and heart. A. Axial thoracic CT image: spontaneous hyperdense aortic wall. B. Axial thoracic CT image: "faded" or "vanishing" appearance of the aorta. C. Axial thoracic CT image: trifoliate appearance of the aorta. D. Axial thoracic CT image: presence of fluid-fluid levels within the cardiac cavities. From Dedouit, F., et al. 2006. Role of modern cross-sectional imaging in thanatology: a pictorial essay. *J Radiol* 87: 619–38, with permission.

Pulmonary Parenchyma

Branches of the pulmonary arteries are visible until they reach the peripheral lung parenchyma (Figure 8.13A; Dedouit et al. 2006). This reflects pulmonary congestion. A diffuse, bilateral ground-glass appearance is frequently seen, probably indicating a congestive state. The trachea and major bronchi are normally aerated. Normally, no pleural effusions are visible. Topographical analysis of internal livor mortis is important and may help to determine the position of the deceased after death because of its gravity dependence (Figure 8.13B). Of course, livor mortis does not develop immediately. Filling of the bronchioloalveolar spaces may have a pseudo-pneumonic appearance that cannot be differentiated from true infectious pulmonary consolidation.

Putrefactive changes consist in the development of effusion in anatomic spaces (pericardium, pleura) and the production of gas, first within and then outside vessels.

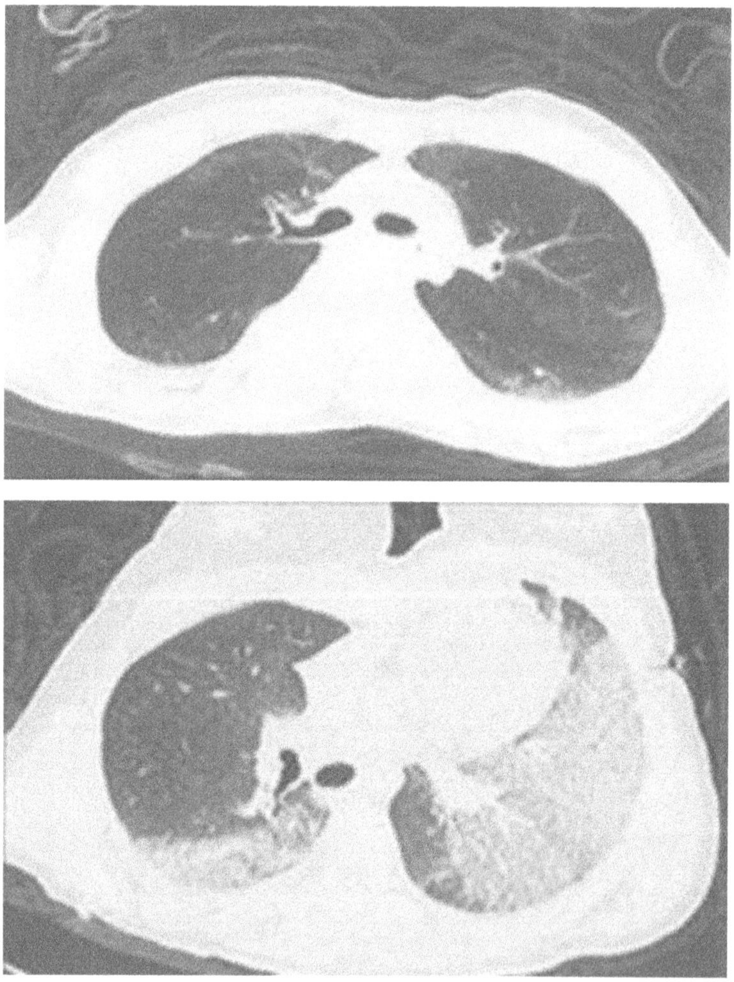

Figure 8.13 Postmortem CT appearance of the pulmonary parenchyma. A. Axial thoracic CT image: normally aerated pulmonary parenchyma. B. Pulmonary hypostasis: axial thoracic CT image: ground-glass and alveolar opacities caused by gravity and the left lateral supine position of the deceased for many days after death giving the lungs a "pseudo-pneumonic" appearance, mainly on the left side. From Dedouit, F., et al. 2006. Role of modern cross-sectional imaging in thanatology: a pictorial essay. *J Radiol* 87: 619–38, with permission.

Abdomen and Pelvis

Usually, gastrointestinal distension may be seen, predominating in the stomach and small-bowel loops (Figure 8.14A; Dedouit et al. 2006). Normally, there is no thickening of the gastrointestinal wall or pneumatosis. In the early postmortem stage, the parenchymas of all organs are homogeneous (Dedouit et al. 2006). With putrefactive changes, they become heterogeneous. The liver is susceptible to putrefactive changes: gas is first seen in the portal veins, then also becomes visible within arteries (Figure 8.14B; Dedouit et al. 2006). This appearance does not reflect the cause of death. The pancreas is also very susceptible to putrefaction and soon resembles a Swiss cheese (Thali et al 2003e; Dedouit et al. 2006).

The aorta may appear collapsed and be difficult to see. In such cases, parietal calcifications are helpful to track the aorta and its visceral branches (Dedouit et al. 2006).

Normally, there is no fluid or gaseous effusion within the intra- or retroperitoneal spaces.

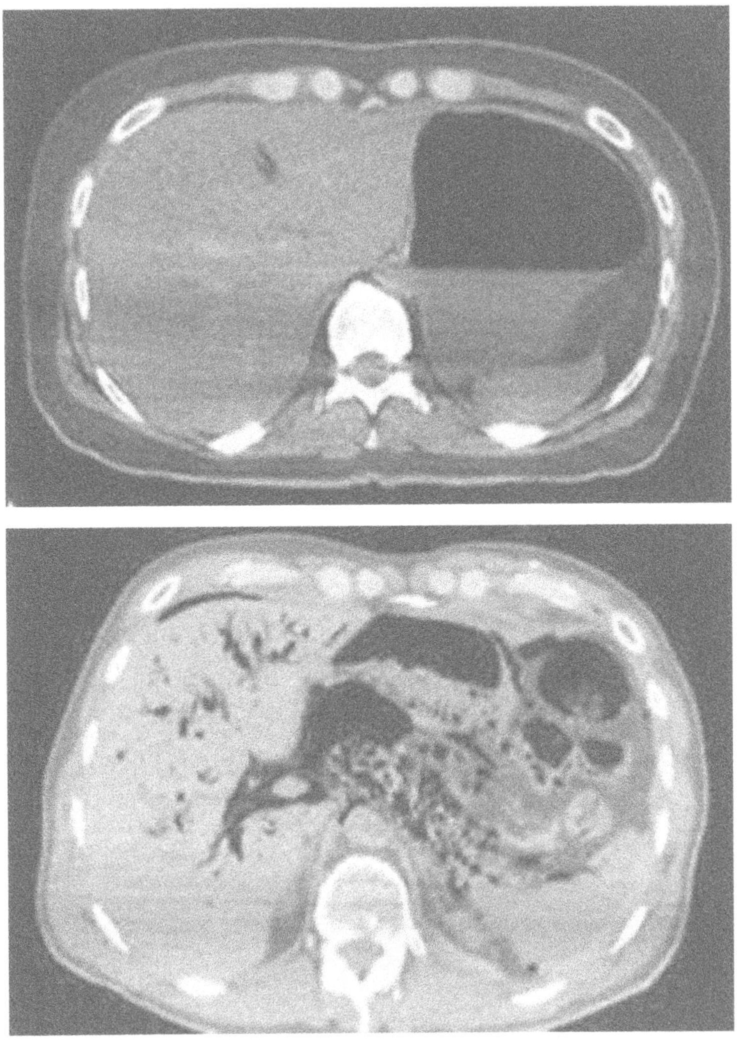

Figure 8.14 Abdomen and pelvis. A. Axial CT image: gaseous gastric distension. B. Portal venous gas and pancreatic putrefaction. From Dedouit, F., et al. 2006. Role of modern cross-sectional imaging in thanatology: a pictorial essay. *J Radiol* 87: 619–38, with permission.

Skin and Muscle

Accumulation of gas in subcutaneous tissues and muscles is often encountered and reflects putrefactive changes (Figure 8.15A; Thali et al. 2009). This gives the subcutaneous fatty tissue and the muscles a feathery appearance. An accumulation of gas located around a cutaneous wound may reflect subcutaneous emphysema (Figure 8.15B; Thali et al. 2003e).

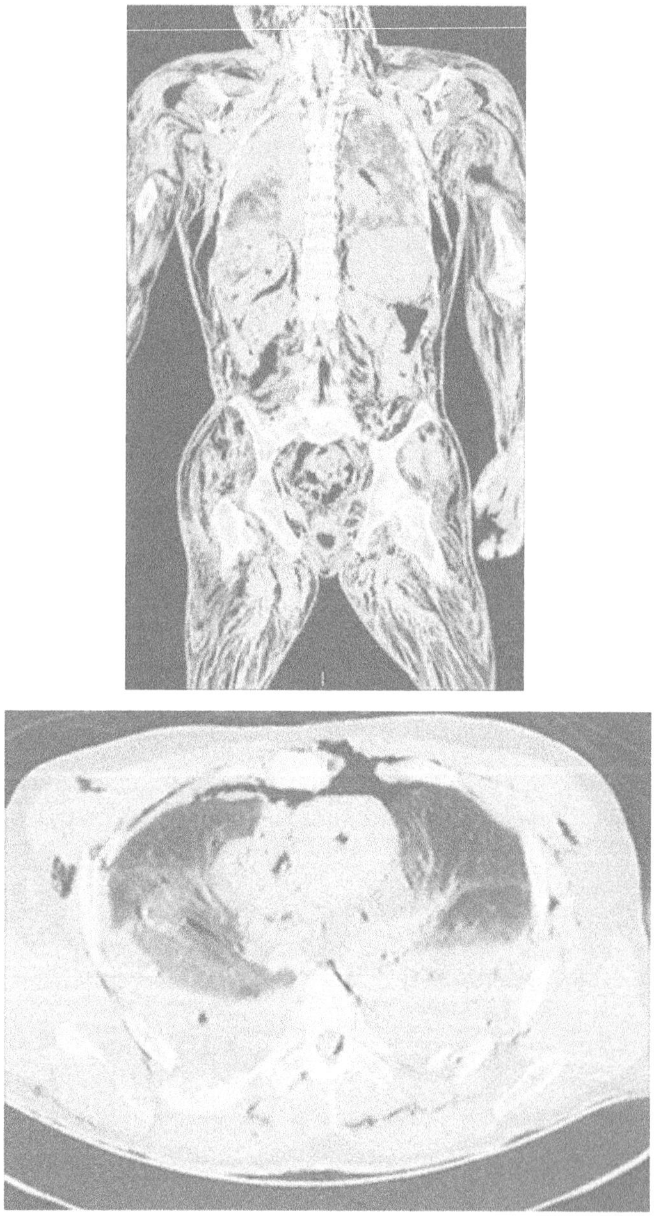

Figure 8.15 Putrefactive changes. A. Frontal MPR: accumulation of gas in subcutaneous tissues and muscles secondary to putrefactive changes. B. Axial thoracic CT image: subcutaneous emphysema with pneumomediastinum and pneumothoraces secondary to a ballistic chest wounds.

Putrefaction

On CT, putrefaction is indirectly reflected by gas formation (Thali et al. 2009). Although experience with forensic imaging in these cases is limited, the potential of CT and MRI is obvious (Thali et al. 2003f). Even in late stages of decomposition, relevant findings can be present at imaging and can even be better displayed and diagnosed than at autopsy. A case of post-traumatic frontal hemorrhage of a cadaver found in a severely decomposed state was examined by MRI and the location of the hemorrhage could be identified far more exactly than at autopsy (Thali et al. 2003e). Moreover, in cases of advanced putrefaction, MCST is valuable for identification of the deceased (Dedouit et al. 2006; Sidler et al. 2007).

Postmortem Lesional Semiology

Postmortem imaging of lesions illustrates the potential of forensic imaging for diagnosis. Of course, we will not give a complete review of the subject because this would involve summarizing the whole field of forensic pathology, impossible in a single chapter. This section will focus only on major topics, reflecting their importance in forensic medicine and showing how they can be illustrated and diagnosed through modern imaging.

Traumatic Deaths: General Aspects

The major interest of postmortem MSCT in forensic medicine is its application to traumatic lesions (Thali et al. 2003d; Dedouit et al. 2006; Thali et al. 2009). The appearance of bone lesions is identical to that seen on clinical imaging (Figure 8.16A). Of course, for diagnosis of traumatic lesions MSCT is superior to plain x-ray imaging and can help us understand the forces causing fractures in indirect trauma (Figure 8.16B). MSCT allows complete skeletal exploration with a single acquisition that takes several minutes (Thali et al. 2003d).

MSCT allows complete examination of the **face** and anatomical regions not easily accessible during autopsy (such as the mandible and sinuses), permitting easy diagnosis of blow-out fracture or nasal skeletal fracture, often suspected at autopsy but sometimes difficult to demonstrate without disfiguring the deceased (Figure 8.16C, D, E; Dedouit et al. 2006; Yen et al. 2007). Postmortem imaging can display such possibly lethal injuries in a rapid and nondestructive manner, thus sparing the face from further disfigurement or the pathologist from missing a potentially important finding. Postmortem imaging can also document subcutaneous hemorrhage or hematomas and intramuscular hematomas (Figure 8.17; Yen et al. 2004). For multiple bone lesions or intersecting **fractures** of the **calvaria** and **skull**, MSCT provides understanding of the chronology of the production of the fracture (Puppe's rule on complex fractures) (Figure 8.30). This is particularly helpful in cases of ballistic trauma or multiple blows (Yen et al. 2007).

Parenchymal brain and **pericerebral** lesions (Figures 8.18 and 8.19):

- Extra-axial hemorrhages include epidural and subdural hematomas, and subarachnoid hemorrhage (Yen et al. 2007).
- Intra-axial hemorrhages include cortical contusions and intracerebral, intraventricular hemorrhages.

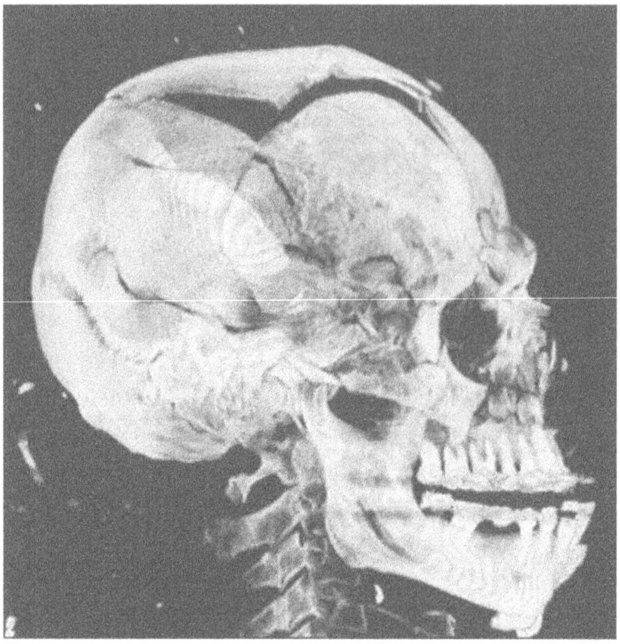

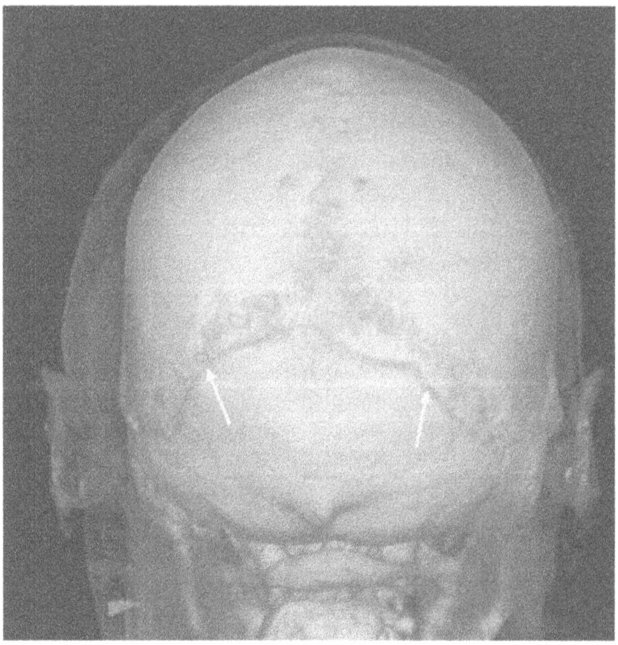

Figure 8.16 Skull and facial trauma. A. Face, motor vehicle accident, direct trauma (collision of a car and an animal). Cephalic VRT CT reconstruction, anterior view: major facial crushing with mandible, facial, and skull fractures with numerous external displaced fractures. B. Skull, fall from a high height, indirect trauma. Cephalic VRT CT reconstruction, posterior view: occipital fracture line immediately below both parieto-occipital sutures (arrows) secondary to hyperflexion of the cervical spine. C. Axial CT image: displacement fracture of the right mandibular condyle (arrow). D. Sagittal MPR reconstruction: fracture of the right mandibular angle (arrow). E. Sagittal MPR reconstruction: displaced fracture of the right orbital roof (arrow). From Dedouit, F., et al. 2006. Role of modern cross-sectional imaging in thanatology: a pictorial essay. *J Radiol* 87: 619–38, with permission.

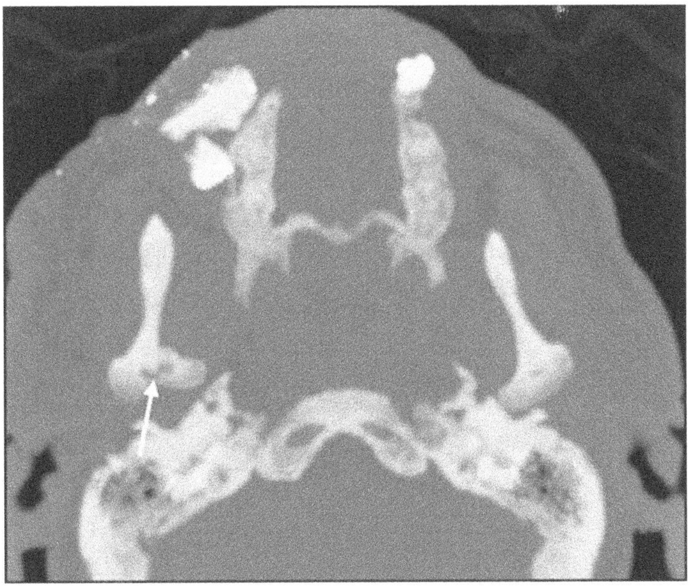

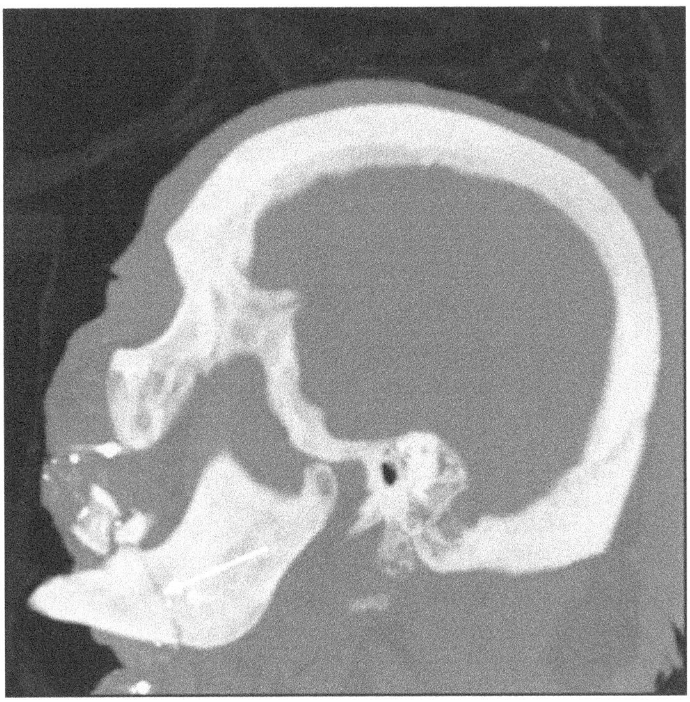

Figure 8.16 (Continued) Skull and facial trauma. A. Face, motor vehicle accident, direct trauma (collision of a car and an animal). Cephalic VRT CT reconstruction, anterior view: major facial crushing with mandible, facial, and skull fractures with numerous external displaced fractures. B. Skull, fall from a high height, indirect trauma. Cephalic VRT CT reconstruction, posterior view: occipital fracture line immediately below both parieto-occipital sutures (arrows) secondary to hyperflexion of the cervical spine. C. Axial CT image: displacement fracture of the right mandibular condyle (arrow). D. Sagittal MPR reconstruction: fracture of the right mandibular angle (arrow). E. Sagittal MPR reconstruction: displaced fracture of the right orbital roof (arrow). From Dedouit, F., et al. 2006. Role of modern cross-sectional imaging in thanatology: a pictorial essay. *J Radiol* 87: 619–38, with permission.

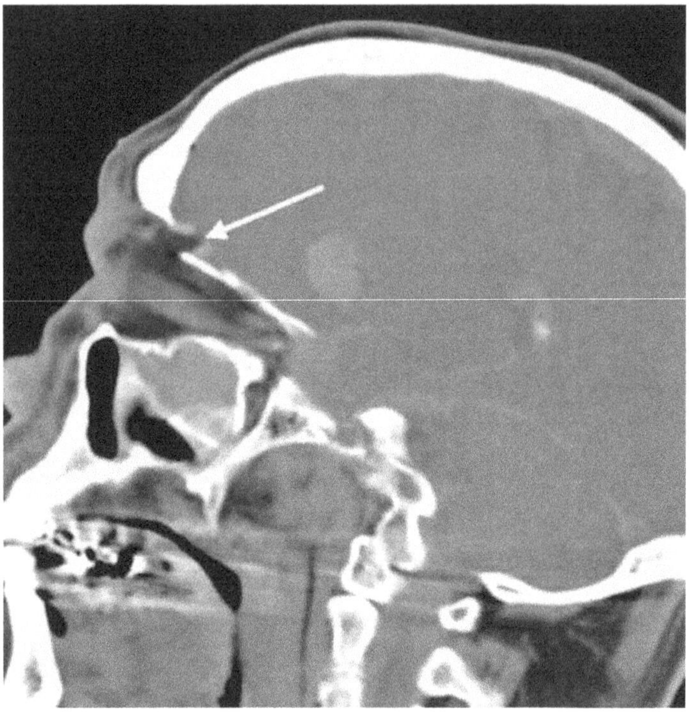

Figure 8.16 (Continued) Skull and facial trauma. A. Face, motor vehicle accident, direct trauma (collision of a car and an animal). Cephalic VRT CT reconstruction, anterior view: major facial crushing with mandible, facial, and skull fractures with numerous external displaced fractures. B. Skull, fall from a high height, indirect trauma. Cephalic VRT CT reconstruction, posterior view: occipital fracture line immediately below both parieto-occipital sutures (arrows) secondary to hyperflexion of the cervical spine. C. Axial CT image: displacement fracture of the right mandibular condyle (arrow). D. Sagittal MPR reconstruction: fracture of the right mandibular angle (arrow). E. Sagittal MPR reconstruction: displaced fracture of the right orbital roof (arrow). From Dedouit, F., et al. 2006. Role of modern cross-sectional imaging in thanatology: a pictorial essay. *J Radiol* 87: 619–38, with permission.

Both CT and 1.5 Tesla MRI regularly fail in the detection of intracerebral hemorrhagic lesions, small contusional hemorrhages, and traumatic intracerebral bleeding smaller than about 3 mm, especially when lesions are solitary or only few in number without accompanying edema (Yen et al. 2007). Using CT and MRI as diagnostic methods, traumatic brain-stem hemorrhage may remain undetected due to current technical limitations concerning image resolution. However, special MRI applications (diffusion tensor imaging) can display traumatic disorganization and rupture of nerve fibers in the brain stem, offering diagnosis based on a "direct" examination of the fiber structures independently from the extent of accompanying hemorrhage (Yen et al. 2006). Diffuse axonal injury (DAI) can be suspected on MSCT and MRI explorations. On MRI, when DAI is present, the apparent diffusion coefficient (ADC) will be markedly reduced in the injured regions (Yen et al. 2006; 2007). However, the value of reduced ADC as a sign of DAI in postmortem cases has to be clarified in future studies.

Generally, subarachnoid hemorrhage and intra- or pericerebral hematomas are also easily visible with MSCT (Dedouit et al. 2006; Yen et al. 2007). In subcutaneous cephalic

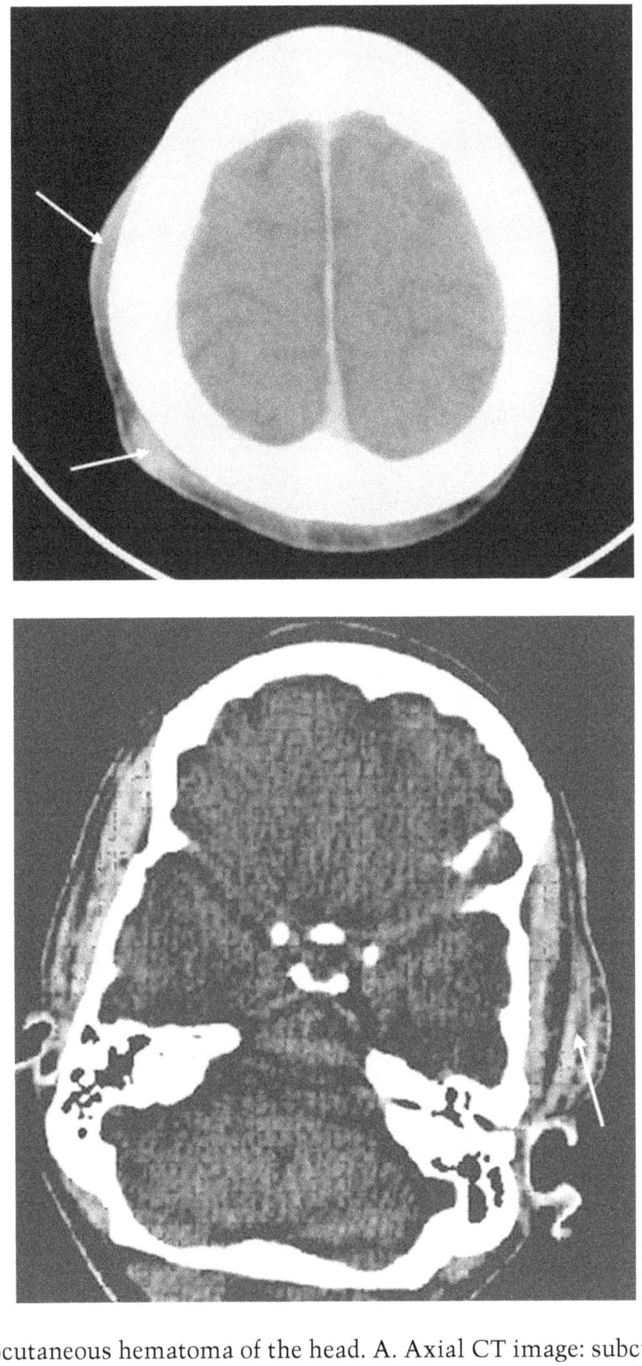

Figure 8.17 Subcutaneous hematoma of the head. A. Axial CT image: subcutaneous hematomas of the vertex (arrow). B. Axial CT image: intramuscular hematoma within the left temporal muscle (arrow).

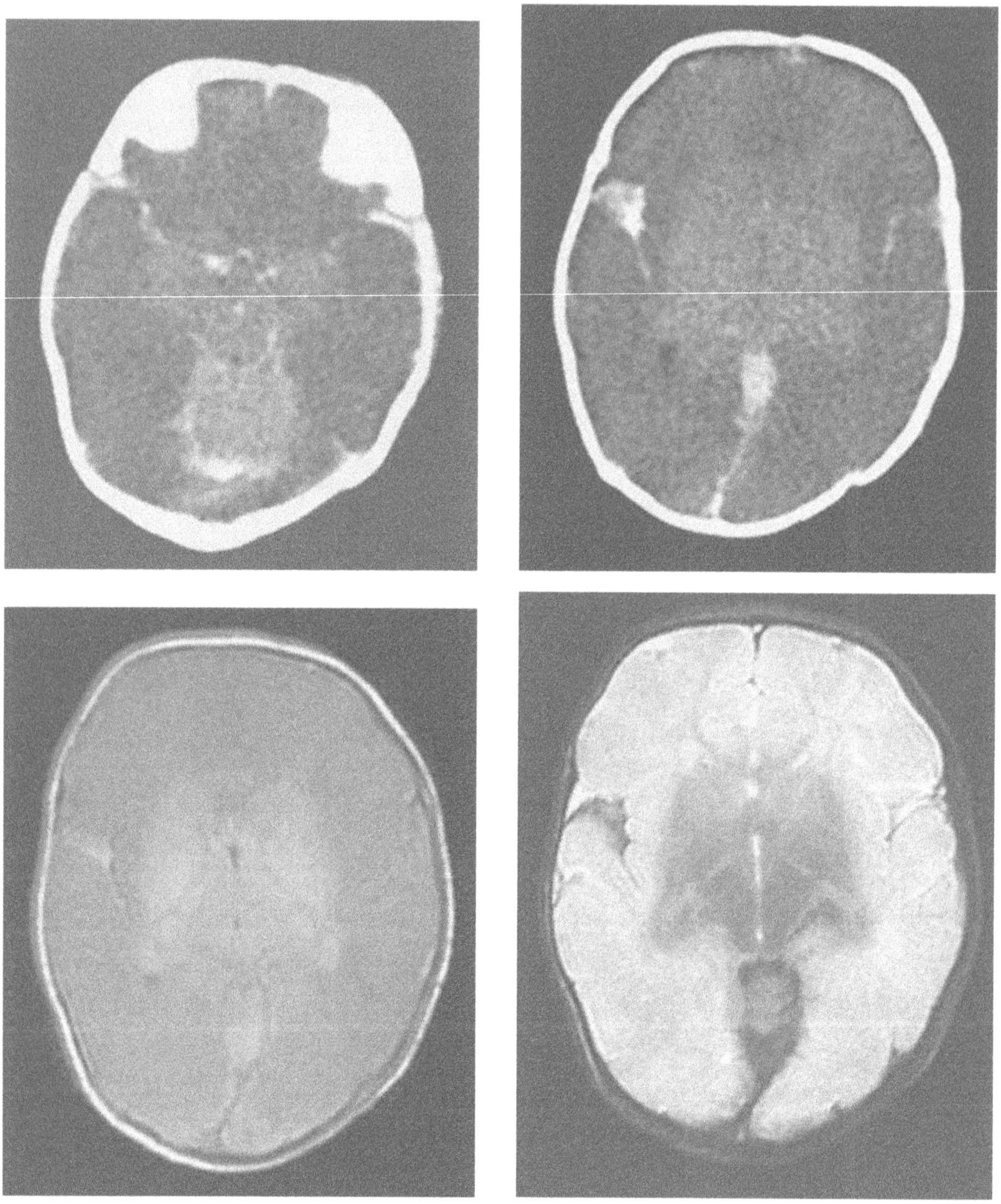

Figure 8.18 Shaken baby syndrome. Subarachnoid hemorrhage and anoxic-ischemic changes. A and B. Axial CT images. Relatively hyperdense appearance of the brain stem and cerebellum compared with the brain parenchyma. Central herniation with obliteration of quadrigeminal and ambient cisterns. Acute tentorial subdural hematoma. Diffuse subarachnoid hemorrhage, acute posterior interhemispheric falx subdural hematoma. Hypodense appearance of thet supratentorial brain parenchyma sparing the basal ganglia, loss of white–gray matter differentiation, compression of the cortical sulci and lateral ventricles, and obliteration of the third ventricle. C. Axial MRI T1-weighted image. Increased signal intensity of the basal ganglia and posterior fossa with diffuse decreased intensity of the rest of the brain parenchyma. D. Axial MRI T2-weighted image. The appearance is the reverse of that observed on the T1-weighted images, with decreased signal intensity of the basal ganglia and diffuse increased intensity of the rest of the brain parenchyma. From Dedouit, F., et al. 2008. Reversal sign on ante- and postmortem brain imaging in a newborn: report of one case. *Forensic Sci Int* 182: e11–14, with permission.

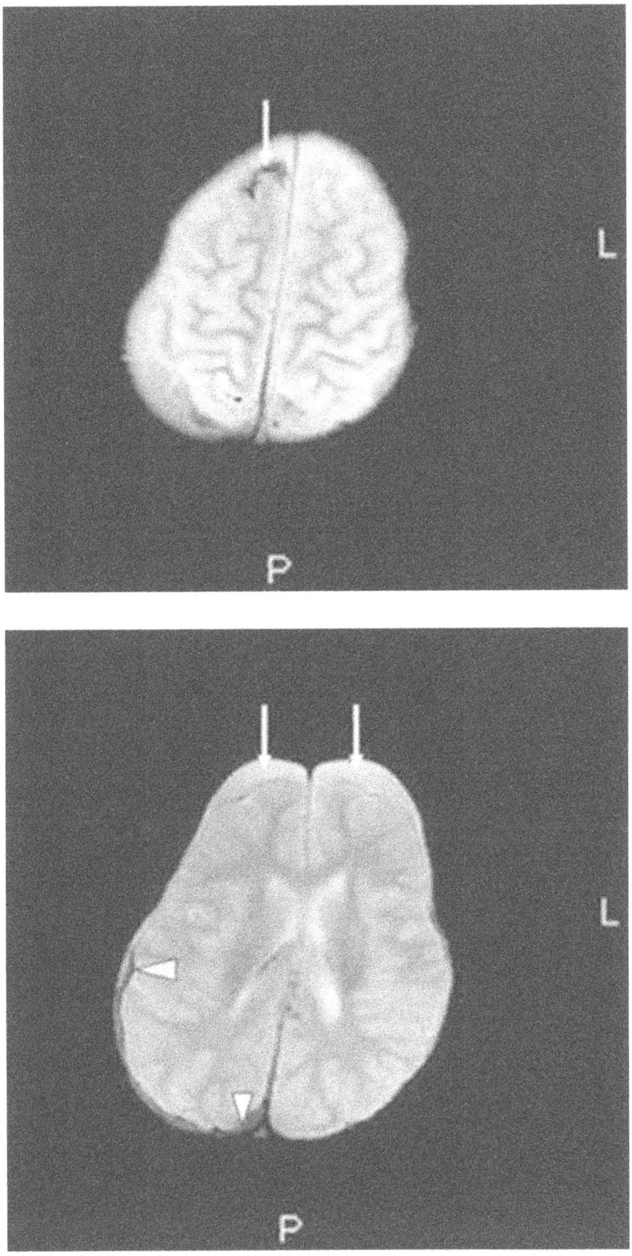

Figure 8.19 Child abuse. Postmortem cerebral MRI study, gradient echo sequences (from superior to inferior level). A. Right frontal meningeal hemorrhage with decreased signal intensity (arrow). B. Bilateral subdural hematomas mainly of increased signal intensity (arrows); decreased signal intensity is visible within the right inferior part of the subdural hematoma (arrowheads). C. Decreased signal intensity of the posterior part of the corpus callosum (arrow); intraventricular hemorrhage within the posterior part of the left lateral ventricle (arrowhead). D. Interpedoncular hemorrhage (arrow). From Dedouit, F., et al. 2008. Child abuse: practical application of autopsy, radiological, and microscopic studies. *J Forensic Sci* 53: 1424–9, with permission.

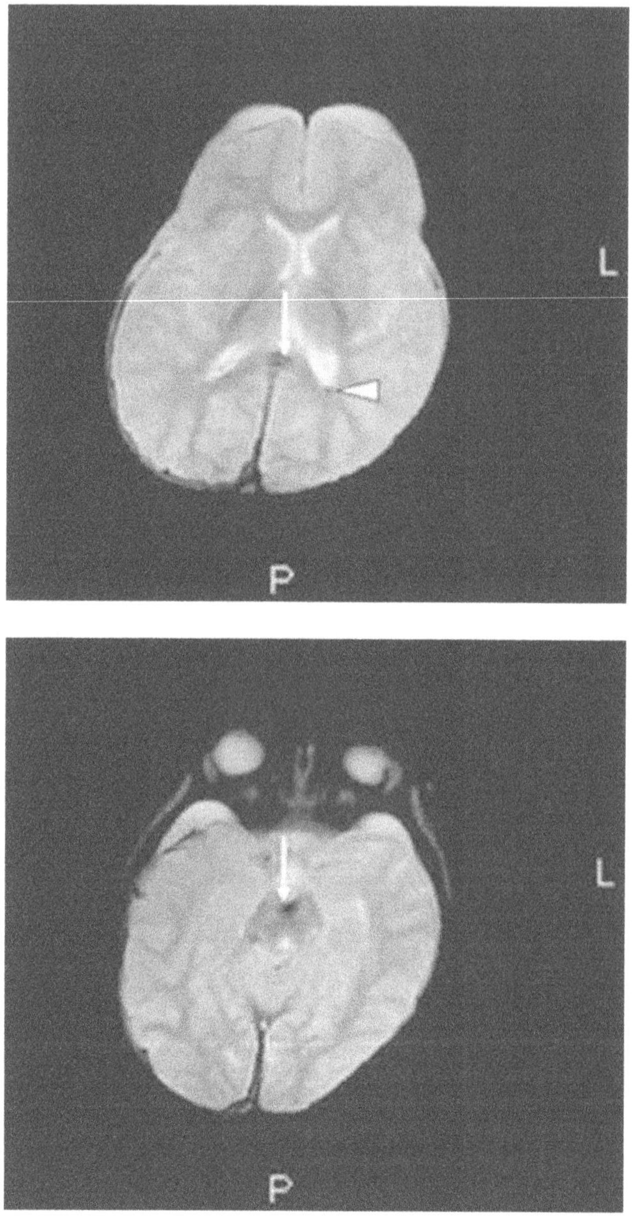

Figure 8.19 (Continued) Child abuse. Postmortem cerebral MRI study, gradient echo sequences (from superior to inferior level). A. Right frontal meningeal hemorrhage with decreased signal intensity (arrow). B. Bilateral subdural hematomas mainly of increased signal intensity (arrows); decreased signal intensity is visible within the right inferior part of the subdural hematoma (arrowheads). C. Decreased signal intensity of the posterior part of the corpus callosum (arrow); intraventricular hemorrhage within the posterior part of the left lateral ventricle (arrowhead). D. Interpedoncular hemorrhage (arrow). From Dedouit, F., et al. 2008. Child abuse: practical application of autopsy, radiological, and microscopic studies. *J Forensic Sci* 53: 1424–9, with permission.

hematomas, it is possible to determine if skull fractures or blood around or within the brain are present (Dedouit et al. 2006). In complement to a single external examination of the corpse, MSCT is very informative and highly useful in determining the cause of death. Furthermore MSCT often demonstrates the discordance between superficial lesions and associated internal lesions (Dedouit et al. 2006).

MSCT can also be useful to estimate the time interval of production of bone fractures (Dedouit et al. 2008b). It can consequently differentiate acute trauma, with non-consolidated fractures, from old trauma, with presence of bone callus (Figure 8.20).

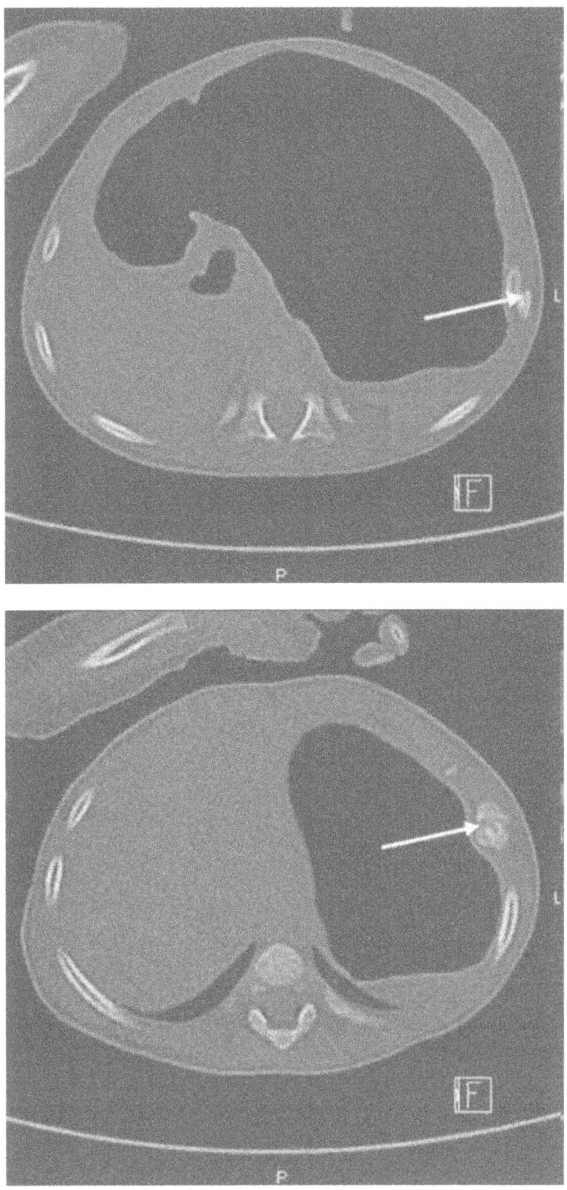

Figure 8.20 Child abuse. Axial chest images. A. Non-healed lateral rib fracture (arrow). B. Healed lateral rib fracture (arrow). From Dedouit, F., et al. 2008. Child abuse: practical application of autopsy, radiological, and microscopic studies. *J Forensic Sci* 53: 1424–9, with permission.

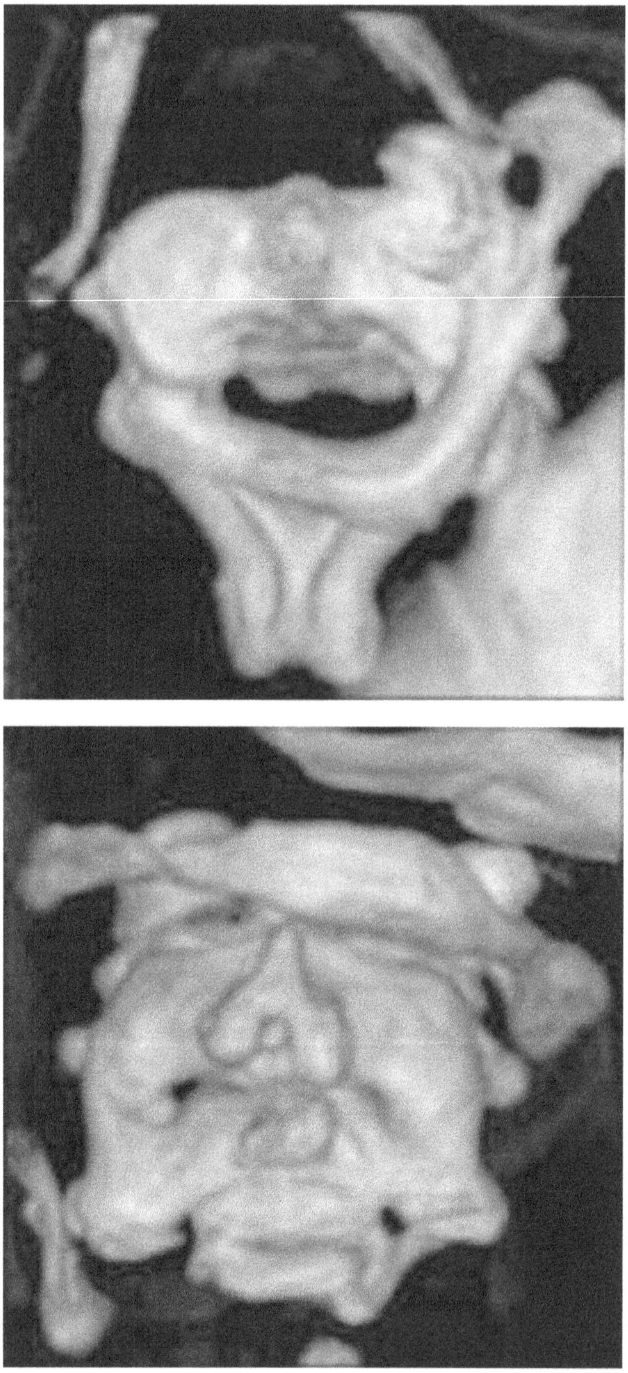

Figure 8.21 Cervical spine: fall from a high height. A. VRT reconstruction of the upper cervical spine, superior view: misalignment of first and second cervical vertebrae caused by a bipedicular fracture. B. VRT reconstruction of the upper cervical spine, posterior view: misalignment of the first and second cervical vertebrae caused by a bipedicular fracture. C. Axial CT image: anterior arch fracture of the first cervical vertebra (arrow). From Dedouit, F., et al. 2006. Role of modern cross-sectional imaging in thanatology: a pictorial essay. *J Radiol* 87: 619–38, with permission. From Dedouit, F., et al. 2007. Virtual anthropology and forensic identification: report of one case. *Forensic Sci Int* 173: 182–7, with permission.

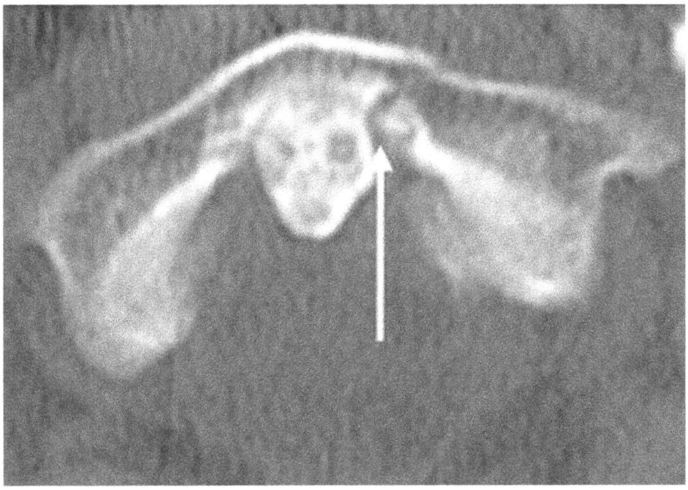

Figure 8.21 (Continued) Cervical spine: fall from a high height. A. VRT reconstruction of the upper cervical spine, superior view: misalignment of first and second cervical vertebrae caused by a bipedicular fracture. B. VRT reconstruction of the upper cervical spine, posterior view: misalignment of the first and second cervical vertebrae caused by a bipedicular fracture. C. Axial CT image: anterior arch fracture of the first cervical vertebra (arrow). From Dedouit, F., et al. 2006. Role of modern cross-sectional imaging in thanatology: a pictorial essay. *J Radiol* 87: 619–38, with permission. From Dedouit, F., et al. 2007. Virtual anthropology and forensic identification: report of one case. *Forensic Sci Int* 173: 182–7, with permission.

Another argument for acute fractures is the infiltrative appearance of the soft tissues around the fracture.

The **cervical spine** may also be difficult to analyze during autopsy (Dedouit et al. 2006). MSCT allows, for example, complete exploration to determine the origin of an intervertebral luxation, such as pedicular fracture or zygapophyseal fractures (Figure 8.21; Yen et al. 2005, 2007).

Extravascular gas detection is also very easy with MSCT (Thali et al. 2003e). Autopsy can miss subtle pneumothorax (Dedouit et al. 2006). Furthermore, MSCT can demonstrate the compressive appearance of a pneumothorax (tension pneumothorax), with deviation of the mediastinal structures (Figure 8.22).

Unfortunately, MSCT often gives poor **intertissular contrast** (Figures 8.23 and 8.24). Consequently, organ lesions such as hepatic or renal fractures or hematomas are not always directly visualized (Dedouit et al. 2006). For such lesions, MRI is more sensitive, either alone or in combination with MSCT (Figure 8.25; Buck et al. 2009; Christe et al. 2009). However, diaphragmatic rupture and other indirect arguments for organ fractures, such as intraperitoneal effusion, can be seen (Figure 8.26; Dedouit et al. 2006). Another limitation is that contrary to clinical cases, the postmortem appearance of fat embolism has not yet been evaluated in forensic cases (Thali et al. 2009).

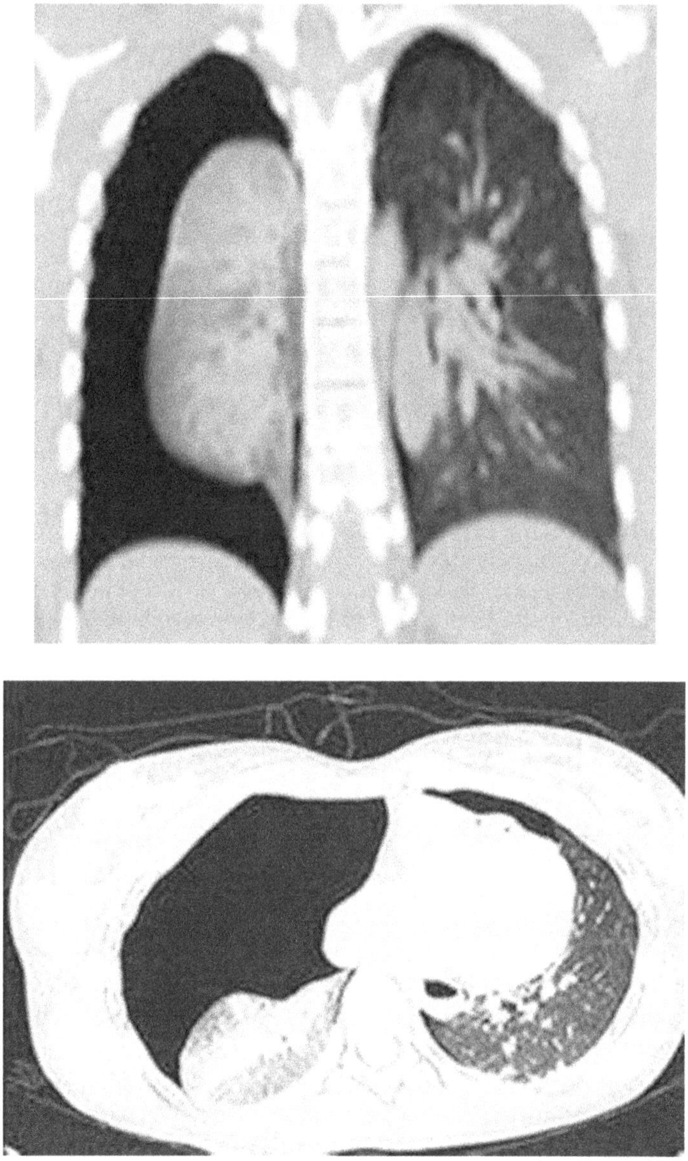

Figure 8.22 Chest: repeated blows. A. Frontal MPR thoracic reconstruction: large right pneumothorax associated with a subtle left pneumothorax. B. Axial chest image: bilateral pneumothoraces; the right one is under tension causing the left mediastinal displacement. From Dedouit, F., et al. 2006. Role of modern cross-sectional imaging in thanatology: a pictorial essay. *J Radiol* 87: 619–38, with permission.

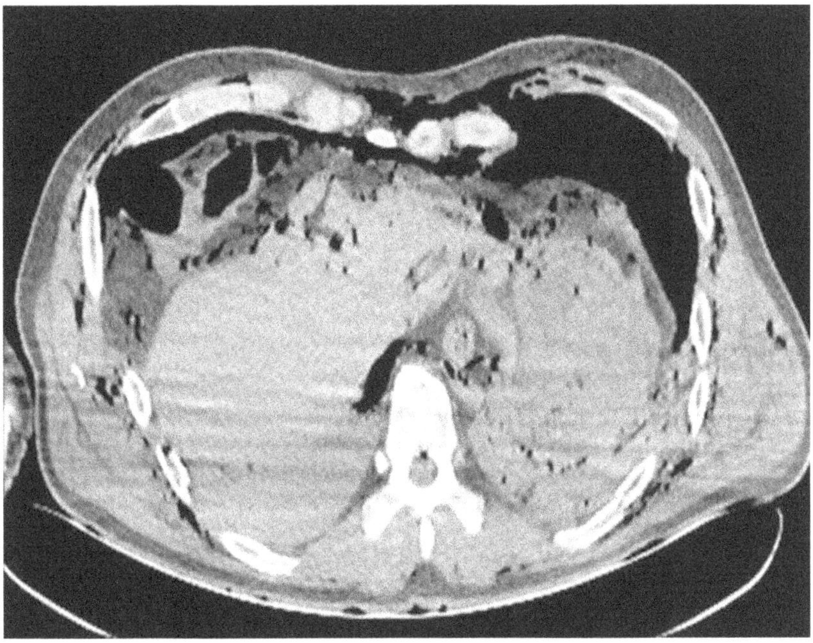

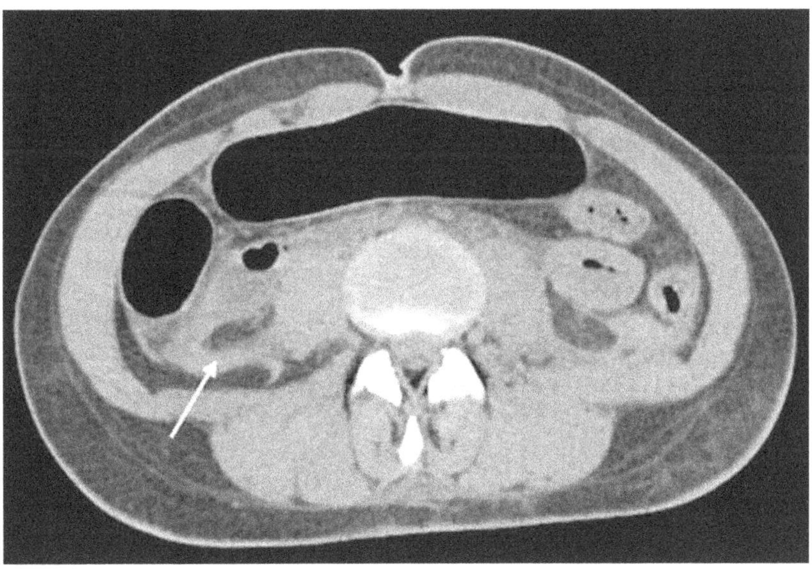

Figure 8.23 Poor spontaneous intertissular MSCT contrast A. Axial CT image. Hepatic fracture not diagnosed and non-visible on CT. B. Axial CT image. Right lateral retroperitoneal hematoma in a context of repeated blows (arrow).

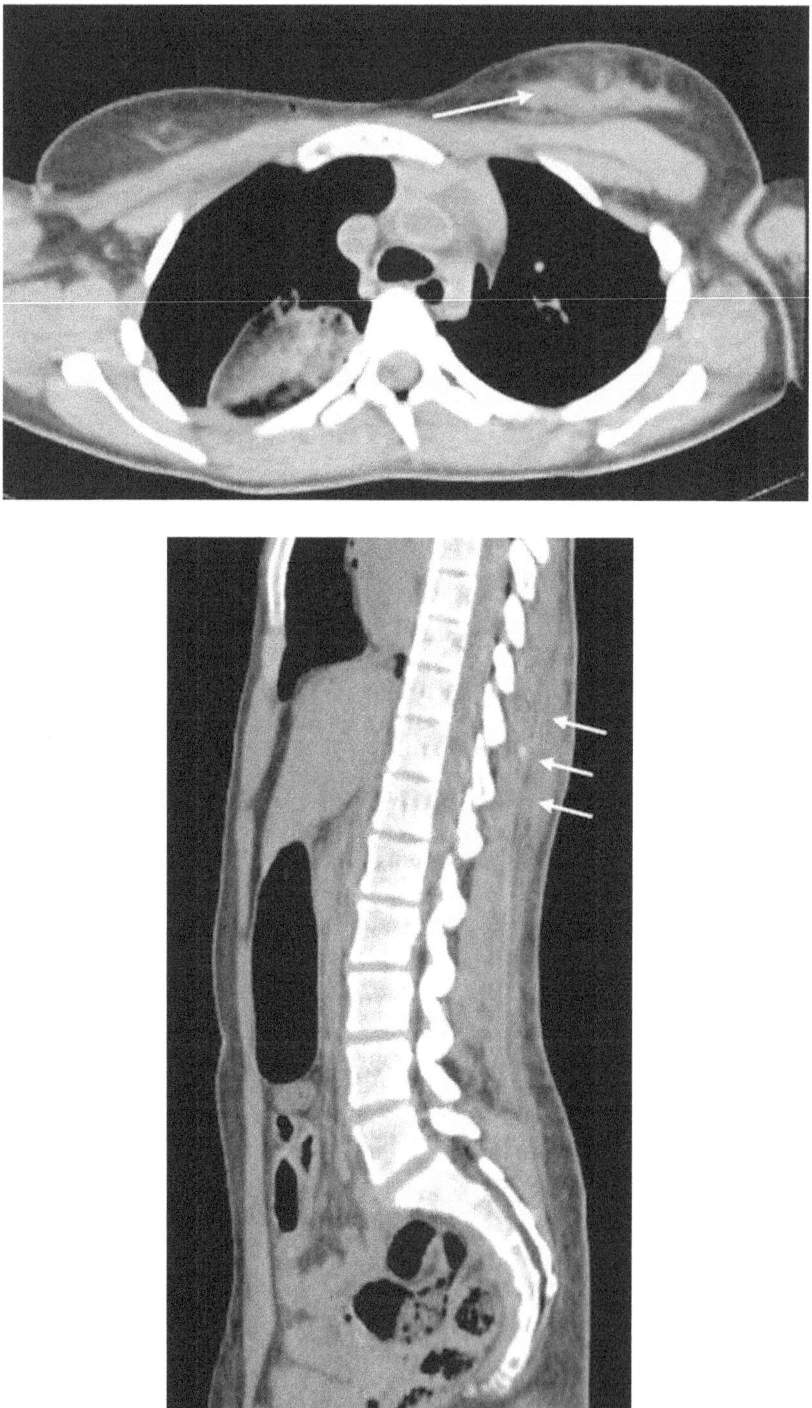

Figure 8.24 Well marked spontaneous intertissular MSCT contrast A. Axial CT image. Trauma of the left breast with subcutaneous bloody effusion (arrow). B. Axial CT image. Large dorsal hematoma secondary to repeated blows (arrows).

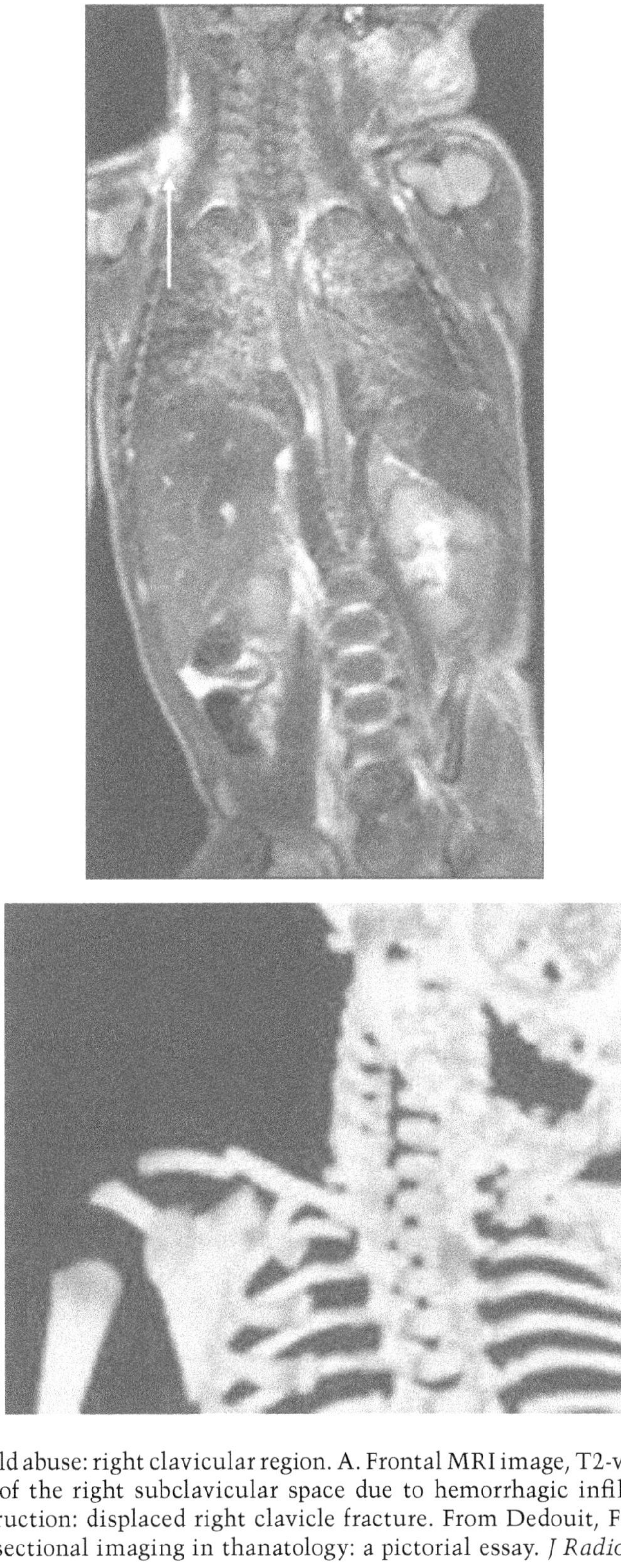

Figure 8.25 Child abuse: right clavicular region. A. Frontal MRI image, T2-weighted sequence: increased signal of the right subclavicular space due to hemorrhagic infiltration (arrow). B. VRT CT reconstruction: displaced right clavicle fracture. From Dedouit, F., et al. 2006. Role of modern cross-sectional imaging in thanatology: a pictorial essay. *J Radiol* 87: 619–38, with permission.

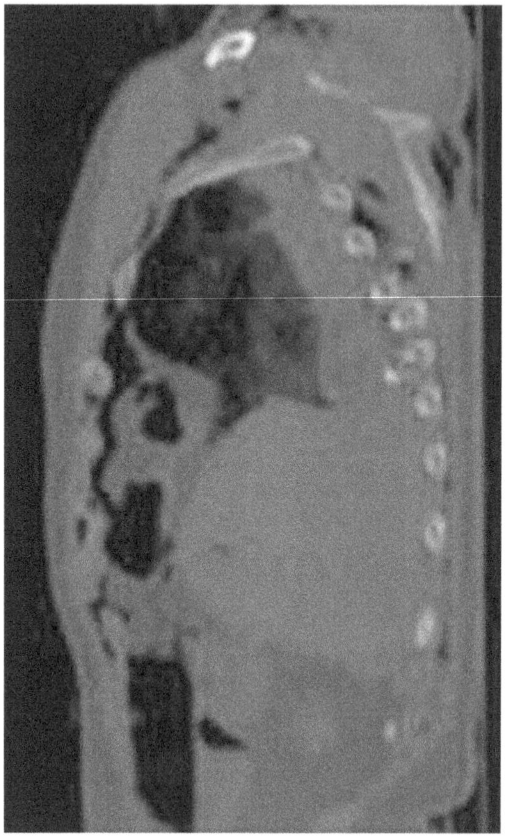

Figure 8.26 Fall from a high height. Sagittal MIP thoracic reconstruction: anterior rupture of the right diaphragmatic dome with intrathoracic migration of the colon and the epiploic fat. From Dedouit, F., et al. 2006. Role of modern cross-sectional imaging in thanatology: a pictorial essay. *J Radiol* 87: 619–38, with permission.

Traumatic Deaths in Children: General Aspects

Where child abuse is suspected, MSCT is highly informative. The entire skeleton can be explored, and also the internal organs if MSCT is combined with MRI (Figure 8.26). The time interval of production of bone fractures can be estimated (Figure 8.20). In child abuse cases, MRI and MSCT also demonstrate intra- and pericerebral hematomas and ischemic changes (Figures 8.18 and 8.19; Dedouit et al. 2008b, 2008c).

Specific Injuries

Gunshot Wounds

Using macroscopic criteria based on those applied in dry bone examination, MSCT characterizes bone defects (entry, exit) and determines their typical or atypical nature (Figures 8.27 and 8.28; Oehmichen et al. 2003; Thali et al. 2003g). MSCT easily

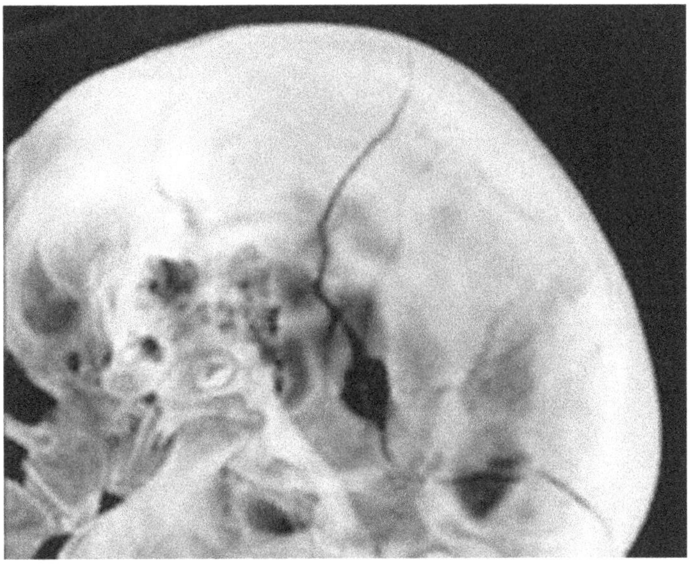

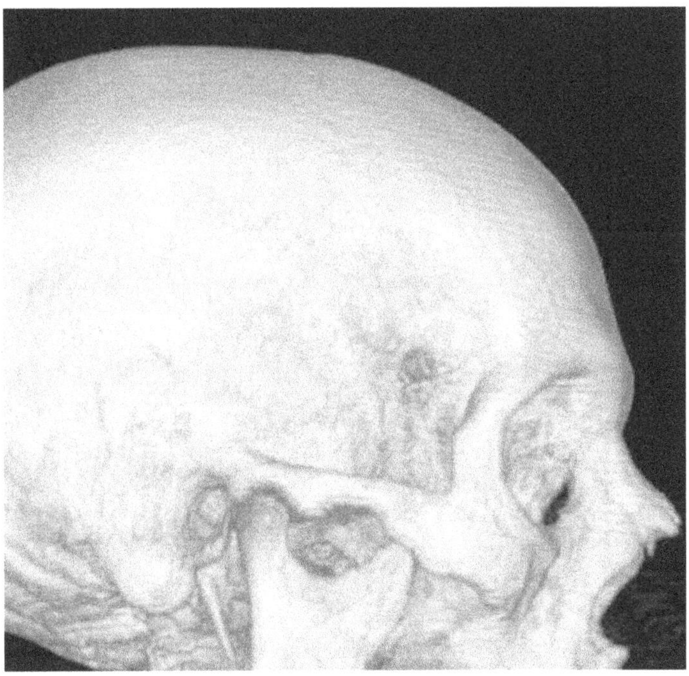

Figure 8.27 Typical gunshot bone entry wounds. A. VRT reconstruction, external view: exocranial visualization of the bone entry wound and associated radial skull fractures. B. VRT reconstruction, external view: exocranial visualization of the bone entry wound with no associated radial skull fractures. C. Axial CT image: presence of pneumencephalon, intracranial bone and bullet fragments, intracerebral hematomas. Spontaneous hyperdense areas are visible at the cutaneous entry wound (soot deposition). The bone entry defect shows internal cone-shaped beveling. From Dedouit, F., et al. 2006. Role of modern cross-sectional imaging in thanatology: a pictorial essay. *J Radiol* 87: 619–38, with permission.

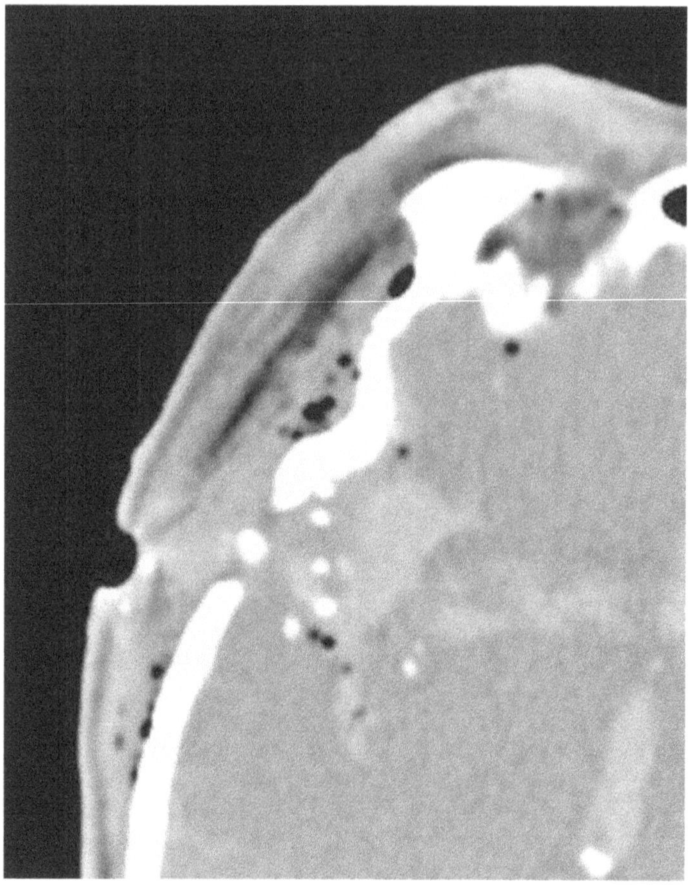

Figure 8.27 (Continued) Typical gunshot bone entry wounds. A. VRT reconstruction, external view: exocranial visualization of the bone entry wound and associated radial skull fractures. B. VRT reconstruction, external view: exocranial visualization of the bone entry wound with no associated radial skull fractures. C. Axial CT image: presence of pneumencephalon, intracranial bone and bullet fragments, intracerebral hematomas. Spontaneous hyperdense areas are visible at the cutaneous entry wound (soot deposition). The bone entry defect shows internal cone-shaped beveling. From Dedouit, F., et al. 2006. Role of modern cross-sectional imaging in thanatology: a pictorial essay. *J Radiol* 87: 619–38, with permission.

identifies fractures, intra-parenchymal bullet paths, injured organs, bone splinters, soot deposition (gunshot residues), and vital reactions such as blood aspiration or gaseous embolism (Figures 8.29–8.33). This is true of all parts of the body. However, trajectory study may be difficult because of ballistic migration and secondary trajectories (Oehmichen et al. 2003). CT and MRI seem to be well suited to determine the location of bullet particles and to identify many gunshot-induced injuries like hemorrhage, contusion, and laceration of the extracranial and intracranial tissues (Yen et al. 2007). In many cases, the bullet path can be reconstructed when not only the intracerebral but also the skull and soft tissue injuries are taken into account (Oehmichen et al. 2003; Dedouit et al. 2006).

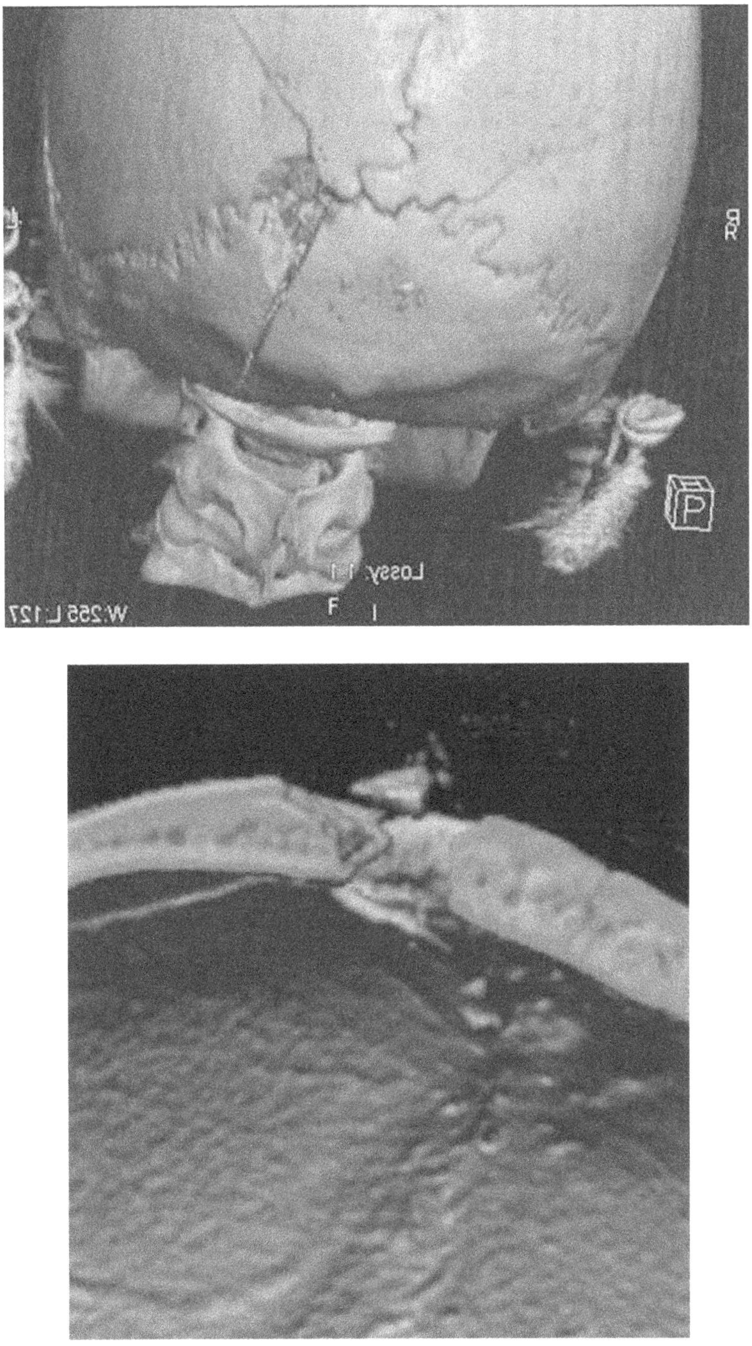

Figure 8.28 Typical gunshot bone exit wounds. A. VRT reconstruction, external view: exocranial visualization of the bone exit wound and associated radial skull fractures. B. VRT reconstruction, virtual cut of the bone: typical external cone-shaped beveling. C. Axial CT image: external cone-shaped beveling.

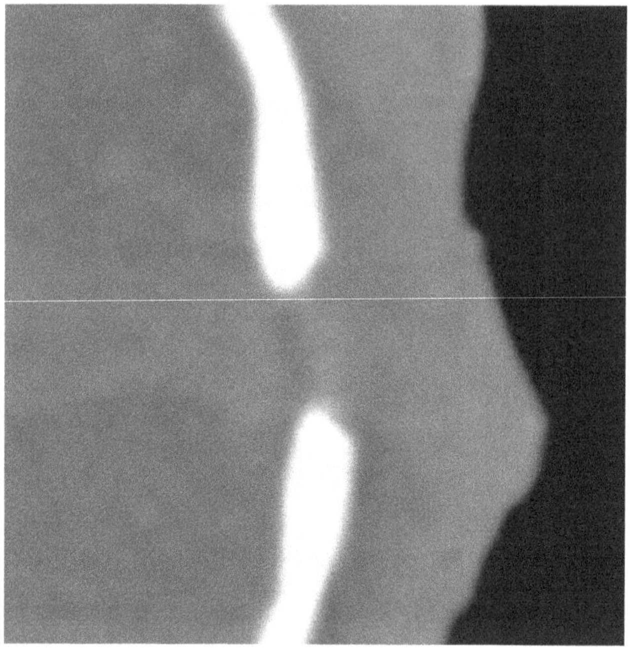

Figure 8.28 (Continued) Typical gunshot bone exit wounds. A. VRT reconstruction, external view: exocranial visualization of the bone exit wound and associated radial skull fractures. B. VRT reconstruction, virtual cut of the bone: typical external cone-shaped beveling. C. Axial CT image: external cone-shaped beveling.

Three-dimensional evaluation of bullet trajectories is also possible and is more precise than during autopsies using steel rods (Oehmichen et al. 2003; Thali et al. 2003g). Along the bullet course, lesions of bone and cartilage can provide evidence of the trajectory and therefore the entry direction (Andenmatten et al. 2008).

Furthermore, three-dimensional reconstructions can better locate the bone splinters which are often removed and manually replaced during autopsy and can give a general overview of the bullet course (Oehmichen et al. 2003; Thali et al. 2003g).

As well as the above, MRI provides detailed information on soft-tissue injuries (Yen et al. 2007). The cause of death is therefore more accurately detailed by MRI than by MSCT examinations. However, MRI does not depict solid objects such as bullets or other foreign particles sufficiently clearly.

In theory, the presence of intracardiac air with a short postmortem interval and without gas in the liver or pancreas is in favor of gaseous embolism (Dedouit et al. 2006).

Stab Wounds

The cutaneous entry can be seen with 3D reconstructions (VRT and MIP) (Figure 8.34; Dedouit et al. 2006; Schnider et al. 2009). MSCT is very sensitive for extravascular gas detection and can give clues as to the cause of death (for example hemorrhage, gas embolism) (Thali et al. 2003e). Gas embolism, a vital sign often encountered in stabbing, is almost impossible to detect on opening the body. Postmortem CT is helpful in determining the general stab direction but is somewhat inadequate in depicting the actual wound channel through soft tissues (Thali et al. 2003e). Stab wound channels are more difficult

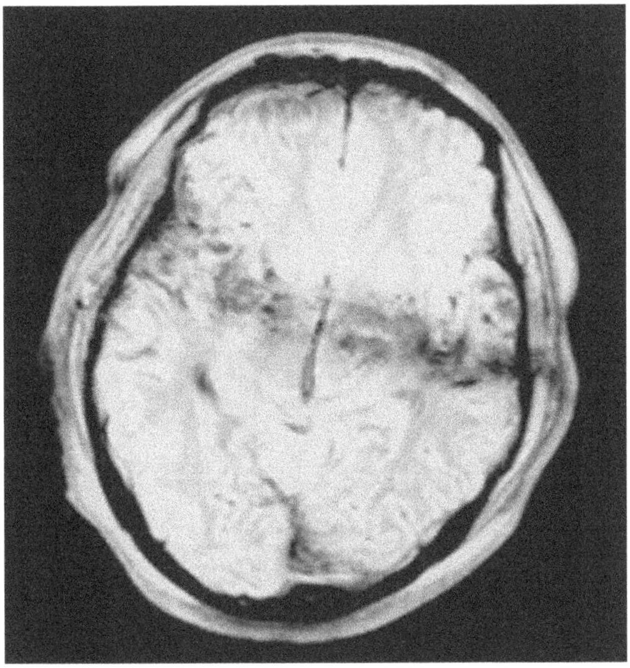

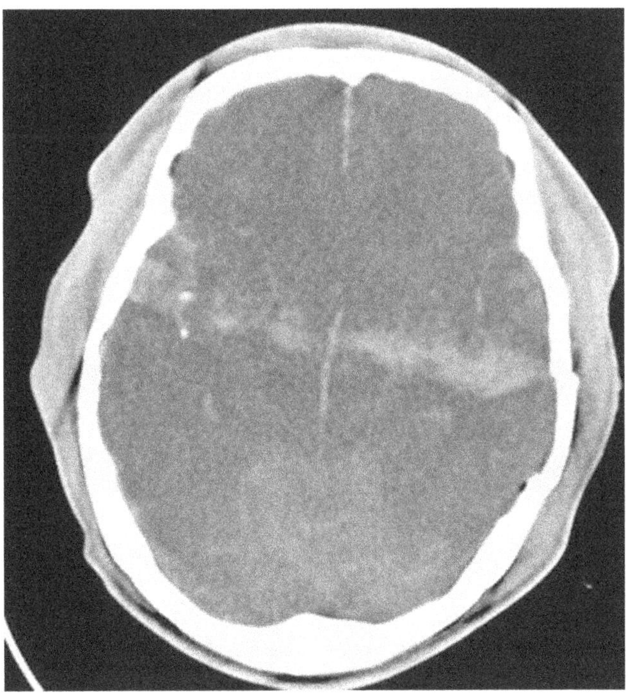

Figure 8.29 Intraparenchymatous ballistic cerebral path. A. Axial MRI image, gradient echo sequence: bullet trajectory from front to back, from right to left and from bottom to top. B. Axial CT image: cerebral path represented by hematoma, air and bone fragments within the brain parenchyma. C. Axial CT image: typical cerebral path. Presence of pneumencephalon, intracranial bone and bullet fragments, intracerebral hematomas, intraventricular hemorrhage. Spontaneous hyperdense areas are visible around the cutaneous entry wound (soot deposition). Entry and exit bone defects are also typical. From Dedouit, F., et al. 2006. Role of modern cross-sectional imaging in thanatology: a pictorial essay. *J Radiol* 87: 619–38, with permission.

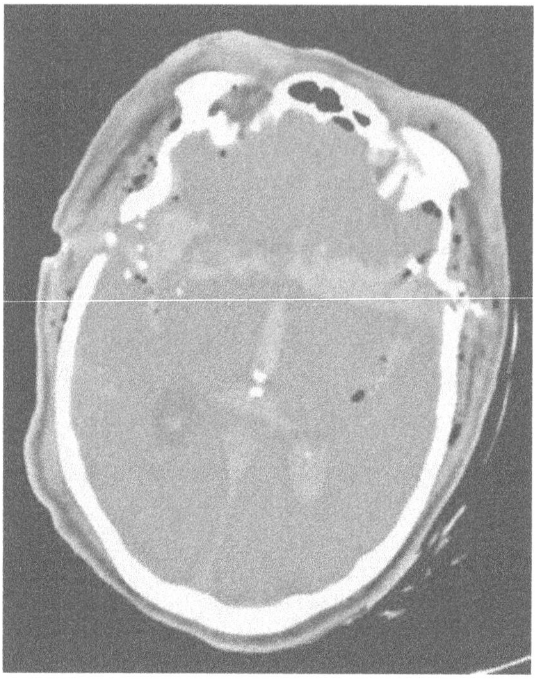

Figure 8.29 (Continued) Intraparenchymatous ballistic cerebral path. A. Axial MRI image, gradient echo sequence: bullet trajectory from front to back, from right to left and from bottom to top. B. Axial CT image: cerebral path represented by hematoma, air and bone fragments within the brain parenchyma. C. Axial CT image: typical cerebral path. Presence of pneumencephalon, intracranial bone and bullet fragments, intracerebral hematomas, intraventricular hemorrhage. Spontaneous hyperdense areas are visible around the cutaneous entry wound (soot deposition). Entry and exit bone defects are also typical. From Dedouit, F., et al. 2006. Role of modern cross-sectional imaging in thanatology: a pictorial essay. *J Radiol* 87: 619–38, with permission.

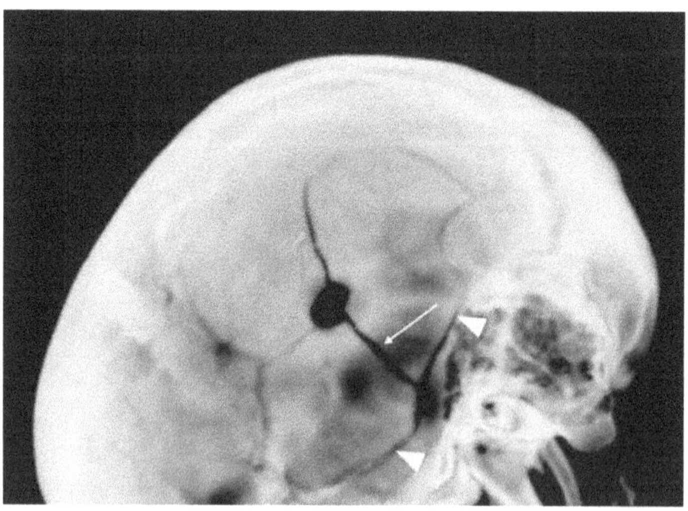

Figure 8.30 Puppe's rule on complex fractures. 3D cephalic VRT reconstruction, external view: exocranial visualization of the bone exit wound and associated radial skull fractures (arrow). Radial inferior fracture ceases where it meets another fracture from the controlateral entry wound (arrowheads).

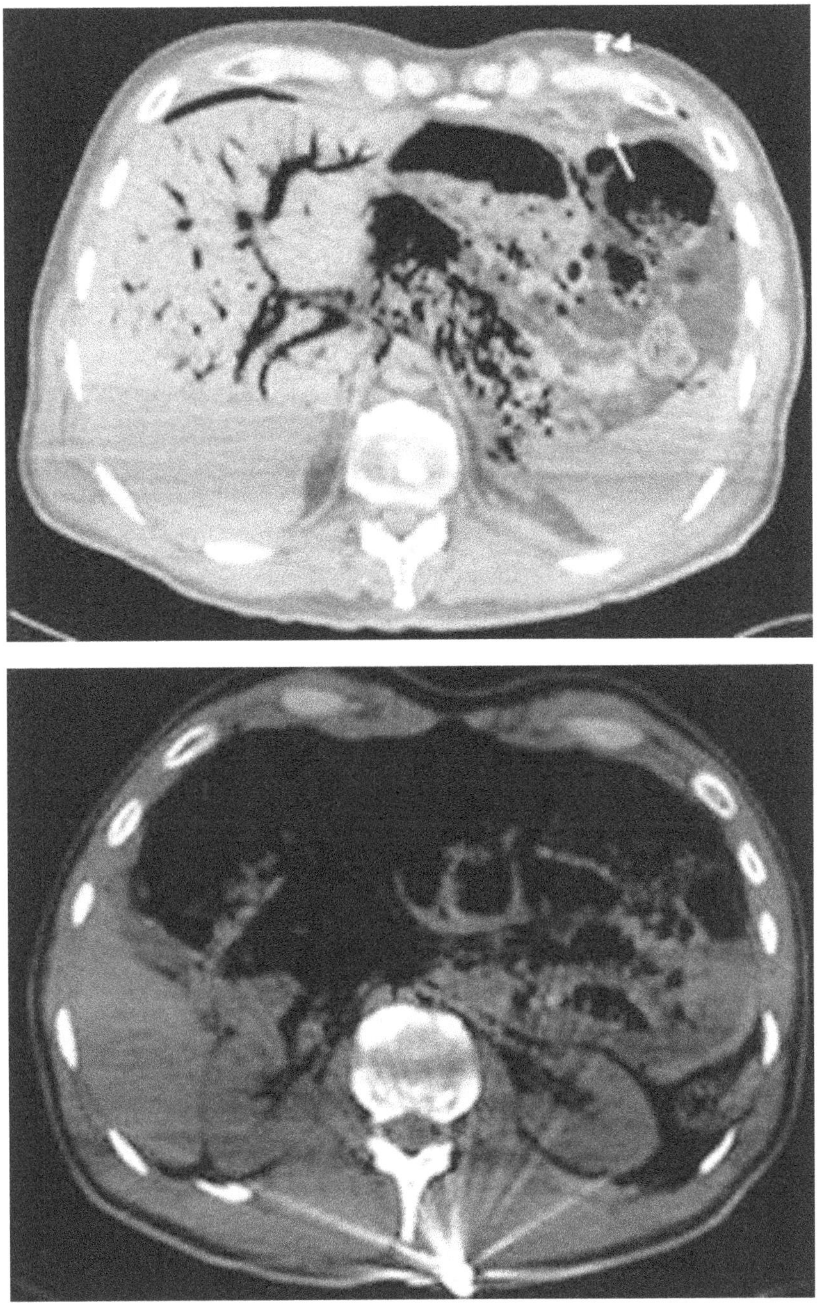

Figure 8.31 Chest and abdominal lesions: shot from a handgun (bullet). A. Axial CT image: visualization of the entry wound with metallic radiopaque fragments of the bullet (arrowhead) and of a peri-orificial hematoma around the soft tissue entry (arrow). B. Axial CT image (level below B): visualization of the subcutaneous left paravertebral bullet; bullet trajectory deviates to the right, back, and downwards. C. MIP CT reconstruction of the chest, lateral view: reconstitution of the bullet trajectory (arrow) bullet trajectory deviates to the right, back and downwards; hemorrhagic left pleural effusion. D. Frontal MPR reconstruction of the chest: pericardial effusion secondary to transfixiant myocardial injuries. From Dedouit, F., et al. 2006. Role of modern cross-sectional imaging in thanatology: a pictorial essay. *J Radiol* 87: 619–38, with permission.

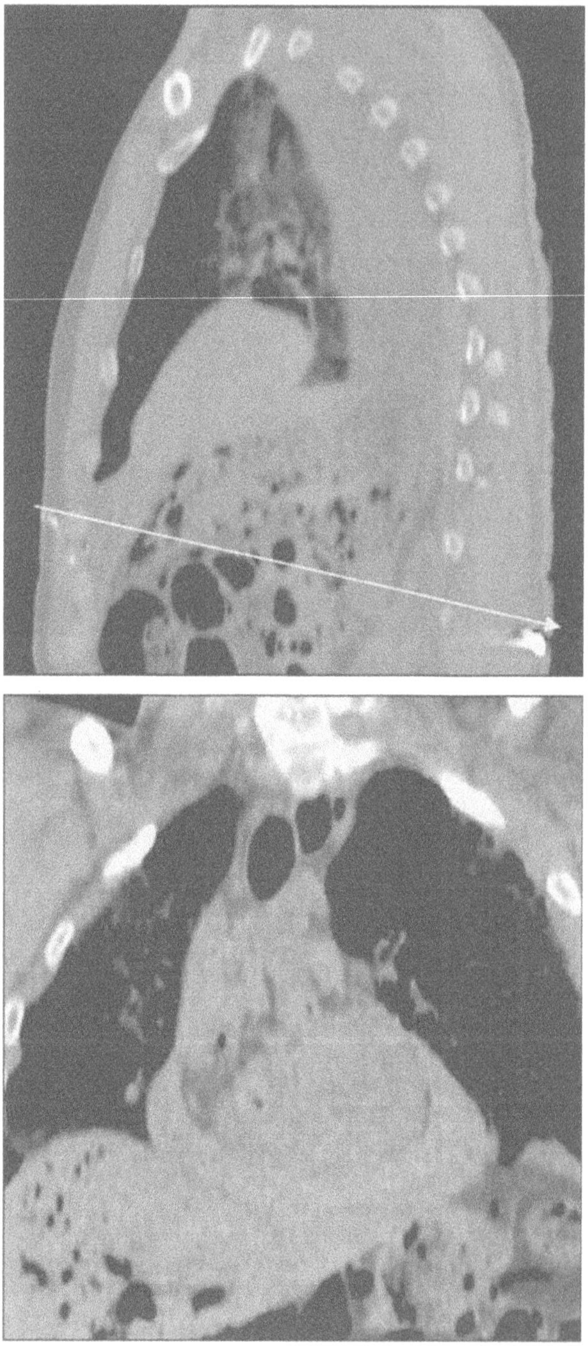

Figure 8.31 (Continued) Chest and abdominal lesions: shot from a handgun (bullet). A. Axial CT image: visualization of the entry wound with metallic radiopaque fragments of the bullet (arrowhead) and of a peri-orificial hematoma around the soft tissue entry (arrow). B. Axial CT image (level below B): visualization of the subcutaneous left paravertebral bullet; bullet trajectory deviates to the right, back, and downwards. C. MIP CT reconstruction of the chest, lateral view: reconstitution of the bullet trajectory (arrow) bullet trajectory deviates to the right, back and downwards; hemorrhagic left pleural effusion. D. Frontal MPR reconstruction of the chest: pericardial effusion secondary to transfixiant myocardial injuries. From Dedouit, F., et al. 2006. Role of modern cross-sectional imaging in thanatology: a pictorial essay. *J Radiol* 87: 619–38, with permission.

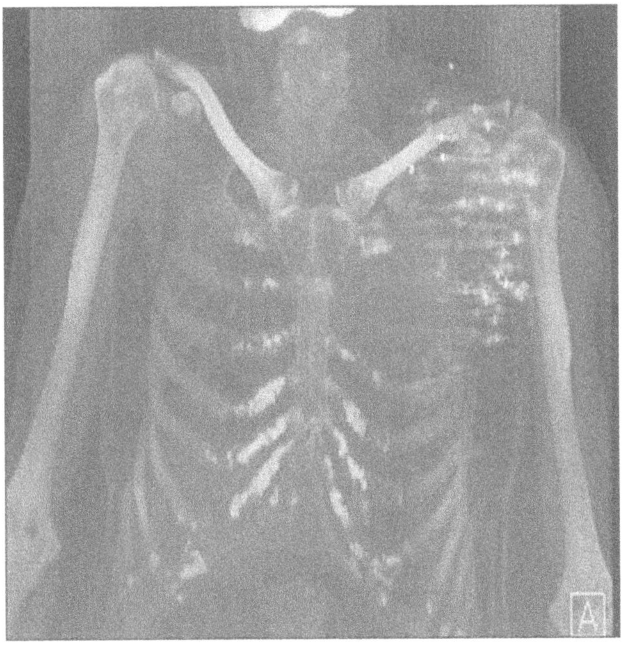

Figure 8.32 Chest, MIP mode, anterior view. Near contact wound from shotgun. Dispersion of the pellets illustrating the billiard effect. From Dedouit, F., et al. 2006. Role of modern cross-sectional imaging in thanatology: a pictorial essay. *J Radiol* 87: 619–38, with permission.

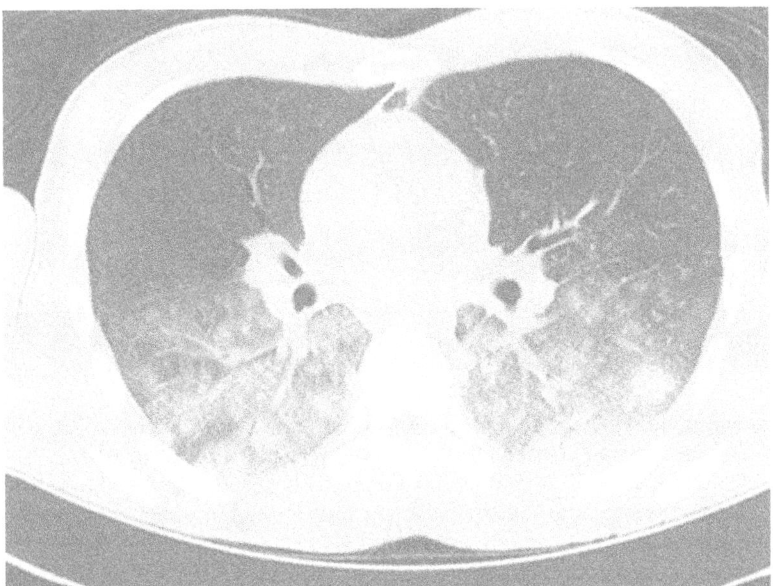

Figure 8.33 Vital reaction signs secondary to ballistic trauma. A. Axial CT image. Parenchyma: alveolar condensation secondary to blood alveolar filling. B. Chest reconstruction, frontal MPR view. Tracheal and bronchial filling secondary to blood alveolar filling. C. Axial CT image. Mediastinum: gas within the trunk and left and right branches of the pulmonary artery secondary to gas embolism. From Dedouit, F., et al. 2006. Role of modern cross-sectional imaging in thanatology: a pictorial essay. *J Radiol* 87: 619–38, with permission.

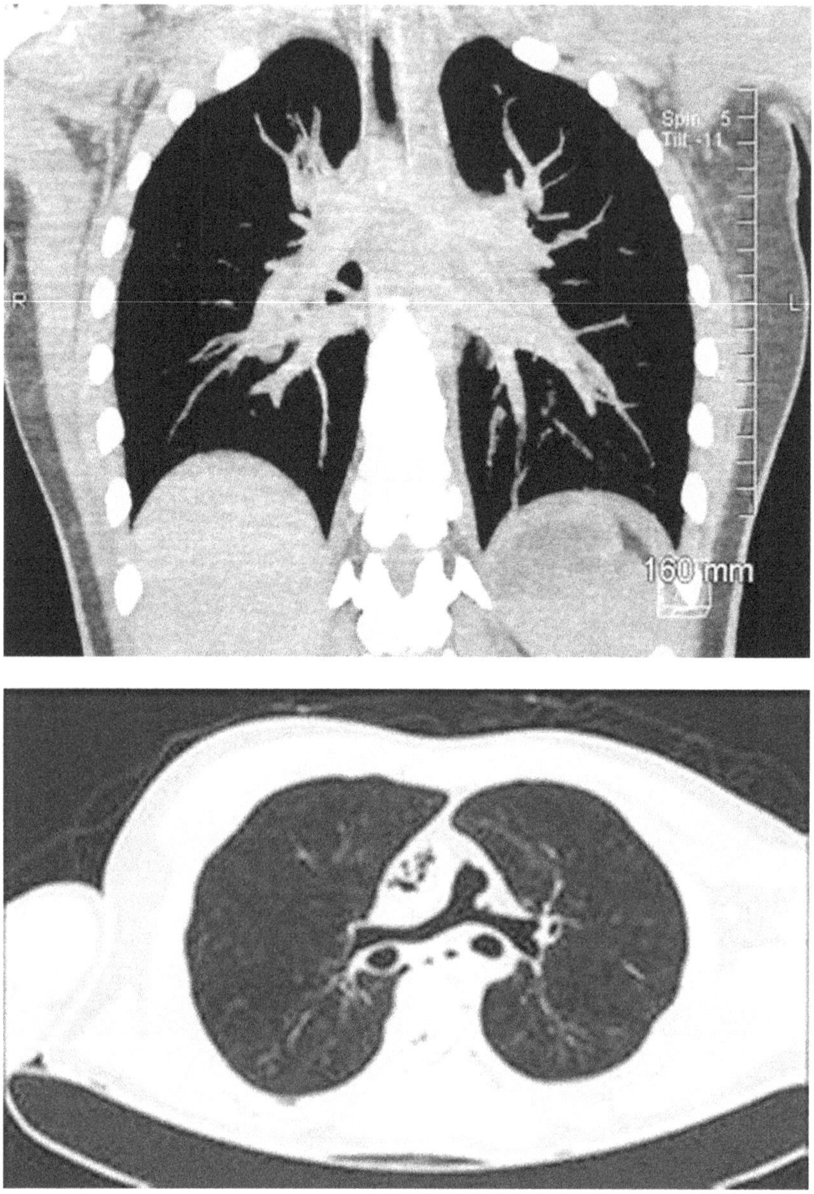

Figure 8.33 (Continued) Vital reaction signs secondary to ballistic trauma. A. Axial CT image. Parenchyma: alveolar condensation secondary to blood alveolar filling. B. Chest reconstruction, frontal MPR view. Tracheal and bronchial filling secondary to blood alveolar filling. C. Axial CT image. Mediastinum: gas within the trunk and left and right branches of the pulmonary artery secondary to gas embolism. From Dedouit, F., et al. 2006. Role of modern cross-sectional imaging in thanatology: a pictorial essay. *J Radiol* 87: 619–38, with permission.

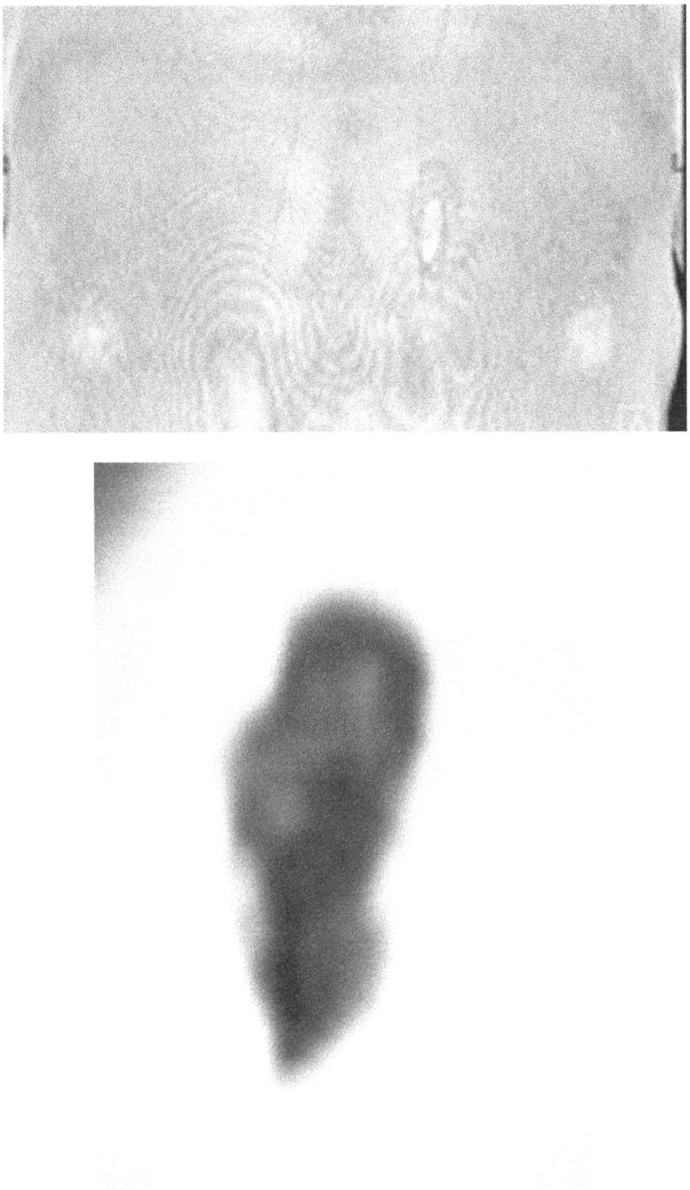

Figure 8.34 Death by knife wound. A. Chest VRT CT reconstruction, anterior view: view of the penetrating wound of the left chest wall. B. Chest MIP CT reconstruction, anterior view: view of the penetrating wound of the left chest wall. C. Axial CT image: large hemopericardium and left pleural effusion; visualization of the cutaneous defect corresponding to the stab entry wound. D. Axial chest CT image: cartilaginous costal section (arrow). From Dedouit, F., et al. 2006. Role of modern cross-sectional imaging in thanatology: a pictorial essay. *J Radiol* 87: 619–38, with permission.

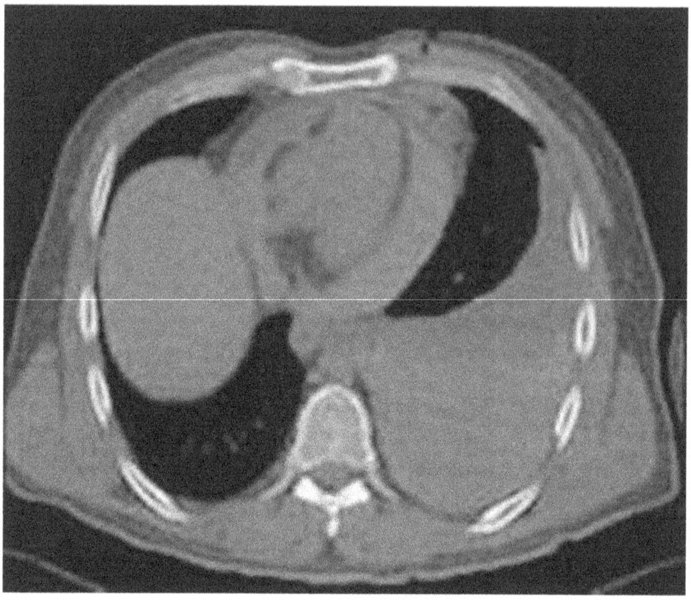

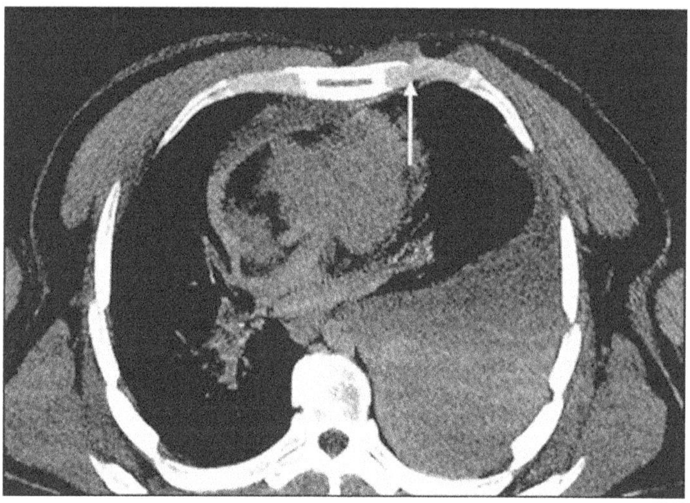

Figure 8.34 (Continued) Death by knife wound. A. Chest VRT CT reconstruction, anterior view: view of the penetrating wound of the left chest wall. B. Chest MIP CT reconstruction, anterior view: view of the penetrating wound of the left chest wall. C. Axial CT image: large hemopericardium and left pleural effusion; visualization of the cutaneous defect corresponding to the stab entry wound. D. Axial chest CT image: cartilaginous costal section (arrow). From Dedouit, F., et al. 2006. Role of modern cross-sectional imaging in thanatology: a pictorial essay. *J Radiol* 87: 619–38, with permission.

to determine than gunshot wound trajectories (Schnider et al. 2009). Myocardial injuries cannot be diagnosed with any precision because spontaneous contrast is poor (Dedouit et al. 2006). However, indirect transmyocardial injuries can be detected when pleural and pericardial blood effusions are seen (Thali et al. 2003e; Schnider et al. 2009). MRI is the method of choice for the depiction of soft tissues and their lesions. The course of wound channels through soft tissues can be very accurately visualized and so determined in a non-destructive fashion (Thali et al. 2003e).

Thermal Damage and Charred Bodies

One basic rule in forensics is that carbonized or putrefied corpses must be radiographed to exclude the presence of hyperdense foreign bodies (gunshot projectiles) and to diagnose fractures (Brogdon 1998; Thali et al. 2002). Fractures of the calvaria appear after 20 minutes of fire exposure and the cranial base is exposed after 45 to 60 minutes of thermal exposure (Knight et al. 2004). It is important to take this into account if we suspect that a cranial base fracture may be of traumatic and not thermal origin. Bronchial filling can be seen on chest CT (Dedouit et al. 2006) (Figure 8.35). An air-fluid level can be seen in maxillary sinuses, which is an argument for regurgitation of vital fluids (Figure 8.35). Heat-induced epidural hematoma is a common postmortem finding in burned bodies (Thali et al. 2003e; Knight et al. 2004). Furthermore, as for putrefied corpses, MSCT can be helpful for identification of the deceased (Dedouit et al. 2007b).

Mechanical Asphyxia

Hanging

Laryngeal fractures are inconstant in suicidal hanging, ranging from 0 to 67% of cases according to the literature (Knight et al. 2004). There are no associations between the number of fractures, type of knot or suspension, or the gender of the deceased. The real discriminant factor is the age of the deceased. This is due to the progressive ossification of the laryngeal cartilage, which increases with advancing age and becomes more fragile. MSCT is an efficient method of evaluating laryngeal trauma: fractures of the upper horns of the thyroid cartilage, fractures of the greater horns of the hyoid bone, or luxation of the greater horns (Figure 8.36; Dedouit et al. 2006). One of the advantages of MSCT is visualization of the displacement of fragments of broken bones. Of course, the cervical spine is easily explored and degenerative changes are differentiated from trauma (Dedouit et al. 2006). However, a hangman fracture is rare (Knight et al. 2004). Such fractures arise only if a large amount of energy is applied to the neck in such a manner as to hyperextend the spine (Dedouit et al. 2007d). This is usually only encountered in vehicle injuries and judicial hangings (Bolliger et al. 2005). Vital reactions such as pulmonary inhalation or fluid regurgitation in the sinuses are seen (Aghayev et al. 2005; Dedouit et al. 2006).

Drowning

MSCT demonstrates air-fluid levels in the paranasal sinuses, which are not routinely seen during autopsy (Figure 8.37; Dedouit et al. 2006; Christe et al. 2008). Intra-esophageal, intra-tracheal, and bronchial fluid filling are also often visible (Figure 8.38; Dedouit et al. 2006). Additionally, the bronchial diameters compared with the diameters of the accompanying pulmonary artery in MSCT can be used as a sign of bronchial constriction, hypothesizing that a ratio of <0.9 (broncho-arterial coefficient) might reflect bronchospasm (Christe et al. 2008). A consecutive mosaic pattern of hypoperfused and hyperperfused lung areas is present in 60% of drowning cases in both autopsy and MSCT.

In diving fatalities, the radiologist performing postmortem imaging must be familiar with the phenomenon of postmortem off-gassing (Figure 8.39; Wheen and Williams 2009).

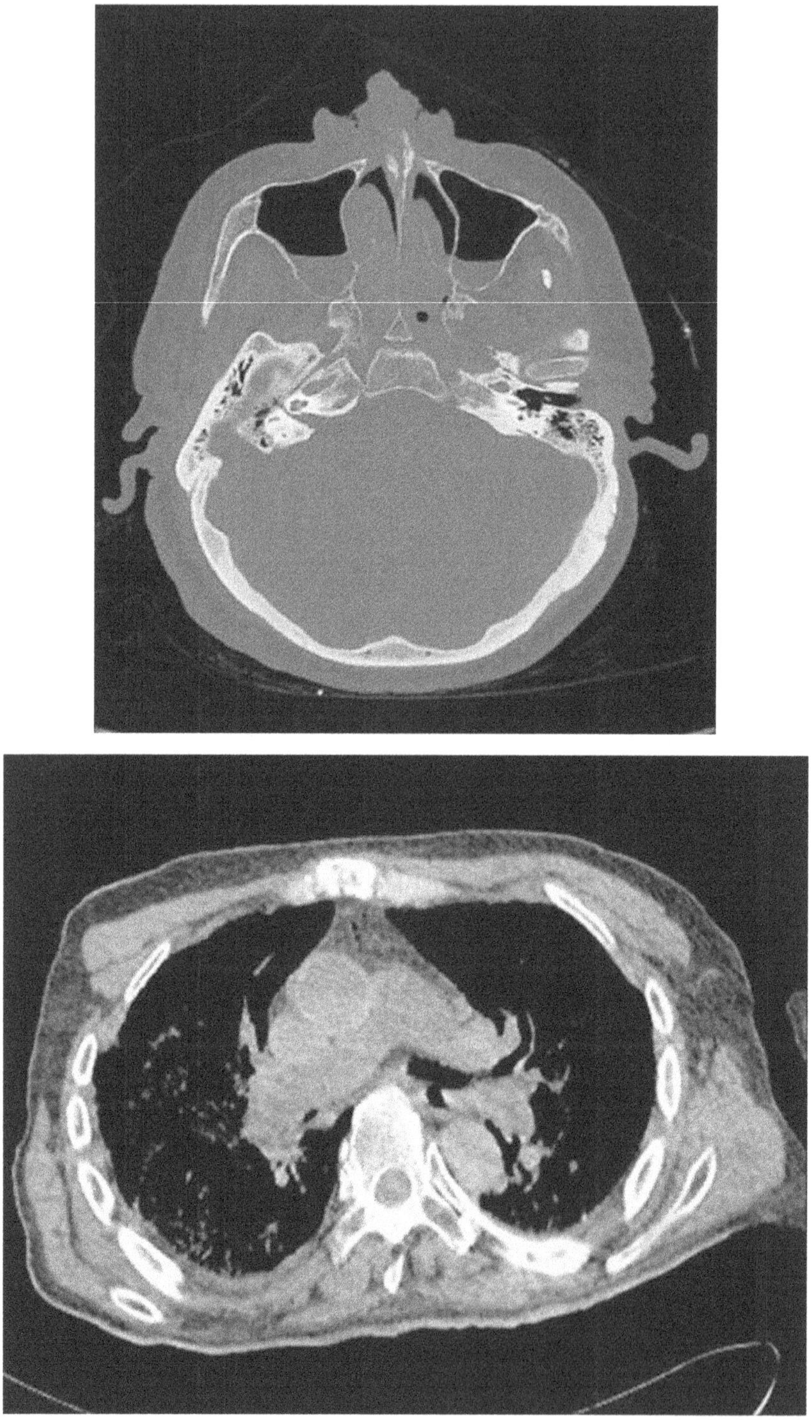

Figure 8.35 Thermal injuries. A. Axial cerebral CT slice: signs of regurgitation with air-fluid levels within the paranasal sinuses. B. Axial chest CT image: bronchial filling secondary to soot inhalation.

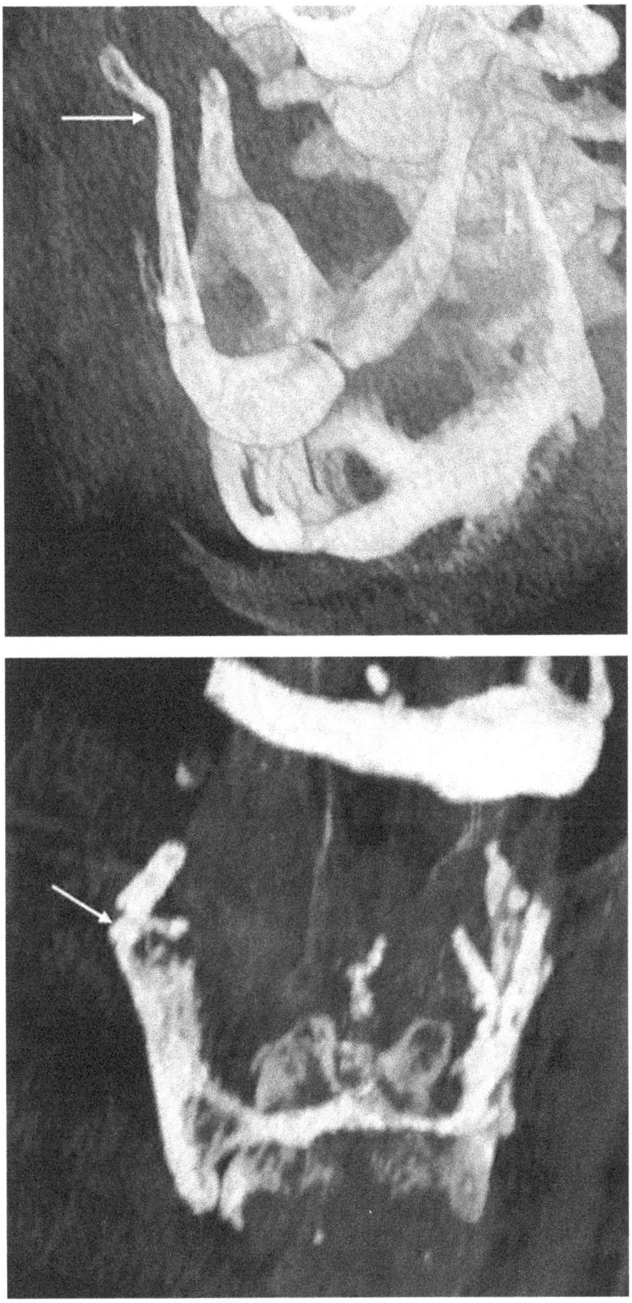

Figure 8.36 Death by hanging. A. Laryngeal VRT CT reconstructions, anterior view: external displaced fracture of the top of the right superior horn of the thyroid (arrow). B. Laryngeal CT reconstruction, superior view: supero-lateral displacement of the end of the right greater hyoid horn due to a fracture (arrow). From Dedouit, F., et al. 2006. Role of modern cross-sectional imaging in thanatology: a pictorial essay. *J Radiol* 87: 619–38, with permission.

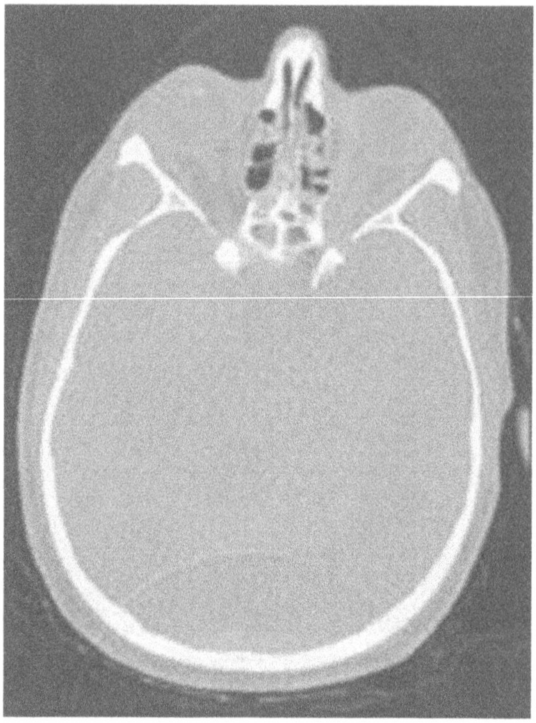

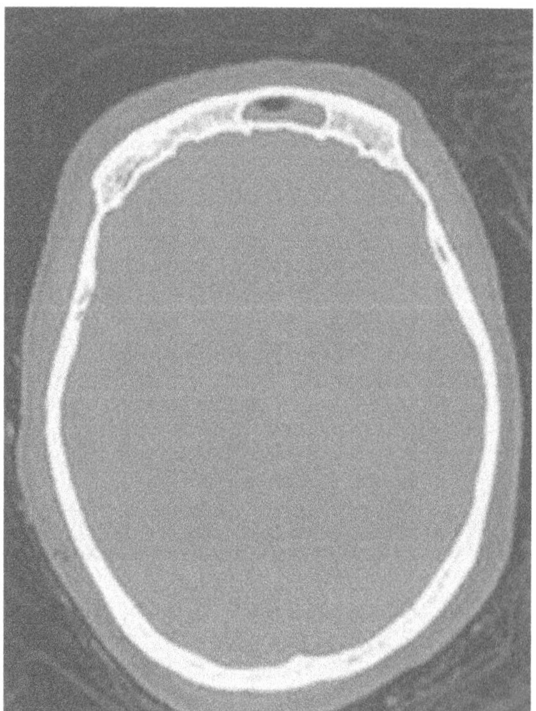

Figure 8.37 Death by drowning: axial CT images of the sinuses. A. Air-fluid level within the left frontal sinus. B. Filling of the anterior and posterior ethmoidal cells. C. Bilateral air-fluid levels within the sphenoid sinuses and filling of the nasal fossae. D. Bilateral air-fluid levels within the maxillary sinuses. From Dedouit, F., et al. 2006. Role of modern cross-sectional imaging in thanatology: a pictorial essay. *J Radiol* 87: 619–38, with permission.

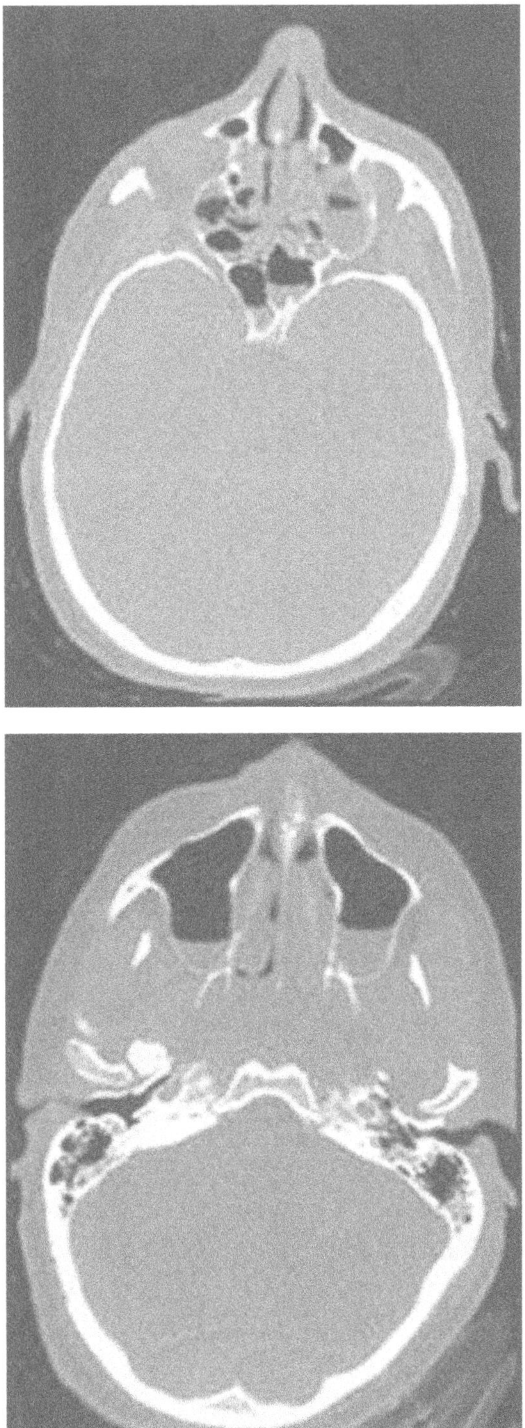

Figure 8.37 (Continued) Death by drowning: axial CT images of the sinuses. A. Air-fluid level within the left frontal sinus. B. Filling of the anterior and posterior ethmoidal cells. C. Bilateral air-fluid levels within the sphenoid sinuses and filling of the nasal fossae. D. Bilateral air-fluid levels within the maxillary sinuses. From Dedouit, F., et al. 2006. Role of modern cross-sectional imaging in thanatology: a pictorial essay. *J Radiol* 87: 619–38, with permission.

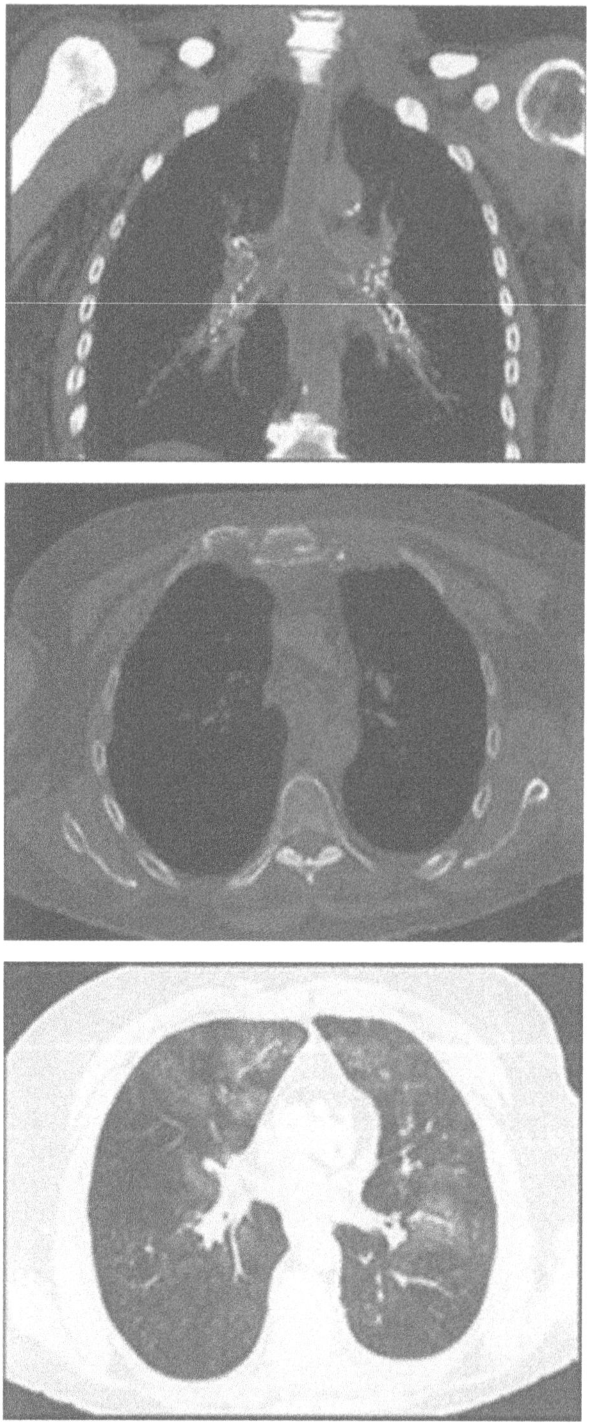

Figure 8.38 Death by drowning: trachea and major bronchi. A. MIP frontal chest reconstruction: fluid filling within the trachea and the major bronchi. B. Axial chest CT image: fluid within the esophagus and major bronchi. C. Axial thoracic CT image: alveolar filling with thickening of inter- and intralobular septa showing the "crazy paving" appearance. From Dedouit, F., et al. 2006. Role of modern cross-sectional imaging in thanatology: a pictorial essay. *J Radiol* 87: 619–38, with permission.

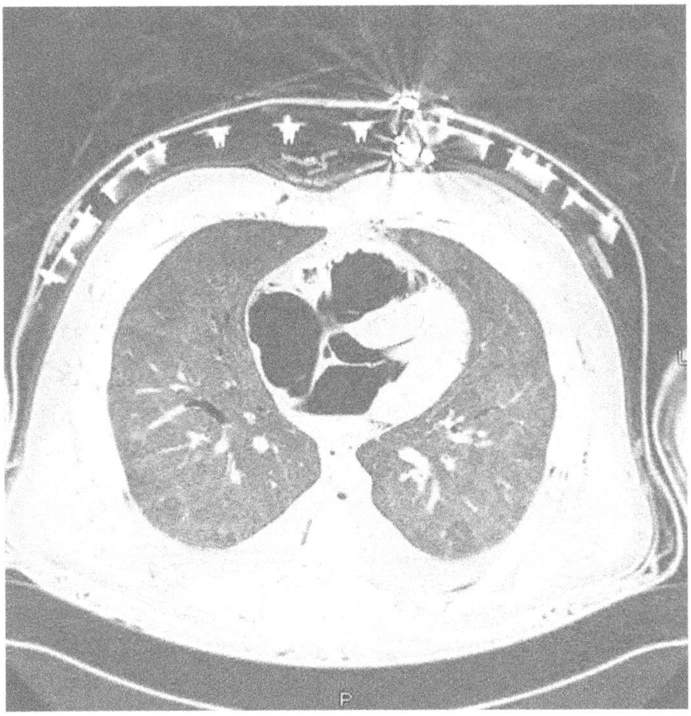

Figure 8.39 Death by drowning (cave diving fatality). Axial chest CT image. Illustration of postmortem decompression or off-gassing. The heart cavities and thoracic vessels (arteries and veins) are completely filled with gas.

Postmortem off-gassing is a diving-related artifact responsible for the presence of gas in the vessels and tissue of cadavers. After a prolonged bottom time at great depths, excess nitrogen is released upon surfacing by a process known as tissue degassing. This can be observed after all types of water-related deaths. It must not be mistaken for vital gas embolism.

Is Postmortem Imaging Useful in Cases of "Sudden Natural Death"?

"Sudden natural death" means different things to different people (Dolinak et al. 2005). The spectrum of diseases causing a sudden natural death varies significantly with the definition used. The truly sudden or "instantaneous" death almost invariably involves diseases of the cardiovascular system, whereas broader definitions can involve virtually any organ system or disease (Knight et al. 2004; Dolinak et al. 2005).

Main Origins of Sudden Natural Deaths

Heart and Vascular Diseases

Diseases of the heart account for approximately 90 percent of all sudden deaths due to natural disease, with atherosclerotic coronary artery disease being the underlying cause of approximately 75 to 90% of sudden cardiac deaths (Dolinak et al. 2005; Di Maio and Dana 2007). The remaining cardiac related deaths can be attributed to hypertension, valvular disease (aortic valve stenosis, membranous subaortic stenosis, supravalvular aortic stenosis, infective endocarditis, mitral valve prolapse), non-atherosclerotic coronary artery disease (coronary artery spasm, spontaneous coronary artery dissection), myocarditis, cardiomyopathy (hypertrophic cardiomyopathy, arrhythmogenic right ventricular cardiomyopathy, dilated cardiomyopathy, alcoholic cardiomyopathy, myotonic dystrophy), or conduction system disorders.

Diseases of the Central Nervous System

A number of the diseases traditionally considered as primary central nervous system pathologies are, in reality, diseases of the cardiovascular system (e.g., ruptured cerebral artery berry aneurysm, hypertensive intracerebral hemorrhage) (Dolinak et al. 2005; Di Maio and Dana 2007). Sudden death due to diseases of the central nervous system can be broadly classified into seizure-related disorders, intracranial hemorrhage of varying etiologies, meningitis, and tumors (Knight et al. 2004).

Diseases of the Respiratory System

The majority of diseases involving the respiratory system present clinical signs and symptoms that result in a clinical diagnosis, such that if and when death occurs it is neither sudden nor unexpected (Dolinak et al. 2005; Di Maio and Dana 2007). This is particularly true for chronic obstructive pulmonary disease and for most pulmonary malignancies. On occasion though, diseases of the respiratory system can cause sudden death and can even be quite dramatic in their presentation (lobar pneumonia, pulmonary artery thromboemboli, reactive airway disease) (Dolinak et al. 2005; Di Maio and Dana 2007).

Diseases of the Gastrointestinal System

In some cases of diseases of the gastrointestinal system, avoidance of physicians, ignoring of symptoms, or vagueness of symptoms can create situations where there is at least an appearance that the death was sudden (Dolinak et al. 2005; Di Maio and Dana 2007). Bleeding gastric or duodenal ulcers (usually benign, but occasionally malignant) are one of the most common gastrointestinal diseases that present in this manner, and the scene can be as dramatic as that for massive hemoptysis. Others are perforation of gastric and peptic ulcers or complications of appendicitis.

Other Causes

Other causes of sudden death relate to the endocrine system (diabetes mellitus, polyglandular autoimmune syndromes), sepsis, or chronic ethanol abuse (Dolinak et al. 2005).

Diagnostic Possibilities of Modern Imaging in Natural Deaths

Attempts to develop techniques for postmortem application of contrast media have yielded promising results (Thali et al. 2009). Future forensic radiological research will define the value and possible applications of these technologies. The main problem of postmortem CT and MRI in detection of venous sinus thromboses is the arrest of blood circulation in the dead. In the near future, it may be possible to detect these thromboses thanks to advances in postmortem angiography.

Aneurysm Ruptures

In clinical and postmortem MSCT and MRI, hemorrhages caused by rupture of major vessel aneurysms are easily visible (Aghayev et al. 2006). Also, the diameter of the major arteries is easily measurable, and medium-sized and large aneurysms as well as hemorrhages to the retroperitoneal soft tissue can be seen.

Thromboembolism

The primary locations of fatal thromboembolism are the pulmonary arteries. There is still a great need for research in this field of postmortem imaging (Thali et al. 2009). Postmortem angiography and image-guided biopsy have potential to diagnose pulmonary embolism in the deceased, but scientific evaluation remains necessary (Grabherr et al. 2007; 2008).

Parenchymal Pulmonary Diseases

At the present time, no postmortem imaging modality can diagnose sudden death due to asthma (Thali et al. 2009). Furthermore, it is sometimes difficult to differentiate between pneumonic infiltration and internal livores (Figure 8.13A; Dedouit et al. 2006).

Gastrointestinal Bleeding

In postmortem radiology the point of bleeding from esophageal varices is not detectable at the present time, but the signs of hemorrhage and cirrhosis of the liver can be identified (Thali et al. 2009). In the future, postmortem angiography may be a valuable tool for the detection of these lesions (Grabherr et al. 2008).

Heart and Vascular Diseases

The first studies in 2003 on isolated human autopsy hearts and entire corpses showed that these imaging techniques have great potential in postmortem diagnosis of heart disease, and they also demonstrated the influence of postmortem reactions on imaging (Jackowski et al. 2005; 2006b). Concerning detection of coronary calcifications, numerous studies have shown the correlation between calcium deposition and narrowing of the artery lumen. However, these are only statistical correlations and do not predict the actual grade of stenosis. CT is an excellent tool for the detection of coronary calcifications and also deposition of calcium on cardiac valves but fails in assessing critical tissue alterations of the myocardium (Figure 8.40). MRI has already been tested to evaluate alterations of the myocardium (Jackowski et al. 2006; Aghayev et al. 2008). A chronology of the MRI appearance of myocardial infarction has already been described for acute, subacute, and chronic infarction. In peracute infarction, MRI failed to visualize myocardial changes, but the series studied was small. Myocardial hypertrophy and cardiac chamber dilatation can also be studied by MRI.

Identification Possibilities

Only three techniques are considered reliable identification methods within the forensic community: DNA profiling, fingerprinting, and comparison of ante- and postmortem dental data (Dolinak et al. 2005; Jackowski et al. 2006a; Beauthier 2008). All other more frequently used methods in forensic practice such as confrontation with relatives, recognition of individual body features (tattoos, piercing, scars), or recognition of personal

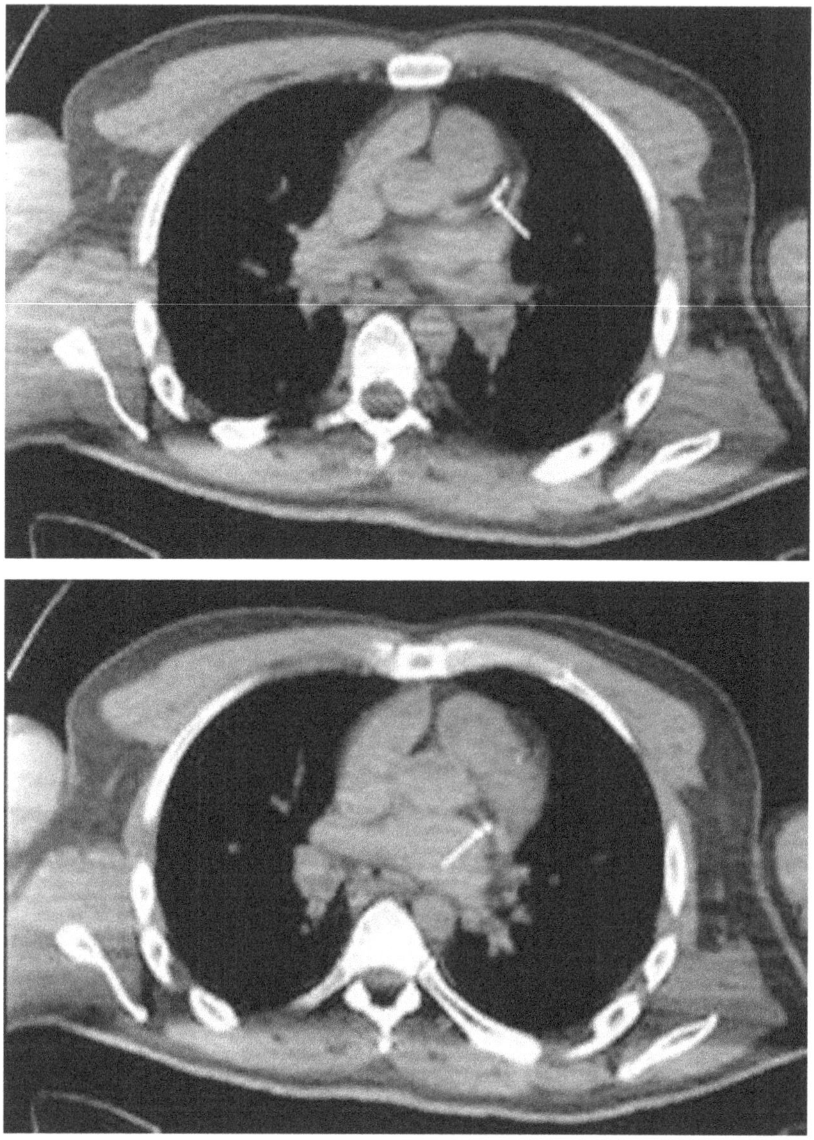

Figure 8.40 Adult sudden death: coronary vessel calcifications. A. Axial CT image: calcifications of the left coronary artery (anterior interventricular vessel) (arrow). B. Axial CT image: calcifications of the left coronary artery (initial part) (arrow). C. Axial CT image: calcifications of the right coronary artery (arrow). From Dedouit, F., et al. 2006. Role of modern cross-sectional imaging in thanatology: a pictorial essay. *J Radiol* 87: 619–38, with permission.

belongings are less reliable, as there are situations when mistakes can occur. These methods are therefore used when the identity of the deceased is highly suspected (Dedouit et al. 2007c).

Furthermore, in some cases, a single MSCT acquisition with forensic purpose on an unidentified body enables performing anthropological analyses simultaneously (Dedouit et al. 2007b, 2007c). The forensic exploration identifies causes of death, possible

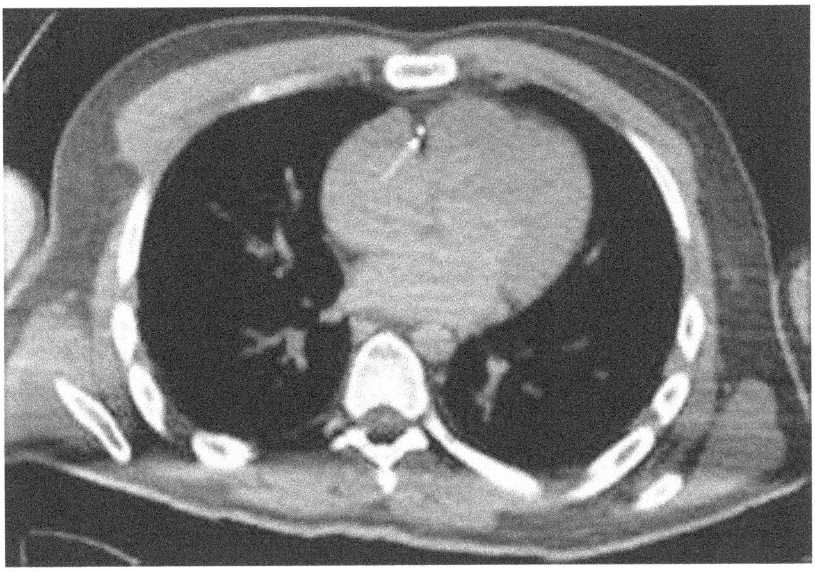

Figure 8.40 (Continued) Adult sudden death: coronary vessel calcifications. A. Axial CT image: calcifications of the left coronary artery (anterior interventricular vessel) (arrow). B. Axial CT image: calcifications of the left coronary artery (initial part) (arrow). C. Axial CT image: calcifications of the right coronary artery (arrow). From Dedouit, F., et al. 2006. Role of modern cross-sectional imaging in thanatology: a pictorial essay. *J Radiol* 87: 619–38, with permission.

premorbid diseases and nonlethal abnormalities; the anthropological exploration detects criteria potentially useful for identification of the deceased (Figure 8.41A). As with plain x-rays, identification may be based on detection of surgical material, variants of normal radiological appearance or preexisting abnormalities (congenital or acquired) (Dedouit et al. 2007a; Pfaeffli et al. 2007; Sidler et al. 2007). As with plain x-rays, ante- and postmortem MSCT images can be compared. With the increasing number of investigations carried out in clinical and surgical situations, such comparisons are more and more frequent.

Foreign material is of great value for identification (Sidler et al. 2007). At the present time the widespread use of many osteosynthesis and endoprosthesis techniques leads to the detection in unknown corpses of a considerable amount of foreign material that is valuable for identification purposes. Normally, use of these surgical techniques means that antemortem x-ray documentation is available. But, it is becoming obvious that 3D computed tomography documentation of foreign bodies has an enormous advantage over plain x-ray documentation. Using 3D computed tomography, radiologists can fit postmortem images to any antemortem x-ray projection that becomes available for identification (Figure 8.41B).

The anthropological use of MSCT is principally based either on specific MSCT criteria and characteristics, or on the transposition of techniques used on dry bones in physical anthropology (Figure 8.42; Dedouit et al. 2007b; Grabherr et al. 2009). Consequently, the radiologist who performs these investigations must be familiar with techniques used in physical anthropology (Dedouit et al. 2008a). Identification can in fact be based on

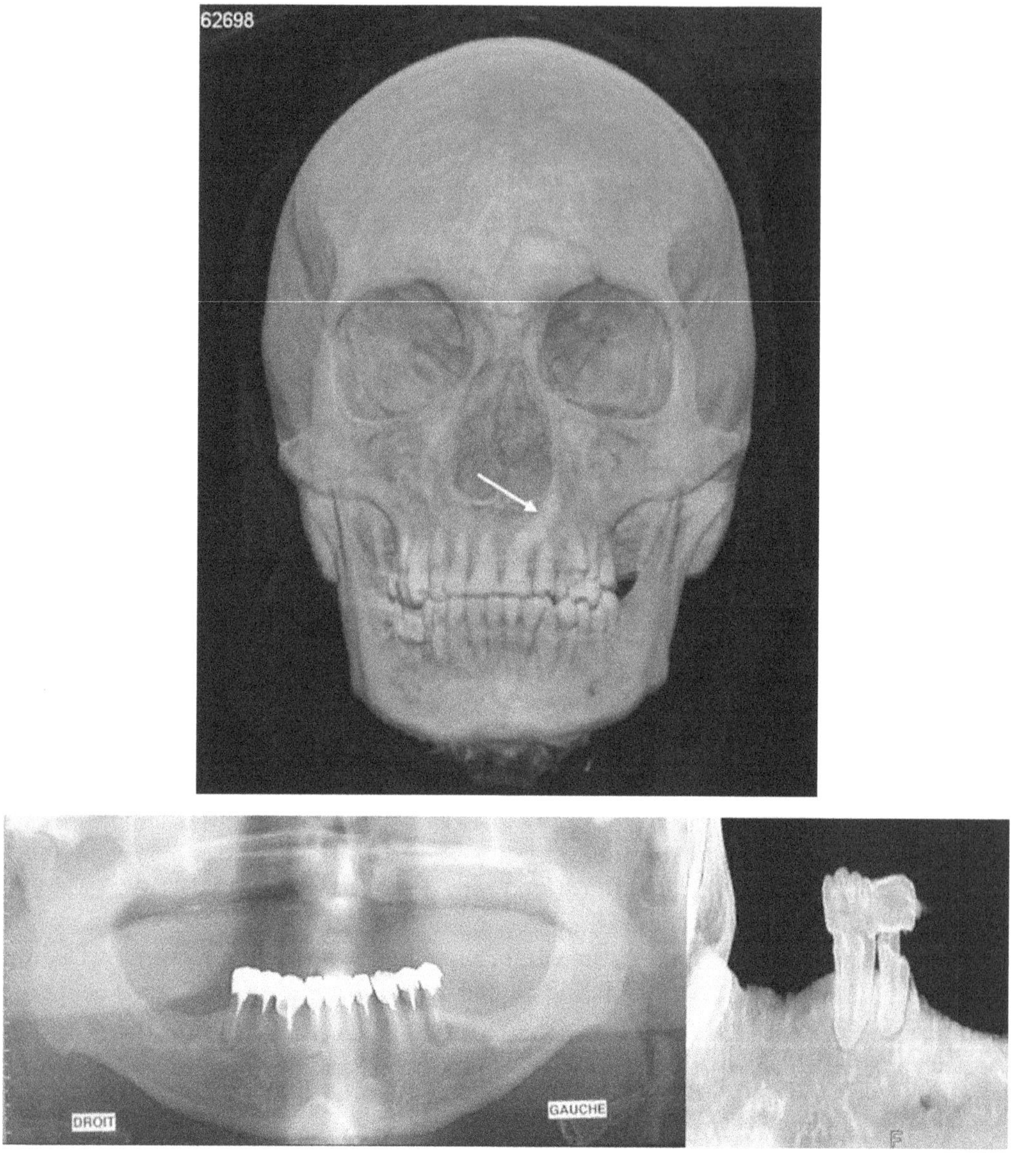

Figure 8.41 Teeth as identification markers. A. VRT facial reconstruction: non-erupted teeth (arrow). From Dedouit, F., et al. 2007. Virtual anthropology and forensic identification: report of one case. *Forensic Sci Int* 173: 182–7, with permission. B. Positive comparison between antemortem dental radiograph (left side) and postmortem VRT mandible reconstruction (right side) in an identification case of skeletal human remains.

determination and assessment of some important anthropological parameters: racial phenotype, age at death, sex, and stature (Dedouit et al. 2007b). Consequently, three-dimensional reconstructions of a scanned skeleton even make it possible to apply anthropological methods to skeletal features if necessary, without the need for time-consuming preparation of bones (Dedouit et al. 2007b).

In mass fatalities, there exists an internationally accepted standard procedure for identification of victims of mass disasters: Interpol's *Disaster Victim Identification Guide*

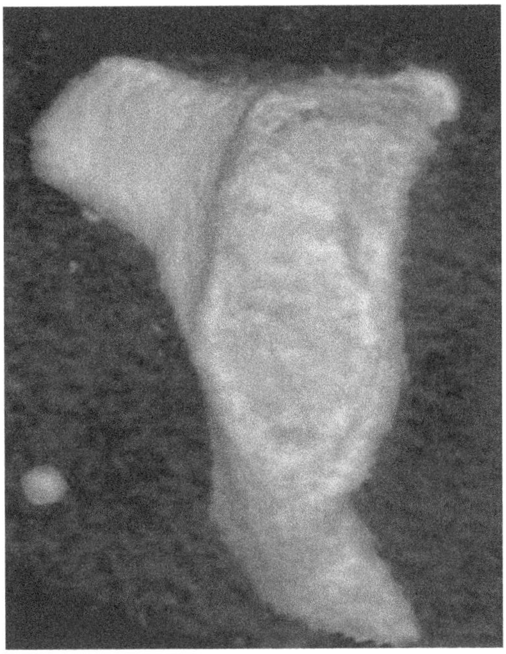

Figure 8.42 Virtual anthropology. VRT reconstruction of the pubic symphysis in an unidentified body. Age markers are clearly seen, permitting Suchey-Brooks staging and consequently determination of an age range. From Dedouit, F., et al. 2007. Virtual anthropology and forensic identification: report of one case. *Forensic Sci Int* 173: 182–7, with permission.

(Jackowski et al. 2006a; Pfaeffli et al. 2007; Beauthier 2008). The three major stages in victim identification are described:

- The search for antemortem information on possible victims
- The recovery and examination of the bodies to establish postmortem evidence from the deceased
- Comparison of antemortem and postmortem data

Conclusion: Possible Indications of Postmortem Imaging

Medicolegal autopsy is always the reference method to determine causes of death. Postmortem imaging must be considered as a complement and not an alternative method. These techniques have numerous limitations that must be known and kept in mind by the users.

Postmortem imaging can be used to document the following:

- Direct and indirect trauma
- Abuse (children, the elderly)
- Gunshot wounds
- Drowning
- Charred, carbonized, putrefied corpses
- Unidentified corpses

Postmortem imaging needs further scientific evaluation in the following areas:

- Most sudden natural deaths
- Toxic deaths
- Determination of postmortem interval
- External body documentation

Postmortem use of modern cross-sectional imaging is a relatively young discipline (Brogdon 1998; Thali et al. 2009). The potentialities it offers in many fields of research have still to be fully explored. Radiology is, of course, a vast specialty and its progress depends on technological advances. Postmortem imaging, like clinical imaging, involves the multidisciplinary participation of numerous actors, among them radiologists, forensic pathologists, anthropologists, pathologists, and toxicologists, opening up a unique path toward future progress and also toward rendering the best possible service to the judiciary system throughout the world.

Bibliography

Aghayev, E., C. Jackowski, M.J. Thali, K. Yen, R. Dirnhofer, and M. Sonnenschein. 2008. Heart luxation and myocardium rupture in postmortem multislice computed tomography and magnetic resonance imaging. *Am J Forensic Med Pathol* 29 (1):86–8.

Aghayev, E., M. Sonnenschein, C. Jackowski, et al. 2006. Postmortem radiology of fatal hemorrhage: measurements of cross-sectional areas of major blood vessels and volumes of aorta and spleen on MDCT and volumes of heart chambers on MRI. *AJR Am J Roentgenol* 187 (1): 209–15.

Aghayev, E., K. Yen, M. Sonnenschein, et al. 2005. Pneumomediastinum and soft tissue emphysema of the neck in postmortem CT and MRI; a new vital sign in hanging? *Forensic Sci Int* 153 (2–3): 181–8.

Andenmatten, M.A., M.J. Thali, B.P. Kneubuehl, et al. 2008. Gunshot injuries detected by postmortem multislice computed tomography (MSCT): a feasibility study. *Leg Med (Tokyo)* 10 (6): 287–92.

Beauthier, J.P. 2008. *Traité de médecine légale*. Bruxelles: De Boeck.

Bolliger, S., M. Thali, C. Jackowski, E. Aghayev, R. Dirnhofer, and M. Sonnenschein. 2005. Postmortem non-invasive virtual autopsy: death by hanging in a car. *J Forensic Sci* 50 (2):455–60.

Brogdon, B.G. 1998. *Forensic radiology*. Boca Raton; London: CRC Press.

Buck, U., A. Christe, S. Naether, S. Ross, and M.J. Thali. 2009. Virtopsy—noninvasive detection of occult bone lesions in postmortem MRI: additional information for traffic accident reconstruction. *Int J Legal Med* 123 (3):221–6.

Christe, A., E. Aghayev, C. Jackowski, M.J. Thali, and P. Vock. 2008. Drowning—post-mortem imaging findings by computed tomography. *Eur Radiol* 18 (2):283–90.

Christe, A., S. Ross, L. Oesterhelweg, et al. 2009. Abdominal trauma—sensitivity and specificity of postmortem noncontrast imaging findings compared with autopsy findings. *J Trauma* 66 (5): 1302–7.

Dedouit, F., S. Bindel, D. Gainza, et al. 2008a. Application of the Iscan method to two- and three-dimensional imaging of the sternal end of the right fourth rib. *J Forensic Sci* 53 (2): 288–95.

Dedouit, F., C. Guilbeau-Frugier, C. Capuani, et al. 2008b. Child abuse: practical application of autopsy, radiological, and microscopic studies. *J Forensic Sci* 53 (6):1424–9.

Dedouit, F., P. Otal, R. Costagliola, et al. 2006. [Role of modern cross-sectional imaging in thanatology: a pictorial essay]. *J Radiol* 87 (6 Pt 1):619–38.

Dedouit, F., A. Sévely, R. Costagliola, et al. 2008c. Reversal sign on ante- and postmortem brain imaging in a newborn: report of one case. *Forensic Sci Int* 182 (1–3):e11–4.

Dedouit, F., N. Telmon, R. Costagliola, et al. 2007a. New identification possibilities with postmortem multislice computed tomography. *Int J Legal Med* 121 (6):507–10.

Dedouit, F., N. Telmon, R. Costagliola, P. Otal, F. Joffre, and D. Rougé. 2007b. Virtual anthropology and forensic identification: report of one case. *Forensic Sci Int* 173 (2–3):182–7.

Dedouit, F., N. Telmon, C. Guilbeau-Frugier, et al. 2007c. Virtual autopsy and forensic identification—practical application: a report of one case. *J Forensic Sci* 52 (4):960–4.

Dedouit, F., G. Tournel, A. Becart, V. Hedouin, and D. Gosset. 2007d. Suicidal hanging resulting in complete decapitation—forensic, radiological, and anthropological studies: a case report. *J Forensic Sci* 52 (5):1190–3.

Di Maio, D.J., and V.J.M. Di Maio. 2001. *Forensic pathology*. 2nd ed. Boca Raton: CRC Press.

Di Maio, V.J.M., and S.E. Dana. 2007. *Handbook of forensic pathology*. 2nd ed. London: Taylor & Francis.

Dix, J. 2000. *Color atlas of forensic pathology*. Boca Raton; London: CRC.

Dolinak, D., E.W. Matshes, and E.O. Lew. 2005. *Forensic pathology: principles and practice*. Amsterdam; London: Elsevier Academic Press.

Doyon, D. 2001. *IRM: imagerie par résonance magnétique*. 3rd ed. *Imagerie médicale. Formation*. Paris: Masson.

Grabherr, S., C. Cooper, S. Ulrich-Bochsler, et al. 2009. Estimation of sex and age of "virtual skeletons"—a feasibility study. *Eur Radiol* 19 (2):419–29.

Grabherr, S., V. Djonov, K. Yen, M.J. Thali, and R. Dirnhofer. 2007. Postmortem angiography: review of former and current methods. *AJR Am J Roentgenol* 188 (3):832–8.

Grabherr, S., E. Gygax, B. Sollberger, et al. 2008. Two-step postmortem angiography with a modified heart-lung machine: preliminary results. *AJR Am J Roentgenol* 190 (2):345–51.

Haaga, J.R., C.F. Lanzieri, and R.C. Gilkeson. 2003. *CT and MR imaging of the whole body*. 4th ed. St. Louis, Mo.: Mosby.

Haglund, W.D. and M.H. Sorg. 1997. *Forensic taphonomy: the postmortem fate of human remains*. Boca Raton: CRC Press.

Jackowski, C., E. Aghayev, M. Sonnenschein, R. Dirnhofer, and M.J. Thali. 2006a. Maximum intensity projection of cranial computed tomography data for dental identification. *Int J Legal Med* 120 (3):165–7.

Jackowski, C., A. Christe, M. Sonnenschein, E. Aghayev, and M.J. Thali. 2006b. Postmortem unenhanced magnetic resonance imaging of myocardial infarction in correlation to histological infarction age characterization. *Eur Heart J* 27 (20):2459–67.

Jackowski, C., W. Schweitzer, M. Thali, et al. 2005. Virtopsy: postmortem imaging of the human heart in situ using MSCT and MRI. *Forensic Sci Int* 149 (1):11–23.

Knight, B. and P.J. Saukko. 2004. *Knight's forensic pathology*. 3rd ed. London: Arnold.

Oehmichen, M., H.B. Gehl, C. Meissner, et al. 2003. Forensic pathological aspects of postmortem imaging of gunshot injury to the head: documentation and biometric data. *Acta Neuropathol* 105 (6):570–80.

Pfaeffli, M., P. Vock, R. Dirnhofer, M. Braun, S.A. Bolliger, and M.J. Thali. 2007. Post-mortem radiological CT identification based on classical ante-mortem X-ray examinations. *Forensic Sci Int* 171 (2–3):111–7.

Schnider, J., M.J. Thali, S. Ross, L. Oesterhelweg, D. Spendlove, and S.A. Bolliger. 2009. Injuries due to sharp trauma detected by post-mortem multislice computed tomography (MSCT): a feasibility study. *Leg Med (Tokyo)* 11 (1):4–9.

Sidler, M., C. Jackowski, R. Dirnhofer, P. Vock, and M. Thali. 2007. Use of multislice computed tomography in disaster victim identification—advantages and limitations. *Forensic Sci Int* 169 (2–3):118–28.

Thali, M.J., M. Braun, and R. Dirnhofer. 2003a. Optical 3D surface digitizing in forensic medicine: 3D documentation of skin and bone injuries. *Forensic Sci Int* 137 (2–3):203–8.

Thali, M.J., M. Braun, T.H. Markwalder, et al. 2003b. Bite mark documentation and analysis: the forensic 3D/CAD supported photogrammetry approach. *Forensic Sci Int* 135 (2):115–21.

Thali, M.J., M. Braun, J. Wirth, P. Vock, and R. Dirnhofer. 2003c. 3D surface and body documentation in forensic medicine: 3-D/CAD Photogrammetry merged with 3D radiological scanning. *J Forensic Sci* 48 (6):1356–65.

Thali, M.J., W. Schweitzer, K. Yen, et al. 2003d. New horizons in forensic radiology: the 60-second digital autopsy-full-body examination of a gunshot victim by multislice computed tomography. *Am J Forensic Med Pathol* 24 (1):22–7.

Thali, M.J., K. Yen, T. Plattner, et al. 2002. Charred body: virtual autopsy with multi-slice computed tomography and magnetic resonance imaging. *J Forensic Sci* 47 (6):1326–31.

Thali, M.J., K. Yen, W. Schweitzer, et al. 2003e. Virtopsy, a new imaging horizon in forensic pathology: virtual autopsy by postmortem multislice computed tomography (MSCT) and magnetic resonance imaging (MRI)—a feasibility study. *J Forensic Sci* 48 (2):386–403.

Thali, M.J., K. Yen, W. Schweitzer, P. Vock, C. Ozdoba, and R. Dirnhofer. 2003f. Into the decomposed body-forensic digital autopsy using multislice-computed tomography. *Forensic Sci Int* 134 (2–3):109–14.

Thali, M.J., K. Yen, P. Vock, et al. 2003g. Image-guided virtual autopsy findings of gunshot victims performed with multi-slice computed tomography and magnetic resonance imaging and subsequent correlation between radiology and autopsy findings. *Forensic Sci Int* 138 (1–3):8–16.

Thali, M.J., R. Dirnhofer, and P. Vock. 2009. *The virtopsy approach: 3D optical and radiological scanning and reconstruction in forensic medicine*. Boca Raton; London: CRC Press/Taylor & Francis.

Wheen, L.C., and M.P. Williams. 2009. Post-mortems in recreational scuba diver deaths: the utility of radiology. *J Forensic Leg Med* 16 (5):273–6.

Yen, K., K.O. Lovblad, E. Scheurer, et al. 2007. Post-mortem forensic neuroimaging: correlation of MSCT and MRI findings with autopsy results. *Forensic Sci Int* 173 (1):21–35.

Yen, K., M. Sonnenschein, M.J. Thali, et al. 2005. Postmortem multislice computed tomography and magnetic resonance imaging of odontoid fractures, atlantoaxial distractions, and ascending medullary edema. *Int J Legal Med* 119 (3):129–36.

Yen, K., P. Vock, B. Tiefenthaler, et al. 2004. Virtopsy: forensic traumatology of the subcutaneous fatty tissue; multislice computed tomography (MSCT) and magnetic resonance imaging (MRI) as diagnostic tools. *J Forensic Sci* 49 (4):799–806.

Yen, K., J. Weis, R. Kreis, et al. 2006. Line-scan diffusion tensor imaging of the posttraumatic brain stem: changes with neuropathologic correlation. *AJNR Am J Neuroradiol* 27 (1):70–3.

9 Forensic Anthropology and Human Identification in Criminal Matters

ANGELIQUE CORTHALS

Contents

Introduction

The discipline of forensic anthropology has only recently received academic attention as a fully recognized academic field after years of being relegated either to archaeology and physical anthropology for the study of ancient human remains or to pathology for the study of contemporary criminal cases involving skeletal remains.

Forensic anthropology is a methodological blend between archaeology, osteology, and pathology. It involves both the recovery of skeletal (or heavily decomposed) remains and the study of these remains to establish pre- and postmortem events (e.g., trauma, pathologies, postmortem damage), as well as possible identification. The noted distinction between forensic anthropology and anthropology resides in the legal aspect of the discipline. The forensic anthropologist will often be called to make statements as an expert witness in court on the cause of death and possible identification of the remains. The study of human remains by the forensic anthropologist can be divided into two main categories: contemporary (usually criminal cases and/or remains considered no more than 100 years old) and ancient (greater than 100 years old).

In this chapter, I will focus on the recovery and study of ancient human remains, in particular the forensic study of mummies.

The Forensic Studies of Mummies

Mummies have always fascinated the greater public at large, both through the emotional link they offer us to our own past as a species, and also through works of fiction in books or movies in which they figure prominently (most often, aberrantly).

Mummies are often mistakenly solely identified with the ancient Egyptian civilization.

The term *mummy* is, in fact, rather misleading. The name originated in the Arabic Peninsula and derives from the word *mummyah*, meaning *bitumen*, describing both the main ingredient and appearance of Egyptian mummified bodies. But not all mummies are "mummies." Ancient civilizations from around the world have been concerned with preserving the bodies of their deceased either naturally or by embalming them (Aufderheide 2003). Not all mummies are anthropogenic (i.e., required the intervention of embalmers). Most are, in fact, naturally made (meaning the body was preserved by natural means, without any man-made intervention).

In this chapter, we will look at the two main types of mummies: natural mummies and anthropogenic mummies. Through examples from South America and Egypt, it is possible to have a closer look at the methods and environmental aspects of mummification and the protocols and difficulties forensic anthropologists face when studying ancient human remains.

Each of these will be exemplified by a preserved ancient body I studied in the last 10 years: these are Copper Man, the Children of Llullaillaco, and the Egyptian Royal mummies. Each exemplified a different type of mummification, a different set of challenges in studying them.

Natural Mummies

Natural mummies are bodies that have not decomposed after death due to environmental causes, rather than by the action of embalming treatments. In this case, the term *mummies* itself is rather erroneous, since this term often describes bodies that have received embalming care.

Natural mummification without human intervention brings forth the question of whether or not naturally mummified bodies were meant to be preserved or not. It is not always possible to determine whether or not the body was meant to be preserved, but clues such as the location of the burial place can indicate such intention. A good example of this is the case of Inca mummies. Although we know that no Inca mummies bear the mark of anthropogenic mummification, the position of the cemeteries in which these bodies were found indicates a knowledge of climactic and environmental conditions which would lead organic matter to be preserved (Ceruti 2003).

The environmental factors leading a body to not decompose are many, and it is usually a combination of factors prevailing that will determine how well a body will be preserved. Chief among all environmental settings preserving organic material is dryness.

Desiccated Mummies

Heat and dryness have been preserving scores of organic matters of all size and forms (bodies, clothes, structure). Hot and dry conditions create a rapid desiccation preventing the soft tissues of the body to decompose. It is the same process used to preserve meat for millennia. It is very likely, in fact, that the observation of bodies (human or nonhuman) being preserved in those conditions have led ancient civilizations, such as the Egyptians, to practice and perfect the art of mummification (Ikram and Dobson 1998).

The best examples of naturally dried preserved bodies have been found in the driest places on earth: "Ginger," the 5,500-year-old Egyptian Predynastic body at the British Museum, was found in the hot sand of the Libyan desert (Southwestern Egypt); the 3,000-year-old "Tarim mummies" were found in the Taklamakan Desert (Northwestern China); Copperman, the 500-year-old preserved body of a copper miner, was found in the Atacama desert (Northwestern Chile).

The latter, Copper Man, is a mummy that I studied while employed at the American Museum of Natural History, where it is currently preserved, and which exemplifies well natural mummification. Copper Man's story is also both unusual and unfortunately familiar for many mummies discovered in the 19th century.

Copper Man: The Mummy Who Visited the World

Currently exhibited at the American Museum of Natural History in New York, Copper Man, one of the best-preserved bodies in the world, has remained a mystery for a hundred years. Limited studies have been published on the mummy, but never quite answered the critical questions everyone faces when gazing upon the graceful remains: Who was he? Where did he come from? To what purpose was he mining copper? Was he a professional or an opportunistic miner? How did he die?

Unlike many desiccated mummies, Copper Man's appearance is not shriveled, brown, and partly skeletonized like most naturally dried bodies (Figure 9.1). On the contrary, his body retains the shape it most likely had during life, with a certain amount of fat, especially in the thigh regions. The skin is not shriveled; the fingernails are still intact (which indicates further that the skin was well preserved). Even Copper Man's braided hair is still beautifully visible. Why was Copper Man not desiccated like most mummies coming from the Atacama Desert? The secret lies in the mine.

Copper Man's discovery and acquisition story is fraught with intrigues and legal battles over ownership of his remains since the very moment he was unearthed. Copper Man

Figure 9.1 Copper Man, preserved at the American Museum of Natural History (photo by the author).

was found in 1899, during mining work at Chuquicamata copper mine in northern Chile. His body was covered with fallen rocks in a shallow shaft (only a few feet from the surface), and had a remarkable greenish appearance. The shallow shaft and the greenish appearance are both clues to the remarkable preservation state of Copper Man. Sealed in a hot, dry, airtight tomb, the body of the miner—more specifically, his subcutaneous fat—went through a chemical reaction called adipocere. Normally encountered in wet and cold environments (see below: the children of Llullaillaco), bodies of persons who were already rotund in life tend to saponify under anaerobic conditions created, for instance, when the mine shaft collapsed on Copper Man (Forbes et al. 2005). This explains why the skin maintained its lifelike appearance. Its greenish color, on the other hand, gave a second clue to its preservation: copper. A film of copper dust envelops completely the body of Copper Man (thus his nickname). At the time of his death, Copper Man was mining the precious metal, which was used ceremonially in the entire Andean region. When the shaft collapsed on him, fine particles of the metal fell on his body, blanketing it completely. Copper is a highly antibacterial and antifungal metal, and most certainly prevented decomposition bacteria, such as *Clostridium sp.*, to attack the soft tissues. The hot, dry, anaerobic conditions of the tomb and the copper both contributed to the beautiful preservation of the body of Copper Man.

However, the very same copper film surrounding the mummy, protecting it so beautifully for centuries, was to prove its downfall. It prompted an immediate ownership battle over Copper Man's remains: the French operator of the mine, Mr. Pidot, claimed him as their property, on the ground that all mineral extract belonged to the mining operation and since Copper Man was covered in copper, the mummy belonged to him, while the American owner, Mr. Matthews claimed that Mr. Pidot had "rented the mines, not the miners." Eventually, it was sold to Mr. Edward Jackson, an American entrepreneur living in Chile, who put the mummy on exhibition in his house in Santiago, Chile. Failing to make a profit, he sold the body to two gentlemen, Torres and Tornero. They took the mummy, again, on exhibition, this time to the United States, at the Pan American Exhibition of 1901 in Buffalo. There, the pamphlets described Copper Man as "Human Petrification: The Only Specimen in Existence of a Perfectly Preserved Body from a Race Which Is Now Entirely Extinct." However, it seems profit was not to be made from Copper Man's remains: Torres and Tornero went heavily into debt and had to return to Chile, with the help of their consul, leaving the body in the United States as security (Bird 1979).

No one knows exactly what happened to Copper Man after Torres and Tornero left. He only reappears in history, a couple of fingers and toes missing, when, in 1905, J. P. Morgan bought it and offered it to the American Museum of Natural History, where he has remained, finally in peace, ever since.

The first studies on Copper Man were performed by Junius Bird in 1975 (Bird 1979). The study took several approaches to resolve the mystery surrounding the origins and chronology of Copper Man. First, a C14 study was made and determined that Copper Man probably died around 550 A.D. Second, a study of x-rays and CT scans was centered on the bone density of the miner, which revealed a remarkably healthy individual. Finally, a study of the loincloth and artifacts associated with Copper Man pointed out that the miner was most probably related to the Tiwanaku culture. The Tiwanaku, though mainly centered on the basin of Lake Titicaca in Bolivia, expanded their influence from southern Peru to northern Chile and Argentina and flourished for nearly a millennium between approximately 200 and 1100 AD.

Since 1979, though, Copper Man had scarcely been studied, and had only been mentioned as an aside in wider studies, with no additional information. It soon became evident that the original studies needed to be revised and complemented.

In 2004, I undertook new sets of studies while employed at the American Museum of Natural History. At the time, I was seeking new answers to the many questions surrounding Copper Man. Chief among those questions were the circumstance of his death and who Copper Man really was in the context of his era.

Having a new look at the physical characteristics of Copper Man provided many new insights. Because the mummy cannot be moved from the museum (due to its extremely fragile state of preservation), new x-rays or CT scans could not be performed. However, research in the archive of the AMNH's Anthropology Department revealed old x-rays which proved to be remarkably revealing.

How Did Copper Man Die?

From his position in the shaft where he was found, it seemed obvious to most who studied him (such as Junius Bird) that Copper Man died crushed by the collapse of the mine. But a closer look at the miner reveals his death was not violent, nor was it sudden. He was not crushed, nor did he suffocate. The very fact that he is still seen clenching his instruments reveals he might have died trying to dig out of the collapsed area. There are also no bone fractures, no evidence of crushing or even abrasions or skin tear which would indicate a violent collapse of the gallery roof on top of the body. He probably died as a result of carbon dioxide poisoning produced by his own breathing. In a tightly confined area, such as the collapsed mine shaft, the displacement of oxygen by the heavier carbon dioxide happens quickly and can result in death with little or no awareness of what is happening to the victim. Copper Man possibly fell quickly unconscious after experiencing the first symptoms of CO_2 poisoning (headache, nausea) and never woke.

Who Was Copper Man?

When Bird wrote his report in the late 1970s, he noted as an aside that "the occiput of the individual was also flattened" (Bird 1979). At the time, Bird could not have seen the implications of such an important feature of the mummy, but nowadays, about a dozen studies have been undertaken on cranial features related to ethnic groups in ancient cemeteries from southern Peru to northern Chile (Torres-Rouff 2002; Rothhammer et al. 1982). It has been quite successfully determined that patterns of body modifications are tied to specific cultures. Thus the Tiwanaku are known to have frequently employed a pronounced form of intentional skull modification (also called "annular vault modification" (Figure 9.2), which resemble Copper Man's type of cranial modification. This, according to recent studies, distinguishes him from the local Atacameño people, who either did not adopt a tradition of cranial deformation or those who would, had developed a different modification (a tabular vault modification; Figure 9.3). This feature, in effect, seems to confirm Bird's assessment of Copper Man's origins: the Tiwanaku State. But the Tiwanaku State encompassed a vast region: from southern Peru to northern Chile and Argentina. The cranial evidence can therefore only point to cultural background, but not to a specific population. More needed to be done to find out if we could pinpoint Copper Man's origins to a specific people.

A new look at old unpublished x-rays from the AMNH archives has revealed another feature which had not been noted until now: despite being outwardly a very healthy looking

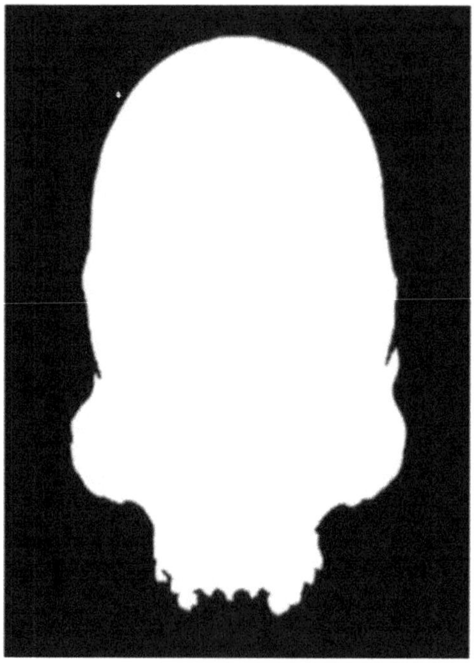

Figure 9.2 Annular cranial vault deformation.

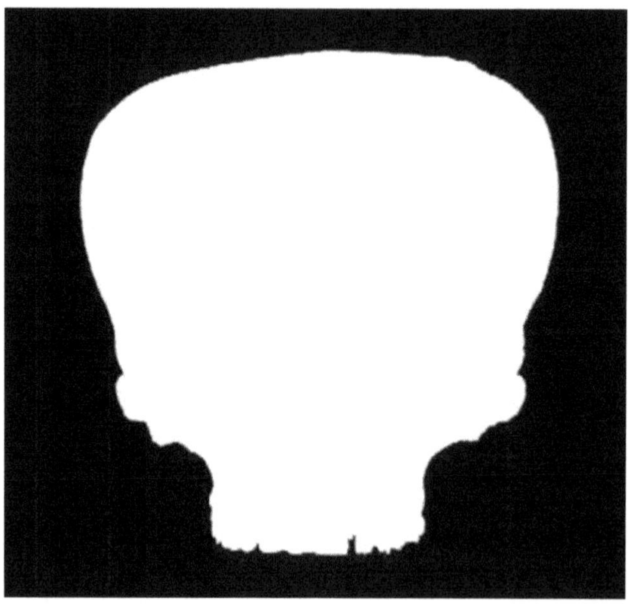

Figure 9.3 Tabular cranial vault deformation.

young adult, Copper Man had lost most of his back teeth. Indeed, though invisible on the surface (mouth is closed), the x-rays reveal that Copper Man is lacking the first premolar, second premolar, and first molar of the upper right mandible. Though the x-rays are of bad quality, it seems that he is also missing the first premolar, second premolar, and first molar on the left side of the upper mandible.

This could, in fact, be indicative of dietary habit, which seems to link Copper Man with many High Andean populations. Copper Man's tooth loss was compared to data from dental effects of nutrition on cultures of northern Chile and southern Peru (Langsjoen 1998). The closest tooth loss pattern to that of the miner was that of the Maitas Chiribayas, who, as descendants of High Andean populations, had kept the practice of chewing coca leaf. This gives us two clues about Copper Man: a dietary habit, coca leaf chewing; and a closer population origin, the High Andes, and possibly southern Peru, which points again to the Tiwanaku culture, and perhaps the subgroup Chiribaya.

Evidence from previous studies suggests strongly that copper mining by the Tiwanaku was performed in the copper-rich region of the Atacama Desert and that a high number of workers migrated from all regions of the Tiwanaku state to northern Chile (Graffam et al. 1996). Once the ore was extracted, the workers would go back to their point of origin, work the metal, or sell it, at high profit. This seems to have been the case of Copper Man, who probably was part of this "migrant workers" class. It is highly possible that Copper Man was in fact more of a coppersmith, than a copper miner. Indeed, Copper Man's remains do not bear the stresses of a professional miner, such as calluses on the elbows and knees, torn skins and multiple lesions in the same area, unusual damage in the joints of the knees and elbows, and so on.

From a purely physical look at Copper Man, we have gathered the following information: Copper Man was a healthy young man, probably in his mid-20s, who died probably asphyxiated by his own CO_2 and compression of his chest. He was not a professional miner, and was most probably a migrant worker in search of profits from selling or working copper. He was not a local Atacameño, and physical evidence, combined with previous artifact studies, seems to point to southern Peru or southwestern Bolivia, the areas of high Tiwanaku influence.

The study of Copper Man exemplifies the necessity for forensic anthropologists to thoroughly examine a mummy not just through the means of technology, but also visually. In our genomic age, this type of study is often discarded as obsolete. Much, however, surfaced from both our visual and our archival research, which could not have been answered by molecular methods.

Ice Mummies

The second most important environmental factor in preserving organic material is freezing temperatures. An environment where temperatures are below 0°C will indeed maintain the integrity of most organic material. But while most of the organic material will be preserved, not all will remain undamaged. The freezing process creates thousands of ice crystals, which shear cell walls, thus leaching bodies of their water content. This explains why most frozen bodies will actually have a very desiccated aspect, as is the case for Otzi, the frozen body found in the Alps at the border between Italy and Austria; the frozen mummies of the Altai mountains of Siberia; and Juanita and El Plomo Prince, the two children mummies found in the Andes mountains of Peru and Chile, respectively (Reinhard 1993; Reinhard and Buikstra 2003; Reinhard 2005).

Possibly the best examples of frozen mummies in the world are the three "Children of Llullaillaco," currently preserved in Salta, Argentina, and which I had the privilege to study in 2004 and 2009.

The Llullaillaco Children

In February 1999, an expedition led by Drs. Reinhard and Ceruti discovered three frozen Inca mummies near the summit of an extinct volcano at the Argentinian-Chilean border, mount Llullaillaco. The three mummies were quickly identified as *capacocha* sacrifices to the earth goddess, *Pachamama*, as indicated by each child's elaborate ceremonial garments, jewels and headdresses as well as the richness of artifacts surrounding them in their tomb (Reinhard 2005; Ceruti 2003). There were three children: an adolescent girl, nicknamed "La Doncella" (~15 years old; Figure 9.4), a little girl, nicknamed "La Niña" (~6 years old; Figure 9.5); and a little boy, nicknamed "El Niño" (~7 years old; Figure 9.6).

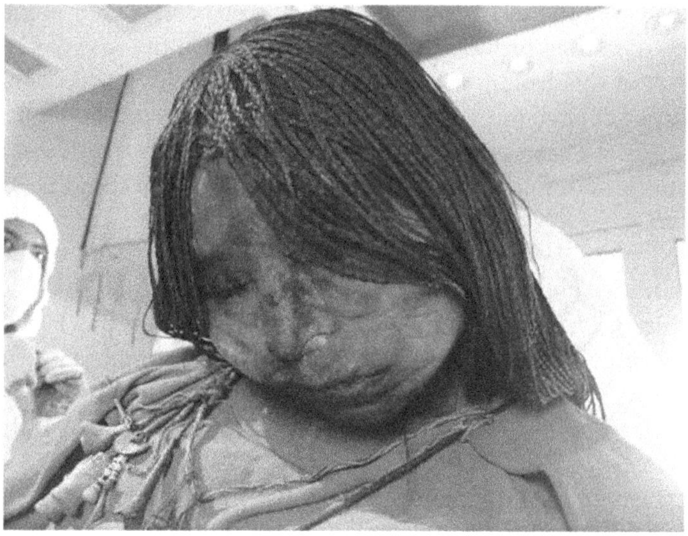

Figure 9.4 La Doncella, preserved at the Museo de Arqueología de Alta Montaña, Salta, Argentina (photo by author).

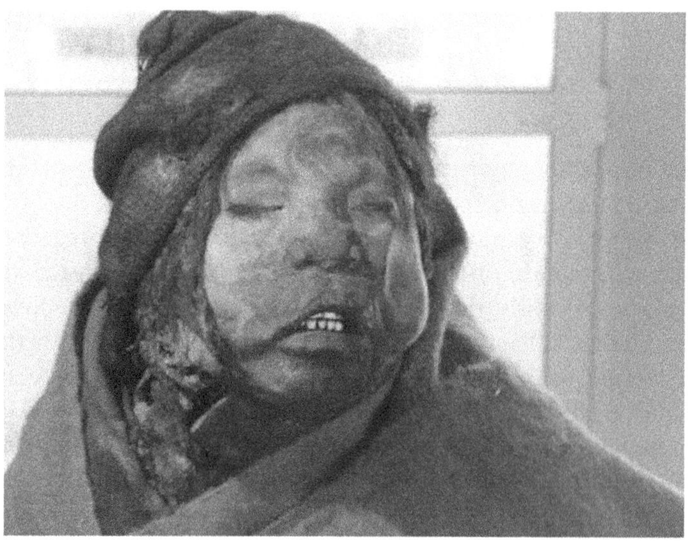

Figure 9.5 La Niña del Rayo (photo by author).

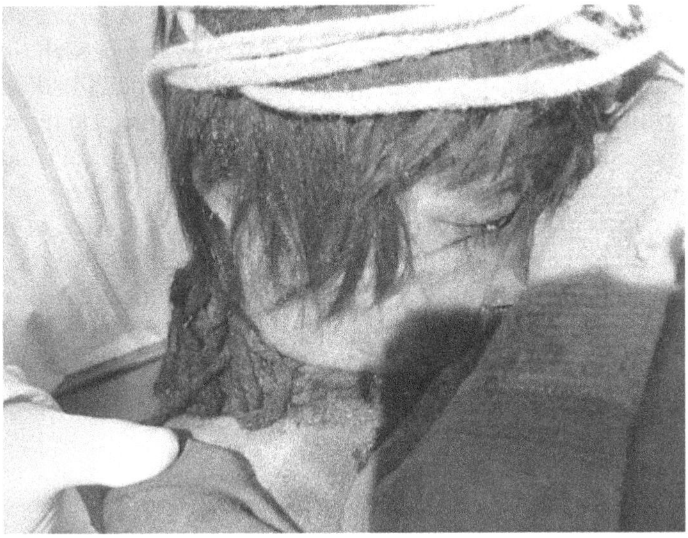

Figure 9.6 El Niño (photo by author).

What makes the children of Llullaillaco unique is their extraordinary state of preservation. But for a few blemishes on the skin due to frost, the children of Llullaillaco appear to be sleeping, their bodies having retained their full integrity. Freezing conditions alone could not have preserved the children (and their surrounding artifacts) as beautifully and vibrantly as they have. What happened at the summit of Llullaillaco is a phenomenon that I like to call the "perfect storm" of environmental conditions needed for perfect preservation.

Mount Llullaillaco sits at 6,700 m above sea level. The temperature at its lowest usually reaches about −40°C in the winter, but on the sheltered platform where the children were found (~6500 m), the temperature tends to stay at a stable 0°C. With low precipitations and dryness, the area is covered in permafrost layers. The permafrost formation comes from melted snow forming sheets of ice in areas of mild winds (Ceruti 2003; Wilson et al. 2007). The platform on which the bodies of the three children were found was covered with a layer of permafrost. The tombs were cylindrical structures with walls of layered stone two meters high and about one meter in diameter, dug in layers of ashes. The bodies were deposited in squatting position and wrapped completely in a ceremonial wool blanket. Each tomb was packed with ashes and other volcanic debris so that no empty space was left between the bodies and the tomb walls. These conditions, both anthropogenic and environmental, played a crucial role in maintaining the perfect integrity of the children's bodies (Reinhard 2005). The enzymes and bacteria involved in decomposition were disabled by the lack of oxygen caused by not only the high altitude but also the permafrost layer cycles of melting and freezing, leaking in the cracks of the tomb walls and freezing, forming an igloo-type shelter and thus sealing the content of the tombs in an anaerobic environment. The bacteria and enzymes were further inhibited by the freezing temperature and the volcanic ash, rich in minerals, which acted as an efficient antibacterial. The bodies of the three children also developed adipocere layers from their subcutaneous fat layers, sealing off their viscera to possible leaking, bacterial attack, and/or enzymatic lysing (Corthals 2004; Egarter-Vigl 2004).

Though the intention surrounding the children's death was evident (sacrifice), the cause of death was difficult to determine. We know from the Spanish chroniclers that sacrificed children were drugged, made to consume chicha, a fermented corn-based alcoholic drink, and then bludgeoned to death. Evidence of that type of death can be seen in other sacrificed children's remains throughout the Andes. But for the children of Llullaillaco, we originally saw no surface traces of deliberate trauma. X-rays and CT scans confirmed no apparent traces of violent trauma, neither on the bones nor on the organs (Previgliano et al. 2003).

In 2008, the Museum of High Mountain Archaeology in Salta, where the mummies are now exhibited, gave our team unique access to the three children of Llullaillaco for a National Geographic documentary (Corthals 2011). During the investigation, we looked for possible cause of death by gathering lip swabs from the three mummies, whose lips were covered by a deep red congealed liquid. An additional sample was taken from the boy's cloak, from an area which covered part of his mouth and which was stained by an unknown substance.

A simple, standard forensic phenolphthalein test quickly revealed that every mummies lip swab contained blood in it. However, this test did not indicate how much blood was present, whether it was the children's blood, or where in the body the blood came from. To answer those questions, I decided to call Dr. Toni Koller at the Proteomics Centre of Stony Brook University. Proteomics, a technique that identifies proteins, would indicate the presence and quantity of not only human hemoglobin (thereby confirming the presence of blood *and* the nature of the blood) but also other proteins laced within the blood that would also indicate a provenance within the body. The mass spectrometry showed clear presence of human blood but also showed that each sample contained a large quantity of it. The presence of mucin in all samples indicated clearly that the blood in fact came from internal bleeding. We could therefore discount any external trauma, which might have been missed by x-rays and CT scans, or made invisible by the fact that clothing could not be removed from the bodies (frozen solid). However, neither the CT scans nor the x-ray assessed by expert radiologists showed any type of internal injuries (Previgliano et al. 2003). One detail, however, on one slice of the little boy's CT scans, showed that the pericardium was slightly enlarged. Could this be an indication of blunt chest trauma? Not necessarily. An enlarged pericardium could also come from a more common condition found in high altitude mountaineers: pulmonary edema. This would explain the blood on all of the three children's lips and clothing. While these findings did not represent a conclusive cause of death, it hinted at the harshness of the conditions these three children faced climbing to 6,500 meters above sea level, with no adequate mountaineering equipment.

Here, a forensic scientific technique was used in a new way in the study of human remains: proteomics helped quantify as well as identify human hemoglobin, as well as gave a possible indication of cause of death by determining the origin of the blood.

Anthropogenic Mummies

Of all the mummies in the world, indeed of all the ancient human remains in the world, the Egyptian mummies are by far those that are most recognized and celebrated by the public at large. Their fascination is tied to the fact that they offer us a glimpse of the past on a more personal level than any golden artifact could ever do. Looking at the godlike exploit of Ramses the Great on his temple walls at Karnak does not compare emotionally to coming face to face with the great pharaoh's remains in his resting place at the Cairo Museum.

Egyptian Mummies

Egyptian mummies are distinct in the mummy world. No other ancient culture researched and applied preservation techniques to its deceased as systematically or as scientifically as the Egyptians did. This is, in part, due to the religious belief tied to a careful observation of the natural world. Indeed, the ancient Egyptians noticed early on that bodies buried in the hot sand of the Sahara, whether animal or human, would not decompose. It is possible that this observation led to the religious belief and then religious decree that both human and animal remains should be preserved if the deceased was to access the afterlife. It is also possible that the observation of preserved cadavers led to the central myth in the Egyptian religion, which revolves around a mummy: that of the god Osiris. The decaying body of Osiris, killed and dismembered in a fight with his brother Seth, was painstakingly reassembled and mummified by his wife, Isis. Because his body was whole again, Osiris "resurrected," becoming the ruler of the Underworld and judge of the dead. Thus, in the image of their god Osiris, Egyptians wanted their bodies to be preserved after death, as they believed that they would be revived in the afterlife (Ikram and Dobson 1998). The belief that only a whole body would grant the deceased a life after death was so strong that mummies were even buried with "spare parts": reserve heads, ears, legs, or arms made of plaster have been found in tombs throughout Egypt. Similarly, mutilated bodies would be given replacement limbs (of unknown origins) or prostheses during embalming (Ikram and Dobson 1998).

Egyptian Embalming

The secret of the Egyptian embalming techniques is one of the greatest paradoxes of Egyptian history. Even though literary and scientific texts, stories of conquests, of expeditions, of liturgical recipes for unguents and incenses were recorded either on temple walls or on papyri, no Egyptian text survives on mummification techniques (Brier 1994). The only source on the subject comes to us secondhand via Herodotus, the 5th century BC Greek historian. Herodotus tells us that the Egyptians practiced three main kinds of embalming depending on the economic background of the deceased:

- The expensive and elaborate embalming: consists in removing surgically (by a small incision on the side of the abdomen) all the organs, except for the heart. The brain is also removed using hooks and softening wax via the nostrils. The body is then placed for 70 days in natron (a sodium bicarbonate–sodium carbonate–sodium chloride–sodium sulfate mixture naturally found in northern Egypt). This allows the body to dry completely. Following that, the body is prepared with expensive resins (made of beeswax and several different plant resins), stuffed with linen cloths containing natron as well as spices for the smell, and wrapped in expensive decorated linen bandages containing precious amulets.
- The moderately expensive embalming: consists in liquefying the internal organs with hot cedar oil, which is then flushed out of the body through natural orifices (anus, mouth). This method does not involve incisions, and only crudely attempts to remove the brain. The body is then dried in natron for 70 days, covered in resin, and returned to the family, unwrapped.
- The least expensive embalming: consists in filling the body with cedar oil, and leaving it to dry in natron for 70 days. There is no attempt at flushing out the

liquefied organs, removing the brain. The body is also not covered in resin and is then returned to the family, unwrapped.

- Though Herodotus did not mention it, the cheapest of all mummification methods was just to place the cadaver in a shallow tomb, and let the heat and the natural salt of the Sahara sand dehydrate the body (Brier 1994; Zimmerman et al. 1998; Aufderheide 2003).

The most famous of the Egyptian mummies are the royal mummies, the bodies of the kings and queens who reigned over Egypt for three millennia. All the royal mummies were preserved using the best methods of embalming at the time, and the most expensive ingredients and materials were utilized. No expense was spared to preserve the bodies of the pharaohs, as exemplified most spectacularly by Tutankhamen's burial chambers, or most beautifully by the preserved regal features of Ramses the Great's face.

Ironically, while the most elaborate embalming methods did wonders to preserve the appearance of the deceased, they have also been the source of problems to modern forensic anthropologists. Not only are the elaborate wrappings preventing a surface observation of the bodies, they also prevent access to potential sampling areas; and while elaborate ingredients have prevented decay, they have also changed the biochemical structure of skin they covered, thereby hindering one of the most important analyses of modern forensic anthropology: DNA analyses (Gilbert et al. 2005b).

A Modern Egyptian Mummy to the Rescue

Extracting DNA from mummies, or any forensic remains, is notoriously difficult. The DNA is often greatly damaged, and when it can be extracted, it is often contaminated with the undamaged DNA of the person(s) who has (have) been handling the body or the samples (Gilbert et al. 2005a; Cooper and Poinar 2000; Poinar and Stankiewicz 1999).

In the case of Egyptian mummies, common sense dictates that time (i.e., time of exposure to environmental conditions) is the greatest culprit in degrading the mummies' DNA. But what of the ingredients of mummification such as natron (a salt) and resins (acidic)? Could they also have damaged the mummies at a molecular level, while protecting them from decay at a tissue level?

To establish which of time or ingredients have had an adverse effect on mummy DNA, Dr. Bob Brier and I ran an experiment on Drs. Brier and Wade's famous mummified corpse (Brier and Wade 2001; Zimmerman et al. 1998). In the 1980s, Drs. Brier and Wade preserved a body donated to science using, for the first time, the ancient Egyptian techniques as described by Herodotus (see above). In 2006, I extracted DNA from samples taken from the modern mummy's skin and from the bones (impervious to the surface treatment, and therefore damage, of mummification). The hypothesis was that if the action of time alone was responsible for such poor-quality DNA in Egyptian mummies, then both soft tissue and bone samples from the modern mummy should produce good results, since they are only 20 years old (not old compared to the 5,000-year-old mummies). However, if the resins and salts of mummification played a role in DNA degradation, then the skin sample from the modern mummy should show much poorer results as opposed to the bone samples, which, being protected from these ingredients, should show good-quality results.

The results of the DNA extraction were clear: while high quality DNA was systematically retrieved from the bone samples of the modern mummy, poor or no DNA was retrieved from the skin samples. This indicated to Dr. Brier and I not only that the ingredients of mummifications were indeed damaging to the DNA contained in skin cells but also that efforts to extract DNA from skin samples of mummies, which has been the traditional method of sampling, are futile. Better and more reliable DNA can be extracted from the bones.

In this case, DNA analysis was used not as identification but rather as a tool to measure damage to forensic samples and as an alternative to better sampling methods. However, DNA studies can offer much more information.

DNA and Mummies

Advances in genetic technologies have recently allowed forensic anthropologists to use the tools of molecular biology to investigate ancient human remains. Svante Paabo made scientific history when he first extracted and amplified DNA from an ancient Egyptian mummy in 1983. Ever since, the subfield of molecular anthropology has grown as techniques were refined and more information could be gathered from ancient human remains, and is now entirely integrated in forensic anthropology.

What Can and Can't DNA Tell Us?

We all carry DNA in every cell of our bodies except in our red and platelet cells. DNA is the genetic material, which in part defines who we are and what we look like. DNA is, to use a common expression, the "blueprint of life." It is passed down from our ancestors with only slight modifications and, as such, helps determine the ancestral origins of all living things by comparing the DNA of the ancestor to that of the descendant.

It is important to know the limitations of DNA. Too often, the media have touted DNA technology as the *deus ex machina* of solving crimes or mysteries tied to ancient populations or famous persons. DNA cannot tell us the full story of an individual; it can tell us neither the age nor the occupation of the individual sampled. DNA can also not, in most cases, tell us the family relationship of an individual if there is no DNA from another member of the family to compare it with. In some cases, DNA can show that an individual would be prone or resistant to some diseases but does not ascertain that the individual was plagued by such diseases.

Above all else, DNA research on ancient remains is about asking the right question (i.e., a question that falls within the possibility of what DNA analysis can tell us). Let's take Copper Man and the Egyptian Royal mummies as examples. We could ask the following questions in these cases: Can we discover Copper Man's origin through his DNA? Can we untangle family relationships between the kings and queens of Egypt? Can we discover whether they were plagued by disease?

mtDNA Haplotypes and Copper Man

To determine an individual's ancestry, like Copper Man, we look at the genetic makeup of populations close to him in location and time and look for tiny mutations, called polymorphisms. The polymorphisms are the slight differences that exist in different population's DNA. There are tiny mutations that occur in different parts of a chromosome and allow forensic anthropologists to characterize a population according to the arrangement of these mutations. The position of the mutations within a chromosome is called an allele. A specific population will have either a single or specific group of alleles differentiating it from another population. This genetic signature is called a haplotype.

In the case of Copper Man, we have to consider the four founding Amerindian mitochondrial haplotype frequencies that make up the genetic signature of native South American populations. These haplotypes are called A, B, C, and D, and they occur at different frequencies in different native South American populations (Horai et al. 1993; Bianchi et al. 1997). The chart in Figure 9.7 clearly shows the mechanism of comparing haplotype frequency to differentiate populations.

One can see that, for example, the haplotype frequency of the Aymara people and the Atacameño people is quite different, in particular in the frequency of haplotype D.

In the case of Copper Man, even though the DNA is highly degraded, the DNA analysis did confirm what the physical examination of the body revealed: that Copper Man is indeed closer, in his genetic makeup, to the population of southern Peru, than to the Atacameño population of northern Chile. However, the DNA could not pinpoint with precision where Copper Man is from. This is because the analysis only indicates a percentage of relatedness to a population frequency. mtDNA never really offers a precise indication of relatedness, neither to a population, nor to a kin. To refine kinship through DNA analysis, one must look at nuclear DNA, and specifically perform a genotyping assay.

DNA Genotyping and the Egyptian Royal Mummies

I was fortunate to be involved in setting up the first DNA laboratory exclusively dedicated to the study of ancient Egyptian mummies at the Cairo Museum under the auspices of the Supreme Council of Antiquities (Hawass et al. 2010). The tests, still going on today, have been set up to determine a DNA-based family relationship between all the royal mummies exhibited in the Cairo Museum (see above). These mummies are the preserved bodies of the

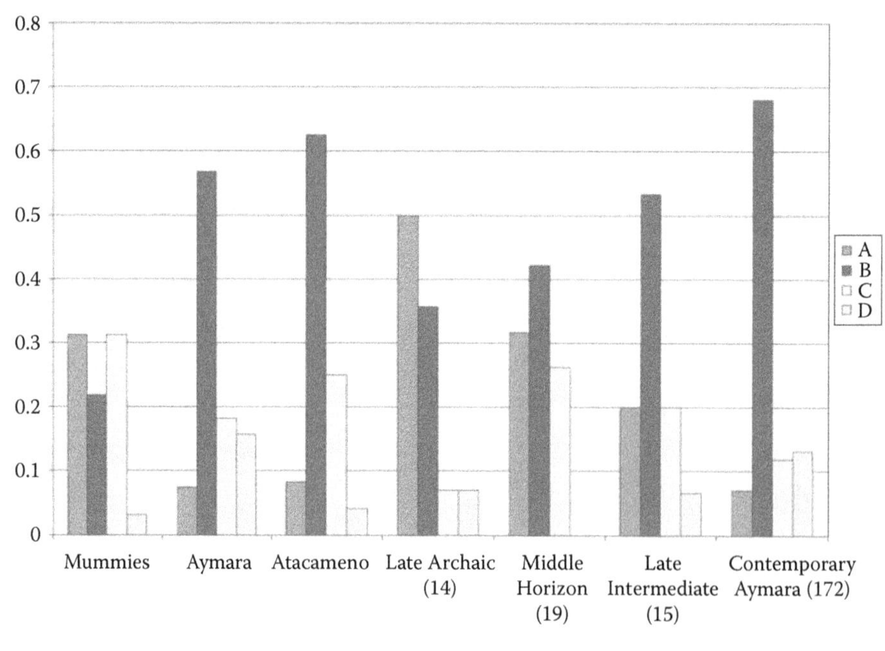

Figure 9.7 Amerindians mtDNA haplotypes.

kings and queens from Egypt's New Kingdom period (16th–11th century BC). Although we have precise ancient texts describing the family relationship of these kings and queens, and magnificent tombs decorated with their names, only *one* of these mummies was found *in situ*, in his tomb: Tutankhamen. All the other royal mummies, from Seti to Ramses V, were found piled up in what is known as *caches*. Caches were hastily dug tombs, which served as temporary shelters for mummies whose tombs had been robbed in ancient times. The treasures of the royal tombs, as splendidly exemplified by the riches of Tutankhamen's tomb, were always appealing to robbers in ancient Egypt. Judicial texts have survived of tomb robbers being tried, convicted, and executed for stealing from the royal tombs of the Valley of the Kings in southern Egypt (Ikram and Dobson 1998). During the period following the New Kingdom, known as the Third Intermediate Period, Egypt's dominion had declined, famines were common, and royal tombs became prey to systematic looting. With little or no policing forces, the Egyptian clergy in charge of the tombs could only protect the bodies of the kings and queens, by hiding them in crude tombs. Most of the mummies would be taken out of their sarcophagus and just piled in small side chapels on top of each other, with no or little indication of who they were (Ikram and Dobson 1998). When one of those caches was discovered in the late 19th century, Egyptologists at the time relied on very few clues to identify the royal jumble. These clues consisted in the names inscribed on the inside of the bandages, the type of amulets, some of the scant funerary material bearing the names of the kings and queens found in the caches, and, when the technology became available, Egyptologists used x-rays to relate the individual kings and queens anthropomorphically (i.e., by comparing the skeletal features, such as skull shapes). However, these identifications were always tenuous and needed additional support from another source to confirm kinship: DNA.

To ascertain kinship using DNA, mitochondrial DNA (mtDNA) is not enough. As we have seen in the case of Copper Man, mtDNA only determines a percentage of relatedness. Patterns of kinship can only truly be determined using nuclear DNA (nuDNA), using an assay known as genotyping (Hawass et al. 2010).

Genotyping is the most common test used in paternity cases and consists in looking for specific mutations in an individual's genome (also called SNPs, short nucleotide polymorphisms). If the member of the family shows the same pattern of specific mutations, it confirms kinship on a much more refined level than mtDNA.

In the case of the Royal mummies, the main problem was to extract nuDNA. As explained earlier, nuDNA only exists in one copy per cell, and is very prone to damage and contamination. In the case of the most famous of all royal mummies, Tutankhamen, recently published by Hawass et al., my colleagues, Drs. Yehia Gad and Albert Zink, succeeded in recovering enough nuDNA from the mummy and supposed members of his family to proceed to genotyping assays (Hawass et al. 2010).

The results were astounding and finally allowed Egyptologists to confirm or reject kinship in the royal Egyptian family tree of the New Kingdom. Furthermore, DNA analysis led to more discoveries about Tutankhamen and elucidated one of King Tut's enduring mysteries: how did he die?

Pathogen DNA Detection and the Sick Tutankhamen

Tutankhamen is without contest the most famous king of ancient Egypt. The discovery of his untouched tomb in the early 20th century by Howard Carter is still the standard by which every archaeological discovery is measured. Everything about the young king has been shrouded in mystery. That Tutankhamen died young (~19 years old) has never been in question, but how he died has remained debated to this day. The mummy of the king is very damaged by multiple handlings, sawing (!), and moves it incurred ever since its discovery. It has been x-rayed and CT scanned many times, and each expert has voiced a different opinion on the visible skeletal trauma: a fractured leg and a possible blow to the head. While some maintain Tutankhamen had been murdered, others explained that the king died of sepsis due to his fractured leg (Aufderheide 2003).

It was not until the DNA analysis performed in 2009 that the mystery of Tutankhamen's death would lift.

DNA can also be recovered from other organisms found in ancient human samples (Yera et al. 2003). Microorganisms, such as bacteria, viruses, or parasites, also leave genetic traces in the body of their hosts. When extracting DNA from an ancient human sample, nothing distinguishes a priori the human DNA from any other DNA that may have been extracted at the same time. It is only by designing specific molecular probes, called primers, which will bind to the DNA of a specific microorganism, that one can identify the presence of a pathogen.

Dr. Albert Zink, a specialist in paleopathology, decided to run tests on the DNA that was recovered from the young king for kinship analysis purposes. He designed molecular probes that would indicate whether or not the young pharaoh suffered from one of the most deadly tropical diseases still plaguing Egypt nowadays: malaria (Hawass et al. 2010).

Malaria is a disease caused by a parasite, *Plasmodium*, that invades blood cells, finally leading to organ failure and death. There are four main strains of *Plasmodium* present in Egypt: *P. vivax*, *P. ovale*, *P. falciparum*, and *P. malariae*. *Plasmodium vivax* and *Plasmodium falciparum* are the most common, and the latter is the most virulent and deadly strain of the parasite, causing what is commonly referred to as "cerebral malaria."

In designing the probes, Dr. Zink had to be specific enough so that they would identify not only *Plasmodium* but also each different species of the parasite. The results revealed that the most deadly form of the parasite plagued the young king: *Plasmodium falciparum*. Though it may not have been the direct cause of death, it certainly was part of the weakening of the king, and certainly aggravated his fractured leg.

Conclusion

Forensic anthropology is a complex and fascinating field of study. It is multidisciplinary and applies the science of many different fields: anatomy, osteology, molecular biology, pathology, and archaeology, among many others.

In the examples based on my own studies, I hope to have conveyed that in the work of a forensic anthropologist it is most important to ask the right questions and find the methodologies that will best allow him or her to answer these questions. The possibilities of scientific exploration in forensic anthropology are endless, and new technology can only help to refine the results.

Forensic anthropologists do not just solve criminal cases. They also have the amazing opportunity to add to our knowledge of our past and warn us of our future as a species.

References

Aufderheide, A. C. 2003. *The Scientific Study of Mummies*. Cambridge: Cambridge University Press.

Bianchi, N. O., G. Bailliet, C. M. Bravi, R. F. Carnese, F. Rothhammer, V. L. MartÌnez-Marignac, and S. D. J. Pena. 1997. Origin of Amerindian Y-chromosomes as inferred by the analysis of six polymorphic markers. *American Journal of Physical Anthropology* 102 (1):79–89.

Bird, J. 1979. The "Copper Man": A Prehistoric Miner and His Tools from Northern Chile. In *Pre-Columbian Metallurgy of South America*, edited by E. Benson, 106–113. Washington D.C.

Brier, B. 1994. *Egyptian Mummies: Unravelling the Secret of an Ancient Art*. New York: Harper.

Brier, B., and R. S. Wade. 2001. Surgical Procedures during Ancient Egyptian Mummification. *Chungará (Arica)* 33 (1):117–123.

Ceruti, M. C. 2003. *Llullaillaco: Sacrificios y Ofrendas en un Santuario Inca de Alta Montaña*. Salta: EUCASA.

Cooper, A., and H. N. Poinar. 2000. Ancient DNA: do it right or not at all. *Science* 289:1139–1139.

Corthals, A. 2004. Los Niños del Lullaillaco: Scientific Investigation Report—Report for the Government of Salta and the Argentinian Ministry of Culture. Salta Governorate, Argentina: Studies performed at the American Museum of Natural History, New York, NY. Unpublished.

Corthals, A., L. M. Dávalos, D. Martin, R. Rieger, E. I. Chen, T. Koller. 2011. Immune system proteins retrieved from a 500-year-old body. *Forthcoming*.

Egarter-Vigl, E. 2004. Los Ninos Del Llullaillaco: Scientific Testimonial on the condition of three Inca mummies of Llullaillaco and proposals for their preservation—Report for the Government of Salta and the Argentinian Ministry of Culture. Salta Governorate, Argentina: Studies performed at the Institute of Pathology, Central Hospital and the South Tyrolean Museum of Archaeology, Bolzano, Italy. Unpublished.

Forbes, S. L., B. H. Stuart, and B. B. Dent. 2005. The effect of the burial environment on adipocere formation. *Forensic Science International* 154 (1):24–34.

Gilbert, M. T. P., H.-J. Bandelt, M. Hofreiter, and I. Barnes. 2005a. Assessing ancient DNA studies. *Trends in Ecology & Evolution* 20 (10):541–544.

Gilbert, M. T. P., I. B. Matthew, J. Collins, C. Smith, J. Eklund, J. Goudsmit, H. Poinar, and A. Cooper. 2005b. Long-term survival of ancient DNA in Egypt: Response to Zink and Nerlich (2003). *American Journal of Physical Anthropology* 128 (1):110–114.

Graffam, G., M. Rivera, and A. Carevič. 1996. Ancient Metallurgy in the Atacama: Evidence for Copper Smelting during Chile's Early Ceramic Period. *Latin American Antiquity* 7 (2):101–113.

Hawass, Z., Y. Z. Gad, S. Ismail, R. Khairat, D. Fathalla, N. Hasan, A. Ahmed, H. Elleithy, M. Ball, F. Gaballah, S. Wasef, M. Fateen, H. Amer, P. Gostner, A. Selim, A. Zink, and C. M. Pusch. 2010. Ancestry and Pathology in King Tutankhamun's Family. *JAMA: The Journal of the American Medical Association* 303 (7):638–647.

Horai, S., R. Kondo, Y. Nakagawa-Hattori, S. Hayashi, S. Sonoda, and K. Tajima. 1993. Peopling of the Americas, founded by four major lineages of mitochondrial DNA. *Mol Biol Evol* 10:23–47.

Ikram, S., and A. Dobson. 1998. *Mummy in Ancient Egypt: Equipping the Dead for Eternity*. London: Thames and Hudson.

Langsjoen, O. 1998. Diseases of the dentition. *The Cambridge Encyclopedia of Human Paleopathology*. Nature Publishing Group, 393–412.

Poinar, H. N., and B. A. Stankiewicz. 1999. Protein Preservation and DNA Retrieval from Ancient Tissues. *Proceedings of the National Academy of Sciences of the United States of America* 96 (15): 8426–8431.

Previgliano, C. H., C. Ceruti, J. Reinhard, F. A. Araoz, and J. G. Diez. 2003. Radiologic Evaluation of the Llullaillaco Mummies. *Am. J. Roentgenol.* 181 (6):1473–1479.

Reinhard, J. 1993. Llullaillaco: An Investigation of the World's Highest Archaeological Site. *Latin American Indian Literatures Journal* 9 (1):31–54.

______. 2005. *The Ice Maiden: Inca Mummies, Mountain Gods, and Sacred Sites in the Andes*. Washington, D.C.: National Geographic Society.

Reinhard, K. J., and J. Buikstra. 2003. Louse infestation of the Chiribaya culture, southern Peru: variation in prevalence by age and sex. *Mem. Inst. Oswaldo Cruz* 98:173–179.

Rothhammer, F., A. Cocilovo, S. Quevedo, and E. Llop. 1982. Microevolution in prehistoric Andean population. Chronologic craniometric variation. *Am J Phys Anthropol* 58:391–396.

Torres-Rouff, C. 2002. Cranial Vault Modification and Ethnicity in Middle Horizon San Pedro de Atacame, Chile. *Current Anthropology* 43 (1):163–171.

Wilson, A. S., T. Taylor, M. C. Ceruti, J. A. Chavez, J. Reinhard, V. Grimes, W. Meier-Augenstein, L. Cartmell, B. Stern, M. P. Richards, M. Worobey, I. Barnes, and M. T. P. Gilbert. 2007. Stable isotope and DNA evidence for ritual sequences in Inca child sacrifice. *Proceedings of the National Academy of Sciences* 104 (42):16456–16461.

Yera, H., M. Tzen, and J. Dupouy-Camet. 2003. Molecular biology for detection and characterization of protozoan infections in humans. *European Journal of Protistology* 39 (4):435–443.

Zimmerman, M. R., B. Brier, and R. S. Wade. 1998. Brief communication: Twentieth-century replication of an Egyptian mummy: Implications for paleopathology. *American Journal of Physical Anthropology* 107 (4):417–420.

Postmortem Chemistry

10

VICTOR W. WEEDN, CHARLES F. SIEBERT, JR.,
AND JOSEPH A. PRAHLOW

Contents

Introduction

Clinical chemistry came into widespread practice with the advent of the automated analyzer by Technicon in the late 1950s and early 1960s and has since burgeoned into a large industry and an integral part of modern medical diagnostic practice. Clinical laboratory tests are also a critical component of the postmortem investigation of death by hospital and forensic pathologists, since most such deaths are from natural causes. In fact, this postmortem testing for clinical disease has begun to broaden beyond traditional clinical chemistry into genetic, metabolic, transcriptomic, proteomic, and other more esoteric testing.

Laboratory testing in clinical practice continues to be debated as either under-utilized or over-utilized depending on skill and trust in clinical history and physical examination. Cases presented to medical examiners commonly have no known clinical history and do not permit the same physical exam; therefore, particularly in the absence of anatomic changes, they may be even more dependent on clinical chemistry. Unfortunately, the clinical chemistries are also altered postmortem. Nonetheless, it has been reported that 5–10% of cases may be resolved or substantially facilitated through postmortem chemistry testing.[1,2,3]

As death ensues, the metabolism of the individual is radically affected. Diminished tissue perfusion results in depleted oxygen reserves, anaerobic metabolism, and lactic acidosis. With loss of membrane integrity, potassium, magnesium, and other small molecules leak out of cells, while sodium, chloride, and calcium ions rush in. Fluid shifts between compartments become manifest. Most enzymes become erratic and fail, while other enzymes are unleashed from their protected environments. In sum, the chemical milieu changes substantially as the patient succumbs to the process of death.

After death, other changes continue to occur. Some enzymatic activity persists, which results in certain continued metabolism. Decomposition, consisting of cellular autolysis and putrefaction (microbial action), begins. Postmortem diffusion results in redistribution, although this is more an issue with exogenous agents. Most postmortem chemistries are of value only in the early postmortem period.

Several analytes are remarkably stable postmortem. Creatinine and urea are the most stable of analytes. They are in relatively high concentration, are robust chemicals that resist the normal environmental insults of early decomposition, and are easy to chemically analyze. However, this cannot be said of most other analytes, and their concentrations may be substantially altered by postmortem changes. Electrolytes, which are at high concentration gradients, immediately begin to diffuse out with postmortem loss of membrane integrity and ion pump activity. Antibody-based tests may not detect analytes that lose their tertiary structure from pH changes, hydration states, and denaturation, while other proteins may become exposed that cross-react. Proteins and other chemicals may be metabolized or become altered by enzymatic activity.

Accordingly, clinical reference testing tables cannot be assumed to be applicable to the interpretation of postmortem tests. Unfortunately there is a relative lack of scientific literature on the subject of postmortem interpretation for many analytes. Although there is an increasing body of literature on the subject, it pales in comparison to the literature on live patient testing. Much basic work has been done, but for only the most common analytes. It is, of course, difficult to obtain data that directly compares postmortem to live patient laboratory test values and relatively few papers are published as such. The bulk of the literature tries to establish postmortem distribution and correlation with pathologist findings. Sadly, postmortem interval is an obvious factor that is usually not well described in most of this literature. Environmental temperature and body mass as well as other environmental factors[4] are simply not issues of concern for clinical testing of live patients, but they confound postmortem testing. Embalming may be another consideration of a forensic autopsy that is not for clinical laboratory testing.[5] Furthermore, the type of sample, site of sampling, sample preparation, and storage[6] are still other important variables. Lastly, the laboratory testing methodology is significant to the results obtained. The bulk of the postmortem chemistry literature is older and has not been updated to more modern equipment and procedures. Within all these parameters measures of "normal" for "postmortem" levels as well as disease cutoff values need to be established. Despite these problems laboratories do attempt to establish reference ranges, and pathologists do find postmortem clinical testing to be valuable.

Postmortem Specimens

Femoral blood, vitreous fluid, and urine are generally the minimal biological fluid specimens from a forensic autopsy; these are generally sufficient for most clinical chemistry testing. Blood for toxicology is most commonly placed in "tiger top" serum separator tubes or standard "red top" tubes. A purple top tube, with EDTA anticoagulant, if the postmortem interval (PMI) is not too long, is also recommended for certain tests. Guidelines for postmortem testing have been recommended.[7,8,9] Postmortem interval (PMI) is the single most important factor affecting all postmortem specimens. Results should be interpreted in light of the PMI.

Blood

Blood is a familiar sample source as the dominant sample source for clinical laboratory testing and has a vast literature. However, postmortem blood is not the same as a fresh pristine clinical sample from a live person. The clinical sample has been mixed within the body, but the postmortem blood has settled out and is no longer in a homogeneous state. Furthermore, the coagulation and complement cascades have been activated and may be in various states of clotting and lysis. Hemolysis is often an indicator that a clinical sample is not a useful sample for valid testing, but some degree of hemolysis is the rule postmortem.

The advantages of blood are that it is usually abundant and readily accessible. It is also a familiar source to laboratories and the medical community and has a large body of literature. Early postmortem testing was largely confined to blood samples. On the other hand, blood also has disadvantages. It is a complex matrix that undergoes great changes postmortem. Postmortem clotting and hemolysis results in variability and confounding factors. The intimate and large surface area of the intravascular spaces exposes it to the release of intracellular materials and to redistribution (e.g., hepatic glycogenolysis). The exposure to gut flora and the excellent nutrient medium renders the blood susceptible to microbial growth. Thus, while blood may be a good source for some analytes relatively unaffected by such processes, it is not a good source for others. Moreover, due to hemorrhage, postmortem clotting, or embalming, blood may not be available for testing.

To reduce the complexity of the matrix, serum or plasma may be extracted. Serum is usually collected from a "tiger top" ("marbled") serum separator tube, which contains a clotting activator and a gel to facilitate uncontaminated separation of the serum. Serum may also be obtained from a "red top" glass tube without additives or "red top" plastic tubes containing clot activators. Plasma is obtained from a "purple top" or "lavender top" tube containing EDTA to chelate potassium and prevent clotting and other metalloenzyme activity; however, since clotting is activated postmortem, pure plasma collection is not possible. "Grey top" tubes contain oxalate to prevent coagulation as well as fluoride to stop enzymatic activity and microbial growth.

Striking differences may be manifest between the right side of the heart (venous blood) and the left side of the heart (arterial blood) in concentrations of postmortem oxygen tension, pH, glucose, insulin, and levels of certain drugs (i.e., digoxin) and thus the site of blood sampling should be noted. Also, postmortem values from peripheral specimens are closest to levels found in living people and are therefore preferred for analysis.

Vitreous Humor

Postmortem degradation and other shortcomings of blood have led the field to explore other sample sources, particularly vitreous humor. Vitreous is a simpler matrix and is protected from early decomposition. The vitreous fluid compartment is relatively small, with a more controlled exchange rate, and thus may reflect blood levels, but is also protected from agonal changes. It should be recognized that this fluid compartment is protected by a blood-brain barrier and thus some analytes are excluded (e.g., bile, most hormones, most enzymes). Moreover, vitreous is accessible and easily obtained.

Since vitreous is not homogeneous, the entire fluid volume should be collected.[3] On the other hand, overly vigorous aspiration will draw fragments of retinal tissues, which will contaminate the fluid; it should be crystal clear. Pairs of vitreous samples, if tested separately, permit some measure of replication and quality control, or conversely, when the samples are combined, an average measurement will be obtained.

A significant issue with interpretation of vitreous values is that data on clinical vitreous chemistries are unavailable.[2] Studies which have been conducted on globe enucleation from ophthalmologic diseases may not be representative due to the disease process for which the enucleation was performed. Studies conducted on animals are also of limited value due to questionable generalizability.

Cerebrospinal Fluid, Pericardial Fluid, Synovial Fluid, Urine

Sample sources from non-vitreous biologic fluids are less commonly tested and often overlooked considerations. CSF may be used as a substitute for vitreous in cases of suspected child abuse where the eyes are saved for histological examination. As filtrates, they all have some advantage over blood: they are simpler matrices and to some extent protected from postmortem decomposition. Cerebrospinal fluid is protected by a blood-brain barrier, but the other fluids are not and may approximate serum values. However, they all suffer from nonspecific fluid accumulations which make quantitative testing difficult to interpret; this is most obvious in the case of urine. Synovial fluid permits replicate testing. Each fluid has potential special significance for organ specific disease associations: CSF for brain, pericardial fluid for heart, synovial fluid for joints, and urine for kidneys.

Solid Organ Tissues

Solid tissues are not generally useful for clinical disease testing. They are complex matrices and are subject to autolysis. However, solid tissues may be appropriate specimens for organ specific chemistries, metabolic studies, and possibly microarray mRNA studies if sufficiently fresh.

Decomposition/Postmortem Interval

As described above, during the process of dying, body tissues and fluids begin to become physiologically deranged due to fluid shifts, ion flows, acid-base disturbances, enzymatic dysfunction, loss of membrane integrity, and so on. Such derangements accelerate after death. Taphonomic changes, particularly autolysis from internal digestive enzymes and putrefaction from microbial enzymes, become dominant. These processes, unless inhibited, continue in some form for weeks, months, and years. It is these processes that so significantly undermine the utility of postmortem chemistry. In general, clinical chemistries are of value only in the early postmortem period. A vitreous potassium of >15 mEq/L is evidence of a prolonged postmortem interval, significant chemical decomposition, and that other clinical chemistries will not likely be of value.[10]

Researchers have investigated various aspects of decomposition as a method to determine the postmortem interval (PMI), the time period between death and the time of analysis, such as pH,[11] non-protein nitrogen,[12] free amino acids,[13] vitreous ammonia,[14] vitreous hypoxanthine,[15–17] calcium,[18] synovial fluid proteoglycans,[19] putrescine and cadaverine production, racemization of amino acid enantiomers, among others.[20] Different decompositional changes would conceivably cover different phases of the PMI. Regardless of the analyte and change measured or the phase of PMI studied, the underlying assumption is that the process follows a relatively predictable linear or curved model that is reproducible. Due to temperature, hydration, clothing, environmental exposures, nature of the death, and biologic variation, attempts to determine PMI through chemical analysis have largely failed to produce narrow time estimates, but rather merely suggest broad windows of time.

By far the most studied effect for PMI determination has been the diffusion of potassium from lining cells into the vitreous humor.[21] Upon death, potassium quickly begins to diffuse out of cells into the extracellular fluids. In the vitreous, the potassium has been shown to have a slower and more gradual rise making it more suitable for the determination of the postmortem interval. According to Sturner, vitreous potassium is a more reliable indicator of PMI than overall body decomposition, rigor mortis, or body temperature.[3]

Factors that cause variation in the vitreous potassium levels include environmental temperature,[22] age of the deceased,[23] terminal illness,[24] renal status,[10] sample collection,[3] and test method.[25,26] An incomplete sampling will cause a spuriously low result, but too vigorous extraction will cause a spuriously high result. Studies have shown differences in potassium of up to plus or minus 10% of the mean for each eye in about 20% of subjects.[27–29]

Despite its shortcomings, vitreous potassium has been shown to be the most reliable chemical method within the first 24 hours of death. Perhaps the most commonly used formulation was derived by Madea:[30]

$$\mathrm{PMI(h)} = 5.26 \times \mathrm{K\,concentration(mmol/L)} - 30.9$$

The confidence limits for this formula are ±20 hours in the first 100 hours postmortem. This assumes that the body has not been kept refrigerated.

By drawing vitreous samples from each eye at different times, Adjutantis and Coutselinis[31] claim to further increase the accuracy. Others (i.e., Schleyer[12]) claim increased accuracy through the use of combinations of chemical determinations.

Hypoxia

Controlled studies in dogs have shown that asphyxial deaths (in which respiratory failure precedes cardiac failure) produce substantially lower arterial (left ventricular heart) blood pO_2 than cardiac deaths (in which cardiac failure precedes respiratory failure)—the former <25 mmHg and the latter >25 mmHg.[2,32] These findings seem to be borne out in humans.[33] However, this difference may become obscured by attempted resuscitation measures prior to death. The analytic method seems to be significant, as oxymetric profiles have found to be of limited value.[34]

Blood carbon dioxide content reflects antemortem levels and remains stable. Vitreous CO_2 levels vary from 4 to 27 mEq/L (average 15 mEq/L) using an AutoAnalyzer.[1] However, such results are method dependent, with some methods (i.e., AutoAnalyzer) showing a rapid decrease from increasing lactic acid and associated decreased CO_2 combining power.

Some investigators have used oxypurines (hypoxanthine, xanthine, uridine, and inosine), as ATP metabolites, to determine hypoxia.[17,35–38] Also, it has been noted that asphyxia produces an increase in terminal blood sugar.

Acid-Base Disorders

Blood pH has been shown to decrease in proportion to the time of death. The value obtained is dependent on the site of the sample. A small study has shown that postmortem pH from a cardiac sample fell from 7.0 at the time of death to 5.5 at 20 hours after death.[11] However, the difference in pH between normal and severely acidotic individuals is sufficient to distinguish the two within the first five hours postmortem.[3]

Plasma lactic acid increases postmortem; it is significantly increased within the first postmortem hour and progressively increases to between 50 and 75 times the normal antemortem values.[2] Vitreous lactic acid also increases but only doubles (from 80–160 to 210–260 mg/dL) at 20 hours. Values are low in sudden cardiac death and are high in cases of prolonged agonal states.[39]

Hydration States

Vitreous sodium and chloride levels remain relatively stable during the early postmortem phase. Sodium levels begin to decline immediately postmortem, but the rate of decrease is variable. Chloride also decreases, but at a relatively constant rate of up to 1 mEq/L/hr (although too variable for PMI determination[3]). Vitreous sodium levels generally range from 135 to 151 mEq/L (average of 143 mEq/L) in adults.[2] However, levels are lower in children (average of 141 mEq/L) and especially newborns (average of 139 mEq/L).[40] Vitreous chloride levels generally range from 104 to 132 mEq/L (average of 120 mEq/L), but are lower in infants (average of 113 mEq/L).[2] However, these results are method dependent, with flame photometry indicating elevated levels compared to normal levels by ion-specific electrodes (such as in an Ektachem determination).[3]

Abnormally high or low salt concentrations can be reliably diagnosed postmortem. Coe has categorized the vitreous electrolyte abnormalities into four patterns:[2,3]

1. *Dehydration or hypertonic pattern.* Increased sodium (>155 mEq/L) and chloride (>135 mEq/dL) and a moderate increase in urea nitrogen (40–100 mg/dL).
2. *Uremic pattern.* Increased urea nitrogen and creatinine without a significant increase in sodium and chloride.
3. *Low-salt or hypotonic pattern.* Decreased sodium (<130 mEq/L) and chloride (<105 mEq/L) with a relatively low potassium (<15 mEq/L).
4. *Decomposition pattern.* Decreased sodium and chloride with an increased (>20 mEq/L) potassium.

Thus, elevated sodium and chloride values may be due to either dehydration[41–43] or impaired renal function, whereas depressed sodium and chloride values may be due to hypotonicity or decomposition. Isolated hypernatremia may be due to hyperosmolar infant formula. Causes for hypotonicity include polydipsia and water intoxication[44,45] and alcoholism with fatty liver or cirrhosis.[3] Isolated hyponatremia has many specific causes including adrenal cortical disease, hypothyroidism, pituitary disorders, acrodynia, beer potomania, and Ecstasy abuse. Isolated hypochloremia may be seen with severe and prolonged vomiting.

Diabetic States

Diabetic hyperglycemia should not normally be diagnosed from postmortem serum values alone.[3,46] It may be considered if the level is above 600 mg/dL from a peripheral blood source, without other explanation for the increased glucose level and if no resuscitative attempt has been performed.[2] Young infants (<3 mo of age) manifest higher postmortem glucose levels than normal adults (170.9 mg/dL v. 96.8 mg/dL). Blood glucose levels in the right atrium may be elevated from hepatic glycogenolysis.[2] Asphyxia and terminal stress has been associated with an increase in blood glucose. Apparently, attempted resuscitation may cause elevated blood glucose due to flushing of the hepatic circulation and terminal glycogenolysis.[2] Fatal hypothermia has also been reported to cause elevated blood glucose, presumably due to decreased glycolysis.[47,48] Thus, elevated postmortem glucose values can be found in diabetics, but also in normal individuals, those dying from asphyxia or hypothermia, and after terminal stress or attempted resuscitation.

Vitreous is the preferred source for glucose determinations. Embalming will not affect establishment of the diagnosis from vitreous chemistries.[5] Diagnosis of fatal diabetic ketoacidosis with severe hyperglycemia is generally obvious, but diagnosis of milder hyperglycemia is problematic. Zilg et al. use 10 mmol/L (~100mg/dL) postmortem vitreous glucose as indicating antemortem hyperglycemia.[49] Coe has reported on 1,000 consecutive natural deaths.[1] He found 103 cases of non-diabetics with serum glucose >500 mg/dL, of which 87 had been resuscitated—in none of these was the vitreous glucose >100 mg/dL. He found that a vitreous level of >200 mg/dL was only found in diabetic fatalities, regardless of resuscitative attempts or death by asphyxia.

Since diabetic ketoacidosis (DKA) is a metabolic state involving more than mere hyperglycemia, testing for lactate and volatile ketone bodies, specifically acetone, acetoacetate, and B-hydroxybutyrate, will permit a definitive diagnosis.[49,50] In fact, vitreous acetone alone has been used to establish DKA in a severely decomposed individual.[51] The presence of glucose and ketone bodies in the urine also suggests DKA. However, an aketotic form of sudden diabetic death has been described.[52–54] Elevated ketones in the absence of elevated glucose suggests malnutrition or potential neglect.[3]

Glycosylated hemoglobin (HbA1c) and glycated protein (fructosamine) are indicators of longer-standing uncontrolled glucose elevation.[55–59]

Although vitreous glucose is useful for diagnosis of hyperglycemia, it is not useful for hypoglycemia. Initial postmortem vitreous glucose levels are approximately 85% of antemortem levels and, due to postmortem glycolysis, may decline to zero within four to five hours.[60] Attempts to combine vitreous lactate levels with vitreous glucose to establish a diagnosis of hypoglycemia have not met with great success.[61–62] Given a clinical picture of starvation, chronic alcoholism, or islet cell tumor, a diagnosis of hypoglycemia might be entertained from a vitreous value of <20 mg/dL when drawn within two hours of death.[2] Sturner has reported a case of a motor vehicle accident caused by hypoglycemia.[63]

Postmortem serum insulin values have been reported to be higher than antemortem levels in healthy individuals, but are variable; however, Coe found generally lower values and decreasing with PMI.[3] Studies have shown values varying by a factor of 10 from different sites in the same body.[64] Nonetheless, the level will generally be below 100 microunits—except in diabetics on exogenous insulin.[2] A diagnosis of insulin poisoning can be made from postmortem serum studies.[67–70] C-peptide may also be measured in postmortem serum.[71] Insulin and C-peptide penetrate the vitreous to a minimal extent.[10] Special considerations are applicable to postmortem insulin analysis.[72,73]

Renal Function

Both urea nitrogen and creatinine in blood, vitreous, and CSF reflect antemortem levels and remain stable for days and despite moderate decompositional changes.[1–3] Apparent postmortem increases reported by some authors, probably represents agonal changes—especially in those hospitalized prior to death.[2] Vitreous urea nitrogen closely parallels antemortem levels, but vitreous creatinine is slightly lower than serum levels (~0.2 mg/dL).[74] After embalming, vitreous urea nitrogen is minimally diluted and will permit a diagnosis of uremia.[8] Creatinine is slower to rise from terminal prerenal elevations and thus is favored by some authors.[2] Uremia is characterized by marked elevations of vitreous and serum urea and creatinine levels without a significant rise in sodium and chloride. Postmortem urea nitrogen and creatinine are sufficiently accurate to support a diagnosis of renal disease despite no antemortem history or autopsy findings.[2,75] As noted above, an associated elevated sodium and chloride indicates dehydration as a basis for the elevated urea and creatinine levels. Other nitrogenous compounds will increase after death and are not useful as postmortem renal function tests.[12]

Hepatic Function

Significant postmortem serum bilirubin values accurately reflect antemortem jaundice, but slight postmortem elevations preclude diagnosis of minimal bilirubin elevations.[1–3,7,10,76] Small amounts of bilirubin have been detected in vitreous, cerebral spinal fluid, and synovial fluid.[77] These results, however, have shown much variation when compared to serum. Neither bile nor urobilinogen are normally present in the urine, and positive tests suggest liver damage.[10] Urinary urobilinogen remains unchanged after death and accurately reflects premortem levels.

Serum liver enzymes (including LDH, SGOT, GPT) become erratically elevated after death.[1-3] A possible exception is gamma glutamyl transferase (GGT), which may be used for documenting chronic alcoholism.[78,79] Vitreous enzyme activities are minimal or absent and highly erratic, bearing no relation to serum levels.

Inversion of the albumin-to-globulin ratio accurately reflects the antemortem state.[1-3] Ammonia concentrations are normally less than 3 mg/dL for the first few hours after death, but rise sharply after an initial eight-hour period.[12] Hepatic coma may be diagnosed by elevated glutamine in the cerebrospinal fluid.[2,3]

Alcoholics will often have a low-salt pattern and low blood sugar, and other markers, such as GGT and CDT.[80-82,3] Sudden death in alcoholics with fatty livers may be due to an alcoholic ketoacidosis (AKA), in which ketone bodies will be present in the blood and vitreous.

Cardiac Function

Clinical use of cardiac markers have evolved with time.[83-85] Lactate dehydrogenase (LDH) isoenzyme analysis was the cardiac biomarker used in the 1950s. LDH becomes elevated in about 10 hours and peaks in 2–3 days after the inception of a myocardial infarction. Myocardial LDH is composed primarily of LDH-1 and LDH-2 isoenzymes, but they are not entirely specific to the heart. Later, creatinine kinase (CK) isoenzyme analysis added further specificity to cardiac necrosis. It usually rises in 4 to 6 hours post-infarction but may not rise until 12 hours post-infarction. Myocardial CK is composed of CK-MB isoenzyme. In the 1990s, cardiac troponins (cTnI and cTnT) began to be used. They rise in a similar fashion to CK-MB. The troponin levels better correlate with severity and prognosis. Plasma norepinephrine, renin activity, antidiuretic hormone (ADH), and particularly beta-natriuretic peptide (BNP) rise after congestive heart failure.

Cardiac deaths constitute the overwhelming caseload of natural deaths seen by medical examiners. Most cardiac deaths do not manifest unequivocal anatomic changes of infarction or other causes of sudden cardiac death. The absence of an acute thrombus in cases of assumed myocardial infarction is the rule rather than the exception. The finding of severe atherosclerotic narrowing (>75%) is not itself a finding of an acute event. Despite the strong need for a useful cardiac marker, forensic pathologists have not found sufficient utility in these cardiac markers for routine use. Investigations of postmortem blood and pericardial fluid CK-MB, troponins, and other markers have yielded varied results—some indicating correlation with supposed ischemia and others not.[86-94] Hemolysis interferes with the analysis of these markers and may have prevented a showing of utility. Also, it appears that concentrations vary by site. Further studies are needed to understand the role of postmortem cardiac markers. Postmortem BNP has not been studied.

As mentioned above, oxygen tensions in left ventricular blood may distinguish between sudden cardiac death and other deaths, but are not totally consistent and will be obscured if resuscitative attempts are made.[33,34] Vitreous lactate has been suggested to assist such analysis.[2]

Cardiac medications may also be determined postmortem.[95]

Hyperlipidemia

Postmortem total serum cholesterol values have been documented to reflect antemortem values—both at high and low ranges.[1–3] Total serum cholesterol remains stable and has been used to identify familial hypercholesterolemia.[96] Other lipid profiles, including lipoproteins and triglycerides, have been found to be generally stable, at least within the first 24 hours, and reflect antemortem values by most, but not all investigators.[97–100] Methods of analysis are likely significant to differences in results between investigators. However, it seems clear that cholesterol esters are reduced by postmortem esterase activity.

Since individuals cannot be assumed to have fasted prior to death, the stomach and upper intestinal tract should be examined for food content. Accordingly, elevated levels should be interpreted with care if the stomach is not empty and a postprandial state inferred. However, one study found marked elevation in triglycerides, low-density lipoproteins, and apolipoprotein B in deaths of young individuals dying from coronary atherosclerosis compared to age matched controls, despite no difference due to stomach contents or postmortem interval.[101]

Attempts have been made to correlate lipid profiles with cardiac deaths.[101–104]

Immunology/Serology and Anaphylaxis

Protein electrophoresis generally retains its profile in postmortem sera.[1–3,105,106] Albumin is somewhat decreased and beta globulins are modestly increased postmortem; other fractions remain generally unchanged. However, hemolysis can alter this profile. Postmortem serum electrophoresis has been used to diagnose agammaglobulinemia and multiple myeloma.[2]

Specific antibodies associated with various viruses and with autoimmune diseases will generally be able to be detected through Western blot techniques.[3]

Postmortem anaphylaxis testing generally involves serum tryptase from mast cell degranulation and radioabsorbent test (RAST) sensitivity analysis for serum IgE antibodies to the specific allergens.[107–115] Human beta tryptase rises rapidly, becoming detectable within 30 minutes and reaching peak levels in 2 to 3 hours; the half-life is 2 hours. Caution must be used in interpretation as elevations of serum tryptase occur in the absence of anaphylaxis.[116–118] Elevated IgE antibodies do not establish anaphylaxis, but rather a potential sensitivity. An insect venom-specific IgE antibody would be confirmatory evidence in a case of a suspected bee sting anaphylactic reaction. Approximately 1% of the population have IgE antibodies to hymenoptera venom. Also, anaphylaxis to an insect sting may occur in the absence of a venom-specific IgE antibody, presumably due to a cross-reactivity from a similar antibody.

Neopterin, a metabolite of GTP and a member of the pteridine chemical group, is a marker of cellular immune system activation under the control of T-helper cells, including viral infections, bacterial infections, parasites, autoimmune disorders, malignant tumors, and allograft rejection. It has been measured postmortem in the serum and urine.[119–120]

Pancreatitis

Amylase levels rise three to four times antemortem levels after two days postmortem.[2] Amylase can enter the vitreous.[121]

Hormonal Disturbances

Thyroid

Serum TSH is stable for approximately 24 hours and reflects antemortem values.[122–124] Some penetration of vitreous by TSH occurs, but levels do not reflect serum values.[124] Postmortem femoral blood thyroxin (T_4) and triiodothyronine (T_3) levels reflect antemortem clinical values.[125–127] T_4 levels decrease after death and may also be depressed agonally; therefore diagnosis of hypothyroidism must be made with caution.[122,128] On the other hand, serum T_4 may permit diagnosis of severe thyroiditis or death due to thyrotoxicosis.[129,130] T_4 does not penetrate the vitreous.[124] Postmortem thyroglobulin (Tg) has been measured by an immunoabsorbent assay.[131]

Steroids

Cortisol levels remain stable postmortem, with an average of about 18.4 ug/dL.[132] 17-hydroxycorticosteroid levels are commonly elevated, but are particularly high after acute illness.[133] Steroids have not been reported to enter the vitreous.[3] Postmortem cortisol can establish a diagnosis of Addisonian crisis.

Other Hormones

Parathormone (PTH) is stable in the early postmortem period and penetrates the vitreous humor.[126] Luteinizing hormone (LH) can be measured in the serum for up to 48 hours but does not pass into the vitreous.[124,134] Human chorionic gonadotropin (HCG) in postmortem blood and urine has been found to reflect antemortem values in the case of HCG-producing tumor.[135] Serum prolactin varies with the cause of death—becoming elevated in postoperative deaths, the chronically ill, and drug-related suicides.[136]

Neuroactive Agents

Marked elevations in catecholamines from pheochromocytomas are manifest after death.[2] In general, catecholamines will be elevated from prolonged deaths and lower for quick deaths, such as from motor vehicle accidents.[2,137] Catecholamine levels are also altered in hyperthermia[138] and hypothermia.[139,140]

Massive increases in glutamine oxalacetic transaminase (GOT) and lactate dehydrogenase (LDH) and the appearance of alkaline phosphatase in clear cerebrospinal fluid is good evidence of brain death.[2] Also, catecholamine excretion[141] and pituitary hormone release[142–143] are depressed after brain death.

Suicide has been associated with depressed serum testosterone levels,[144] elevated serum prolactin[136] and CSF corticotropin-releasing factor (CRF) levels,[145] and mixed results with the monoamine, serotonin, and its metabolite, 5-hydroxy indole acetic acid (5-HIAA).[3,146–150]

Metabolic Screening

Most medical examiner offices now routinely perform metabolic screens on infants.[151–162] Tandem mass spectrometry (MS/MS) can interrogate amino acids and acylcarnitines useful for screening for 20 or more inherited metabolic conditions, some of which have been associated with sudden death, including medium chain acylCoA dehydrogenase (MCAD) deficiency and rarer disorders such as MSUD (maple syrup urine disease), citrullinemia, VLCAD (Very Long Chain Acyl CoA dehyrdogenase) deficiency, GA-I and GA-II, propionic acidemia, and methylmalonic acidemia. This testing is expensive and available from only a few sources; however, it appears that federal funding may become available for this. It should also be noted that this testing is becoming part of required panels of screening tests for all newborn infants. Testing for channelopathies appear on the horizon as a further screen of sudden unexpected infant deaths.

Creatine is not formed postmortem in the urine; its presence indicates significant breakdown of body tissue. Amino acids in urine have allowed diagnosis of methylmalonic acidemia and maple syrup urine disease.

Genetic Screening

Genetic testing is still considered expensive and is not widely performed after death. Nonetheless, the promise of such testing looms large and will undoubtedly become increasingly commonplace. The concept of a molecular autopsy is already being discussed.

DNA, unlike RNA, is remarkably robust and survivable after extremely harsh environments. However, endogenous nucleases and bacteria will eventually enzymatically destroy the DNA. These processes are largely arrested when samples are taken and dried or cooled. Furthermore, formalin will hydrolyze and cross-link the DNA strands and thus may be problematic, yet will not necessarily preclude testing. Polymerase chain reaction (PCR)-based testing is extremely sensitive, permitting testing of only a relatively few remaining intact molecules. Thus, the most important factors for most postmortem testing are generally postmortem interval and the size of the DNA target tested.

It should not be forgotten that testing can also be performed on the relatives of the deceased in the case of hereditable genetic disease. Whenever testing of relatives is performed, the discovery of non-paternity must be considered.

Traditional genetic testing may be performed for known genetic disease, but there are many other postmortem applications that are possible.

Nucleic acid tests (NAT) for viral, bacterial, and even parasitic pathogens are widely available and may prove tremendously valuable. However, since RNA is less stable, tests for RNA viruses and RNA-based tests may be less valuable in a postmortem setting. The tests can take the form of a laboratory-based test on the tissue or fluid, or they may take the form of fluorescent hybridization in situ on a histologic slide. There is interest in a "zebra chip" as a microarray for a panoply of pathogens.

Genetic testing may be useful for toxicologic testing, so-called pharmacogenomic testing. Certain tests can define a person as a fast or slow acetylator. For example, only half an oral dose of the antihypertensive hydralazine will reach the blood of a fast acetylator (FA) compared to that of a slow acetylator (SA). Such testing has been applied to toxicology.[163–165]

Spontaneous thromboembolism may particularly suggest testing for hereditary thrombophilias. Three sets of DNA tests have become common in this setting: antithrombin-III deficiency, Protein C and Protein S deficiency, and Factor V Leiden (activated protein C resistance from a variant form of Factor V).

Sudden death may suggest testing for a "channelopathy"—in which genetic mutations result in defects in cardiac ion channel proteins that may lead to fatal arrhythmias. These are generally characterized as a long Q-T syndrome (primarily Romano-Ward syndrome) or Brugada's syndrome in which the Q-T interval is normal.

One can envision the day that atherosclerosis, hypertension, diabetes, and other diseases, or subsets thereof, will someday be routinely tested at death, as they are currently becoming routine at birth.[166] The characterization of families may drive future health care.

References

1. Coe JI, 1976. Postmortem chemistry of blood, cerebrospinal fluid, and vitreous humor, in *Legal Medicine Annual 1976*, ed by C.H. Wecht, New York, NY, Appleton, Century Croft, pp. 55–92.
2. Coe JI, 1977. Postmortem chemistry of blood, cerebrospinal fluid, and vitreous humor, in *Forensic Medicine*; vol 2, ed by C.G. Tedeschi, W.C. Eckert, L.G. Tedeschi, Philadelphia, WB Saunders, pp. 1030–60.
3. Sturner WQ, 2006. Chemical considerations, in *Medicolegal Investigation of Death*, 4th ed., ed by W.U. Spitz, Springfield, IL, Charles C Thomas, pp. 128–148.
4. Zhu BL, Ishida K, Taniguchi M, Quan L, Oritani S, Tsuda K, Kamikodai Y, Fujita MQ, Maeda H, 2003. Possible postmortem serum markers for differentiation between fresh-saltwater drowning and acute cardiac death: a preliminary investigation, *Leg Med* (Tokyo) 5(sup 1): 298–301.
5. Coe JI, 1976. Comparative postmortem chemistries of vitreous humor before and after embalming, *J For Sci* 21:583–6.
6. Bray M, 1984. The effect of chilling, freezing, and rewarming on the postmortem chemistry of vitreous humor, *J For Sci* 29:404–11.
7. Fekete JF, Brunsdon DFV, 1974. The use of routine laboratory tests in postmortem examinations, *Can Soc For Sci* 7:238–54.
8. Flanagan RJ, Connally G, Evans JM, 2005. Analytical toxicology: guidelines for sample collection postmortem, *Tox Rev* 24(1):63–71.
9. Uemura K, Shintani-Ishida K, Saka K, Nakajima M, Ikegaya H, Kikuchi Y, Yoshida K, 2008. Biochemical blood markers and sampling sites in forensic autopsy, *J For Leg Med* 15(5): 312–7.
10. Coe JI, 1993. Postmortem chemistry update, *Am J For Med & Path* 14(2):91–117.
11. Sawyer WR, Steup DR, Martin BS, Forney RB, 1988. Cardiac blood pH as a possible indicator of postmortem interval, *J For Sci* 33(6):1439–1444.
12. Schleyer F, Determination of time of death in the early postmortem interval, in *Methods of Forensic Science*, vol. 2, New York Interscience, John Wiley and Sons, pp. 253–293, 1963.
13. Durham DG, Dickinson JC, Hamilton PB, Ion-exchange chromatography of free amino acids in human intraocular fluids, 1971. *Clin Chem* 17(4):285–289.

14. van den Oever R, 1978. Postmortem vitreous ammonium concentrations in estimating the time of death, *Z Rechtsmed* 80(4):259–263.
15. Rognum TO, Hauge S, Oyasaeter S, Saugstad OD, 1991. A new biochemical method for estimation of postmortem time, *For Sci Int* 51(1):139–146.
16. James RA, Hoadley PA, Sampson BG, 1997. Determination of postmortem interval by sampling vitreous humor, *Am J For Med & Path* 18(2):158–162.
17. Madea B, Kaferstein H, Herman N, Sticht G, 1994. Hypoxanthine in vitreous humor and cerebrospinal fluid—A marker of postmortem interval and prolonged (vital) hypoxia? Remarks also on hypoxanthine in SIDS, *For Sci Int* 65(1):19–31.
18. Nowak R, Balanova S, 1989. Determination of calcium and magnesium in postmortem human vitreous humor as a test to ascertain the cause and time of death, *Z Rechtsmed* 102(2–3):179–183.
19. Hansen LM, Donnell M, Robinson S, Heimer R, Molinaro L, Laposata EA, 1990. Changes in synovial fluid proteoglycans as a possible marker of time of death, abstract G25, in the 42nd Annual Meeting, Amer Acad of For Sci publication no. 90–92.
20. Vass AA, Barshick SA, Sega G, Caton J, Skeen JT, Love JC, Synstelien JA, 2002. Decomposition chemistry of human remains: a new methodology for determining the postmortem interval, *J For Sci* 47(3):542–53.
21. Coe JI, 1989.Vitreous potassium as a measure of the postmortem interval: an historical review and clinical evaluation, *For Sci Int* 42:201–13.
22. Pex JO, Menneely KD, Andrews FC, 1983. Time of death estimations in blacktail deer by temperature and aqueous humor glucose, *J For Sci* 28:594–600.
23. Blumenfeld TA, Blanc WA, Devlin J, 1974. Postmortem vitreous humor concentrations of Na, K, Cl, Ca, and Mg in children, *Ped Res* 8:356.
24. Sturner WQ, Gantner GE, 1964. The postmortem interval: a study of potassium in the vitreous humor, *Am J Clin Path* 42(2):137–144.
25. Coe JI, Apple FS, 1985. Variations in vitreous humor chemical values as a result of instrumentation, *J For Sci* 30(3):828–835.
26. Tagliaro F, Manetto G, Cittadina F, Marchetti D, Bortolotti F, Marigo, M, 1999. Capillary zone electrophoresis of potassium in human vitreous humor: validation of a new method, *J Chromatography* 733(1–2):273–9.
27. Balasooriya BAW, St. Hill CA, Williams AR, 1984. The biochemistry of vitreous humor: a comparative study of potassium, sodium, and urate concentrations in the eyes at identical time intervals after death, *For Sci Int* 26(2):85–91.
28. Madea B, Henssge C, Honig W, Gerbracht A, 1989. References for determining the time of death by potassium in the vitreous humor, *For Sci Int* 40:231–43.
29. Pounder DJ, Carson DO, Johnston K, Orihara Y, 1998. Electrolyte concentration differences between left and right vitreous humor samples, *J For Sci* 43(3):604–607.
30. Madea B, Herrmann N, Henssge C, 1990. Precision of estimating the time since death by vitreous potassium: comparison of two different equations, *For Sci Int* 46:277–84.
31. Adjutantis G, Coutselinis A, 1972. Estimation of the time of death by potassium levels in the vitreous humor, *For Sci* 1:55–60.
32. Mithoefer JC, Mead G, Hughes JMB, Iliff LD, Campbell EJM, 1967. A method of distinguishing death due to cardiac arrest from asphyxia, *Lancet* 2:654–6.
33. Patrick JR, 1970. Cardiac or respiratory death, in *Sudden Infant Death Syndrome: Proceedings of the Second International Conference on Causes of the Sudden Death in Infants* (Seattle), ed by A.B. Bergman, J.B. Beckwith, C. Ray, Univ of Washington Press, p. 131.
34. Maeda B, Fukita K, Oritani S, Ishia K, Zhu BL, 1997. Evaluation of postmortem oxymetry with reference to causes of death, *For Sci Int* 87(3):201–210.
35. Harkness RA, Lund RJ. 1983. Cerebrospinal fluid concentrations of hypoxanthine, xanthine, urdine, and inosine: high concentrations of the ATP metabolite, hypoxanthine, after hypoxia, *J Clin Path* 36:1–8.

36. Saugstad OD, Rognum TO, 1988. High postmortem levels of hypoxanthine in the vitreous humor of premature babies with respiratory distress syndrome, *Pediatrics* 81:395–8.
37. Poulsen, JP, Rognum, TO, Hauge S, Oyasaeter S, Saugstad OD, 1993. Postmortem concentrations of hypoxanthine in the vitreous humor—A comparison between babies with severe respiratory failure, congenital abnormalities of the heart, and victims of sudden infant death syndrome, *J Perinatal Med* 21(2):153–163.
38. Opdal, SH, Rognum, TO, Vege, A, Saugstad, OD, 1998. Hypoxanthine levels in vitreous humor: a study of influencing factors in sudden infant death syndrome, *Ped Res 44* (2):192–196.
39. Sturner WQ, Sullivan A, Suzuki K. 1983. Lactic acid concentrations in vitreous humor: their use in asphyxial deaths in children, *J For Sci* 28:222–30.
40. Blumenfeld TA, Blanc WA, Devlin J, 1974. Postmortem vitreous humor concentrations of Na, K, Cl, Ca, and Mg in children, *Ped Res* 8:356.
41. DiMaio VJM, DiMaio SJ, 1980. Fatal water intoxication in a case of psychogenic, *J For Sci* 25:332–5.
42. Huser CJ, Smialek JE, 1986. Diagnosis of sudden death in infants due to acute dehydration, *Am J For Med & Path* 7(4):278–282.
43. Moder KG, Hurley DL, 1990. Fatal hypernatremia from exogenous salt intake: report of a case and review of the literature, *Mayo Clinic Proc* 65:1587–94.
44. Hyashi T, Ishida Y, Miyashita T, Kiyokawa H, Kimura A, Kondo T, 2005. Fatal water intoxication in a schizophrenic patient—an autopsy case, *J Clin For Med* 12(3):157–9.
45. Madea B, Lachenmeier DW, 2005. Postmortem diagnosis of hypertonic dehydration, *For Sci Int* 155(1):1–6.
46. Gormsen H, Lund A, 1985. The diagnostic value of postmortem blood glucose determinations in cases of diabetes mellitus, *For Sci Int* 28:103–7.
47. Bray M, 1984. The eye as a chemical indicator of environmental temperature at the time of death, *J For Sci* 29(2):396–403.
48. Coe JI, 1984. Hypothermia: Autopsy findings and vitreous glucose, *J For Sci* 29(2):389–395.
49. Zilg, B. Alkass, K. Berg, S Druid, H., 2009. Postmortem identification of hyperglycemia, *For Sci Int* 185:89–95.
50. Osuna E, Vivero G, Conejero J, Abenza JM, Martinez P, Luna A, Perez-Carceles MD, 2005. Postmortem vitreous humor beta-hydroxybutyrate: its utility for the postmortem interpretation of diabetes mellitus, *For Sci Int* 153:189–95.
51. Smialek JE, Levine B, 1998. Diabetes and decomposition: a case of diabetic ketoacidosis with advanced postmortem change, *Am J For Med Path*, 19(1):98–101.
52. DiMaio VJM, Sturner WQ, Coe JI, 1977. Sudden and unexpected deaths after the acute onset of diabetes mellitus, *J For Sci* 22(1):147–151.
53. Irwin J, Cohle SD. 1988. Sudden death due to diabetic ketoacidosis, A*m J For Med Path* 9:119–21.
54. Cohle SD, 1989. The authors reply, *Am J For Med Path* 10:270.
55. Chen C, Glagov S, Mako M, Rochman H, Rubenstein AH, 1983. Postmortem glycosylated hemoglobin (HbA1c): evidence for a history of diabetes mellitus, *Annals Clin Lab Sci* 13(5):407–410.
56. John WG, Scott KW, Hawcroft DM, 1988. Glycated haemoglobin and glycated protein and glucose concentrations in necropsy blood samples, *J Clin Path* 41:415–8.
57. Valenzuela A. 1988. Postmortem diagnosis of diabetes mellitus: quantitation of fructosamine and glycated hemoglobin, *For Sci Int* 38:203–8.
58. Ritz S, Mehlan G, Martz W, 1996. Postmortem diagnosis of diabetic metabolic derangement: elevated alpha 1-antitrypsin and haptoglobin glycosylation levels as an index of antemortem hyperglycemia, *J For Sci* 41(1):94–100.
59. Winecker RE, Hammett-Stabler CA, Chapman JF, Ropero-Miller JD, 2002. HbA1c as a postmortem tool to identify glycemic control, *J For Sci* 47(6):1373–9.

60. Coe JI, 1973. Further thoughts and observations on postmortem chemistry, *For Sci Gaz* 5(5):2.
61. De Letter EA, Pierre MH, 1998. Can routinely combined analysis of glucose and lactate in vitreous humour be useful in current forensic practice? *Am J For Med Path* 19(4) 335–342.
62. Peclet, C, Picotte P, Jobin, F, 1994. The use of vitreous humor levels of glucose, lactic acid, and blood levels of acetone to establish antemortem hyperglycemia in diabetic, *For Sci Int* 65(1):1–6.
63. Sturner, WQ, Sullivan A, 1983. Hypoglycemia as the responsible factor in a truck driver accident fatality, *J For Sci* 28(4):1016–1020.
64. Lindquist O, Rammer L, 1975. Insulin in postmortem blood, *Z Rechtsmed* 75(4):275–277.
65. Oksanen A, 1976. Insulin in postmortem blood: a comment, *Z Rechtsmed* 77:311–2.
66. Dickson SJ, Cairns ER, 1977. The isolation and quantitation of insulin in postmortem specimens: a case report, *For Sci* 9:37–42.
67. Sturner WQ, Putnam RS, 1972. Suicidal insulin poisoning with nine day survival: recovery in bile at autopsy by radioimmunoassay, *J For Sci* 17:514–21.
68. Hood I, Mirchandani H, Monforte J, Stacer W, 1986. Immunohistochemical demonstration of homicidal insulin injection site, *Arch Path Lab Med* 110:973–4.
69. Patel F, 1992. Fatal self-induced hyperinsulinaemia: a delayed post-mortem analytical detection, *Med Sci Law* 32:151–9.
70. Winston DC, 2000. Suicide via insulin overdose in nondiabetics: the New Mexico experience, *Am J For Med Path* 21(3): 237–240.
71. Iwase H, Kobayashi M, Nakajima M, Takatori, T, 2001.The ratio of insulin to C-peptide can be used to make a forensic diagnosis of exogenous insulin overdosage, *For Sci Int* 115 (1,2) 123–127.
72. Fletcher SM, 1983. Insulin: a forensic primer, *J For Sci Soc* 23:5–17.
73. Kernbach-Wighton G, Puschel K, 1998. On the phenomenology of lethal applications of insulin, *For Sci Int* 93(1): 61–73.
74. Piette M, 1989. The effect of postmortem interval on the level of creatinine in vitreous humor, *Med Sci Law* 29:47–54.
75. Zhu BL, Ishida K, Quan L, Taniguchi M, Oritani S, Li DR, Fujita MQ, Maeda H, 2002. Postmortem serum uric acid and creatinine levels in relation to the causes of death, *For Sci Int* 24;125(1):59–66.
76. Coe JI, 1974. Postmortem chemistries on blood: particular reference to urea nitrogen, electrolytes, and bilirubin, *J For Sci* 19:33–42.
77. Naumann HN, Young JM, 1960. Comparative bilirubin levels in vitreous body, synovial fluid, cerebrospinal fluid, and serum after death, *Proc Soc Exp Biol Med* 105:70–2.
78. Devgun MS, Dunbar JA, 1985. Postmortem estimation of gamma-glutamyl transferase in vitreous humor and its association with chronic abuse of alcohol and road-traffic deaths, *For Sci Int* 28:179–80.
79. Piette M, DeSchrijver G, 1987. Gamma-glutamyl transferase: applications in forensic pathology: I: study of blood serum recovered from human bodies, *Med Sci Law* 27(3):152–160.
80. Sturner WQ, Coe JI, 1973. Electrolyte imbalance in alcoholic liver disease, *J Forensic Sci* 18:344–50.
81. Sadler, D.W., Girela, E, Pounder, DJ, 1996. Post mortem markers of chronic alcoholism, *For Sci Int* 82 (2):153–163.
82. Osuna E, Perez-Carceles MD, Moreno M, Bedate A, Conejero J, Abenza J, Matinez P, Luna A, 2000. Vitreous humor carbohydrate-deficient transferrin concentrations in the postmortem diagnosis of alcoholism, *For Sci Int* 108(3):205–213.
83. Perez-Carceles MD, Osuna E, Vieira DN, Martinez A, Luna A, 1995. Biochemical assessment of acute myocardial ischaemia, *J Clin Path* 48(2):124–8.
84. Harrison A, Kirchick H, Mader S, Goldsmith BM, 2004. An analysis of cardiovascular biomarkers, *Advance/Laboratory.*

85. Jaffe AS, Babuin L, Apple FS, 2006. Biomarkers in acute cardiac disease: the present and the future, *J Am Coll Cardiol* 48(1):1–11.
86. Luna A, Carmona A, Villanueva E, 1983. The postmortem determination of CK isoenzymes in the pericardial fluid in various causes of death, *For Sci Int* 22:23–30.
87. Stewart RV, Zumwalt RE, Hirsch CS, Kaplan L, 1984. Postmortem diagnosis of myocardial disease by enzyme analysis of pericardial fluid, *Am J Clin Pathol* 82:411–7.
88. Arroyo A, Valero J, Marron T, Vidal C, Hontecillas B, Bernal J, 1998. Pericardial fluid postmortem: comparative study of natural and violent deaths, *Am J For Med Path* 19 (3):266–268.
89. Cina SJ, Thompson WC, Fischer JR Jr., Brown DK, Titus JM, Smialek JE, 1999. A study of various morphologic variables and troponin I in pericardial fluid as possible discriminators of sudden cardiac death, *Am J For Med Path* 20 (4):333–337.
90. Ooi DS, Isotalo PA, Veinot JP, 2000. Correlation of antemortem serum creatine kinase, creatine kinase-MB, troponin I, and troponin T with cardiac pathology, *Clin Chem* 46(3):338–344.
91. Ellingsen CL, Hetland O, 2004. Serum concentrations of cardiac troponin T in sudden death, *Am J For Med & Path* 25(3):213–215.
92. Davies SJ, Gaze DC, Collinson PO, 2005. Investigation of cardiac troponins in postmortem subjects: comparing antemortem and postmortem levels, *Am J For Med & Path* 26(3):213–215.
93. Khalifa AB, Najjar M, Addad F, Turki E, Mghirbi T, 2006. Cardiac troponin T (cTnT) and the postmortem diagnosis of sudden death, *Am J For Med & Path* 27(2):175–177.
94. Takeichi S, Nakajima Y, Osawa M, Yukawa N, Saito T, Seto Y, Nakano T, Adachi M, Jitsukata K, Horiuchi K, Wang T, Nakajima K, 1997. The possible role of remnant-like particles as a risk factor for sudden cardiac death, *Int J Legal Med* 114(4):213–9.
95. Coe JI, 1981. Forensic aspects of cardiac medications, *Am J For Med & Pathol* 2:329:32.
96. Leadbeatter S, Stansbie D, 1984. Postmortem diagnosis of familial hypercholesterolaemia, *BMJ* 289:1656.
97. Tilvis R, Miettinen TA, 1980. Squalene, methyl sterol, and cholesterol levels in human organs, *Arch Pathol Lab Med* 104:305–40.
98. Sarkoja T, Yla-Herttuala S, Solakjui T, Nikkari T, Hirvonen J, 1988. Stability of plasma total cholesterol, triglycerides, and apolipoproteins B and A-1 during the early postmortem period, *J For Sci* 33:1432–8.
99. Sarikioja T, Yla-Hettuala S, Solakivi T, Nikkari T, Hirvonen J, 1988. Stability of plasma total cholesterol, triglycerides, and apolipoproteins B and A-1 during the early postmortem period, *J For Sci* 33(6):1432–1438.
100. Lehtimaki T, 1991. Determination of apolipoprotein E phenotypes from stored or postmortem serum samples, *Clin Chim Acta* 203(2–3):177–182.
101. Hiserodt JC, Perper JA, Koehler SA, Orchard TJ, 1995. A comparison of blood lipid and lipoprotein values in young adults who die suddenly and unexpectedly from atherosclerotic coronary artery disease with other noncardiac deaths, *Am J For Med & Path* 16(2):101–106.
102. Enticknap JB, 1962. Lipids in cadaver sera after fatal heart attack, *J Clin Path* 14:496–499.
103. Sturner WQ, 1971. Postmortem lipid studies: attempts to correlate with death from arteriosclerotic heart disease in the young age group, *For Sci Gaz* 2(1):5–7.
104. Hart AP, Zumwalt RE, Dasgupta A, 1997. Postmortem lipid levels for the analysis of risk factors of sudden death: usefulness of the Ektachem and Monarch analyzers, *Am J For Med & Path* 18(4):354–359.
105. Brazinsky JH, Kellenberger RE, 1970. Comparison of immunoglobulin analyses of antemortem and postmortem sera, *Am J Clin Pathol* 54:622–4.
106. McCormick GM, 1972. Nonanatomic postmortem techniques: postmortem serology, *J For Sci* 17:57–62.
107. Schwartz HJ, Squillace DL, Sher TH, Tiegland JD, Yunginger JW, 1986. Studies in stinging insect hypersensitivity: postmortem demonstration of antivenom IgE antibody in possible sting related sudden death, *Am J Clin Pathol* 85:607–610.

108. Yunginger JW, Sweeney KG, Sturner WQ, Giannandra LE, Teigland JD, Bray M, Benson PA, York JA, Biedrzycki L, Squillace DL, Helm RM, 1988. Fatal food induced anaphylaxis, *JAMA* 260(10):1450–2.
109. Yunginger JW, Nelson DR, Squillace DL, Jones RT, Holley KE, Hyma BA, Biedrzycki L, Sweeney KG, Sturner WQ, Schwartz LB, 1991. Laboratory investigation of deaths due to anaphylaxis, *J For Sci* 36(3):857–865.
110. Prahlow JA, Barnard JJ, 1998. Fatal anaphylaxis caused by fire ant stings, *Am J For Med & Path* 19(2):137–142.
111. Pumphrey RSH, Roberts IS, 2000. Postmortem findings after fatal anaphylactic reactions, *J Clin Path* 53(4):273–276.
112. Horn KD, Halsey JF, Zumwalt RE, 2004. Utilization of serum tryptase and immunoglobulin e assay in the postmortem diagnosis of anaphylaxis, *Am J For Med Pathol* 25(1):37–43.
113. Nishio H, Takai S, Miyazaki M, Horiuchi H, Osawa M, Uemura K, Yoshida K, Mukaida M, Ueno Y, Suzuki K, 2005. Usefulness of serum mast cell-specific chymase levels for postmortem diagnosis of anaphylaxis, *Int J Legal Med* 119(6):331–4.
114. Perskvist N, Edston E, 2007. Differential accumulation of pulmonary and cardiac mast cell-subsets and eosinophils between fatal anaphylaxis and asthma death: a postmortem comparative study, *For Sci Int* 169(1):43–9.
115. Greenberger PA, Rostkoff BD, Lifschulz B, 2007. Fatal anaphylaxis: postmortem findings and associated comorbid diseases, *Ann Allergy Asthma Immunol* 98(3):252–7.
116. Randall B, Butts J, Halsey JF, 1995. Elevated postmortem tryptase in the absence of anaphylaxis, *J For Sci* 40(2):208–211.
117. Nishio H, Suzuki K, 2005. Three cases of suspected hyperthermia with remarkable elevation of serum mast cell tryptase, *For Sci Int* 149(1):51–5.
118. Edston E, Eriksson O, Van Hage M, 2007. Mast cell tryptase in postmortem serum-reference values and confounders, *Int J Legal Med* 2007 121(4):275–80.
119. Ambach E, Tributsch W, Fuchs D, Reibnegger G, Henn R, Wachter H, 1991. Postmortem evaluation of serum and urine neopterin concentrations, *J For Sci* 36:1089–93.
120. Ambach E, Tributsch W, Rabl W, Fuchs D, Reibnegger G, Henn R, Wachter H, 1991. Postmortem neopterin concentrations: comparison of diagnoses with and without cellular immunological background, *Int J Leg Med* 104:259–62.
121. Devos C, Piette M, 1989. Hypothermia and combined postmortem determination of amylase and isoamylase in the serum and vitreous humor, *Med Sci Law* 29(3):218–228.
122. Coe JI, 1973. Postmortem values of thyroxine and thyroid stimulating hormone, *J For Sci* 18:20–4.
123. Ross IS, Moffat MA, Reid IW, 1983. Thyroid hormones in the sudden infant death syndrome (SIDS), *Clin Chim Acta* 129:151–5.
124. Chong APY, Aw SE, 1986. Postmortem endocrine levels in vitreous humor, *Ann Acad Med Singapore* 15(4):606–609.
125. Edston, E., Druid, H., Holmgren, P., and Ostrom, M., 2001. Postmortem measurements of thyroid hormones in blood and vitreous humor combined with histology, *Am J For Med Path* 22(1): 78–83.
126. Rachut E, Rynbrandt DJ, Doutt TW, 1980. Postmortem behavior of serum thyroxine, triiodothyronine, and parathormone, *J For Sci* 25:67–71.
127. Bader M, 1982. Normal thyroxine levels in sudden death syndrome, *JAMA* 248:3095.
128. Bonnell HJ, 1983. Antemortem chemical hypothyroxinemia, *J For Sci* 28:242–8.
129. Simson LR, 1976. Thyrotoxicosis: postmortem diagnosis in an unexpected death, *J For Sci* 21:831–2.
130. Herman GE, Kanluen S, Monforte J, Husain M, Spitz WU, 1986. Fatal thyrotoxic crisis, *Am J For Med Path* 7:174–6.
131. Tamaki K, Sato K, Katsumato Y, 1987. Enzyme-linked immunosorbent assay for determination of plasma thyroglobulin and its application to postmortem diagnosis of mechanical asphyxia, *For Sci Int* 33:259–65.

132. Finlayson NB, 1965. Blood cortisol in infants and adults: A postmortem study, *J Pediatr* 67:284–92.
133. Done AK, Ely RS, Kelly VC, 1958. Studies of 17-hydroxycorticosteroid concentrations at death in human subjects, *Am J Dis Child* 96:655–65.
134. Mendelson JH, Dietz PE, Ellingboe J, 1982. Postmortem plasma luteinizing hormone levels and antemortem violence, *Pharmacol Biochem Behav* 17(1):171–173.
135. Ludwig J, in *Current Methods of Autopsy Practice*, Philadelphia, W.B. Saunders, p. 220, 1972.
136. Jones TJ, Hallworth MJ, 1999. Postmortem prolactin as a marker of antemortem stress, *J Clin Pathol* 52(10):749–51.
137. Hirvonen J, Huttunen P, 1996. Postmortem changes in serum noradrenaline and adrenaline concentrations in rabbit and human cadavers, *Int J Legal Med,* 109(3):143–146.
138. Kortelainen M, Huttunen P, Lapinlamppi TD, 1990. Urinary catecholamines in hyperthermia-related deaths, *For Sci Int* 48:103–10.
139. Hirvonen J, Huttunen P, 1982. Increased urinary concentrations of catecholamines in hypothermia deaths, *J For Sci* 27:264–71.
140. Lapinlampi TD, Hirvonen JI, 1986. Catecholamines in the vitreous fluid and urine of guinea pigs dying of cold and the effect of postmortem freezing and autolysis, *J For Sci* 31:1357–67.
141. Feibel H, 1981. Reduced catecholamine excretion at onset of brain death, *Lancet* 1:890.
142. Powner DJ, Hendrich A, Lagler RG, Ng RH, Madden Rl, 1990. Hormonal changes in brain dead patients, *Crit Care Med* 18:702–8.
143. Zaloga GP, 1990. Endocrine function after brain death, *Crit Care Med* 29:785–6.
144. Roland BC, Morris JL, Zelhart PF, 1986. Proposed relation of testosterone levels to make suicide and sudden death, *Psychol Rep* 59:100–2.
145. Arato M, Banki CM, Bissette G, Nemeroff CB, 1989. Elevated CSF CRF in suicide victims, *Biol Psych* 25(3):355–359.
146. Ricci LC, Wellman MM, 1990. Monoamines: biochemical markers of suicide? *J Clin Psychol* 46:106–16.
147. Stanley M, Stanley B, 1990. Postmortem evidence for serotonin's role in suicide, *J Clin Psychol* 51(suppl): 22–8.
148. Endo T, Hara S, Kuriiwa F, Kano S, 1990. Postmortem changes in the levels of monoamine metabolites in human cerebrospinal fluid, *For Sci Int* 44:61–8.
149. Karkela J, Scheinin M, 1992. Tryptophan and biogenic amine metabolites in postmortem human cisternal fluid: effects of postmortem interval and agonal time, *J Neurol Sci* 107:239–45.
150. Molcho A, Stanley B, Stanley M, 1991. Biological studies and markers in suicide and attempted suicide, *Int Clin Psychopharm* 6(2):77–92.
151. Morrow G, Barness LA, Auerbach VH, DiGeorge AM, Ando T, Nyhan WL, 1969. Observations on the coexistence of methylmalonic academia and glycinemia, *J Ped* 74:680–90.
152. Hallock J, Morrow G, Karp LA, Barness LA, 1969. Postmortem diagnosis of metabolic disorders, *Am J Dis Child* 118:649–51.
153. Bennet MJ, Marlow N, Pollit RJ, Wales JKH, 1986. Glutaric aciduria type I: biochemical investigations and postmortem findings, *Eur J Ped* 145:403–5.
154. Emery JL, Variend S, Howat AJ, Vawter GF, 1988. Investigation of inborn errors of metabolism in unexpected infant deaths, *Lancet* 1988(2):29–31.
155. Coude M, Bonnefont JP, Charpentier C, Chadefaux B, Saudubray JM, Kamoun P, 1989. Aqueous humor, a possible material for postmortem methylmalonic acidaemia, *J Inherited Metab Dis* 12:95–6.
156. Bennett MJ, Hale DE, Coates PM, Stanley CA, 1991. Postmortem recognition of fatty acid oxidation disorders, *Ped Pathol* 11:365–70.
157. Touma EH, Charpentier C, 1992. Medium chain acyl-CoA dehydrogenase deficiency, *Arch Dis Child* 67:142–5.
158. Bennett MJ, Rinaldo P, 2001. The metabolic autopsy comes of age, *Clin Chem* 47(7):1145–6.
159. Green A, Preece MA, Hardy D, 2002. More on the metabolic autopsy, *Clin Chem* 48(6):964–5.

160. Christodoulou J, Wilcken B, 2004. Perimortem laboratory investigation of genetic metabolic disorders. *Semin Neonatol* 9(4):275–80.
161. Olpin SE, 2004. The metabolic investigation of sudden infant death, *Ann Clin Bichem* 41(4): 282–93.
162. Ernst LM, Sondheimer N, Deardorff MA, Bennett MJ, Pawel BR, 2006. The value of the metabolic autopsy in the pediatric hospital setting, *J Ped* 148(6):779–83.
163. Jannetto PJ, Wong, SH, Glock SB, Laleili-Sahin E, Schur BC, Jentzen JM, 2002. Pharmacogenomics as molecular autopsy for postmortem forensic toxicology: genotyping cytochrome P450 2D6 for oxycodone cases, *J Analytical Toxicology* 26(7):438–447.
164. Wong SH, Wagner MA, Jentzen JM, Schur C, Bjerke J, Glock SB, Chang CC, 2003. Pharmacogenomics as an aspect of molecular autopsy for forensic pathology/toxicology: does genotyping CYP 2D6 serve as an adjunct for certifying methadone toxicity? *J For Sci* 48(6):1406–1415.
165. Jin M, Glock SB, Jannetto PJ, Jentzen JM, Wong SH, 2005. Pharmacogenomics as molecular autopsy for forensic toxicology: genotyping cytochrome P450 3A4*1B and 3A5*3 for 25 fentanyl cases, *J Analytical Toxicology* 29(7):590–8.
166. NIH newborn screening website: http://www.nlm.nih.gov/medlineplus/newbornscreening.html (accessed 5/21/09).

The Recent Evolution of Animal Cruelty Law and Veterinary Forensic Medicine

11

ROBERT W. REISMAN

Contents

Introduction

The last quarter of the American 20th century saw an encouraging evolution in the perception and treatment of animals that has, if anything, accelerated during the first decade of the 21st century. These changes, which are societal, medical, and legal, have impacted the attitude and approach to the problem of animal cruelty. Truthfully, there have been stirrings of change in the perception and treatment of animals across the globe.

Animals do not commit crimes; people do. One of the crimes they commit is the crime of animal cruelty. People neglect and abuse animals to extreme degrees. Animals are starved, beaten, shot, and stabbed. Basically, whatever people do to each other, they do to animals.

People often ask the question, how can somebody do this to an animal? Maybe a better way to phrase the question would be, how can somebody do this to a living being? As we know, if somebody is capable of hurting an animal, they are capable of hurting any living being, including humans. This awareness, that animals and humans can be hurt by the same person, contributes to the changing perception of the place animals hold in our society. We share our existence, good and bad.

Animals and Society—The Human–Animal Bond

Animals have a heightened importance in our society. Central to this change is recognition of the importance of the human–animal bond. The term *companion animal*, a substitute for the less appropriate term *pet*, is itself a meaningful evolutionary change in the description of domesticated animals who live with people. It signals how completely animals are integrated into society. It reflects the valued role animals have in our lives. Companion animals are recognized and accepted as family members, whatever your definition of family.

In a study of companion animal-owning households in the United States (AVMA, 2007), 49.7% of the people surveyed considered their companion animals to be family members. There were an estimated 72,114,000 dogs and 81,721,000 cats in the United States. In a British study (McNicholas, 2005), 90% of people considered their companion animals to be family members. The conclusion: companion animals are a very important part of our lives.

The attachment people feel to their animal companions is such that individuals have demonstrated that they would jeopardize their own life in order not to abandon an animal companion. This has been documented in disasters, such as Hurricane Katrina, where people refused to leave life-threatening situations if rescue was not available for their animals. It is also seen with victims of domestic abuse who have similarly stated that they would not leave an abusive environment unless there was a solution for their animal companions as well (Ascione, 2007; Faver, 2003).

Laws have changed in response to recognizing that people will jeopardize their own lives to save their pets. After Hurricane Katrina, the federal government amended the Robert T. Stafford Disaster Relief and Emergency Assistance Act to ensure that state and local emergency preparedness plans address the needs of individuals with household pets and service animals following a major disaster or emergency. This amendment is called the Pets Evacuation and Transportation Standards Act of 2006 (PETS Act). To qualify for Federal Emergency Management Agency (FEMA) funding, a city or state is required to submit a plan detailing its disaster preparedness program. Those plans now have to include plans for companion animals (Library of Congress, 2006).

Animal Abuse and the Connection to Interpersonal Human Violence

The same criminals who commit crimes against people may also commit crimes against animals. In some instances there is a progression from a violent criminal abuse of animals to violent abuse of people. This is called the Progression Thesis (Beirne, 2004). The progression from violent abuse of animals to violence against people is most sensationally illustrated in biographical information of serial murderers (Arkow, 1995; Lockwood, 1999). Another study showed that violent offenders incarcerated in a maximum-security prison were significantly more likely than nonviolent offenders to have committed childhood acts of cruelty toward companion animals (Merz-Perez, Heide, & Silverman, 2001). Intervention at the time when an individual abuses animals clearly benefits society.

Another connection between crimes against animals and crimes against people is the link between animal abuse and other forms of family violence—abuse of children, partners, disabled persons, and the elderly. The term *family violence* communicates that there are not uncommonly multiple victims of one violent individual in a particular household (Lockwood, 1998). The importance of this concept is undeniable. Where there is one victim, there may be more. If an animal is the victim of abuse there may be human victims as well. This is the reason that interdisciplinary and interagency collaboration is so important; these crimes are not separate and unrelated. We share our existence with animals—good and bad.

Henry Bergh, the founder (1866) of the American Society for the Prevention of Cruelty to Animals (ASPCA), succinctly stated the connection between animals and people in society: "Mercy to animals is mercy to mankind." In the case of family violence, it is frequently the case that animal abuse is the more visible crime simply because animals spend time outdoors. They may live outdoors, they are walked outdoors, they are taken to veterinarians for health care, and as a result health problems caused by criminal neglect and abuse become public. If the abused animal is not reported to law enforcement, or the law is not enforced, a chance may be missed to help an animal or to help an abused child, spouse, or other family member.

Fifty-three families in New Jersey with pets who met state criteria for child abuse or neglect were surveyed: 60% of these families' pets were abused or neglected. Animals were abused in 88% of households where children were physically abused (Deviney, Dicker, & Lockwood, 1983). In one study, 71% of women (with companion animals) in a battered women's shelter said that their companion animals were threatened, hurt, or killed by the batterer (Ascione, 1998).

One outcome of the expanding scientific documentation of the link between animal abuse and other forms of family violence is that some state legislatures have signed into law or are considering the need to legally protect the animal victims of family violence. In New York State (2006), for example, a bill was signed into law that allows petitioners for "Orders of Protection" to include companion animals owned by the petitioner or a minor child residing in the household to be included in the order (AnimalLaw.info). In fact, there are cases where companion animals have been included in orders of protection in domestic violence situations (Arkow, 2009).

Another connection between animal abuse and interpersonal human violence is that the same triggers put both animals and children at risk in a household with a violent individual (Loar, 1999).

- The need for constant supervision
- Urination and defecation in the house
- Chronic illnesses that require long-term care and/or result in a significant financial burden
- Destructive, aggressive, and/or noisy behavior

Animal Cruelty Is Not a New Problem

With all the recent attention to animal cruelty, it must be pointed out that animal cruelty has been recognized as immoral, if not illegal, for a long time. In 1751, the British artist William Hogarth produced a series of printed engravings titled *The Four Stages of Cruelty.*

Each print depicts a different stage in the life of the fictional animal abuser and criminal, "Tom Nero." The set of four images, which were circulated among the general public, begin with the abuse of a dog by Tom Nero as a child. The story progresses with an illustration of Nero as an adult beating a horse (at the time an animal of more importance than the dog). The third engraving, titled "Cruelty in Perfection," shows Nero committing theft and murder. The final engraving, titled "The Reward of Cruelty," shows the deceased body of Tom Nero, after his execution by hanging, as it is publically dissected, with a dog eating his entrails (Wikipedia). Interestingly, in these engravings Hogarth showed the connection between the act of animal cruelty by a child and subsequent crimes against humans when the child became an adult—an illustration of the Progression Thesis mentioned previously.

Animal Protection and Humane Societies

In 1822, Englishman Richard Martin MP (Member of Parliament) helped give cattle, horses, and sheep some protection from mistreatment by facilitating the passage of a bill in the British parliament. The legislation, known as Martin's Act, was titled the Ill Treatment of Cattle Bill. It made it a criminal offense to "wantonly beat, abuse…any horse, cow, ox, heifer, steer, sheep or other cattle" (Lynam, 1989). In 1824, Richard Martin and 21 others founded the Society for the Prevention of Cruelty to Animals in London—the first national animal protection society in the world. In 1840, Queen Victoria became the first British monarch to serve as the Society's royal patron. In 1844, the society's name was changed to the Royal Society for the Prevention of Cruelty to Animals (RSPCA; http://www.rspca.org.uk/home).

The American Society for the Prevention of Cruelty to Animals (ASPCA) was formed in New York City in 1866. The ASPCA was modeled after the RSPCA in London, England. On April 10, 1866, the New York State legislature granted a special charter for the formation of the American Society for the Prevention of Cruelty to Animals (http://www.aspca.org/), the first animal protection society in the western hemisphere. Henry Bergh, the ASPCA's first president, socially and politically connected in New York City, New York State, and Washington DC, was the driving force behind the formation of the ASPCA.

Many organizations devoted to the welfare of animals have been formed in the United States since the founding of the ASPCA in 1866. The following are some of these organizations:

- Massachusetts Society for the Prevention of Cruelty to Animals (MSPCA) (1868): The second-oldest animal protection society in the Western Hemisphere.
- American Humane (1877): http://www.americanhumane.org/. American Humane is dedicated to protecting both children and animals.
- The Latham Foundation for Humane Education (1918): http://www.latham.org/index.html.
- Humane Society of the United States (1954): http://www.hsus.org/. HSUS is a national nonprofit group that is at the forefront of fighting the problem of animal cruelty.
- American Welfare Institute (1951): http://www.awionline.org/.

- Friends of Animals (1957): http://www.friendsofanimals.org/index.html.
- People for the Ethical Treatment of Animals (1980): http://www.peta.org/. PETA is the largest animal rights organization in the world.
- Pet-Abuse.com (2002): http://www.pet-abuse.com/.

The History and Evolution of Animal Law

The field of animal law is experiencing a spectacular evolution. Not only are there remarkable changes in state and federal laws, but the practice of law as it pertains to animal issues is changing as well. Changing state and federal laws are discussed below. Other changes are reflected in academia and legal practice (Alexander, 2009). Ten years ago, in 2000, there were nine animal law courses offered at ABA-accredited law schools. Currently there are more than 100 such courses. In 2000 there were 12 Student Animal Law Defense Fund (SALDF) chapters. In 2010, there are more than 140 SALDF chapters across the United States and Canada. In April 2010, a conference titled "The Future of Animal Law," cosponsored by the Animal Legal Defense Fund (ALDF) and the Harvard Law School Student ALDF chapter, was held at Harvard Law School.

As a result of the formation of the ASPCA, the first animal cruelty laws in this country were passed by the New York State legislature. These laws pre-dated child cruelty laws in the United States. The first child cruelty laws, in fact, followed the ASPCA involvement in the well-known Mary Ellen Wilson child abuse case (1874) and the formation of the New York Society for the Prevention of Cruelty to Children (NYSPCC)—yet another connection between animal and human welfare. The NYSPCC, still in existence, celebrated its 135th anniversary in 2010. Many state animal cruelty laws are modeled after New York State laws.

Another evolutionary change in the American legal system is the formation of groups whose primary focus is animal law. The Animal Legal Defense Fund was established in 1979 by attorneys interested in the new field of animal law. In 2002, the Michigan State University College of Law created the "Animal Legal and Historical Center" (http://www.animallaw.info/), a remarkable resource for national and international animal law.

Animal cruelty is defined by laws at the state and federal level. Today, every state has an anti-cruelty statute. These laws do not afford animals legal rights but serve as the primary legal protection for animals in our society. There is no overarching federal anti-cruelty law; rather, all 50 states have different individual anti-cruelty laws.

The majority of animal cruelty crimes in this country are prosecuted under state laws. The legal definition of animal cruelty varies from state to state. Some state laws criminalize behavior that endangers an animal's well-being in addition to criminalizing neglect and physical abuse that injures animals. Many state law cruelty prosecutions, however, hinge on proof of an animal's compromised health. This is determined by a veterinary medical examination.

States prosecute animal cruelty laws at the misdemeanor and felony (aggravated animal cruelty) levels. Felony animal cruelty laws exist in 46 states plus the District of Columbia. Idaho, Mississippi, North Dakota, and South Dakota do not have felony animal cruelty laws (American Humane: Summary of Animal Cruelty Laws).

Exemptions from the application of the animal cruelty statutes are common and may include veterinary practice, research, hunting, fishing, trapping, food production, pest control, rodeos, zoos, circuses, and killing of one's own animals on his or her property (if done humanely). There are no exemptions in the anti-cruelty statutes of Minnesota, Mississippi, and Oklahoma (Wisch, 2005).

The language in state laws that define animal cruelty varies. Some examples follow (AnimalLaw.info—Anti-Cruelty: Related Statutes). New York State has the oldest law, and some of the language sounds as if it was written in another century when animals of "importance" were used for agriculture. Obviously, a full reading of an individual state law is necessary for real comprehension, and that is not possible in this text, but it is appropriate and informative to include some of the language as it exists.

New York State—A person who overdrives, overloads, tortures or cruelly beats or unjustifiably injures, maims, mutilates, or kills any animal, or deprives any animal of necessary sustenance, food, or drink, is guilty of a misdemeanor. A person is guilty of aggravated cruelty to animals when, with no justifiable purpose, he or she intentionally kills or intentionally causes serious physical injury to a companion animal with aggravated cruelty. For purposes of this section, "aggravated cruelty" shall mean conduct which: (i) is intended to cause extreme physical pain; or (ii) is done or carried out in an especially depraved or sadistic manner.

New Mexico—Cruelty to animals occurs when a person negligently mistreats, injures, kills without lawful justification, or torments an animal or abandons or fails to provide necessary sustenance to an animal under that person's custody or control. Extreme cruelty to animals, a fourth-degree felony, consists of a person intentionally or maliciously torturing, mutilating, injuring, or poisoning an animal or maliciously killing an animal.

Illinois—No person or owner may beat, cruelly treat, torment, starve, overwork, or otherwise abuse any animal. No owner may abandon any animal where it may become a public charge or may suffer injury, hunger, or exposure. A person convicted of violating this Section is guilty of a Class A misdemeanor. A second or subsequent conviction for a violation of this Section is a Class 4 felony. Illinois also defines an owner's duties: Each owner shall provide for each of his animals: (a) sufficient quantity of good quality, wholesome food and water; (b) adequate shelter and protection from the weather; (c) veterinary care when needed to prevent suffering [the requirement for veterinary care tends to be the exception in state anti-cruelty laws]; and (d) humane care and treatment.

Nothing can be assumed when considering how animal cruelty is legally defined—even the definition of the word *animal*. The following are some representative definitions of the word *animal* in state anti-cruelty statutes (AnimalLaw.info):

Arizona—*Animal* is defined as a mammal, bird, reptile, or amphibian.

Delaware—The definition of *animal* excludes fish, crustacea, or molluska.

Florida—The word *animal* includes every living dumb creature.

Georgia—*Animal* does not include any fish or any pest that might be exterminated or removed.

Illinois—*Animal* means every living creature, domestic or wild, but does not include man.

Massachusetts—All animals except an animal if used as lure or bait in fishing.

New Jersey—*Animal* or *creature* includes the whole brute creation.
New Mexico—*Animal* does not include insects or reptiles.

United States Federal Law Affecting the Lives of Animals

In 1966, the United States federal government created the Laboratory Animal Welfare Act (now called the Animal Welfare Act, AWA) to regulate the use of certain animals in research in the United States. It is an evolving approach to regulating how animals are treated in our society. It is the only federal law designed to regulate use of animals by breeders, dealers, exhibitors, and researchers (AAVS.org). The AWA sets minimum standards for the care, housing, sale, and transport of dogs, cats, primates, rabbits, hamsters, guinea pigs, and other animals held on the premises of animal dealers or laboratories. The act also requires the licensing of cat and dog dealers and research facilities and the identification of dogs and cats to prevent their theft.

The AWA has been frequently amended over the years to, for example, extend coverage to all species of warm-blooded laboratory animals, the sale of pets and animals used in exhibitions, and the "appropriate use of anesthetic, analgesic, and tranquilizing drugs" (1970).

Enforcement of laws of course will affect a law's impact. The U.S. Department of Agriculture (USDA), who enforces the AWA, adopted regulations that specifically excluded birds, mice, rats, horses, and farmed animals from the act's definition of *animal* (1972).

AWA amendments have also addressed exercise of dogs, the physical environment and the psychological well-being of primates, and a minimum holding period (five days) for sheltered animals sold to research facilities (1985). In 2002, the USDA amended the AWA to reflect the Farm Bill definition of *animal*, which excludes "birds, mice of the genus *Mus*, and rats of the genus *Rattus*, bred for use in research."

The passage of the Food Security Act of 1985 contained an amendment titled the Improved Standards for Laboratory Animals Act. This amendment strengthened AWA standards for laboratory animal care, increased enforcement of the act, mandated training for those who handle animals, and required the creation of Institutional Animal Care and Use Committees (IACUC's: http://www.iacuc.org/) at every institution that uses animals for federally funded laboratory research. Each local IACUC reviews research protocols and conducts evaluations of the institution's animal care and use including facility inspections. IACUC committees also look at alternatives to experiments that cause pain or suffering.

Enforcement and Prosecution of Animal Cruelty Law

Law enforcement of animal cruelty cases is the responsibility of the government (i.e., local, state, and federal law enforcement). In actual practice this is not always the case. This is due to a combination of circumstances including historical lack of perceived relative importance of animal issues, assumption of responsibility by private nonprofits, lack of familiarity with animal cruelty law (often not found in the penal code where most state crimes are defined), and lack of resources. It is the elected officials who need to provide law enforcement with adequate resources to investigate and enforce animal cruelty. This includes resources for a forensic veterinary medical investigation.

Changes are in the wind, and it is the case across the country that public (federal, state, and local law enforcement) and private partnerships are forming to investigate and prosecute animal cruelty. It is not uncommon to read media reports of animal cruelty investigations where there is collaborative effort of federal, state, and local law enforcement and private nonprofit groups, such as a local, regional, and/or national SPCA or humane society (see section on dog fighting).

Despite these encouraging recent changes it is still the case that in some localities private nonprofits are still primarily responsible for cruelty investigations. The ASPCA in New York City for instance, with a humane law enforcement department and an animal hospital, is primarily responsible for most NYC animal cruelty investigations (law enforcement and medical). NYPD, while not primarily responsible for the animal cruelty investigations, frequently provides significant support to the ASPCA Humane Law Enforcement agents during difficult and dangerous investigations. There is also a strong interest by both parties to work collaboratively in the future. Similarly, the MSPCA (1868) and Animal Rescue League (1899) in Boston is another example where law enforcement of a private nonprofit agency is responsible for animal cruelty investigation.

The costs associated with a criminal prosecution, including the criminal investigation, seizure and holding evidence, and veterinary forensic evaluation, are government charges. This happens in some localities; however, it is also the case that these costs are often passed along to nonprofit agencies that handle cruelty investigations. In many situations government support of criminal prosecution for animal cruelty begins when the district attorney's office is contacted.

The Recent Evolution of Veterinary Medical Practice

Veterinary practice in the United States has changed significantly in the last 30 to 40 years. Farm animal and equine medicine, once the mainstay of the profession serving an agricultural society, now have companion animal medicine as an equal partner. The creation of specialty and emergency care hospitals in more populated areas are representative of the importance of companion animals as family members in the 21st century. As mentioned above, laboratory animals are provided with better care in recognition of their place in the animal world and the sacrifice they make to improve human health.

One of the more significant changes in veterinary practice in recent years is the attention to animal pain. Not that long ago (1990s), animal surgical patients did not routinely receive postoperative pain relief medications. Nonsteroidal anti-inflammatory drugs (NSAIDS), a foundation of pain relief in human medicine, were not available for use in animals. The first NSAID available for use specifically for animals (carprofen) came on the market in 1997 (Senior Dog Project website, 2010). The first veterinary association devoted to the pain in animals, the International Veterinary Academy of Pain Management (IVAPM), was established in 2003 (IVAPM website, 2010).

Shelter Medicine and Forensic Veterinary Medicine

Shelter animal medicine and forensic veterinary medicine are two areas of veterinary medicine that to a great degree did not exist 20 years ago. Shelter animals, once an ignored group of animals, are now recognized as an important group of animals, whose health problems impact the privately "owned" animal community. Their welfare is ignored now only to the detriment of all companion animals. These two areas, shelter and forensic veterinary medicine, are allied areas, as it is not unusual for abused animals to show up at an animal shelter and the staff of shelters in many localities includes individuals who investigate complaints of animal cruelty. Veterinarians who manage the health care of shelter animal populations are frequently the same veterinarians who are asked to conduct a forensic medical examination of animal victims of suspected cruelty.

There are now courses in shelter medicine taught at veterinary schools across the country. There are multiple veterinary schools with shelter medicine residencies. In 2004 the first veterinary text devoted to shelter medicine, *Shelter Medicine for Veterinarians and Staff*, was published by Blackwell Publishing (Miller & Zawistowski, 2004). There are five sections: Animal Shelters and Their Functions, Husbandry, Disease Management, Shelter and Community Programs, and, importantly, Animal Cruelty.

In 1997, the American Humane Association published the first veterinary text (in the world) on the topic of animal cruelty: *Recognizing and Reporting Animal Abuse*. Important topics, such as the link between animal abuse and violence to humans, recognizing and reporting animal abuse, the veterinarian's role in investigating animal cruelty, and animal abuse case prosecution and punishment, are covered for the first time in any text. Since 2007, four books on forensic veterinary medicine have been published (Lockwood, 2006; Merck, 2007; Cooper, 2008; Munro 2008).

Forensic veterinary medicine is the use of veterinary scientific information to answer questions raised in a public forum—a court of law. Depending on the case, veterinary forensic evidence may be a weekly weight chart showing an emaciated dog gaining weight with no medical intervention (starvation), or DNA from an object used to physically injure an animal, thus identifying the weapon. The information that is described as forensic evidence is not determined by the type of information, but how that information is used to explain an animal's health in a court of law.

Forensic veterinary medicine is a new field that in some form or another has been practiced for a long time (i.e., veterinarians have testified in court about animal cruelty previously). It is only recently, however, that there is a focused effort by a critical mass of veterinarians and other experts to work in and advance the field of forensic veterinary medicine. In the last 10 years there have been many more educational opportunities (e.g., veterinary school lectures, continuing education conferences) for veterinarians to learn about animal cruelty and forensic veterinary medicine.

There is currently no certification process for veterinary forensic medicine. When a veterinarian testifies in court in an animal cruelty case, he or she testifies as an expert in veterinary medicine. A veterinary forensic certification program is being developed at the University of Florida at Gainesville. It is a joint effort of the ASPCA, the William R. Maples Center for Forensic Medicine, and the University of Florida Veterinary School at Gainesville.

There is not always awareness by law enforcement and veterinarians that the abused animal is evidence. Veterinarians are the individuals responsible for evaluating an animal's state of health. Forensic evaluation of the animal is, however, a relatively new role for most veterinarians. The idea that an animal's health has been compromised to the extent a crime has been committed is something most veterinarians do not think about, or do not want to think about. The information that should be collected in the context of a potential criminal prosecution, by definition, a forensic veterinary medical examination, may be unfamiliar to someone who is unfamiliar with abuse cases.

The lack of attention to deceased animals can be particularly concerning. There may be minimal crime scene investigation. The author has multiple experiences where a deceased animal has been frozen, buried, or cremated without a forensic veterinary medical evaluation. A complete necropsy (animal autopsy) at a minimum requires radiographs, a gross dissection and examination of the animal, and microscopic tissue analysis (histopathology). In certain localities, there is no veterinarian experienced with forensic medical investigations, or if there is veterinary support, there may not be adequate resources to allow a complete veterinary medical forensic investigation.

Veterinary Reporting of Animal Cruelty

All 50 states mandate certain professionals and institutions to report suspected child abuse. There is no equivalent established reporting of animal abuse. Currently, 28 states have some law related to veterinary reporting of animal cruelty (Wisch, 2010). This means that 22 states make no specific legal provision for veterinary reporting of animal cruelty. The laws that do exist vary from state to state. In some states veterinarians are *allowed* to report suspected animal cruelty. This gives the veterinarian the authority to break doctor-client confidentiality. In some states veterinarians are provided with immunity from criminal and civil prosecution when making a good faith report of suspected animal cruelty. In Arizona, California, Colorado, Illinois, Minnesota, Nebraska, and Oklahoma veterinarians are mandated to report animal cruelty. In Arizona and Wisconsin veterinarians are mandated to report dog fighting (legally considered different than animal cruelty). In Oregon veterinarians are mandated to report aggravated animal cruelty (felony level). Interestingly, because of the recognition of animals as "family members," in some states veterinarians are mandated to report child abuse (Miller, 2010). Some states protect all citizens who make a good faith report of animal cruelty. Alaska law allows any citizen to make a complaint of animal cruelty to a public or private animal control agency or organization, the department, or a peace officer.

Organized Veterinary Medicine and Animal Cruelty

There is recognition of the problem of animal cruelty by organized veterinary medicine. In the 1994 position statement on animal welfare, the American Veterinary Medical Association (AVMA) included the following text:

> The AVMA recognizes that veterinarians may have occasion to observe cases of cruelty to animals, animal abuse, or animal neglect as defined by state law or local ordinances. When these observations occur, the AVMA considers it the responsibility of the veterinarian to report such cases to appropriate authorities. Such disclosures may be necessary to protect the health and welfare of animals and people.

The AVMA Model Veterinary Practice Act is intended to serve as a model for state practice acts. In the current AVMA Model Practice Act, there is a recommendation for immunity from prosecution when a veterinarian makes a good faith report of animal abuse:

> Any veterinarian licensed in this state who reports, in good faith and in the normal course of business, a suspected incident of animal cruelty, as described by law, to the proper authorities shall be immune from liability in any civil or criminal action brought against such veterinarian for reporting such incident.

Making a Good Faith Report of Animal Abuse

In 1962, Dr. C. Kempe wrote, "Physicians have great difficulty both in believing that parents could have attacked their children and undertaking the essential questioning of parents on this subject. Many physicians find it hard to believe that such an attack could have occurred and they attempt to obliterate such suspicions from their minds, even in the face of obvious circumstantial evidence." Veterinarians have a similar difficulty recognizing and acknowledging that the injured animal before them may be the victim of abuse, and they have difficulty making the report to law enforcement.

The following case history illustrates many aspects of the problem of animal cruelty. The dog was battered (i.e., it was beaten over a period of time, similar to the battered child syndrome) by the husband an example of the link between animal abuse and other forms of family violence. The woman, who suspected the animal abuse, was herself abused by her husband. The veterinarian, even with knowledge of the animal abuse (the husband confessed to beating the dog in front of his wife and the veterinarian), failed to make a report. Finally, a complete veterinary forensic evaluation provided evidence that the dog had been physically abused over a period of time.

A number of years ago, a married physician beat the family dog to death. This individual also abused his wife. There were no children. After killing the dog, the perpetrator called his wife to tell her what he had done. She forced him to take the deceased dog with her to their veterinarian on the Upper West Side of Manhattan. During this visit the husband confessed to killing the dog in front of his wife and the veterinarian. During the fatal beating the husband was bitten by the dog. The husband claimed that the fatal beating was in response to being bitten by the dog. People who abuse animals usually claim that the physical abuse is in self-defense. (At trial in 2009 for a fatal attack of a cat, a six-foot-tall, 200-pound man claimed he was knocked down by a declawed eight-pound cat.) It is important to consider that in reality it is the animal who is acting in self-defense; the human physically abused the animal first. This is especially important to keep in mind during court testimony. The animal, because it is an animal, should not automatically be considered the initiator of the violence. There is always a story, and frequently that's all it is: a story.

During the visit to the veterinarian, at a time when the husband was out of the room, the wife asked the veterinarian if he thought that the dog had been beaten previously. She knew or had an awareness of what was happening. She was also a victim; maybe it was her way of asking for help.

The veterinarian's only action in this case was to call the NYC Department of Health to report a dog bite. The Department of Health's only interest in a case like this would be to test the dog for rabies. The dog was well vaccinated against rabies virus, and there had not been a rabid animal in Manhattan for 40 years. There was no possibility that this dog was rabid.

It was Friday afternoon and the Health Department asked the veterinarian to refrigerate the animal over the weekend. They would pick up the dog's body the following Monday to test it for the rabies virus. The dog walker who found out about the incident flagged down an ASPCA Humane Law Enforcement vehicle. On Monday before the dog could be tested, HLE agents seized the dog's body to the protests of the Health Department. A necropsy was performed. During the necropsy, the cause of death was clear. The dog had extreme subcutaneous and muscular hemorrhage, broken ribs, severe lung contusions, a hemothorax (a chest full of blood), and a brain injury. But, just as importantly, histopathology showed fibrosis (scarring) of the liver and kidney, and the presence of hemosiderin in the lungs, liver, and kidney. Hemosiderin is the pigment that is formed from the red blood cell pigment, hemoglobin, as the body cleans up tissue hemorrhage. It is responsible for an older bruise's yellowish golden color. Hemosiderin is not present at the time of the injury. Its presence is evidence of an older injury. The internal organ scarring and hemosiderin were evidence of previous physical injury sustained by this dog. The claim of self-defense no longer applied.

Five years after the dog's death, the wife called and asked for a copy of the necropsy report. She was finally divorcing her abusive husband, and she wanted documentation of his abuse. This case had it all: a battered animal with scientific evidence of previous physical abuse, a fatal attack, domestic violence, and failure of the veterinarian to report known animal cruelty.

Reasons a Veterinarian Might Suspect Animal Abuse

"A marked discrepancy between clinical findings and historical data as supplied by the parents is a major diagnostic feature of the battered child syndrome" (Kempe, 1962). It is this same discrepancy between the story and the clinical findings that may lead a veterinarian to suspect animal abuse. The perpetrator always has a story (e.g., animals falling while being bathed, animals falling off of the couch, self-defense). In the *Veterinarian's Guide to Recognizing and Reporting Animal Abuse*, Dr. Helen Munro ("The Battered Pet Syndrome," 1997) lists reasons a veterinarian might suspect physical abuse.

1. The account of the accident does not fit with the injury observed.
2. The owner refuses to comment on how the injury came about.
3. The owner shows a lack of concern for the animal's injuries.
4. There is a delay in seeking veterinary treatment.

In another case some years ago, a very astute veterinarian did pick up on a problem with an owner's story as to how an indoor cat had broken its leg. Although the veterinarian did not suspect that the young woman had hurt her cat, she was uncomfortable with the woman's lack of interest in how the cat had been injured. How does an indoor cat in a small Manhattan apartment break its leg? The veterinarian contacted a mental health professional who was available to interview the woman.

The psychologist found out that the woman, who had moved to New York from the Midwest a few years earlier, had unfortunately become a prostitute. It was one of her "clients" who had hurt the cat. As a result of this intervention, the woman got back in touch with her family, from whom she had become estranged. They paid for the cat's care, and the woman moved back home. Two lives were saved, because "the owner refused to comment on how the injury came about," and the veterinarian took action.

The Veterinarian's Role in Investigating Animal Cruelty

The animal who is a victim of cruelty is also evidence for a criminal prosecution, and in the case of a live animal, the evidence is changing. If the animal is receiving medical care, its health status needs to be completely documented on the first day, or crucial evidence of the animal's compromised health may be lost as it responds to care and heals.

Veterinarians may become involved in animal cruelty cases in a variety of ways. Abused animals may present in an exam room or at a shelter directly to the veterinarian; suspected abuse cases should be referred to law enforcement. In other situations, law enforcement may request veterinary participation in a case. The animals may be alive and/or deceased. The animals may be brought to the veterinarian or the veterinarian may have to travel to the animal(s) location (e.g., farm animals, dog fighting raids, puppy mill raids): the crime scene. If the latter is the case, then the veterinarian becomes involved in crime scene investigation. Some crime scene evidence will be most suited to veterinary interpretation. Seeing the abused animals and where they have lived and/or died will provide additional information to that which is gathered in the animal hospital. Many protocols available to human forensic investigation are applicable to animal forensic investigation. The bodies of deceased animals can be exhumed, using a mapping technique of the animal's body. Forensic entomology can provide information about time of burial. DNA analysis can help identify the crime scene and/or weapon used to injure the animal.

Forensic Veterinary Medical Examination

A forensic veterinary evaluation of a live animal victim of cruelty must be approached in the context of a potential criminal prosecution for animal cruelty. Questions must be considered and answers sought in this context. Consideration of clinical signs and choice of diagnostic tools are made in this context. There are some key elements of the forensic medical investigation that must be considered in all cases. Foremost is the determination of whether an animal has been injured and is in pain or some state of discomfort as a result of human neglect and/or abuse.

A physical exam is the most important part of a forensic examination. This should ideally be supplemented with a standard group of blood, urine, and fecal tests. Radiography is similarly a very valuable tool in the veterinary forensic examination of a suspected victim of animal abuse. Photography is an essential part of veterinary forensic documentation of a crime victim. Figure 11.1 shows photos of a starved dog before and after an 84% increase in body weight. Figure 11.2 shows photographs of a dog with a severely matted hair coat before and after grooming. Photographs provide visual documentation of an animal's presenting physical appearance, which as mentioned previously can change dramatically with care.

While some state laws criminalize behavior that endangers and/or injures animals, many state law cruelty prosecutions hinge on proof of physical injury and or the presence of pain. In these states where there is no endangerment law, the central medical questions in animal cruelty cases are always whether the animal was injured and whether the animal experienced pain as a result of human action or inaction.

The identification of pain in animals is difficult. The standard for identifying pain in human patients is to ask the patient if they are in pain. The patient, if conscious and able

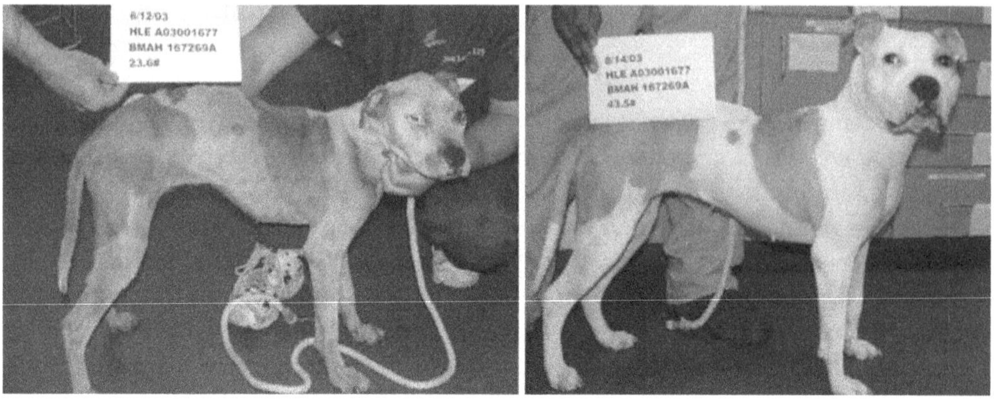

Figure 11.1 A dog named "Gucci", before and after an 84% increase in body weight.

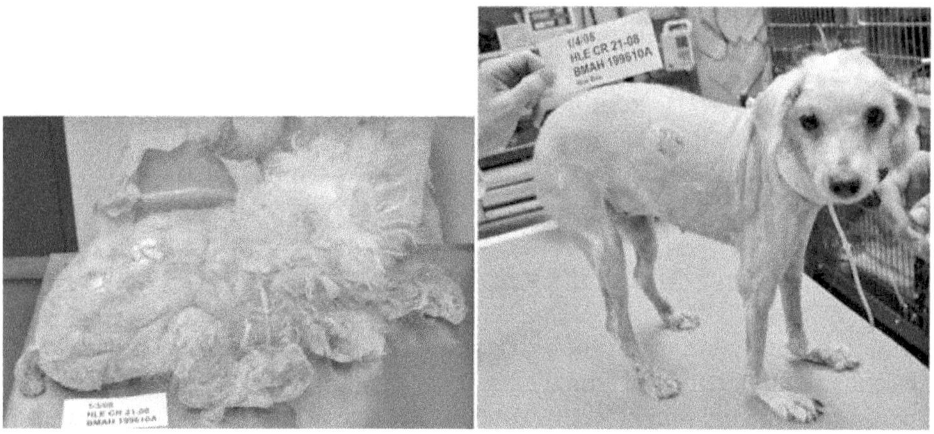

Figure 11.2 A dog named "Miss Bea", before and after grooming. Notice the fecal and urine.

to speak, can give a definitive description of the deviation of their health from a state of comfort. In hospitals, patients are now frequently given control of the delivery of their own pain medicines. None of this is possible for animal patients. The assessment of animal pain, so important to a criminal prosecution of animal cruelty, relies completely on the observations of the veterinary medical staff. Common behaviors such as eating, drinking, sleeping, and movement provide information as to whether the animal is comfortable, uncomfortable, distressed, and/or in pain. The animal's reaction to physical handling may be informative as to the animal's state of comfort. If the animal cries, threatens to bite, or actually bites the handler, a deviation from a state of comfort must be considered.

There are two general types of cases where veterinarians perform live animal forensic evaluations: (1) cases where there is one or a relatively small group of animals, (2) cases where there are a large number of animals (puppy mills, hoarding situations, dog fighting raids). These two types of cases are approached differently. In cases where there is one or a few animals, the animal(s) health status may be understood to a very fine level of detail. This is simply not possible in a case where there are hundreds of animals. In these cases an organized approach is necessary and a minimum database of information to gather about each animal's health must be decided upon.

General Classification—Types of Abuse: Neglect and Nonaccidental Injury

Types of animal abuse have been classified as neglect and nonaccidental injury. Neglect does not imply lack of intent to compromise the animal's health. *Neglect* means that lack of action (e.g., not grooming an animal, not feeding an animal, "failure to treat" a serious medical condition) has resulted in an animal having compromised health. *Nonaccidental injury* means that a person's actions have resulted in compromised health. Examples would be blunt force trauma and sharp force trauma injuries, drowning, and asphyxiation. Table 11.1 is a summary of the types of abuse seen at the ASPCA in New York City in 2007 and 2008.

Large-Scale Animal Abuse

There are many situations where many animals, sometimes numbering in the hundreds, are abused at the same location. This is called *large-scale animal abuse* and includes hoarding

Table 11.1 Summary of the Types of Animal Abuse Seen at the ASPCA in New York City in 2007 and 2008.

Abuse Category	Number of Animals in 2007	Number of Animals in 2008
Abandonment	17	14
Blunt Force Trauma	49	49
Buried Alive	0	1
Burns	3	3
Decapitation	0	1
Embedded Collar	4	3
Failure to Provide Treatment	23	32
Fighting	1	15
Heat Stroke	0	26
Illegal Selling of Chicks	1	0
Improper Disposal	2	0
Improper Transport	1	0
Inadequate Shelter	11	9
Matted Hair Coat	0	12
Neglect	8	22
No Known Cause of Death	7	4
Poison	2	6
Sexual Abuse	1	0
Sharp Force Trauma	1	2
Shooting Victim	1	2
Spray Painting	0	1
Starvation	154	107
Violation of Probation	2	0
Total Animals	288	309

situations. A hoarding situation may involve a single individual and/or may be publicly presented as sanctuaries, shelters, and farms. These are situations where large groups of animals are suffering from extreme neglect that involves starvation and rampant infectious disease. Mortality rates are very high and mass graves are common. Puppy mills represent another type of large-scale abuse and similar to the hoarding situation, extreme neglect and high mortality is common. Dog fighting is an especially abhorrent example of large-scale animal abuse because of the extreme neglect and brutality that these dogs experience. In all of these cases it is essential that the health of the animals be evaluated by a veterinarian.

Dog Fighting

Animal fighting is one of the worst abuses of animals. Dogs caught up in dog fighting suffer their entire lives. They live permanently tethered to a six-foot chain with no significant human or dog interaction. Frequently these dogs are poorly cared for, experiencing starvation, severe parasitism, and other illnesses with no proper medical care. In general they have a short lifespan. Mortality rates in a particular group of dogs are commonly over 50% because of lack of care. (See Figure 11.3.)

The injuries sustained by the dogs who actually fight are horrendous and usually result in a painful death, either because of lack of medical attention, or because they are killed by their "owners" in a cruel and horrifying manner (drowning, beaten to death, asphyxiation, and shooting).

Dog fighting is widespread across the United States in both rural and urban communities. The devastation caused by dog fighting is not limited to the dogs. Generations of American children have their lives affected by exposure to the violent brutality of dog fighting and associated crimes of gambling, drugs, and illegal weapons (Gibson, 2005). We intimately share our lives with these animals, good and bad.

In 1975 no states had felony dog fighting laws. By 2005, dog fighting was illegal in all 50 states and the District of Columbia. In addition, the United States Animal Welfare Act

Figure 11.3 This is a sick, emaciated dog at a dog fighting breeding location. The dog is permanently tethered on this six foot chain, she is starved and the plastic drum is her only shelter regardless of the weather.

prohibits the interstate transport of dogs for fighting purposes. In 2005 the Animal Fighting Prohibition Enforcement Act was passed establishing felony-level penalties for violation of the federal animal-fighting law (Lockwood, 2006). Dog fighting laws are generally separate from state anti-cruelty statutes. In some states veterinarians are mandated to report suspected dog fighting. Some dog fighting laws make it a crime to be a spectator at a dog fight.

Recently, there has been a concerted effort by federal, state, and local law enforcement with support of private nonprofits and veterinarians to investigate and prosecute dog fighting operators. In 2007, four men including Michael Vick, the highest-paid player in the National Football League, pleaded guilty to dog fighting charges. Vick served 19 months of a 23-month sentence. Many of the dogs were placed in new homes, in contrast to the generally accepted notion that all dog fighting dogs must be euthanized. The case was tried in federal court. In 2009, the Humane Society of Missouri and the FBI led the largest dog fighting raid in U.S. history. The raid extended across eight states. Twenty-six people were arrested and 407 dogs were rescued (Humane Society of Missouri, 2009; von Drehle, 2009). The list of agencies involved in the law enforcement and rescue effort is impressive: Humane Society of Missouri, Missouri State Highway Patrol, the United States Department of Agriculture's Office of the Inspector General, the Federal Bureau of Investigation, the U.S. Marshals Service, the United States Attorney, the ASPCA, and the Humane Society of the United States. Many other humane groups were involved in the subsequent sheltering effort.

There has been, in the last 15–20 years, an encouraging evolution in the perception and treatment of animals in the United States. These changes are societal, medical, and legal. The problem of animal cruelty is being addressed nationwide and in some instances internationally, by governments, and the legal and veterinary professions. The optimistic view is that as the years go by we will finally see a reduction in the horrible abuse of animals with whom we share our lives. We will all benefit from a less violent, more caring society.

References

Alexander, P. Animal Law and Your Practice. *Animal Legal Defense Fund,* http://www.aldf.org/downloads/GPSolo_ALpractice_palexander.pdf (accessed online April 5, 2010; originally published in GP Solo, Volume 26, Number 5, July/August 2009, © 2009 by the American Bar Association).

The American Anti-Vivisection Society (AAVS). Animal Welfare Act: Act for All. AWA History. http://www.aavs.org/campAWAHistory.html (accessed online April 5, 2010).

American Humane. Animal Cruelty Statutes by State. http://www.americanhumane.org/assets/docs/advocacy/ADV-laws-state-animal-cruelty-state.pdf (accessed April 5, 2010).

American Humane. Summary of Animal Cruelty Laws. http://www.americanhumane.org/advocacy/animal-protection/animal-cruelty-summary.html (accessed April 5, 2010).

American Veterinary Medical Association. *AVMA Market Statistics 2007, U.S. Pet Ownership and Demographic Sourcebook.* http://www.avma.org/reference/marketstats/ownership.asp (accessed April 5, 2010).

Animal Legal & Historical Center. Anti-Cruelty: Related Statutes. http://www.animallaw.info/statutes/topicstatutes/sttoac.htm (accessed April 5, 2010).

Arkow, Phil. 1995. Breaking The Cycles of Violence—A Practical Guide. *The Latham Foundation.* Alameda California. p. 5.

Arkow, Phil, Coppola Tracy. 2009. Expanding Protective Orders to Include Companion Animals. *American Humane Resources section.* http://www.americanhumane.org/assets/docs/advocacy/ADV-ppo-report-09-v2.pdf (accessed April 5, 2010).

Ascione, F.R. 1998. Battered Women's Reports of Their Partners and Their Children's Cruelty to Animals. *Journal of Emotional, Abuse.* pp. 119–133.

Ascione, F.R, Weber, C.V, Thompson, T.M, Heath, J., Maruyama, M., Hayashi, K. 2007. Battered pets and domestic violence: animal abuse reported by women experiencing intimate violence and by nonabused women. In *Violence Against Women.* 13(4):354–73.

Beirne, Piers, 2004. From Animal Abuse to Interhuman Violence? A Critical Review of the Progression Thesis. *Society & Animals* 12:1 Koninklijke Brill NV, Leiden.

Cooper, John E., Cooper. Margaret E. 2007. *Introduction to Veterinary and Comparative Forensic Medicine.* Blackwell Publishing Ltd, Oxford.

Deviney, E., Dicker, J., and Lockwood, R. 1983. The Care of Pets Within Child Abusing Families, *International Journal for the Study of Animal Problems.* 4:321–329.

Faver, C.A., Strand, E.B. 2003. To leave or to stay?: Battered women's concern for vulnerable pets. *Journal of Interpersonal Violence.* 18(12):1367–77.

Flynn, C. 1999. Animal Abuse in Childhood and Later Support for Interpersonal Violence in Families. *Society and Animals.* 7(2).

Gibson, Hannah. 2005. Dog Fighting Detailed Discussion, *Animal Legal & Historical Center, Michigan State University College of Law.* http://www.animallaw.info/articles/ddusdogfighting.htm (accessed April 5, 2010).

Hogarth, William. *Wikipedia.* http://en.wikipedia.org/wiki/William_Hogarth (accessed April 5, 2010).

Humane Society of Missouri. 2009. HSMO's Animal Cruelty Task Force Works with State and Federal Agencies on Largest Dog Fighting Raid and Rescue in U.S. History; Nearly 500 Pit Bulls Seized in Multi-State Operation, http://member.hsmo.org/site/PageNavigator/Federal_dog_fighting_case_7_8_09 (accessed April 5, 2010).

International Veterinary Academy of Pain Management, http://www.ivapm.org/ (accessed April 5, 2010).

Kempe, C.H, Silverman, F.N. Steele, B.F. Droegemuller, W. and Silver. H.K. 1962. The Battered Child Syndrome. *Journal of the American Medical Association.* 181:17–24.

Library of Congress, 2006. H.R. H.R.3858, http://thomas.loc.gov/cgi-bin/bdquery/z?d109:h.r.03858 (accessed April 5, 2010).

Loar, Lynn. 1999. I'll Only Help You If You Have Two Legs. In *Child Abuse, Domestic Violence, and Animal Abuse, Linking the Circles of Compassion for Prevention and Intervention.* Purdue University Press. West Lafayette, Indiana.

Lockwood, Randall Ph.D. 1999. Animal Cruelty and Societal Violence: A Brief Look Back from the Front. In *Child Abuse, Domestic Violence, and Animal Abuse, Linking the Circles of Compassion for Prevention and Intervention.* Purdue University Press, West Lafayette Indiana. p3.

Lockwood, Randall Ph.D., Ascione Frank. 1998. *Cruelty to Animals and Interpersonal Violence: Readings in Research and Application,* Purdue University Press, West Lafayette, Indiana.

Lockwood, Randall Ph.D., Sinclair, Leslie DVM, Merck, Melinda D. DVM. 2006. *Forensic Investigation of Animal Cruelty: A Guide for Veterinary and Law Enforcement Professionals.* Humane Society Press.

Lynam, Shevawn. *Humanity Dick Martin: "King of Connemara," 1754–1834.* Lilliput Press, Dublin, 1989.

McNicholas, June, Gilbey Andrew, Rennie Ann, Ahmedzai Sam, Dono, Jo-Ann Ormerod Elizabeth. 2005. Pet ownership and human health: a brief review of evidence and issues. *British Medical Journal.* 331:1252–1254.

Merck, Melinda D. DVM. 2007. *Veterinary Forensics, Animal Cruelty Investigations.* Blackwell Publishing. Ames, Iowa.

Merz-Perez, L., Heide, K. M., Silverman, I., & Lockwood, R. 2000. Childhood Cruelty to Animals and Subsequent Violence Against Humans. *Fifty-Second Annual Meeting of the American Society of Criminology, San Francisco.* November 2000.

Merz-Perez, L., Heide, K.M., & Silverman, I.J. 2001. Childhood Cruelty to Animals and Subsequent Violence Against Humans. *International Journal of Offender Therapy and Comparative Criminology. 45*, 556–573.

Miller, Grant. 2010. The Veterinarian's Role in Child Abuse Reporting. *California Veterinary Medical Association (CVMA).* http://www.cvma.net/doc.asp?id=3021&pid=1258 (accessed April 5, 2010).

Miller, Lila DVM; Zawistowski, Stephen Ph.D. Editors. 2004. Section 5. Animal Cruelty. In *Shelter Veterinary Medicine for Veterinarians and Staff.* Blackwell Publishing. Ames, Iowa.

Munro, Helen MC, BVMS. 1997. The Battered Pet: signs and Symptoms. In *Recognizing & Reporting Animal Abuse: A Veterinarian's Guide*. American Humane Association. Colorado.

Munro, Ranald BVMS MSc. MRCVS, Munro Helen M. C. BVMS MRCVS. 2008. *Animal Abuse and Unlawful Killing: Forensic Veterinary Pathology.* Saunders Ltd. Philadelphia, Oxford.

New York Society for the Prevention of Cruelty to Children (NYSPCC). http://www.nyspcc.org/nyspcc/ (accessed April 5, 2010).

Reid, Czerne M. 2009. New forensics program to investigate crime against animals, *University of Florida News.* http://news.ufl.edu/2009/01/15/csi-animals/ (accessed April 5, 2010).

The Senior Dogs Project. The History of Rimadyl. http://www.srdogs.com/Pages/rimadyl.html.

USDA Animal Welfare Page, including; .pdf and .doc versions of the Animal Welfare Act. http://www.aphis.usda.gov/animal_welfare/publications_and_reports.shtml (accessed April 5, 2010).

von Drehle, David. 2009, Dec. 7. Can Attack Dogs Be Rehabilitated? *Time Magazine.* http://www.time.com/time/magazine/article/0,9171,1942950,00.html (accessed April 5, 2010).

Wisch, Rebecca F. 2010. Table of Veterinary Reporting Requirement and Immunity Laws. *Animal Legal & Historical Center. Michigan State University College of Law.* http://www.animallaw.info/articles/ddusvetreporttable.htm (accessed April 5, 2010).

Wisch, Rebecca F. 2005. Overview of State Cruelty Laws. *Animal Legal & Historical Center, Michigan State University College of Law.* http://www.animallaw.info/articles/ovusstatecrueltylaws.htm (accessed April 5, 2010).

Index

C

D

Q

R

S

T

U

V

W

X

Y

Z

For Product Safety Concerns and Information please contact our EU
representative GPSR@taylorandfrancis.com
Taylor & Francis Verlag GmbH, Kaufingerstraße 24, 80331 München, Germany

www.ingramcontent.com/pod-product-compliance
Ingram Content Group UK Ltd.
Pitfield, Milton Keynes, MK11 3LW, UK
UKHW050756180926
475701UK00007B/1085

* 9 7 8 0 3 6 7 7 7 8 5 7 6 *